D0772398

EARLY MUSIC HISTORY 19

STUDIES IN MEDIEVAL AND EARLY MODERN MUSIC

Edited by

IAIN FENLON
Fellow of King's College, Cambridge

Printed in the United Kingdom at the University Press, The Edinburgh Building, Cambridge CB2 2RU, United Kingdom
40 West 20th Street, New York, NY 10011–4211, USA
10 Stamford Road, Oakleigh, Melbourne 3166, Australia

First Published 2000

Phototypeset in Baskerville by Wyvern 21 Ltd, Bristol
Printed in Great Britain at the University Press, Cambridge

ISSN 0261–1279

ISBN 0 521 790735

SUBSCRIPTIONS The subscription price (excluding VAT) of volume 19, which includes postage, is £60 (US $99 in USA and Canada) for institutions, £40 (US $63 in USA and Canada) for individuals ordering direct from the Press and certifying that the annual is for their personal use. Airmail (orders to Cambridge only) £10.00 extra. Copies of the annual for subscribers in the USA and Canada are sent by air to New York to arrive with minimum delay. Orders, which must be accompanied by payment, may be sent to a bookseller, subscription agent or direct to the publishers: Cambridge University Press, The Edinburgh Building, Shaftesbury Road, Cambridge CB2 2RU. Payment may be made by any of the following methods: cheque (payable to Cambridge University Press), UK postal order, bank draft, Post Office Giro (account no. 571 6055 GB Bootle – advise CUP of payment), international money order, UNESCO coupons, or any credit card bearing the Interbank symbol. EU subscribers (outside the UK) who are not registered for VAT should add VAT at their country's rate. VAT registered subscribers should provide their VAT registration number. Japanese prices for institutions (including ASP delivery) are available from Kinokuniya Company Ltd, P.O. Box 55, Chitose, Tokyo. Orders from the USA and Canada should be sent to Cambridge University Press, 40 West 20th Street, New York, NY 10011–4211, USA.

BACK VOLUMES Volumes 1–18 are available from the publisher at £60 ($99 in USA and Canada).

NOTE Each volume of *Early Music History* is now published in the year in which it is subscribed. Volume 19 is therefore published in 2000. Readers should be aware, however, that some earlier volumes have been subscribed in the year *after* the copyright and publication date given on this imprints page. Thus volume 8, the volume received by 1989 subscribers, is dated 1988 on the imprints page.

INTERNET ACCESS This journal is included in the Cambridge Journals Online service which can be found at www.journals.cup.org. For further information on other Press titles access http://www.cup.cam.ac.uk or www.cup.org.

CONTENTS

Early Music History (2000) Volume 19. © Cambridge University Press
Printed in the United Kingdom

CLIVE BURGESS AND ANDREW WATHEY

MAPPING THE SOUNDSCAPE: CHURCH MUSIC IN ENGLISH TOWNS, 1450–1550*

Topography and its metaphors have long dominated the historiography of towns and they continue to do so in the modern renaissance of what might be called 'urban musicology'. Maps, plans and townscapes – likewise 'soundscapes' – have proved valuable in representing the diversity and disposition of activity, alongside the interplay of time and space and of private and public spheres. Yet at the same time a number of implications present in these constructs have yet to be fully explored, with consequences in turn for the ways in which we theorise the structures and dynamics of musical cultures. In this article we propose a redrafting of the institutional and historiographic 'map' of church music in English towns during the century or so before the Reformation. This serves as a preliminary to two larger questions, to be more fully investigated elsewhere but inevitably also touched upon here. First, how did the liturgy function within the temporal and physical space of

* Parts of this paper were presented in earlier versions at the seminar 'Produzione, circolazione e consumo: per una mappa della musica sacra del tardo Medioevo al primo Seicento', held at the Fondazione Ugo e Olga Levi, Venice, in October 1999. We are grateful to colleagues present there, and others who read the text, for their comments and advice, in particular Caroline Barron, David Bryant, Tim Carter and Iain Fenlon. Work on this article forms part of a larger research project, 'Church Music in English Towns, *c.* 1450–1500' (Directors: Caroline Barron and Andrew Wathey), funded at Royal Holloway, University of London by the Arts and Humanities Research Board, whose generous support we here gratefully acknowledge.

The following abbreviations have been used:

BL	London, British Library
BRO	Bristol Record Office
CLRO	London, Corporation of London Record Office
GL	London, Guildhall Library
GLRO	London, Greater London Record Office
PRO	London, Public Record Office

Dates given in the form '1507/8' indicate the year of account.

individual churches? Second, how did the broader material, devotional and musical experience of the liturgy cohere, and how did it interact with urban spaces and with the social institutions of the parish and the town?

Recent years have witnessed significant advances in three related areas of late medieval study. Religious historians have rehabilitated the late medieval Church and have looked more closely at parish life and management to explain the vitality of these local communities.[1] Urban historians have mapped the cultural dynamics of pre-industrial towns.[2] Musicologists have begun to study the roles played by musicians in towns and have increasingly sought urban contexts for repertories and activities that were formerly studied exclusively in the setting of the court.[3] That these strands have not yet merged is evident from recent historical literature.[4] Conversely, the reception in musicology of the revolution that English Reformation historiography underwent in the 1970s and 1980s has not yet been especially marked, even though histo-

1 See in particular E. Duffy, *The Stripping of the Altars: Traditional Religion in England, 1400–1580* (London, 1992); C. Burgess, '"By Quick and by Dead": Wills and Pious Provision in Later Medieval Bristol', *English Historical Review*, 102 (1987), pp. 837–58; *idem*, 'London Parishes: Development in Context', in R. Britnell (ed.), *Daily Life in the Late Middle Ages* (Stroud, 1998), pp. 151–74. See also, among numerous other studies, N. P. Tanner, *The Church in Late Medieval Norwich, 1370–1532* (Pontifical Institute of Mediaeval Studies: Studies and Texts, 66; Toronto, 1984); R. Whiting, *The Blind Devotion of the People: Popular Religion and the English Reformation* (Cambridge Studies in Early Modern History; Cambridge, 1989).

2 See, for example, G. Rosser, *Medieval Westminster, 1200–1540* (Oxford, 1989); G. Rosser and R. Holt (eds), *The English Medieval Town: A Reader in English Urban History, 1200–1540* (Readers in Urban History; London, 1990); A. Dyer, *Decline and Growth in English Towns, 1400–1640* (New Studies in Economic and Social History; Cambridge, 1991).

3 Earlier studies of English material include most obviously H. Baillie, 'London Churches and their Musicians' (Ph.D. thesis, University of Cambridge, 1958), *idem*, 'A London Church in Tudor Times', *Music & Letters*, 36 (1955), pp. 55–64, and 'A London Guild of Musicians, 1460–1530', *Proceedings of the Royal Musical Association*, 83 (1956–7), pp. 15–28. For the renaissance of 'urban musicology' in the 1970s and 1980s, see T. Carter, 'The Sound of Silence: Models for an Urban Musicology', forthcoming, and more particularly R. Strohm, *Music in Late Medieval Bruges* (Oxford, 1985). More recent studies include F. Kisby, 'The Royal Household Chapel in Early Tudor London, 1485–1547' (Ph.D. thesis, University of London, 1996). See also the remarks in A. Wathey, *Music in the Royal and Noble Households in Late Medieval England: Studies of Sources and Patronage* (New York and London, 1989), pp. 165–7; *idem*, 'Editorial [Music in Tudor London]', *Early Music*, 25 (1997), pp. 180–2.

4 For example, Duffy, *The Stripping of the Altars*; K. L. French, G. G. Gibbs and B. A. Kümin (eds), *The Parish in English Life 1400–1600* (Manchester and New York, 1997), and P. Collinson and J. Craig (eds), *The Reformation in English Towns, 1540–1640* (Basingstoke, 1998).

rians of adjacent periods, the late Middle Ages and the early seventeenth century, have now been responding to its challenges for some time.[5] In what follows, we first trace the influence of historical and musicological historiographies on the 'map' (I–II). We then suggest how notions of urban layout and its origins (III) and parish and legal sources (IV) may be used to reshape this picture. Finally (V), we essay a tentative framework for the production, circulation and consumption of vocal polyphony in towns, though these notions too are called into question to some degree by the character of urban musical environments. We adopt the usage of much writing in English medieval history in defining towns as trading/service centres with a social identity separate from that of their surroundings, but do not distinguish them from cities on the basis of chartered status or size. Although most – the majority, perhaps – of our examples are drawn from the well-documented case of London, our argument is directed at English towns more broadly, among which Bristol and Norwich (alongside London) featured as the largest and most important.

I: REVISIONISM AND THE PRE-REFORMATION CHURCH

For those who work on any aspect of the late medieval Church, the Reformation inevitably looms large. This transformation and the ways in which it has been understood and explained, in England at least, have cast a long, deep shadow which has done much to obscure the Church as it existed and functioned before the mid-sixteenth century. History, as ever, has been to the victor; but, in this particular instance, denominational pressures have intensified the processes discounting and denigrating the pre-Reformation Catholic establishment in England, markedly lowering estimates and expectations of its achievements and of its appeal to contemporaries.

It used to be relatively simple, in England at least, where even twenty-five years ago the Reformation seemed cut and dried. It

[5] Among much else, see R. Hutton, *The Rise and Fall of Merry England: The Ritual Year 1400–1700* (Oxford, 1994); C. Russell, *The Causes of the English Civil War: The Ford Lectures Delivered in the University of Oxford 1987–1988* (Oxford, 1990); C. Rawcliffe, *Medicine for the Soul: The Life, Death and Resurrection of an English Medieval Hospital, St Giles's, Norwich, c.1249–1550* (Stroud, 1999).

happened, 'self-evidently', as the result of the Roman Church's abuses. Internationally, these abuses were typefied by the Schism, the deep-seated rapacity of the administration, the unseemly influence of certain families, and the Inquisition with its unfortunate predisposition to punish by burning any who objected. In England they were characterised by the arch-pluralist Cardinal Wolsey, by the endemic absenteeism of the bishops, the ineradicable ignorance of the lower clergy and the rampant immorality of monks and nuns. All demonstrated, on the one hand, the degeneracy of the Roman Church; all led, on the other, to virulent anti-clericalism. Luther's objections in Germany had set the process of reform in motion; Henry VIII in England, one of Luther's opponents in the 1520s, had mercifully seen the light by the 1530s. With Parliament on his side, he had only to give the sign to unleash long pent-up forces of discontent. The Reformation had been driven by general demand and by the natural propensity of the English to turn their backs on Europe. A 'national' Church was thus established, with King (or Queen) in Parliament in control of religion. A combination of establishment control and xenophobia, helped undoubtedly by the ringing English of Cranmer's Prayer Book and, later, of the Authorised Version of the Bible, proved potent; but it was a settlement which distilled the national genius for compromise. The novelty of 'King in Parliament' was rendered palatable because the traditional organisation of the Church 'on the ground', in dioceses and parishes, was unchanged; similarly, the novelty of Scripture and liturgy in English was the medium, ultimately, only of 'watered-down' Protestantism. While Anglicanism proved broadly acceptable by not asking too much of anyone, it bolstered its claims by heaping censure on what it had replaced – a Church in thrall to a foreign potentate, doctrinally in error, morally degenerate and a stranger to Scripture. The Reformation had been right because it was necessary.

The above is a caricature, but it is not entirely unrepresentative of views once advocated by even reputable historians.[6] However, such explanations have buckled under increasing pressure in the last two decades as revisionist historians have taken

[6] The most influential exposition, following in the footsteps of many predecessors, is A. G. Dickens, *The English Reformation* (London, 1964); for its effects, see for example C. Cross, *Church and People, 1450–1660* (London, 1976).

issue with their predecessors and have insisted on new emphases. First, revisionists would argue that the Reformation was not a movement 'from below'. Henry VIII was the son of a usurper and, without a legitimate male heir in the late 1520s, he stopped at nothing to secure the dynasty; the Pope would not grant a divorce, so alternatives were found. Moreover, Henry was desperate to play the role of the Renaissance prince but was poor by comparison with his Continental counterparts: the Church in England was very richly endowed, and Henry was greedy. The English Reformation has thus come to be seen as a 'top-down' act of state, precipitated by an anxious and avaricious king who was, nevertheless, cautious about doctrinal change. Second, the English Reformation was metropolitan, political and anything but clean-cut. Doctrinal change came with Edward VI (1547–53), only to be reversed by Mary (1553–8), and reversed again by Elizabeth (1558–1603). Longevity assisted the success of Elizabeth's settlement, but her feeling for moderation undoubtedly helped. She could not countenance excess, which the 'godly', who saw themselves as her most loyal subjects, found irksome in the extreme; but to have done so would have jeopardised the real and more valuable loyalty of the many. Some revisionists, Christopher Haigh in particular, have argued that 'the Reformations' ultimately altered little.[7] Given that, in the 1620s, Bishop Laud, with Charles I's full support, was *inter alia* emphasising 'the beauty of holiness' and insisting on the restoration of altars and proper vestments, it is permissible to question whether profound religious change ever did result from mid-sixteenth-century reform.

Revisionism has undermined the notion of the 'popular' Reformation. It has also forced reappraisal of the Church in England before the 1530s. If the Reformation was an Act of State, there is no need to argue that the Church was either generally corrupt or unpopular. Much of the reputation for 'corruption' is now understood as Protestant propaganda, some of which, like Foxe's *Book of Martyrs* (1563), was very powerful. Documentary and

[7] Haigh's views, many of which had first been aired in articles, are most conveniently and extensively summarised in his *English Reformations: Religion, Politics and Society under the Tudors* (Oxford, 1993); see also J. J. Scarisbrick, *The Reformation and the English People* (Oxford, 1984), whose conclusions are more pessimistic.

building evidence, by contrast, reveal a Church whose members were generous, keen to participate and far from discontent. Thus 'traditional' religion, to employ the phrase coined by Eamon Duffy, has been rehabilitated as a vital force in the lives of a laity caught up in parish life and liturgy.[8] This is one reason why change was slow: English men and women had invested considerable sums of money and prodigious effort 'to benefit the old religion' and their appetite for change was limited. But revisionism is young, and the reception of revisionism among late medievalists – less firmly focused on the Reformation itself – is arguably younger still, particularly in the period before 1530. Much is still to be done, and some historians, keen to distance themselves from what all too easily appears a denominational tussle, may be criticised for reclothing prejudice as a means of coming to terms with new interpretations.[9] Only very recently, freed from the constraints of knee-jerk criticism, has the fifteenth-century Church come to be studied for its own sake and in its broader aspects, ranging from the vitality of individuals' devotional lives to the corporate parish ceremonial, including liturgical celebration, from which all might benefit.

As we have suggested, the laity participated in Church affairs and worked hard for the benefit of their parish, the rich especially investing very considerable sums of money in the process. This produced beautiful buildings; the achievement of the laity in this respect was remarkable, if often overlooked for reasons outlined above.[10] It also produced an elaborate and powerful liturgy in smaller churches as well as in larger ones. We make some comments below on the nature of the provision, the infrastructures of

[8] Duffy, *The Stripping of the Altars*, especially Part I, pp. 9–376.

[9] See for example the appraisal of the rebellions in Edward VI's reign in S. J. Loach, *Edward VI* (New Haven and London, 1999), p. 183: 'Moreover, without following in their entirety the romantic notions of pre-Reformation Catholicism offered to us by Eamon Duffy, I should also suggest that what Protestantism stood for in the eyes of many parishioners by 1553 must have been looting and sacking, and the stripping by the state of the objects of beauty which bound them to their locality and its past.'

[10] See A. H. Thompson, *The English Clergy and their Organization in the Later Middle Ages* (Oxford, 1947), p. 128, who led the way with the judgement that 'There is no period at which money was lavished so freely on [the fabric of] English churches as in the fifteenth century'; Duffy and others have followed in considering the implications of structural remains. H. Munro Cautley, *Suffolk Churches and their Treasures* (5th edn, Woodbridge, 1982) remains one of the most useful compendia charting the laity's achievement, albeit in a wealthy county.

liturgy, that fed on this process but, as a preliminary, it is worth examining the doctrinal tradition that both supported the social dimension of participation and brought forth hard cash. One result of the long tradition of criticising the pre-Reformation English Church is a relative ignorance of its teachings. The key to understanding what motivated contemporaries is the Church's teaching on Purgatory, dismissed by Protestants with particular ferocity because of its lack of explicit Scriptural authority.[11]

The aspiration which explains why contemporaries responded so enthusiastically was the promise of an eased salvation. What did the Church prescribe for those whose sought to be saved? One had to believe the Gospel, to attend church, and to participate in the sacraments: the 'rites of passage' sacraments (including Baptism, Confirmation, and Extreme Unction) and, on a more regular basis, the central sacraments of Eucharist and Penance. The Eucharist was, and was to remain, the pivotal ritual of church life; but penance, which dealt with the all-important barrier which sin had erected between God and mankind, had a much higher profile in corporate life and ceremonial before the Reformation than it did after. Pre-Reformation penance demanded a response more ostentatious and public than that subsequently envisaged by reformers. Its most important aspect, dealing with the guilt consequent on sin, was confession. The Fourth Lateran Council of 1215 decreed that every Christian of either sex had an obligation to confess at least once annually: the properly penitent and shriven Christian might then rest assured that he or she would not be damned. But among the most auspicious of the doctrinal developments of the twelfth and thirteenth centuries, dealing admittedly with a subsidiary aspect of penance, was the formulation of a feasible means of dealing with the penalties due to sins committed – penalties which had to be undergone before the soul could enter Heaven. Where, previously, the penances were to be satisfied in life, they might, as a result of new teachings (emanating particularly from Paris), be completed, or indeed fully satisfied, in

[11] Discussed by Duffy, *The Stripping of the Altars*, chapter 10; see also C. Burgess, '"A fond thing vainly invented": An Essay on Purgatory and Pious Motive in Late Medieval England', in S. J. Wright (ed.), *Parish, Church and People: Local Studies in Lay Religion, 1350–1750* (London, 1988), pp. 56–84.

Purgatory.[12] And it was the definition and development of the doctrine of Purgatory, the 'third place' and staging post to Heaven, which created 'a workable scheme of religious discipline for everyone' and which, by the fifteenth century, had wrought so profound an effect in shaping the response of Christians.[13]

As Christians sought to expedite their progress through Purgatory, they responded to teachings which emphasised the need for good works and for intercession, two principles which in practice intertwined. Good works, including charity to the poor, the support of the clergy, or contribution towards church building, benefited the soul through intrinsic merit; but in giving, the donor obliged beneficiaries – paupers, clergy or fellow parishioners – to pray for their benefactors, and the intercession of the faithful was essential both to speed and ease the process of purgation. Purgatory set up powerful forces, stimulating generosity with time and money and instilling a desire for remembrance. While the honest poor might rest assured that their main duty was to pray for their benefactors,[14] the wealthy were left in no doubt (by written, preached and visual admonition) of their need for intercession, and their interest to stimulate it by generosity. The craving for intercession which the doctrine of Purgatory generated had an undeniable potency in persuading the wealthy to part with very substantial sums in charity to the poor, in building and rebuilding churches, in employing priests and other clergy, in furnishing and beautifying churches, and in providing often sumptuous vestments and equipment.[15] England's wealthier classes were, in all probability, more generous towards the Church in the century or more preceding the Reformation than at any time since.

[12] Earlier penitential systems were severe, rendering salvation almost impossible for the great majority who were neither monks nor able to procure adequate substitutive penance.

[13] The concept of Purgatory, and concomitant emphases on charity, prayer and good works to benefit the souls of the departed, had a pedigree of at least two centuries by the time they received official definition at the Council of Florence in 1439; see J. Le Goff, *La Naissance du Purgatoire* (Paris, 1981), and more particularly the review of this work by R. W. Southern, *Times Literary Supplement*, 18 June 1982, pp. 651–2.

[14] Just as Christ and His apostles had been paupers, so the honest poor were thought to be close to Christ and their prayers particularly efficacious; see B. L. Manning, *The People's Faith in the Age of Wyclif* (2nd edn, Hassocks, 1975), chapter 10.

[15] It is striking that, as a result of the Reformation, charity had to be sustained by statute, particularly the Poor Laws of the 1590s (although these still relied very much on the parish); moreover, for the most part, church-building languished.

II: MUSIC AND URBAN CHURCHES: A REAPPRAISAL

The consequences of this large extra influx of resources into the late medieval English Church have been studied by historians for the last two decades. But musicological studies have turned to the question more recently as the certainties of older historical writings have receded, in tandem with a broader critique of the arguments underpinning the formation of the 'map' of musical activity.[16] Earlier attempts to frame the 'map' (quite literally in the case of Anselm Hughes's 'Topography'), as well as studies of individual institutions or groups of institutions, quite often suffered from a narrow conception of what the 'institution' actually was, and also sometimes from the preoccupations and/or shortcomings of a yet earlier generation of secondary historical writing. Thus, for example, smaller institutions (parishes and hospitals) and monasteries after 1400 still fare poorly in musicological narratives by comparison with cathedrals and the new collegiate foundations of the fifteenth century. Chantries and (until recently) endowed services are virtually ignored. Equally problematic is the 'constitutionalist' view adopted of the individual church, set by the musicologist in social, political and (usually) musical isolation. Much as a fixation with the Borough Charter shaped the nineteenth-century historiography of English towns,[17] earlier musicological studies were dominated by the apparent certainties of statutes and formal constitutions, valuable for the study of internal governance and legal frameworks but not always helpful for the purposes of mapping the extent of a given activity. (As their present-day counterparts demonstrate, the legalistic, top-level focus of such documents can be misleading in the extreme.)

The consequences of this approach have been far-reaching. For the sake of discussion they can conveniently be divided into three:

[16] To the classic account in F. Ll. Harrison, *Music in Medieval Britain* (London, 1958) may be added Dom A. Hughes, 'The Topography of English Mediaeval Polyphony', in H. Anglès *et al.* (ed.), *In memoriam Jacques Handschin* (Strassburg, 1962), pp. 127–39 and R. Bowers, 'Choral Institutions Within the English Church: Their Constitution and Development' (Ph.D. thesis, University of East Anglia, 1975). See also Wathey, *Music in the Royal and Noble Households*; B. Haggh, 'Foundations or Institutions? On Bringing the Middle Ages into the History of Medieval Music', *Acta musicologica*, 58 (1996), pp. 87–128.

[17] For example, Rosser, *Medieval Westminster*, pp. 1–2, and the remarks in R. Sweet, *The Writing of Urban Histories in Eighteenth-Century England* (Oxford, 1997), pp. 75–80.

internal, local and global. Internally, it can be argued that institutions have been framed too much in terms of their prescribed complement of clergy, singers and other staff – irrespective of the realities of day-to-day attendance – and in ignorance of other frameworks imposed by the liturgical calendar and/or internal space. The same exclusivity colours the functions of individual personnel, often viewed in the image of their duties with again little regard for their potential for interaction. Locally, churches have been treated as islands, unrelated to their neighbours save by an occasional accident of pluralism, even when surrounded by similar institutions, as they inevitably were in even modest-sized settlements. Thirdly, at a global level, a hierarchy of institutions by wealth and size has come to dominate – or even to serve as a proxy for – the overall map of musical activity, uncomplicated by geographic, political or musical variables or indeed by the scope for normal human interaction.

The realities are, unsurprisingly, emerging as much more fluid. First, within the walls of most churches, it is clear that a variety of practices flourished and that plurality of function, formally or informally organised, made a radical difference to effective size. The statutes of a church might prescribe a complement of, for example, eight priests, twelve clerks and six boys; but even assuming the absence of vacancies or supernumeraries, the number of those present might be cut by the operation of rotas, or massively boosted by special events and/or collaboration with other staff in the institution.[18] Pluralism by definition affects more than one party, as the case of St Paul's Cathedral, London, demonstrates. For much of the mid-fifteenth century, the residentiary canons (*stagiarii*) at the cathedral were often either King's chaplains or, as in the case of the Old Hall composers Thomas Damett and Nicholas Sturgeon, senior chaplains in the royal household chapel.[19] As the numerous dispensations granted by the chapter

[18] This point is explored in relation to the English royal household chapel in the fifteenth century in Wathey, *Music in the Royal and Noble Households*, pp. 92–134.

[19] Of the dean and six residentiary canons in 1442, at least four also held such positions. Damett was a canon 1419–36, becoming a residentiary in May 1427; Sturgeon was a residentiary canon 1440–54, becoming Precentor in July 1442; see GL MS 25513, fol. 118, and *John Le Neve: Fasti Ecclesiae Anglicanae 1300–1541*, v: *St Paul's, London*, ed. J. M. Horn (London, 1963), pp. 17, 28, 58.

reveal, short-term absence from services was the norm for this group and was frequently tailored to the changing distance between cathedral and court. Thus, for example, a number of the dispensations made to Sturgeon in the early 1440s coincided with the court's arrival at Westminster.[20] Henry VI's more extended visits to Windsor and other royal residences on the Thames similarly appear to have precipitated requests for absence, often presented at short notice. Dispensations from the day or night Hours at the cathedral, or from all but one service each day, may have been intended to enable the residentiaries to 'commute' to court. In other cases, repeat absences granted for three or four days in successive weeks may perhaps reflect more extensive ceremonial commitments in royal service.[21] The longest absence appears to be that of Thomas Damett, who resumed residence on Easter eve 1432 after half a year with the king 'in partibus transmarinis', presumably for the Paris coronation expedition of 1430–2.[22] But more striking in the present context is the regularity with which absences from St Paul's occurred on principal feasts in the church's calendar when these were also celebrated as 'days of estate' or crown wearings at court.[23] Attendance was enforced by royal

[20] For example, from prime on 5 February 1441 to prime on the following Saturday, 10 February, coinciding with the King's presence at Westminster between 3 and 16 February, and from prime on 14 October 1441 for 10 days, coinciding with the King's presence there between 12 and 27 October (GL MS 25513, fols. 183^{r-v}, 190; B. Wolffe, *Henry VI* (London, 1981), pp. 362–3). Almost thirty dispensations were made to Sturgeon between 1441 and 1447, and his ready availability at St Paul's may have been one element in his appointment by the Privy Council to choose 'vj singers of England' for the Emperor Friedrich III; see *Proceedings and Ordinances of the Privy Council*, ed. H. Nicolas, 7 vols. (London, 1834–7), v, p. 218 (16 October 1442).

[21] See GL MS 25513, fols. 180–254 *passim*; for the use of royal licences sanctioning absence, see fol. 201^{v} (Thomas Lyseux). For repeat absences granted to Sturgeon in the late spring of 1441 while the King was at Windsor and Sheen, see fols. 185–186^{v}.

[22] GL MS 25513, fol. 138.

[23] The list of such days changed marginally over time but in the 1440s and early 1450s comprised All Saints, St Nicholas, the Conception of the BVM, Christmas, Circumcision, Epiphany, the Purification and Annunciation of the BVM, Good Friday, Easter, Pentecost, Trinity Sunday, Corpus Christi and the Assumption and Nativity of the BVM (see, for example, PRO, E 101/409/9, fol. 32^{v} (1441/2), E 101/410/9, fol. 37^{v} (1451/2), and other accounts cited in Wathey, *Music in the Royal and Noble Households*, p. 127). For crown wearings, with which this list overlaps substantially, see *Liber regie capelle: A Manuscript in the Biblioteca Publica, Evora*, ed. W. Ullmann (Henry Bradshaw Society, 92; London, 1961), pp. 18, 61–2, and for the observance of such days at the early Tudor court, see F. Kisby, '"When the King Goeth a Procession": Chapel Ceremonies and Services, the Ritual Year and Religious Reforms at the Early-Tudor Court, 1485–1547', *Journal of British Studies*, 40 (2001), forthcoming.

authority, as the *Liber regie capelle* of 1448 makes clear.[24] Dispensations granted to Sturgeon account for about a quarter of the sixteen such days in each of 1444 and 1445, mostly occurring when the court was within easy reach at Windsor or Westminster, and in one case when it was at Berkhamstead.[25] Nevertheless, since Dammet, Sturgeon and other royal chaplains were at St Paul's on at least some of the 'days of estate' it is clear that even the royal household chapel celebrating a major feast at court did not necessarily require its full complement.

Classic notions of attendance compelled by a celebratory hierarchy – strongly encouraged by medieval statutes and modern writers alike – thus fade in some cases to reveal more flexible and negotiated structures. For those, including Sturgeon and Damett, who held canonries at St George's Chapel, Windsor in addition to positions at St Paul's and at court, the matrix of obligation and identity, driven in part by the itinerations of the king, emerges as more complex still. The royal household chapel almost certainly operated rotas from an early date, formalised in the 1478 Ordinance into half-year tours of duty in which absent chaplains were obliged to reside at their benefices.[26] The few surviving attendance registers from St George's Windsor make amply clear that rotas of some form operated at court during the 1380s and 1460s/70s, revealing individual members of the royal household chapel present when the court was absent, and vice versa, alongside the numerous instances in which royal chaplains and royal chapel coincided.[27] These registers also suggest that organised absence operated among groups of the St George's canons, singing-

[24] *Liber regie capelle*, p. 66: 'Excusantur etiam omnes de Capelle Regis a residencia in beneficiis suis quibuscumque, licet in cathedralibus, ecclesiis dignitates fuerint maiores et necessariam requirant residenciam, quamdiu in obsequio vel servicio Regis aut Regine fuerint.'

[25] GL MS 25513, fols. 225, 227, 228, 229v, 232v.

[26] *The Household of Edward IV: The Black Book and the Ordinance of 1478*, ed. A. R. Myers (Manchester, 1959), p. 215: 'the chaplains make their attendaunce from halve year to halve year, som at oo tyme and som at another; and that for the same half yere they shalbe absent from their saide attendaunce they kepe and be reseant and abiding on their cures'. See also Wathey, *Music in the Royal and Noble Households*, p. 62; Kisby, 'The Royal Household Chapel', pp. 192–4.

[27] Windsor, The Erary, MS V.B.1 (October 1384–January 1386) and MS V.B.2 (June 1468–July 1479); an analysis of the latter appears in H. Jeffries, 'John Plummer, the Royal Household Chapel and St George's Chapel, Windsor Castle' (M.Mus. thesis, Royal Holloway, University of London, 1999).

men, chantry priests or clerks, and similar impressions emerge from comparable materials elsewhere.[28]

Even if not strictly operated, rotas and fluctuating attendance have implications for the use of space, the size of the performing group and the projection of institutional identity. They also predispose towards a flexibility of function which in many institutions may already have been semi-implicit. At St Paul's there is clear evidence that the cathedral's legion of chantry priests, numbering forty-seven by the Reformation, was expected not only to perform the post-obit services whose endowments paid their salaries but also to sing in the choir and sometimes to attend other services outside the cathedral in addition.[29] The terms of some chantries reported in 1548 explicitly required attendance at 'all maner processions, specially, generally and rogations', or, in one case, to keep a library 'founded for studients' by the benefactor, and some made additional provision to support the choir or the education of boy choristers.[30] The small regular complement of canons at St Paul's has sometimes encouraged scholars to believe that it supported a relatively low level of musical activity; the reality, however, was probably that singers elsewhere in this large institution and its surrounding area in the metropolis helped to staff its main round of services.

From a local perspective it is clear that institutions interacted musically, and almost inescapably so in dense urban environments where they were already floating on a lagoon of tenurial, residential, political, legal and personal interrelationships. The implications of this point for London – where 107 parishes, numerous monasteries and hospitals, and St Paul's cathedral occupied under 1.6 km^2 – have barely been recognised (see Figure 1). Yet it is

[28] Relatively few such records survive; for chaplains and clerks in the attendance registers of the household of John of Gaunt in the 1380s and 1390s, see A. Wathey, 'John of Gaunt, John Pycard and the Negotiations at Amiens, 1392', in C. Barron and N. Saul (eds), *England and the Low Countries in the Late Middle Ages* (London, 1995), pp. 29–42.

[29] See GL MS 25526, the original return to the commissioners in 1548, *passim*, and *London and Middlesex Chantry Certificate, 1548*, ed. C. J. Kitching (London Record Society, 16; London, 1980), pp. xxviii–xxx, 52–9.

[30] GL MS 25526, fols. 12^v, 20, and T. Hearne, *The History and Antiquities of Glastonbury, to which are added the Endowment and Orders of Sherington's Chantry, Founded in Saint Paul's Church, London* (Oxford, 1722), pp. 161–223. For chantries supporting the choir or choristers, see *London and Middlesex Chantry Certificate, 1548*, ed. Kitching, pp. xxx, 53, and MS 25526, fols. 2, 4^v.

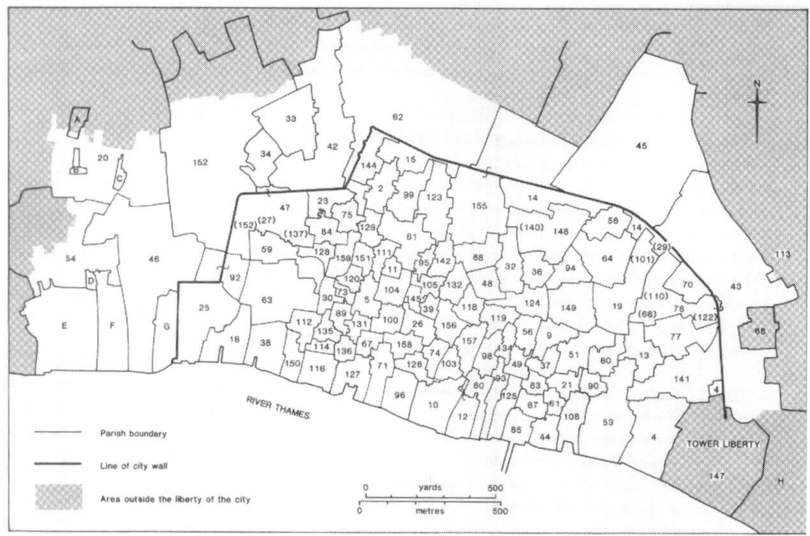

MAP OF LONDON PARISHES

The map is based on the boundaries shown on the Ordnance Survey 1:2500 plan, 1878 edition, with minor adjustments. It shows the boundaries as they existed on the eve of the Great Fire. The numbers represent parishes: only those marked * in the list are shown. Numbers in parentheses represent parishes, or parts of parishes, which had been suppressed, and their approximate location. The letters represent extra-parochial precincts or liberties as follows: A, Furnival's Inn; B, Barnard's Inn; C, Thavie's Inn; D, Serjeants' Inn; E, Temple; F, Whitefriars; G, Bridewell (formerly part of *46*); H, St. Katharine's Hospital.

For notes on the compilation and form of the parish list, see above, p. xvii.

KEY TO PARISH REFERENCES

1 St. Agnes (alias *23*, *24*)
* *2* St. Alban Wood Street
3 All Hallows (unspecified)
* *4* All Hallows Barking (by the Tower; alias *102*)
* *5* All Hallows Bread Street (Watling Street)
6 All Hallows Colemanchurch (alias *50*, *77*)
7 All Hallows Cornhill (probably identical with *9*)
8 All Hallows Fenchurch (alias *60*, *106*, *107*)
* *9* All Hallows Gracechurch (Lombard Street; probably identical with *7*)
* *10* All Hallows the Great (*ad fenum*, at the Hay Wharf, in the Ropery; earlier *Semannescyrce*)
* *11* All Hallows Honey Lane
* *12* All Hallows the Less (on the Cellars, on the Solars)
* *13* All Hallows Staining
* *14* All Hallows on the Wall (London Wall; *29* added, 1442)
* *15* St. Alphage
16 St. Amand (alias *159*, *160*)
17 St. Andrew (unspecified)
* *18* St. Andrew Castle Baynard (by the Wardrobe)
* *19* St. Andrew Cornhill (*atte Knappe*, Undershaft; *101* added, 1565)
* *20* St. Andrew Holborn
* *21* St. Andrew Hubbard (Eastcheap, towards the Tower)
22 St. Anne (unspecified)
* *23* St. Anne & St. Agnes (alias *1*, *24*)
24 St. Anne Aldersgate (alias *1*, *23*)
* *25* St. Anne Blackfriars (created after the Dissolution from Blackfriars precinct)
* *26* St. Antonin (later St. Antholin)
(*) *27* St. Audoen (alias St. Ewen, St. Owen; taken into *47*, 1547)
28 St. Augustine (unspecified)
(*) *29* St. Augustine Papey (on the Wall; joined to *14*, 1442)
* *30* St. Augustine by St. Paul (*parvus*, Watling Street)
31 St. Bartholomew (unspecified)
* *32* St. Bartholomew the Little (by the Exchange)
* *33* St. Bartholomew the Great (created after Dissolution from precinct of St. Bartholomew's Priory)

Figure 1 London parishes before the Great Fire (from D. Keene and V. Harding, *A Survey of Documentary Sources for Property Holding in London Before the Great Fire* (London Record Society, 22; London, 1985), pp. xvi, xviii–xix)

* 34 St. Bartholomew the Less (created after Dissolution from precinct of St. Bartholomew's Hospital)
35 St. Benet (unspecified)
* 36 St. Benet Fink
* 37 St. Benet Gracechurch
* 38 St. Benet Paul's Wharf (Hithe, Woodwharf)
* 39 St. Benet Sherehog (alias *40*, *153*)
40 St. Benet & St. Sithe (alias *39*, *153*)
41 St. Botolph (unspecified)
* 42 St. Botolph without Aldersgate
* 43 St. Botolph without Aldgate
* 44 St. Botolph Billingsgate
* 45 St. Botolph without Bishopsgate
* 46 St. Bride (Fleet Street)
* 47 Christ Church Newgate Street (created 1547 from Grey Friars precinct, *27*, *137*, intramural part of *152*)
* 48 St. Christopher (le Stocks)
* 49 St. Clement (Candlewick Street, Eastcheap)
50 Colemanchurch (alias *6*, *77*)
* 51 St. Dionis Backchurch
52 St. Dunstan (unspecified)
* 53 St. Dunstan in the East (towards the Tower)
* 54 St. Dunstan in the West (Fleet Street)
55 St. Edmund (unspecified)
* 56 St. Edmund Lombard Street (King and Martyr)
57 St. Edmund without Newgate (alias *152*)
* 58 St. Ethelburga
* 59 St. Faith (by St. Paul's)
* 60 St. Gabriel (Fenchurch; alias *8*, *106*, *107*)
* 61 St. George (Botolph Lane, Eastcheap)
* 62 St. Giles Cripplegate
* 63 St. Gregory (by St. Paul's)
* 64 St. Helen (Bishopsgate)
65 Holy Trinity (unspecified)
(*) 66 Holy Trinity Aldgate (absorbed by *78* or precinct of Holy Trinity Priory)
* 67 Holy Trinity the Less
* 68 Holy Trinity Minories (created after the Dissolution from the Minoresses' precinct)
69 St. James (unspecified)
* 70 St. James Duke's Place (created 17C from former precinct of Holy Trinity Priory)
* 71 St. James Garlickhithe (Vintry)
72 St. John (unspecified)
* 73 St. John the Evangelist (Watling Street; earlier *162*)
* 74 St. John Walbrook
* 75 St. John Zachary
76 St. Katharine (unspecified)
* 77 St. Katharine Coleman (alias *6*, *50*)
* 78 St. Katharine Cree (Christ Church)
79 St. Lawrence (unspecified)
* 80 St. Lawrence Candlewick Street (Pountney)
* 81 St. Lawrence Jewry
82 St. Leonard (unspecified)
* 83 St. Leonard Eastcheap
* 84 St. Leonard Foster Lane
* 85 St. Magnus (Bridge, the Martyr)
86 St. Margaret (unspecified)
* 87 St. Margaret Bridge Street (New Fish Street)
* 88 St. Margaret Lothbury
* 89 St. Margaret Moses (Friday Street)
* 90 St. Margaret Pattens
91 St. Martin (unspecified)
* 92 St. Martin Ludgate
* 93 St. Martin Orgar (Candlewick Street)
* 94 St. Martin Outwich
* 95 St. Martin Pomary (Ironmonger Lane)
* 96 St. Martin Vintry (Bermanchurch)
97 St. Mary (unspecified)
* 98 St. Mary Abchurch
* 99 St. Mary Aldermanbury
* 100 St. Mary Aldermary
(*) 101 St. Mary Axe (joined to *19*, 1565)
102 St. Mary de Berkyngcherch (alias *4*)
* 103 St. Mary Bothaw
* 104 St. Mary le Bow (*de Arcubus*)
* 105 St. Mary Colechurch
106 St. Mary Fenchurch (alias *8*, *60*, *107*)
107 St. Mary & St. Gabriel Fenchurch (alias *8*, *60*, *106*)
* 108 St. Mary at Hill
109 St. Mary Magdalen (unspecified)
(*) 110 St. Mary Magdalen Aldgate (absorbed by *78* or precinct of Holy Trinity Priory)
* 111 St. Mary Magdalen Milk Street
* 112 St. Mary Magdalen Old Fish Street (*in* (*nova*) *piscaria*, *Westpiscaria*; earlier *161*)
* 113 St. Mary Matfellon (Whitechapel)
* 114 St. Mary Mounthaw
115 St. Mary Olaf (alias *144*)
* 116 St. Mary Somerset
* 117 St. Mary Staining
* 118 St. Mary Woolchurch (Newchurch)
* 119 St. Mary Woolnoth
* 120 St. Matthew Friday Street
121 St. Michael (unspecified)
(*) 122 St. Michael Aldgate (absorbed by *78* or precinct of Holy Trinity Priory)
* 123 St. Michael Bassishaw
* 124 St. Michael Cornhill
* 125 St. Michael Crooked Lane (Candlewick Street)
* 126 St. Michael Paternoster (Paternoster Royal, in the Riole)
* 127 St. Michael Queenhithe (*Ripa Regine*)
* 128 St. Michael le Querne (*ad bladum*, *ubi bladum venditur*, atte Corne, *in foro*)
* 129 St. Michael Wood Street (Huggin Lane)
130 St. Mildred (unspecified)
* 131 St. Mildred Bread Street
* 132 St. Mildred Poultry (Walbrook)
133 St. Nicholas (unspecified)
* 134 St. Nicholas Acon (Hakon)
* 135 St. Nicholas Cole Abbey (Old Fish Street, *in piscaria*, *Westpiscaria*)
* 136 St. Nicholas Olave (Bernard, ? *in piscaria*; alias *139*)
(*) 137 St. Nicholas in the Shambles (alias *143*; taken into *47*, 1547)
138 St. Olave (unspecified)
139 St. Olave Bread Street (alias *136*)
(*) 140 St. Olave Broad Street (absorbed by Austin Friars' precinct and later *148*)
* 141 St. Olave Hart Street (Crutched Friars, Mark Lane, by the Tower)
* 142 St. Olave Old Jewry
143 St. Olave in the Shambles (alias *137*)
* 144 St. Olave Silver Street (Cripplegate, Monkwell Street; alias *115*)
* 145 St. Pancras (Soper Lane)
146 St. Peter (unspecified)
* 147 St. Peter in the Bailey (in the Tower, *ad Vincula*)
* 148 St. Peter Broad Street (the Poor; incl. former Austin Friars' precinct and *140* from 16C)
* 149 St. Peter Cornhill
* 150 St. Peter Paul's Wharf (the Less)
* 151 St. Peter Westcheap (Wood Street)
* 152 St. Sepulchre (without Newgate; alias *57*; part taken into *47*, 1547)
153 St. Sithe (alias *39*, *40*)
154 St. Stephen (unspecified)
* 155 St. Stephen Coleman Street
* 156 St. Stephen Walbrook
* 157 St. Swithin (Candlewick Street, London Stone)
* 158 St. Thomas the Apostle
* 159 St. Vedast (Foster Lane; alias *16*, *160*)
160 St. Vedast & St. Amand (alias *16*, *159*)
161 St. Wandrille (later *112*)
162 St. Werburga (later *73*)

clear that the cathedral, parish churches and hospitals borrowed singers from one another. They used singers from royal and aristocratic chapels who were resident in the metropolis.[31] They also drew on the large, well-organised workforce of parish clerks, whose own mid-fifteenth-century guild statutes explicitly defended (rather than prohibited) a monopoly in cross-parish activity.[32] At St Mary at Hill, which was not exceptional in this respect, singers were engaged from neighbouring parishes, from the royal household chapel and variously from the large pool of freelance clerics supported by the metropolis.[33] There is evidence also that parish clerks took part in services at St Paul's. Conversely, chantry priests from St Paul's were paid on occasion to sing at St Mary at Hill and other parish churches.[34] More various arrangements may have obtained in London's suburbs but for those areas that were close to the metropolis and its resources the organisation of labour was clearly similar. St Stephen's and St Margaret's, Westminster, used singers from Westminster Abbey. John Medwall, the parish clerk at St Margaret's Southwark, not only copied polyphony, played the organ and ran the choir for his own parish, but also subcontracted with the Abbot of Bermondsey to perform obits at the abbey 'with

[31] For examples in contrasting parishes see *The Medieval Records of a London City Church (St. Mary at Hill) A.D. 1420–1559*, ed. H. Littlehales, 2 vols. (Early English Text Society, O.S. 128; London, 1904–5), i, pp. 270, 309–10 and other references at i, pp. xxi–xxii; *The Churchwardens Accounts of the Parish of All Hallows, London Wall in the City of London, 33 Henry VI to 27 Henry VIII*, ed. C. Welch (London, 1912), p. 50: 'Item payd to master Corbrand for hellpyng of the quere at ester [1510]'. Littlehales prints only extracts from the St Mary's accounts (GL MS 1239/1) for the years after 1495, where further comparable references remain unpublished.

[32] See J. Christie, *Some Account of Parish Clerks, More Especially of the Ancient Fraternity (Bretherne and Sisterne) of St. Nicholas Now Known as the Worshipful Company of Parish Clerks* (London, 1893), pp. 71–2. See also R. Lloyd, 'Provision for Music in the Parish Church in Late Medieval London' (Ph.D. thesis, University of London, 2000), chapter 3, and Baillie, 'A London Guild of Musicians', pp. 19–20.

[33] See for example the accounts for 1477–9: 'to iiij childre of St Magnus [the neighbouring parish] for syngyng, 4d.'; 1527/8 'paid at the son tavern for the drinking of Mr Colmas with others of the kinges chapple that had songen in the churche, 9d.'; 1512/13 'paid to a condukte for the Ester halydays, for lak of the Clerkes absence, for to play at orgons, 2s. 4d.' (*The Medieval Records*, ed. Littlehales, i, pp. 81, 344, 281, and for further examples i, pp. 197, 229, 233, 256, 270, 309, 310, 373, 411). See also the index to *The Church Records of St Andrew Hubbard, Eastcheap, c1450–c1570*, ed. C. Burgess (London Record Society, 34; London, 1999), pp. 307–8 *sub* 'Clergy'.

[34] *The Medieval Records*, ed. Littlehales, ii, p. 411.

other helpe of men and childern', acting in addition as the Abbot's rent-collector in London and Southwark.[35]

It is implicit in this – thirdly and at a global level – that while size and wealth were important they were not the unique passport to an involvement with composed polyphony. Here rich/poor, and perhaps also metropolitan/provincial, polarities require realignment. London parishes and hospitals have been shown to be more fully involved in polyphony than previously thought and over a longer period, and a similar picture is emerging for guilds and parish churches in some small market towns. The London Hospital of St Anthony of Vienne maintained choristers and an instructor, apparently importing adult singers; several parishes maintained a priest and only one or two parish clerks and yet paid for the copying of four- or five-part music.[36] At Boston, the Guild of the Blessed Virgin in the early sixteenth century not only hired singers *ad hoc* to support its permanent staff but also regularly bought the services of prominent musicians working in London and for royal and sub-royal chapels.[37] At St James's, Louth, vestments were made in 1535/6 'for strange syngyng men when they cum to sett in the qwere to the honour of God and the honeste of the

[35] For Westminster, see for example PRO, E 28/90 (43); Rosser, *Medieval Westminster*, p. 255. For Medwall see PRO, C 1/81/49 (between October 1486 and March 1487): under this agreement, Medwall was to meet the costs of the obit in return for an annual pension of 5 marks; however, he alleged that he had met the costs of the obit for eighteen months and had then been dismissed without payment. The Abbot's answer is C 1/81/50. See also A. F. Johnson and S.-B. MacLean, 'Reformation and Resistance in Thames/Severn Parishes: The Dramatic Witness', in French, Gibbs and Kümin (eds), *The Parish in English Life*, pp. 178–200, at p. 185. The inventory of goods at St Margaret's parish church, taken by the churchwardens on 16 November 1485, includes 'a prykyd songboke of parchment þat syr John Docheman gave, prise 6s. 8d. . . . anoder prykyd songboke of papyr bowght of John Medwale, prise 9s.' (GLRO, P92/SAV/24, fol. 5^{v}); see also M. Carlin, *Medieval Southwark* (London and Rio Grande, 1996), pp. 89–93.

[36] For St Anthony's, see Baillie, 'London Churches'; D. Knowles and R. N. Hadcock, *Medieval Religious Houses: England and Wales* (2nd edn, London, 1971), p. 373, and more recently on John Benet, instructor of the choristers there, *c.* 1443–9, C. M. Barron, 'Education in London', in J. Blair and B. Golding (eds), *The Cloister and the World: Essays in Medieval History in Honour of Barbara Harvey* (Oxford, 1996), at pp. 228–9. An inventory of the Hospital's books in 1499 included 'a lytyll grayle for the organys. Item ij pryksong bookys one of paper and theother of parchment. Item a boke of brevys and longys' (Windsor Erary, XV.37.23).

[37] See BL Egerton MS 2886, at, for example, fol. 263 (1524/5), which records payments to clerics from King's Lynn, Leicester, Tattershall, St Paul's and Revesby Abbey, and from the household of Cardinal Wolsey. We are grateful to Magnus Williamson for drawing our attention to this information.

towne'.[38] What in an older construction might be cast as a 'minimal choral establishment' thus emerges as a significant consumer of polyphony, networked with – albeit not located at – the apex of the system. The position of English monasteries in the fifteenth and sixteenth centuries is similarly ripe for review. Some were of course vast, but even here perceived provinciality and/or Protestant echoes in their recent historiography have damped down attention for all but a handful of the largest.[39] Yet, as is clear (though not always from their own records), they were significant employers of seculars, well integrated into singers' career paths, and when located in or near small market towns they played important roles in relation to other churches. The networking fostered by even middle-ranking monastic houses emerges clearly from cases such as that of William Preston, lured from secure employment as 'maister of the singing childern' in the Benedictine abbey at Tavistock to perform the same service at Cerne,[40] or from the payments made at Thetford Priory to singers from the royal chapel, including William Cornyshe, or for transporting 'le prikesongbokes' from London.[41] None of these houses was exceptional; Thetford only narrowly escaped the 1536 dissolution of the 'smaller monasteries' and of these three only Tavistock features among the fifty or so houses with annual incomes over £600 in *c.* 1535.[42]

[38] See Lincolnshire Archives Office, Louth, St James' Parish 7/2, fol. 53; cited in M. Williamson, 'The Role of Religious Guilds in the Cultivation of Ritual Polyphony in England: The Case of Louth, 1450–1550', in F. Kisby (ed.), *Music and Musicians in Renaissance Cities, c.1350–c.1650* (Cambridge, forthcoming).

[39] Harrison, *Music in Medieval Britain*, pp. 38–45, 185–94 mentions only six (Glastonbury, Leicester, Muchelney, St Albans, Syon and Waltham) in addition to monastic cathedrals; see also the remarks in Bowers, 'Choral Institutions', p. 2062.

[40] Under less auspicious circumstances as it turned out, since Preston later brought a suit, at some point between 1518 and 1529, alleging non-payment over a period of four years; see PRO, C 1/557/60. The larger abbeys provide similar cases: James Renynger, engaged as organist at Glastonbury in 1534, had previously been organist at Eton and subsequently worked at St Dunstan in the East, London (Harrison, *Music in Medieval Britain*, p. 462; M. Williamson, 'The Early Tudor Court, the Provinces and the Eton Choirbook', *Early Music*, 25 (1997), pp. 229–44, at p. 239).

[41] See *The Register of Thetford Priory*, ed. D. Dymond, 2 vols. (Records of Social and Economic History, NS; Oxford, 1995–6), i, p. 284 (1511/12); ii, p. 600 (1532/3).

[42] *The Register of Thetford Priory*, i, p. 54. The annual incomes of Tavistock, Cerne and Thetford *c.* 1535 were respectively £902, £575 and £312; some twenty-three monastic houses had incomes over £1,000 (for details see Knowles and Hadcock, *Medieval Religious Houses*). At Tutbury Priory, whose income at dissolution was £199, the Prior and Convent retained a layman, Thomas Alenson, 'to kepe oure lady masse daily with priksong and

A final pernicious thread in all of this is the implicit linkage that has grown up between two of the musicologist's favourite hierarchies: size and musical sophistication. It is of course true that much of the most demanding music was found in the largest, richest institutions and performed there by the some of the best singers. The polar opposite of this position, however – that small churches knew nothing of these repertories – is a view both widespread and unsustainable. Parish churches and hospitals achieved access to complex composed polyphony by a variety of means, for example by importing expert singers; they sometimes also had it written down, as demonstrated, for example, by the copying of the *Caput* mass at St Margaret's Westminster in 1480/1.[43] Some owned whole collections of such music at least a generation earlier, as at St James Garlickhithe, London in 1448/9, where one choirbook contained music attributed to named composers and organised by setting in the manner of the Old Hall manuscript and other lavishly prepared choirbooks.[44] So-called 'simple polyphony' – often assumed to have been confined to singers and institutions of limited capabilities – turns out to be more widely found and its presence, perhaps unsurprisingly, to be more functionally than hierarchically determined. Faburdens and similar pieces share the ritual functions of the books, typically processionals and hymnals, in which they were copied; 'simplified' notations may be better understood as 'abbreviated', conveying less information without the presumption of inferior reading skills. The performing personnel and environments for these repertories emerge as not very different from those in which more lavish music was performed. And this in turn may help to explain why borrowed musical material could filter reasonably readily between repertories at different levels of complexity, as for example in several large-scale works incorporating squares or faburdens.

organs and every night after evensong an antem of oure lady and odur divine servyce of festivall dais . . . and to be at mattens at mydnyght in such principall feestes as hath been or hereafter shalbe accostomed to be kept with organs and priksong and to teche vj children playnsong and priksong and descant' (PRO, C 1/603/3). Alenson was engaged in 1495/6 and dismissed in 1527 following, it was alleged, a series of violent disagreements and having 'giffen playn answere that he wold be no daily plair opon thorgans'.

[43] F. Kisby, 'Music and Musicians of Early Tudor Westminster', *Early Music*, 23 (1995), pp. 223–42, at p. 226.

[44] See Appendix, no. 2, item 30. The remainder of the inventory makes clear the church's overall lavishness in provision.

The effects of post-obit provision in urban churches have only recently begun to be studied for their impact on overall provision and on the musically skilled urban workforce. But a number of important preliminary conclusions can be drawn, broadening significantly Harrison's limited taxonomy of polyphonic activity (organs, rood lofts, conducts and books of polyphony).[45] Singers in large urban centres appear to have formed a sizeable pool of labour, variously but often flexibly available to smaller as well as larger churches. 'Freelance' working appears commonplace, undertaken by those with positions in churches as well as by those without. Overall, the workforce grew, to at least the extent implied by increased post-mortem provision. Recent work on clerical residence patterns in London suggests that the lower reaches of the business were highly transient, with about 80 per cent of chantry priests and clerks moving within or out of the capital within a two-year period.[46] By contrast, the remaining 20 per cent often remained for an average of a decade or more. Details of these more settled arrangements are frequently revealed in wills and those in more senior posts had the opportunity to dig themselves deep into local networks, with all the plurality of interests and connections that this entails.

In this setting, Walter Frye provides a case in point, as in different ways do Nicholas Sturgeon, John Dunstable and Gilbert Banaster (see Figure 2). Frye joined the London parish clerks' guild in 1455/6 and at his death in 1475 he owed tithes, indicating residence and perhaps property ownership, in the parishes of All Hallows the Less and of St Gregory by St Paul.[47] Association with the first probably reflected his employment, documented between 1464 and 1472, with Anne, Duchess of Exeter, sister of Edward IV, whose palace of Coldharbour was the main landmark of the parish. His second parish connection may disclose a link

45 *Music in Medieval Britain*, p. 197.

46 Lloyd, 'Provision for Music', chapter 3.

47 Frye's membership of the parish clerk's guild, which began in the year from Ascension (15 May) 1455, is redated together with those of many others in N. James, *The Bede Roll of the Fraternity of St Nicholas* (London Record Society, forthcoming); we are grateful to Dr James for allowing us to see the text of his edition before publication. For Frye's will (12 August 1474, proved 5 June 1475), see PRO, PROB 11/6, fol. 141v. For Frye and Anne, Duchess of Exeter, see A. Wathey, 'Walter Frye and the Brussels Choirbook', forthcoming.

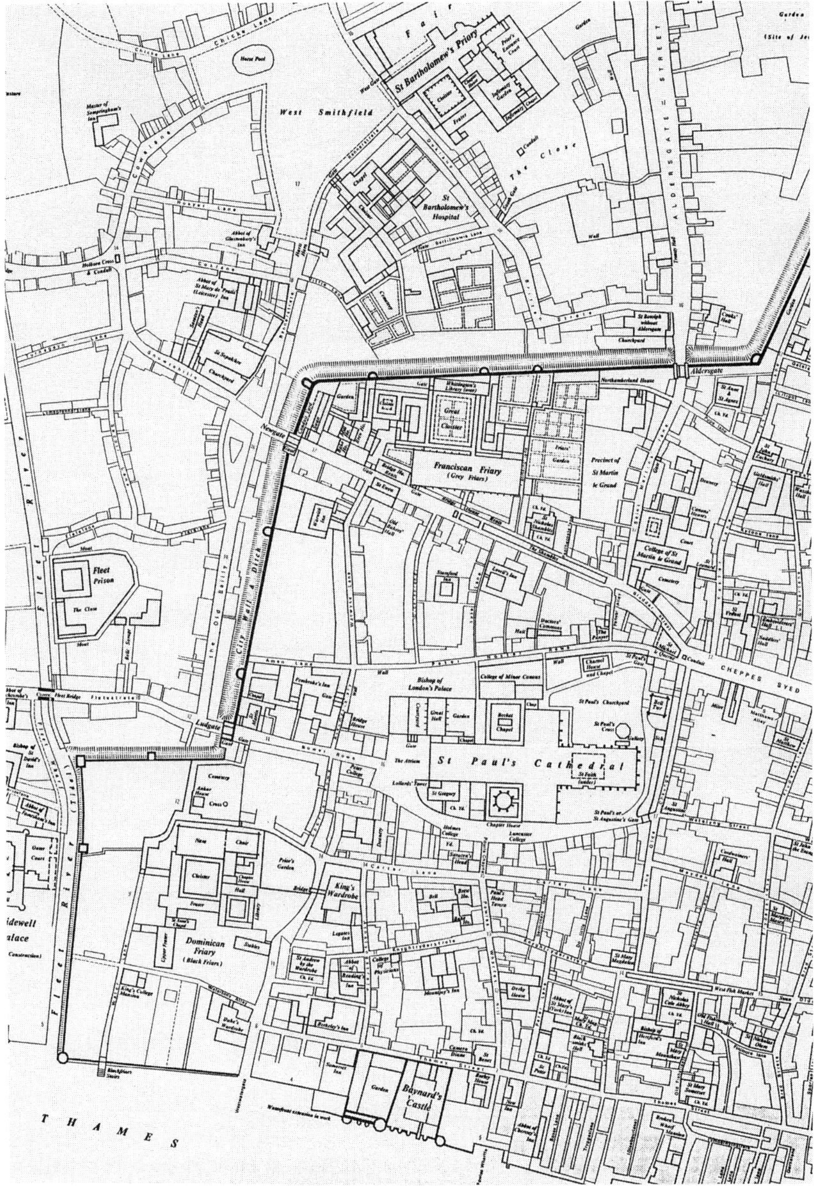

Figure 2 Detailed plan of St Paul's, Blackfriars and Smithfield, London (from *The City of London from Prehistoric Times to c. 1520*, ed. M. D. Lobel (The British Atlas of Historic Towns, 3; Oxford, 1989), Map 2)

with St Paul's, since St Gregory's embraced the area surrounding the cathedral, and it probably also reflects his membership of the confraternity at the neighbouring Blackfriars, where he bequeathed further sums for *post mortem* services.[48] In Sturgeon's case, residence reveals both occupational and familial networks. At Easter 1442, he leased from the St Paul's chapter a property known as Stamford's Inn in Warwick Lane, close to the cathedral. But his first residence as a canon lay in the precinct of the Hospital of St Bartholomew, Smithfield, where his brother Richard Sturgeon was also resident and later endowed an extensive obit.[49] John Dunstable appears to have held property in thirteen parishes by the time of his death, including St Stephen Walbroke, where he was buried, and the neighbouring parish of St Benet Sherehog (see Figure 3).[50] For an armiger, one step below knighthood, this number of holdings is probably unremarkable. More striking in the present context is their spread within the city and the implications that this holds for their owner's connections, interests and obligations across London.

One further by-product of the expanding labour force, feeding equally on such networks, was the strong and emerging professional linkage, reflected by interchangeable personal styles between parish clerks, scriveners and writers of court letter. As a group the parish clerks had long formed a mid-ranking executive layer in the parish, directly charged by the churchwardens with the security and upkeep of the goods of the church, including its books, on occasion merging occupationally with the ranks of conducts and chantry priests.[51] Parish clerks were, moreover, also frequently the local copyists of polyphony, and their links with

[48] See PRO, PROB 11/6, fol. 141^{v}: 'Item volo quod littere fraternitatis mee pro conventum [*sic*] fratrum predicatorum London' michi sigillate post obitum meum eidem conventui deportetur unacum xl s. ut faciant me participem magis suffragiorum suorum prout in litteris predictis continentur.'

[49] See GL MS 25513, fol. 202^{v}. For Richard Sturgeon, see PRO, PROB 11/3, fol. 65^{r-v} (will of 14 May 1456; proved 1 June 1457).

[50] See, for example, CLRO, Hustings Rolls 172, 175; A. Wathey, 'Dunstable in France', *Music & Letters*, 67 (1986), pp. 1–36, at p. 27.

[51] Discussed in Lloyd, 'Provision for Music', chapter 5. See also, for example, *The Medieval Records*, ed. Littlehales, i, pp. 133, 314, 350, 382; ii, pp. xix, lvii. Two late fifteenth-century cases concerning the theft of church goods from St Giles Cripplegate (PRO, C 1/76/111) and St Mary Woolnoth (C 1/66/292) throw further light on the detail of this relationship.

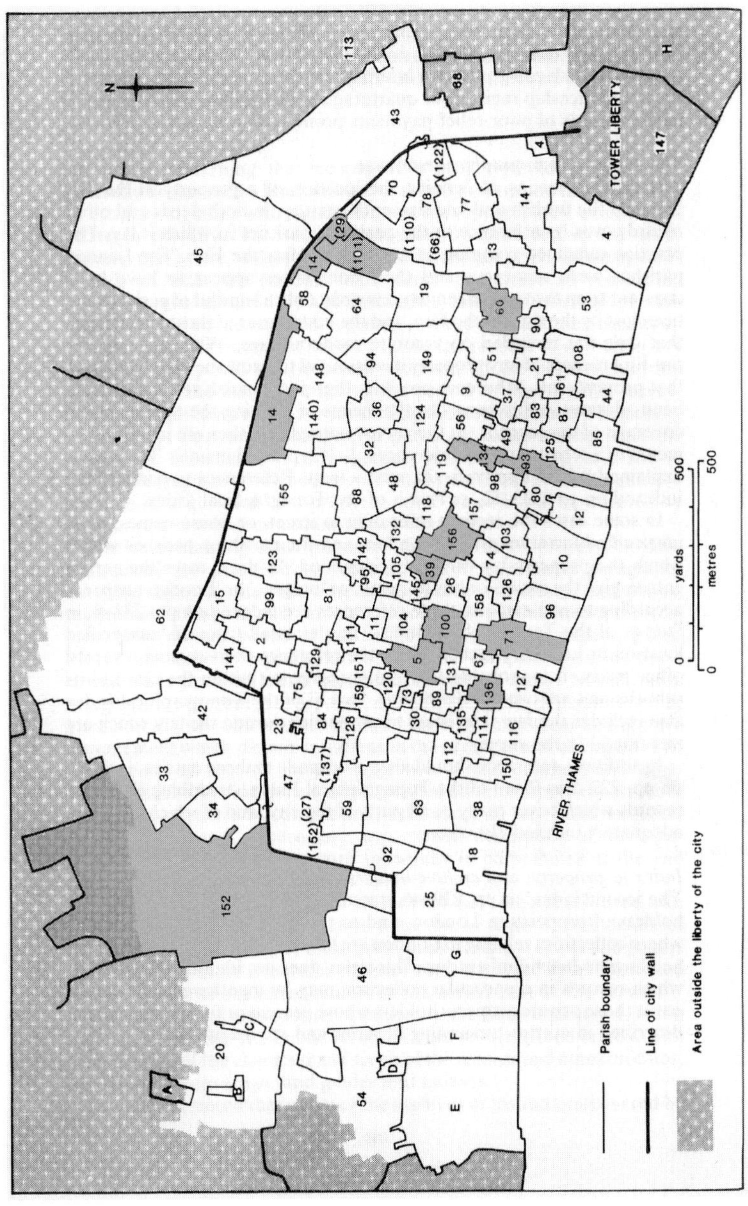

Figure 3 Parishes in which John Dunstable held lands
(map adapted from Keene and Harding, *A Survey*, p. xvi)

commercial production (as semi-professional stationers) puts the urban circulation of liturgical or ritual texts of all types – whether texts, plainsong or polyphony – into a new and dynamic relationship with both the workforce and the extended workplace.

III: THE CONTEXT: A CASE STUDY

The late-medieval urban Church was the result of generations of endowment; but it was also the product of an interplay between history and geography in individual locations. How did these factors mesh to produce an urban environment, the backdrop against which the boundaries and contours of the map, as well as institutional and personal networks, were projected? London, the largest and most influential city in England throughout the Middle Ages, repays attention as a case study.[52] While not typical, its size, wealth and sheer diversity yield models for numerous developments elsewhere.

The City stood on the northern bank of the Thames on two hills, Cornhill in the east and Ludgate hill in the west, between which flowed the Walbrook stream. The Roman city was walled on all sides but in the early Saxon period this area was deserted when most habitation and commerce moved west to the Aldwych.[53] The Viking threat in the ninth century prompted the reoccupation of the City, given the relative safety afforded by the walls to inhabitants, trade and manufacture, and there London stayed and flourished. The City evolved a sophisticated and effective system of government, based on territorial units (wards) which appointed aldermen and elected Common Councillors. Participation in this government was restricted to men who had achieved civic franchise, the freedom of the City, by service and success in one of its craft gilds. In common with other trading settlements, two themes dominate its development: ease of access for trade, and the emergence of complex social arrangements 'on the ground'.

[52] The following account is indebted to the essays and maps in M. D. Lobel (ed.), *The City of London from Prehistoric Times to c.1520* (The British Atlas of Historic Towns, 3; Oxford, 1989).

[53] The walled area was not left void, however; on the western hill, closest to the *wic*, were a royal residence, a possible place of public assembly in the former amphitheatre, the cathedral and the bishop's house and a number of lesser residential enclosures.

The Thames was London's main artery, facilitating trade and supply with western Europe, the eastern and southern coasts of England, the rich hinterland of the Thames valley and thence much of southern England. It afforded easy contact with royal and administrative centres at Westminster and Greenwich. A bridge over the Thames had been built in the twelfth century and for long remained an object of wonder to visitors; more important, it provided the only easy river crossing below Kingston, further concentrating commercial activity in and around the City. The bridge also afforded ready access to Southwark, free of the City's jurisdiction and therefore a magnet for its outcasts: prostitutes, aliens, those practising without the freedom of a craft, bear-pits, other leisure pursuits and (eventually) theatres. Within the City, communications determined settlement patterns. London's street plan evolved in the ninth and tenth centuries independent of the earlier Roman scheme. The grid of streets in each of its two halves, separated by the Walbrook, gathered around two great market thoroughfares, Westcheap (or Cheapside) and Eastcheap.[54] By the twelfth century, a great food market ran down Westcheap from St Paul's to the Poultry, a development greatly assisted by the relative ease of supply via the roads running into Newgate and Aldersgate.[55] Proximity to river and roads introduced a greater variety of goods and by the late Middle Ages Cheapside was the City's main trading artery. East of the Walbrook, the ease of sea, river and land access stimulated markets for fish and meat in and around Eastcheap, and for fish particularly around New Fishstreet, running north from the bridge just to the west of Billingsgate. The grid of streets which grew around the western and eastern 'cheaps' or markets contrasted with the sparser pattern of streets in the north and north-eastern sectors of the city which, at least in the high Middle Ages, were also less densely inhabited.

The development of wards when habitation returned to the walled area was the fundamental on which much of the subsequent

[54] The following rests on the discussion in C. Brooke, 'The Central Middle Ages: 800–1270', in Lobel (ed.), *The City of London*, pp. 30–41, at p. 33.

[55] From west to east: the Shambles, or meat market, between Newgate and Westcheap; a fish market, in Old Fish Street linked to Cheapside by Friday Street; Bread Street and Milk Street, populated by bakers and dairymen; Honey Lane, and the Coneyhope (rabbit market), and finally, at the east end of Cheapside, the Poultry.

neighbourhood and civic government of London rested. The tenth and eleventh centuries also saw the evolution of London's other basic territorial division: the parish. Significantly, parishes developed separately from and seldom if ever meshed with or shared the boundaries of the larger wards.[56] They were small, organic growths, representing the results of local devotion and initiative that crystallised into the provision of a neighbourhood church; the communities thus served ultimately resolved themselves into parishes. This development pre-dates effective ecclesiastical supervision. Thus parishes were small and numerous; the church almost always lay at the centre of the parish, as eventually defined; major streets were thoroughfares, not boundaries. Together these characteristics suggest spontaneous, localised action; an official or planned process would undoubtedly have imposed tidier regularity. Like the street pattern, parishes reflected economic determinants and population density; in the centre of the City they were thus small and concentrated, and larger towards its periphery.

The conspicuous wealth of many inhabitants and the steady proximity and strength of royal and noble influence prompted a constant stream of voluntary, intercessory foundation, earlier of large monasteries, nunneries and hospitals, later of smaller institutions, including colleges and almshouses. In this sense, London presents only an exaggerated version of a phenomenon found in other English towns. It is a striking feature of pre-Reformation London that these institutions were sited in the less heavily inhabited sectors of the City, in an arc around its periphery. Some older houses stood just inside or just outside the walls, among them St Martin le Grand, St Bartholomew's Priory and Hospital, the hospital and priory of St Mary Bethlehem, St Helen's nunnery near Bishopsgate, the Priory of Holy Trinity, Aldgate, and the hospital of St Katherine near the Tower. Surrounding this inner arc was another further outside the walls: St Peter's Abbey, Westminster to the west; the Cluniac priory of Bermondsey and Augustinian Priory of St Mary Overy, Southwark, to the south; the Cistercian house of St Mary Graces and the House of the Minoresses (the 'Minories') dedicated to St Clare to the east. At some distance out-

[56] Brooke, 'The Central Middle Ages', p. 34.

side the different gates were St Mary Spittal, the Charterhouse, St John's Clerkenwell and the fifteenth-century Hospital of St John the Baptist on the site of the Savoy. Predating all of these foundations was St Paul's on Ludgate hill, over 600 feet in length and with a spire rising to some 500 feet. Some small foundations were, however, sited more centrally, including the colleges founded by Poultney and Whittington and the hospitals of St Thomas of Acon and St Anthony of Vienne, and many noble and episcopal dwellings in the City had private chapels. The friaries complete this panorama of London's extra-parochial institutions: the Carmelite house lay west of the City near Fleet Street, the other four lay round the City just inside the walls. London's 107 parish churches stretched a close pastoral web over the City and by the late Middle Ages almost all had been enriched by noteworthy intercessory provision, in particular chantry foundation. The sum of these elements – a central cluster and sparser peripheral network of parishes, overlaid by a wide variety of larger intercessory and other institutions – reveals a remarkable density and diversity in religious provision. The forest of spires and towers sprouting into the skyline, so notable a feature of Wyngaerde's panorama of London in the early 1540s,[57] symbolised the cumulative ecclesiastical and intercessory investment made by generations of Londoners (see Figure 4). Each of the City's ecclesiastical institutions, moreover, provided a more or less sophisticated liturgy. London's wealth, the proximity of the court, the mobility and expertise of its workforce, the taste for novelty and spirit of competition which wealth in a densely populated environment can foster, alongside the constant need for spiritual solace, were, it can be argued, all factors combining to make London a liturgical hothouse. While London was exceptional, a similar atmosphere prevailed in other towns.

IV: REAPPRAISING THE SOURCES

Redrawing the urban ecclesiastical map poses significant questions about sources, particularly those at parish level where the extent and sophistication of liturgical provision has been least clear. It is

[57] *The Panorama of London circa 1544 by Anthonis van den Wyngaerde*, ed. H. M. Colvin and S. Foister (London Topographical Society, 141; London, 1996).

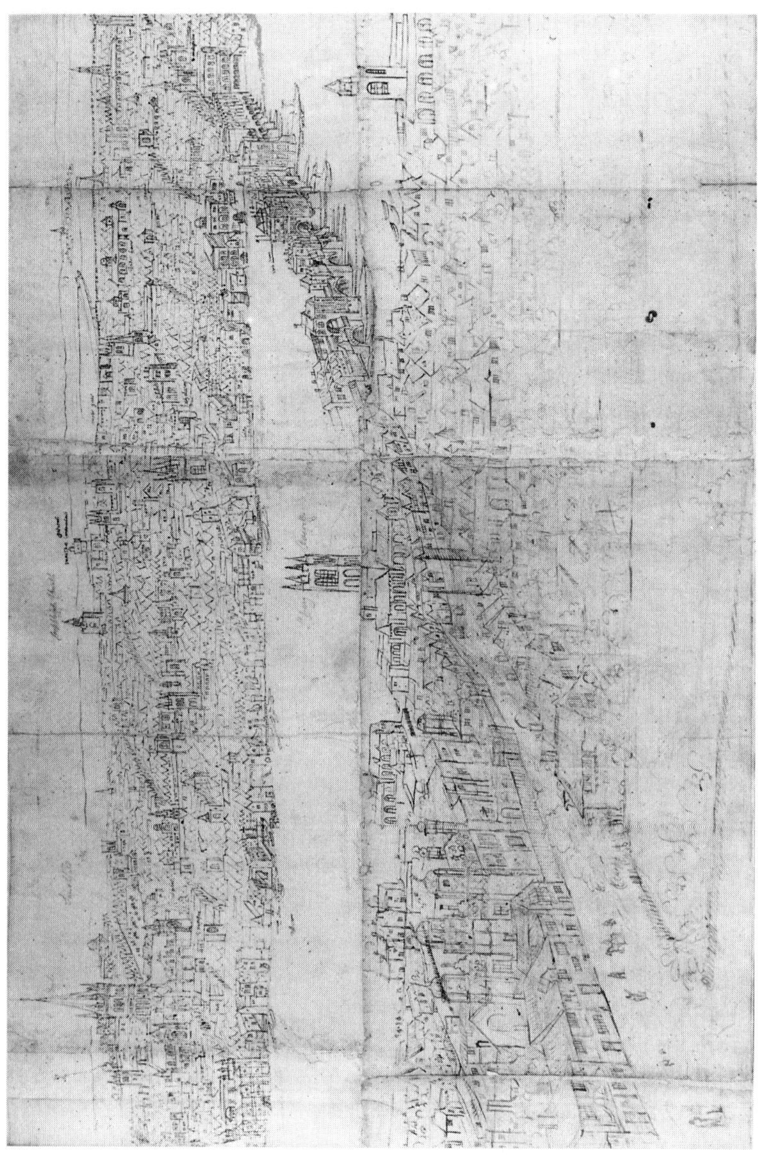

Figure 4 The western parts of the City of London, in Anthony van der Wyngaerde's panorama, *c.* 1544 (reproduced by permission of the Ashmolean Museum, Oxford)

to the most important of these, the churchwardens' accounts, that we now turn. Churchwardens' accounts survive in greater abundance in England than elsewhere in Europe: the earliest dates from the mid-fourteenth century and by the late fifteenth century they are relatively numerous. They survive for both urban and rural parishes, but distribution is patchy. Many more survive for the south of England than for the north, and towns are better represented. Some, including London and Bristol, have a number of surviving sets (for London see Figure 5); others, among them York and Norwich, have almost none. Overall they are not plentiful, nor do they often survive in a complete series over a sustained period. But, while they can be made to yield a detailed impression of the laity's management of and investment in parish life, systematic use has yet to be made of them. In part this is symptomatic of the wider neglect of the pre-Reformation Church.

If we seek to use them we have to establish a methodology.[58] Churchwardens usually served in pairs for a one- or two-year stint, and were charged by their fellow parishioners to act as agents for the benefit of the parish community. They were responsible for maintaining the building of the parish church (strictly, for the nave and tower) and the vestments and equipment necessary for the seemly celebration of rites within the church. They were obliged to keep accounts so that, at visitation, the bishop or his deputy might ascertain that the parish community had an adequate building in which to worship and that the incumbent had the equipment appropriate for the discharge of his duties. Less formally, fellow parishioners had a natural interest in the churchwardens' accountability for funds. Churchwardens therefore presented accounts to the parish for audit at the end of their term of office; these were kept so that they might be produced at visitation and, presumably, to assist future management by facilitating comparisons with previous conduct. This leads to a number of points. First, the churchwardens' brief was restricted: they were not in charge of every aspect of parish life and provision, nor do they record in

[58] Much of the following rests on C. Drew, *Early Parochial Organisation in England: The Origins of the Office of Churchwarden* (St Anthony's Hall Publications, 7; York, 1954); see also B. Kümin, *The Shaping of a Community: The Rise and Reformation of the English Parish, c.1400–1560* (Aldershot, 1996), chapter 2.

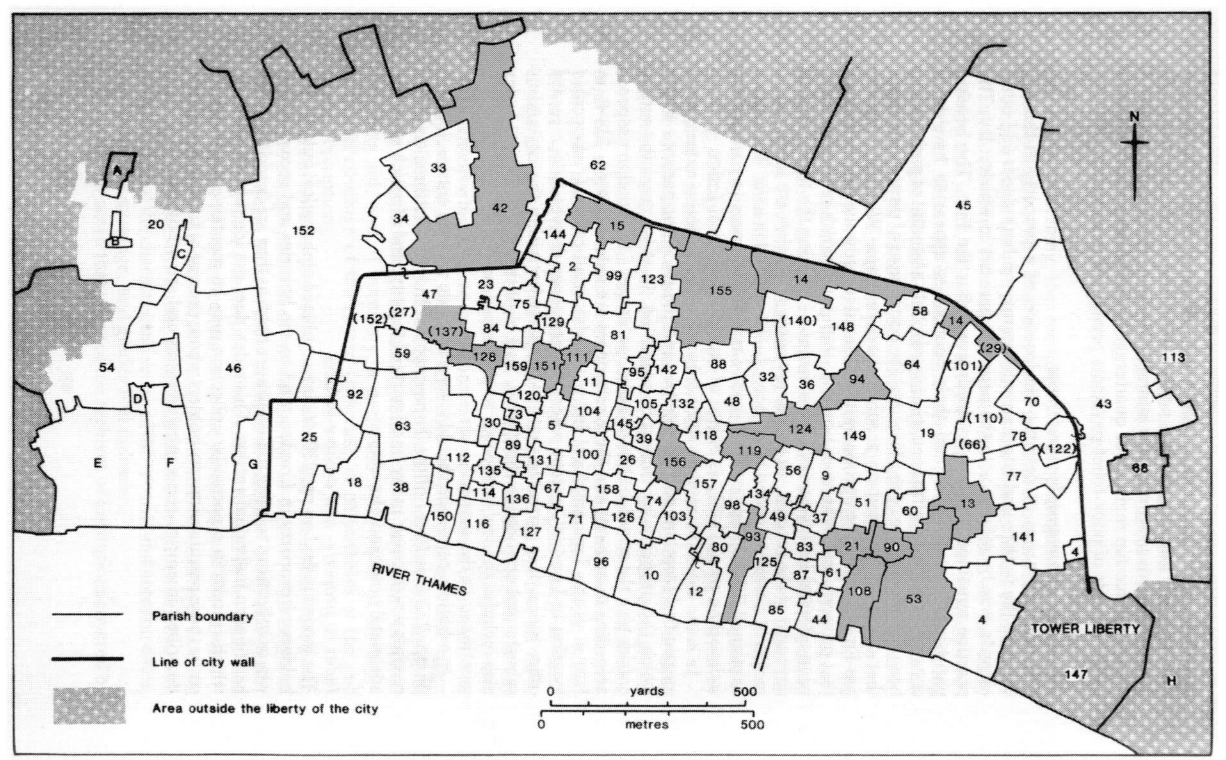

Figure 5 Survival of pre-Reformation churchwardens' accounts by parish (map adapted from Keene and Harding, *A Survey*, p. xvi)

their accounts the character of their duties from year to year. Their accounts are thus limited and variable from year to year, with never an indication of the proportion of the parish budget represented. Second, churchwardenship was a 'rung on the ladder'; there were other individuals, about whom we know much less because they did not preserve accounts so assiduously, who had previously served as churchwardens and who were now referred to as 'the masters' or 'the worshipful'. This group was in effective control of parish life, but depended on the churchwardens for day-to-day management.[59] This leads to a division. Churchwardens were responsible for basic maintenance; more flamboyant provision was in the hands of 'the masters'. Others in the parish might be responsible for rebuilding programmes (as opposed to maintenance) or for the provision of a more elaborate or impressive liturgy (as opposed to canonically required basic observance), but their records seldom survive. Churchwardens' accounts, therefore, offer a restricted impression of parish life.

In addition, the accounts as they survive are not ordinarily the audited documents but fair copies, tidied and presented at a later date. To celebrate the good work that wardens had done for the parish community, accounts were often rendered into a memorial fair copy. Churchwardens were benefactors and deserved to be remembered; the tidied versions of their accounts were intended to facilitate seemly remembrance and even intercession from the body of the parish that benefited from the wardens' work.[60] At All Saints', Bristol, accounts both tidied and audited are preserved for the later 1460s and early 1470s, and comparison reveals that 'tidied' means drastically abbreviated.[61] Not only was the wardens'

[59] For a more detailed discussion of these points based on two of London's parishes in Billingsgate ward, see C. Burgess, 'Shaping the Parish: St Mary at Hill, London, in the Fifteenth Century', in Blair and Golding (eds), *The Cloister and the World*, pp. 246–86; *The Church Records of St Andrew Hubbard*, ed. Burgess, pp. xxi–xxx; and as a summary, *idem*, 'London Parishes'.

[60] This was explicitly done in Bristol's All Saints' Church Book, where long-obsolete accounts were copied up to celebrate the good deeds of the parish's churchwardens, just as other material in the Church Book commemorates the generosity of other benefactors 'so that they should not be forgotten but be had in remembrance and be prayed for of all this parish'; see *The Pre-Reformation Records of All Saints', Bristol: Part 1*, ed. C. Burgess (Bristol Record Society Publications, 46; Bristol, 1995), pp. xxvi–xxxvi, xxxviii–xli, 4.

[61] The much fuller audited accounts are printed in *The Pre-Reformation Records of All Saints', Bristol: Part 2*, ed. C. Burgess (Bristol Record Society Publications; Bristol, forthcoming, 2001).

brief limited, but their accounts as preserved are frequently summaries.

In the absence of additional material against which they might be measured and checked, it has usually been assumed that churchwardens' accounts convey a comprehensive impression of the laity's contribution to parish life. This is emphatically not the case. Flamboyant provision, over and above canonical requirements, is either absent from or, at best, severely underrepresented. Music is a case in point. Although music was central to parish liturgies, certainly in towns, by the later Middle Ages it is mentioned relatively seldom in churchwardens' accounts, if only because it was far less prominent in parish provision during the thirteenth century when churchwardens' duties were initially defined. Churchwardens' accounts itemise the purchase and installation of organs; they mention the acquisition of written polyphony; they register payments to singers and players, particularly at Christmas, Candlemas, Easter and other major festivals when parish provision was swelled by supernumeraries. But churchwardens also recorded many more payments for the refreshments provided to singers than they did for the singers' stipends.[62] As far as music was concerned, wardens took care of the extras, of supplementary payments; others, apparently the 'masters' of the parish, shouldered the main burden, collecting and paying for musicians and singers. Parishes were benefiting from much more than their churchwardens provided. This principle is important and helps to make sense of the extraneous, often surprising material which survives in parish memoranda – surprising because it so often depicts a situation wildly at variance with the circumspect payments and provision which churchwardens made.

Three examples will make the point. The first is from the records of St Mary at Hill, London, and is a later memorandum on the version of William Cambridge's will copied into one of the Church Books.[63] Cambridge had been Mayor of London and, a very

[62] It is, for instance, striking that in both All Saints', Bristol, and St Andrew Hubbard, Eastcheap, churchwardens paid for the wine given to the singers on Palm Sunday, but did not pay for the singers.

[63] For a transcript see *The Medieval Records*, ed. Littlehales, i, p. 16; the will, copied in 1486, is GL MS 1239/2, fols. 10–12; the memorandum is copied later and in a different hand on fol. 12^{v}. For a summary, see also Burgess, 'Shaping the Parish', p. 280.

wealthy man, was a major benefactor to the parish, building the chapel of St Stephen on the north side of the church. He died in 1431 and established a perpetual chantry in the church, a priest being provided to sing divine service daily in St Stephen's chapel; Cambridge had requested also that his anniversary be kept 'cum nota'. The memorandum on his will, however, which was written some time after the 1480s, reveals that much more was customarily being provided for Cambridge's benefit. At the Magnificat during evensong on Christmas day (St Stephen's eve), it was customary to distribute fifteen lighted candles, one to every surpliced priest, clerk and child providing the service; holding a lighted candle, all proceeded to Cambridge's tomb, in the chapel of St Stephen, singing a respond of St Stephen with the prose, followed by a versicle with the collect of St Stephen; after this they proceeded into the choir singing an anthem of Our Lady. As well as adding to the liturgical elaboration of the parish, it is clear from this memorandum that benefactors could rely and build on a sophisticated round of observance already present. If, however, one were to rely only on churchwardens' accounts, one would never assume the existence of a choir of fifteen, apparently readily available, that this memorandum implies. And the resources of St Mary at Hill were by no means unique; they were not even unusual in London by the end of the fifteenth century.[64] The will of Jane, Viscountess Lisle, made in 1500, reveals a similar situation in her parish church, St Michael Cornhill, London, where she was to be buried.[65] She requested that in the forty days following her burial the priests and clerks of St Michael should sing solemnly by note a mass of Requiem and dirige for her soul and the souls of her late husbands and parents, 'and the number of priests daily shall be twelve, or ten at least'. The resources were there, but what did they sing?

To attempt some answer to this question, we turn finally to the parish of All Saints', Bristol, a smaller community in a town that,

[64] *London and Middlesex Chantry Certificate, 1548*, ed. Kitching, records a number of churches in London with more stipendiaries than St Mary at Hill, including two (St Magnus and St Dunstan in the East) in the Billingsgate area.

[65] Printed in *Sede Vacante Wills: A Calendar of Wills proved before the Commissary of the Prior and Chapter of Christ Church Canterbury during Vacancies in the Primacy*, ed. C. E. Woodruff (Kent Archaeological Society Records Branch, 3; London, 1914), pp. 127 ff.

though smaller than London, was rich and prominent by contemporary standards. Among the end papers of the 1522/3 accounts for the Halleways' chantry, a perpetual chantry kept in All Saints', is an inventory, apparently in the hand of one Jerome Grene, one of the churchwardens for that year.[66] The inventory, dated 1524, lists the music left to the parish by the parish clerk, William Brigeman, who is known as a clerk at Eton College in 1503 and who died in Bristol in 1524. Among the items listed in the inventory are at least four sets of part-books, containing masses, votive antiphons, Magnificats and responsorial items in five and four parts; two choirbooks, containing Kyries, Alleluias, masses, antiphons, Lady-mass sequences, a passion and Fayrfax's mass 'Dobull Desolre' [*O bone iesu*] and Magnificat; books and rolls for children, other rolls containing anthems, carols and processional items 'with diverse other small songes, abowte the number of xl Rolls'. Brigeman had bequeathed these materials 'in his testament to the use of the said church (All Saints') under the condition that no children should be taught upon the said books, scrolls and rolls'. Harrison uses this document to show that five-part music was sung throughout the year at All Saints' (a parish of some 180 communicant members in the 1540s), concluding that 'the church's remarkably comprehensive liturgy bears comparison with that of the King's College Cambridge inventory of 1529, with which list All Saints' has much in common'.[67] One would not chance this conclusion if the churchwardens' accounts were all that survived for the parish; they do survive, they are detailed, and they include payments for copying polyphony.[68] But there is no a priori reason

[66] BRO, P/AS/C1; printed in F. Ll. Harrison, 'The Repertory of an English Parish Church in the Early Sixteenth Century', in J. Robijns *et al.* (eds), *Renaissance-muziek, 1400–1600: donum natalicium René Bernard Lenaerts* (Musicologica Lovaniensia, 1; Leuven, 1969), pp. 143–7 and in Appendix, no. 1 below; see also E. G. C. F. Atchley, 'The Halleway Chauntry at the Parish Church of All Saints, Bristol, and the Halleway Family', *Transactions of the Bristol and Gloucestershire Archaeological Society*, 24 (1901), pp. 74–135.

[67] 'The Repertory', p. 147.

[68] Particularly in the late 1520s, though whether this was a new development or resulted from a change in the brief determining accounting methods is open to debate. In 1527 the wardens paid 6*s*. 8*d*. and 8*s*. 10*d*. respectively to the clerk of St Thomas for five pricksong books containing eight masses and to John Beche for pricking four books of masses and anthems 'of the trebuls and the meanes' (both entries probably refer to sets of partbooks). They also paid 3½*d*. for a quire of paper to 'perform the said pricksong book[s]' and 4*d*. to the clerk of St Thomas for binding a book. All Saints' had an altar dedicated to St Thomas and it is likely that this clerk was one of the parish's own clergy; the iden-

for assuming that such provision was unique in Bristol; many of the other parish churches in the town were markedly larger and wealthier. As the main set of accounts makes clear, moreover, this list simply commemorates Brigeman's bequest; a subsequent inventory of 1535/6, recorded in the churchwardens' accounts, reveals that the church maintained a separate collection of its own books, some of which had been purchased from, and were probably copied by, former churchwardens and parish clerks.[69] Our ignorance of the equivalent situation in other parishes, when combined with powerful preconceptions of pre-Reformation conditions, has tended to suppress any such paradigm – wrongly, it would appear.

A parallel impression emerges from legal sources. A full survey remains to be made of the English material, but equity suits in Chancery emerge as particularly rich in cases involving the personnel and goods of urban churches.[70] These are often informative well beyond the scope of the church's own records, but, more important, go some way to revealing variety and flexibility in practice, as well as the shape of informal arrangements. Two examples can illustrate this point. First, a case concerning sums due to the executors of John Wetwood, a canon of St Mary's Warwick (a collegiate church that also served the parish) who died on St Katherine's day 1542, reveals not only that he was receiving sums for boarding a chorister that were identified in the accounts as the chorister's own dues, but also that he received a dividend over and above his stipend, paid only in years showing a profit and then at varying rates.[71] The church's own accounts are blind at this level of detail, recording the first sum as a liability rather than as a transfer of hard cash (and thus overlooking Wetwood) and the second not at all.

tity of John Beche is uncertain. In 1528 Beche received 4*d*. for 'pricking a song against St Nicholas Night' and possibly also the payment of 12*d*., immediately following, 'for making and pricking a part that was lost'. See BRO, P/AS/ChW 3, *sub* 1527, fol. 4 and *sub* 1528, fol. 5.

69 Appendix, no. 1.

70 For a general guide, see H. Horwitz, *A Guide to Chancery Equity Records and Proceedings* (2nd edn, Public Record Office Handbooks, 27; London, 1998).

71 See PRO, C 1/1092/42, the bill of complaint of Richard Wetwood, administrator of John Wetwood's goods; C 4/23/127, the Dean and Chapter's answer, and C 1/1092/43, Richard Wetwood's replication. For payments in 1540/41, see the sub-treasurer's accounts in PRO, E 315/64, fols. 17–34; see also D. Styles, *Ministers' Accounts of the Collegiate Church of St. Mary, Warwick, 1432–85* (Dugdale Society, 26; Oxford, 1969), pp. xxix–xxxi for the payment of stipends in the early fifteenth century, and p. lv for John Wetwood.

A second example concerns the acquisition of an antiphonal, in effect sold by one London parish church to another via a series of informal arrangements and loans.[72] John Motram, a chantry priest at St Mary at Hill and subsequently priest of St Paul's, owned the antiphonal, which he 'loved as his principall jeuell' and for several years before his death he appears to have intended to bequeath it to St Mary's. At the instigation of the St Mary's churchwardens, who received the proceeds, he sold the antiphonal to the churchwardens of St Botolph Billingsgate, the neighbouring parish, via their agent John Benyngton. This took place a some point between 1466 and 1471, but nine years later Motram alleged that the book had been lent to Benyngton only so that he might have the book at his house 'to the intent that he myght shewe the same to a conyng man for to have anoþer made of lyke fynenes both in stuffe and writtyng'. Motram's complaint demanded the return of the book; Benyngton's answer claimed that proceeds of the sale had already been paid to the St Mary's churchwardens. Eventually, as their accounts reveal, Motram's antiphonal, or the proceeds of its sale, supported a twenty-year obit in Holmes College (the College of chantry priests) at St Paul's.[73] Important here is less that parishes were in the habit of selling books to one another, even those that they did not yet own, but that it was plausible to allege an arrangement of such informality as the domestic loan of an illuminated antiphonal for the purpose of making a copy. This is unexpected even if we believe that the market was largely bespoke and such cases are invisible to most classic definitions of the market (though whether they should be is another matter), as well as to the churchwardens' accounts.

[72] For the following, see the bill of complaint, answer and replication in PRO, C 1/51/253–255 (quotations from C 1/51/253). The bill was addressed to the Bishop of Lincoln as chancellor, thus locating the case within the chancellorship of Thomas Rotherham, 1474–80. Mortram was still a priest serving the chantry of William Cambridge at St Mary at Hill in 1481 but had vacated this position by 1489 (see *The Medieval Records*, ed. Littlehales, i, pp. 89, 97, 155); his will was proved before 21 January 1493 (p. 182).

[73] *The Medieval Records*, ed. Littlehales, i, pp. 181–2, 197, 213; the annual cost to the churchwardens was 6*s*. 8*d*.

V: PRODUCTION, CIRCULATION AND CONSUMPTION

Such informal arrangements emerge as particularly important in what have generally been regarded as the production, circulation and consumption of polyphony, in part for reasons of scale of demand and of textual uniqueness. But informal arrangements, proximity and other constants in urban society also invite scrutiny of these terms. It is easier to trace the production of written media that transmitted polyphony than of the performed 'product' even though the latter was almost certainly the more prevalent activity. What we have traditionally represented as circulation is often closer to transmission, especially in situations where the market was barely in evidence. Consumption prompts the question: who was consuming what? To replace production, circulation and consumption with the less materialist trio of creation, transmission and reception resolves some of these issues. Yet, as has recently been argued, work-centred notions of the market are still only partly appropriate, especially for musical cultures that were intensely performative.[74] A broad model for the century and a half before the Reformation – of which probably the outlines and certainly the detail could be refined – might thus be elaborated along the following lines.[75]

Production. Written polyphonic music for use in church appears to have been largely if not exclusively the work of singers who doubled as copyists, most obviously because musical skills were required to ensure the textual integrity and coherence of the final product. A variety of models emerges from this constant, here described in ascending order of the church's financial commitment. Singers might provide written polyphony themselves, as a modern-day workman would his own tools; such copies are financially invis-

[74] Carter, 'The Sound of Silence'.

[75] An initial exploration of some of the following, to be treated at greater length as part of the Church Music in English Towns project, appears in A. Wathey, 'The Production of Books of Liturgical Polyphony', in D. Pearsall and J. Griffiths (eds), *Book Production and Publishing in Britain, 1375–1475* (Cambridge, 1989), pp. 143–61. For supporting documentation see *idem*, 'Lost Books of Polyphony in Medieval England: A List to 1500', *Royal Musical Association Research Chronicle*, 21 (1988), pp. 1–19, and the supplement covering additions to 1500 and a list to 1548, by F. Kisby, A. Wathey and M. Williamson, forthcoming in the same journal.

ible and are disclosed only by inventories and bequests (as in the case of Brigeman).[76] Churches might pay for materials only, assuming labour to be covered. Or they might pay for labour and materials, effectively meeting the cost of the whole book, though rarely from outside the institution and then usually on the basis of a personal connection. During the fifteenth century there is a gradual increase in institutional involvement, reflecting perhaps the growing page-size of choirbooks – for which the raw materials were now a significant expense – and a more formalised approach to the employment of specialists. By contrast with liturgical books, choirbooks are almost never bought or commissioned from, or copied by, stationers. But stationers did perform tasks for which the ability to read notation was not required, including illuminating and binding. In the early sixteenth century, however, the growth of liturgical printing (though almost never of polyphony) fed a market whose polyphonic needs were met in the shift to part-books and single sheets, physical formats that were portable and cheap and (to judge from the archival evidence) readily taken up.[77] These formats may have increased the potential for stationers' involvement; they certainly suggest an increased volume of copying activity. At the same time, and against the background of an expanding market, some of the parish clerks who had doubled as scriveners or writers of court letter, and who had been the primary copyists of polyphony in parishes, made the natural diversification into printing and the mainstream of the book trade.

Circulation. Implicit in the above is that some polyphonic pieces did not circulate, either for reasons of technical difficulty or because they were yoked to specific performing groups and situations. Whether the same can be said of genres is another matter, as implied above. Faburdens, though not textually stable, are widely transmitted and sometimes appear in multiple copies made

[76] Above, p. 34; see also Wathey, 'The Production', pp. 149–50. For a later example, see the will of Thomas Allen, chantry priest at St Dunstan in the East, London, 24 April 1520, in *London Consistory Court Wills, 1492–1547*, ed. I. Darlington (London Record Society, 3; London, 1967), p. 56 ('I bequethe to the seyde chirche a blake booke of masses in prikson, also 4 quayres of antymes in prikson').

[77] See also the comments in J. Milsom, 'Songs and Society in Early Tudor London', *Early Music History*, 16 (1997), pp. 235–93, at pp. 237–9.

for the same institution.[78] Some large-scale works also appear widely, particularly in the early sixteenth century but also earlier, as demonstrated by the copying of the *Caput* mass at St Margaret's Westminster. By 1480 this work was between thirty and forty years old, and its appearance here helps to challenge the notion that, because of their limited lifespan, English works did not achieve canonic status until the Tudor period. Parish churches in Bristol, London and elsewhere had access to complex repertory and – where the process is transparent – seem to have acquired it, as did numerous establishments of other types, by borrowing and copying from other institutions. For example, King's College Cambridge sent one of its conducts to Fotheringhay 'pro quadam cantu' in 1507/8 and in the following year rewarded the royal chapel composer Prentis and another singer (neither formally attached to King's) for copying masses by Fayrfax.[79] The parish church at Louth sent one of its chantry priests to York to copy polyphony in 1510; similarly, Winchester College sent one of its chaplains to Salisbury in 1548 for 'cantilenis'.[80] Geographic proximity inevitably reduces the noteworthiness of this process, and hence its prominence in the record, but a similar pattern is implicit in urban churches where the copyist is known to have been employed elsewhere and probably also operated when the copying was undertaken by the parish's own clerks.[81] Even standard service books sometimes circulated by peculiar and informal routes that reveal the importance of personal connections between individual urban residents.

[78] For a list, see B. Trowell, 'Faburden – New Sources, New Evidence: A Preliminary Survey', in E. Olleson (ed.), *Modern Musical Scholarship* (London, 1980), pp. 28–78.

[79] See Cambridge, King's College, Mundum Book 10 (unfoliated), *sub* 'Custus equitancium' 1507/8, 'Item xiiij° die Aprilis pro expensis Bourman equitant' ad Fodringay pro quadam cantu ex mandato magistri prepositi, ix d.', and *sub* 'Custus ecclesie' 1508/9, 'Item in regardis datis Prentise et Domino Nicholo Thomas pro missa Fayrfax et aliis cantulis, v s.'; cited in M. Williamson, 'The Eton Choirbook: Its Institutional and Historical Background' (D.Phil. thesis, University of Oxford, 1997), chapter 4.

[80] See *The First Churchwardens' Book of Louth, 1500–1524*, ed. R. C. Dudding (Oxford, 1941), p. 131 (1510/11): 'William Prince prest for songs prekyng at Yorke xvj d.'; Winchester College Muniment 2206 (Bursar's Account, 1548/9): 'Item domino Godwyn pro expensis suis eunti Sarum pro cantilenis, v s. iij d. . . . Item pro cantalenis emptis hoc anno pro choro, v s.'. For what may be a parallel case, see *The Register of Thetford Priory*, ii, p. 600.

[81] As, for example, in *The Medieval Records*, ed. Littlehales, i, pp. 131, 133; ii, p. 350, or at All Saints' Bristol, where the churchwardens paid for five books of 'songs of square note' to be copied at 'Gaunts', the Hospital of St Mark in Bristol (BRO, P/AS/ChW3, sub 1524/25, fol. 5).

Reception/Consumption. Parish churches were arguably more active as users of performed polyphony than as producers of high-art composition in its written form. They copied it but were unsurprisingly more dependent than larger churches on the networking of their own singers who could themselves act as copyists or arrange for others to do so. Consumption of polyphony thus becomes substantially a workforce issue, particularly when informal arrangements between singers rob us of hard evidence in the form of documented payment. The consumers, moreover, were not churches, but at one level singers and at another those members of urban communities who supported the experience of which composed polyphony formed a part. For service books, however, which by contrast had a real market value and whose possession was compelled by canon law, urban parish churches emerge as important consumers, with several in London acquiring printed copies at a relatively early date.[82] The regional and/or national scale of this market – reflecting on general liturgical provision – emerges in a list of books supplied wholesale by Richard Pynson *c.* 1496 to a 'retailer', John Russhe. This reveals print-runs in the region of 500–600 for small format 'massbooks', *c.* 200 for 'greate gylt primers', and *c.* 1,000 for 'journals' and other books with an obvious private sale. Pynson also supplied some more expensive works, including some old stock printed by Caxton, so that Russhe could have 'good utteraunce' with potential customers.[83] Here liturgical books are in the majority and it may be significant that at least some urban churches (for example in London and Warwick) figure among the institutions from which copies survive.[84]

Finally, reception by definition embraces the later fates of polyphony written for the pre-Reformation church, which via their consequences have a pivotal role in the historiography of music in

[82] See, for example, F. Kisby, 'Books in London Parish Churches, 1400–1603', *Proceedings of the 1999 Harlaxton Symposium* (Harlaxton Medieval Studies, 11; Stamford, 2001), forthcoming.

[83] See H. R. Plomer, 'Two Lawsuits of Richard Pynson', *The Library*, NS 10 (1909), pp. 114–33, at pp. 124–30, printing PRO, C 1/1510/43–47; *idem*, 'Pynson's Dealings with John Russhe', *The Library*, 3rd ser. 9 (1919), pp. 150–2; S. H. Johnstone, 'A Study of the Career and Literary Publications of Richard Pynson' (Ph.D. thesis, University of Western Ontario, 1977), pp. 12–18.

[84] See, for example, M. Bent, 'New and Little-Known Fragments of English Medieval Polyphony', *Journal of the American Musicological Society*, 21 (1968), pp. 137–56, at p. 142.

Reformation England. It has long been clear that although losses were vast, religious reform in the mid-sixteenth century could not have been the sole culprit.[85] Much fell victim to earlier destruction as choirbooks followed their contents into obsolescence and, once discarded, fell prey to binders and other consumers of scrap parchment. At the same time, it could be argued, the visibility of written polyphony in dissolution inventories is reduced by a predisposition to personal and semi-personal ownership and by the low material value and high portability of the product (in stark contrast to organs, for example).[86] The obverse of this coin is that, for these books, abstraction from the official process of destruction and from subsequent concealment were both more straightforward and less noteworthy than for other church goods. Old repertory probably remained in the hands of parish clerks and other singers, or even unremarked among larger caches of books and ornaments; perceptions of its utility were constrained by stylistic change, but less perhaps than was once assumed by the finality of religious reform. This argument has implications well beyond the mid-century – at which moment an older historiography, framed in the organ loft, formally appoints the origins of the English choral tradition – as well as, more obviously, for the task of mapping pre-Reformation repertories, practices and continuities. Thus, the Eton Choirbook, completed *c.* 1504, was pressed once more into service during Mary's reign.[87] A fragmentary choirbook from the early sixteenth century, of which more leaves are still coming to light, was demonstrably broken up only in 1609/10;[88]

85 See, for example, Harrison, *Music in Medieval Britain*, pp. 156–219; Wathey, 'Lost Books', p. 1.

86 Harrison noted that nine of 109 reformation inventories from London parishes include polyphony (*Music in Medieval Britain*, p. 201; see also his earlier comments, reported in the discussion of Baillie, 'A London Gild', pp. 26–7); most list no more than a single set of part-books.

87 See N. R. Ker, *Medieval Manuscripts in British Libraries*, 4 vols. (Oxford, 1969–92), ii, pp. 773–4; Williamson, 'The Eton Choirbook', pp. 432–8.

88 The connection between the fragments in All Souls College, MS 330 and London Royal College of Physicians, MS 734 was first signalled in N. R. Ker, *Fragments of Medieval Manuscripts Used as Pastedowns in Oxford Bindings, with a Survey of Oxford Binding c.1515–1620* (Oxford Bibliographical Society Publications, NS 5; Oxford, 1954), pp. 83, 105 (nos. 872, 1128); further leaves and fragments in New College, Oxford and Chester Town Archive, identified by Wathey, are listed *sub* 'Lost Choirbook 2' in G. Curtis and A. Wathey, 'Fifteenth-Century English Liturgical Music: A List of the Surviving Repertory', *Royal Musical Association Research Chronicle*, 27 (1994), pp. 1–69, at p. 23.

another, whose leaves were reused as backing for ceiling-paintings at New College, Oxford, may possibly have perished at about the same time.[89] As in other areas of the church's material and spiritual history, it is arguable that permanent change arrived only in the 1580s, after the execution of Mary Queen of Scots and the defeat of the Armada. The drift towards the destruction of choirbooks may have been irreversible only when revivalist aspirations were extinguished with the accession of James.

In conclusion we make three observations. First, both the quantity and the diversity of activity are underestimated by established approaches to music and liturgy in English institutions. The grail of documentary certainty is partly responsible for this, but so too is the inherited historiography, some of which has proved remarkably durable both within and outside the academic discipline of history. Second, we argue that the urban church is much more fully integrated than previously thought, both with its surrounding community and with other institutional players (guilds, courts and other churches). Third, and in consequence, the contribution of these communities provided liturgical, celebratory and commemorative activity with a substantial part of its rationale and material support, alongside the actions of the church's own managers. This last point is of course not wholly novel. But here too it is possible to underestimate the level of activity and the broader implications of such support for musical and liturgical practice have, in an English setting, yet fully to be traced out.

Royal Holloway, University of London

[89] Oxford, New College, MS 368; see *Manuscripts at Oxford: An Exhibition in Memory of Richard William Hunt (1908–1979), Keeper of Western Manuscripts at the Bodleian Library, Oxford, 1945–1975*, ed. A. C. de la Mare and B. C. Barker-Benfield (Oxford, 1980), pp. 115–16.

APPENDIX

1. Inventories of books at All Saints' Bristol

The first inventory lists the books given to All Saints' by William Brigeman, and was copied as an appendix to the account for Halleways' Chantry for 1522/3 by Jerome Grene, the senior churchwarden at All Saints' in that year. The second list, drawn up by William Young, proctor of All Saints', appears at the end of the account for 1535/6. For earlier transcriptions, each with minor errors, see above, n. 66.

(i) BRO, P/AS/C1, 1522–3, fol. 5^{v}
Anno domini 1524
Here affter foloweth sutch books Roolls and Skrowys of Pricke song that William Brigeman late Clerke of this Parish Church hath bequethis in his Testament to the use of this same Church under the Condicion that no Childern shuld be tawte apon the seid bookes scrowis and Rools

[1] In primis .v. bokes of a mene volume conteyning .v. massis

[2] Item .v. bookes of a mene volume conteyning xvi antems besides diverse *Exultavit* [and] *Salve festa dies* with j masse scilicet *ascendo ad patrem* quod W. Brigeman

[3] Item a booke of a large volume conteyning dyvers Kyreleyson, Alleluia, Masses, antems, *Salve festa dies*, Sequences of our lady, *In nomine Jhesu*, *Sospitati*, with many other songes for a grete parte of the yere necessary

[4] Item iiij boks of a mene volume conteyning iij masses with antems to sing the saturdays at Evynsong byfore the Crosse wyth *Vidi aquam* etc.

[5] Item a thyn boke of a large volume conteyning *Kyre Alleluia*, a masse of iij partes etc.

[6] Item a boke of paper Riall with owte a forell conteyning the passion for palme sonday and a masse of docter farfex makyng callid *Dobull Desolre* with an *Exultavit*

[7] Item dyverse other small boks and scrows for childern of *Sancte deus* with other songs as *Te lucis*, *Saluater* etc.

[8] Item dyverse small queres conteynyng antems of our lady scilicet *Sancta maria*, *Ascendit Cristus*, *Tota pulchra*, *In pace in idipsum* etc.

[9] Item other boks of a mene volume conteyning supra

[10] Item Rolles of paper conteyning dyverse antempnes, Carells, passions for palme sonday, *Salve festa dies*, *Sospitati*, *Ad sepulchrum*, *Ex mortuis*,

Te Deum, *In pace*, *Inventor rutili*, *Confitemini*, *Dicant nunc*, *Quia viderunt*, *Asperges*, *Gloria in excelsis*, *Nesciens mater*, *Regina celi*, *En rex venit*, *Gloria laus* with diverse other small songes abowte the number of xl Rolles.

(ii) BRO, P/AS/ChW3, 1535–6, fol. 8v
We have in the church of the church bokys whych ys now delyvered to Umffrey Wally then beying clarke

[1] Item v Antem boks ffor men and chylder

[2] Item v mass boks ffor men [and] chylder

[3] Item more v Masse boks of *Regaly* and *O bone Jhesu*

[4] Item a old boke of massys of iiij partys

[5] Item iiij Square boks

[6] Item v masse boks whych were bought of Mr Mawnsell for men and chylder

[7] Item more bought of Sir Wyllyam Deane iiij boks of massys for men and chylder

[8] Item more iiij boks of ij massys of iiij partes and a *exultavyt* of v partes

[9] Item iiij boks of keryes and Allaluyas ffor men and chylder

2. Inventory of service books at London, St James Garlickhithe, 1449
Made by William Huntingdon, parson of the church of St James Garlickhithe, 1448/9.

Westminster Abbey Muniment 6644

[1] Item a principall portoos noted of the yeft of Robert Chichele[1] perpetuelly to lye afore the parson, prise £20.

[2] Item a principall portoos lyeng tofor the parson notid and lymned in the begynnyng with a capitall lettre of gold and theryn the figure of God sittyng in þe dome, prise £16.

[3] Item an oþer old portoos notid, prise 33s. 4d.

[4] Item a greet antiphonary lyeng afore the redynge preest lymned in the begynnyng with a greet capitall lettre florisshid, prise £20

[5] Item an oþer fair antiphonarie notid lyeng apon þe parsons side

[1] Citizen and Grocer, d. 1440.

lymned with a capital lettre of gold florisshid in the beginning, prise 106s. 8d.

[6] Item an oþer antiphonarie notid lyeng upon the other side lymned in the begynnyng with a lettre of asur and vys, prise 66s. 8d.

[7] Item a middell portoos notid of salesburyes use lymned in the begynnyng with a lettre of azure, prise 66s. 8d.

[8] Item a faire sawter with a kalender in the begynnyng with a capital lettre of gold *Beatus vir* and theryn the figure of David and Golye lymned covered with a rough contour, prise 20s.

[9] Item an other brode sauter with invitatories and ympnes ferialx notid the whiche begynnyth with preocupenins of Powles use, prise 20s.

[10] Item an other litill sawter with *placebo* and *dirige* and ympner in þe end \whiche John Trillow haþ/, prise 10s.

[11] Item a martlage lymned in the begynnyng with a capitall lettre of gold and theryn a figure of God, prise 6s. 8d.

[12] Item a fair legent lymned with an lettre of gold florisshid in the begynnyng, prise 10s.

[13] Item a legenda aurea in latyn, prise 40s.

[14] Item a missall principall þe whiche begynneth with *Deus creator* and the letanye followynge and the capitall lettre of *Exorcizo* lymned with gold with a figur of a prest theryn and through lymned with lettres of gold, prise £12.

[15] Item an oþer missal with a kalender in the begynnyng with clapses of copre and ouergilt of the gift of Gilbert Boneyt servyng for seint John Baptist auter, prise £8.

[16] Item an other fair missall cotidiane for the high auter with a kalender in the begynnyng and lettre capitall of gold lymned and therynne a figur of a prest halowyng a clerk to fore him and a prest behynd him, prise £6 13s. 4d.

[17] Item an other missal servyng afore our Lady auter of the yift of Alice Kyng[2] somtyme wif of William Kyng draper with a kalender in the begynnyng, prise £4.

[18] Item an other missall with a kalender in the begynnyng lymned with lettres of vys, prise 40s.

[2] d. 1394.

[19] Item an other missall for the morowe masse auter, prise 26s. 8d.

[20] Item another missall of Sir John Peny yift, prise 106s. 8d.

[21] Item a principall grayell with *Salve mater salvatoris* notid in the begynnyng, prise 53s. 4d.

[22] Item an other grayell with epistolary with *Ecce venit rex* in the begynnyng of the yift of Thomas Say, prise £6

[23] Item an other grayell which begynneth *Deus venerunt gentes* with a capitall lettre of gold *ac omnibus dominicis per annum*, prise 46s. 8d.

[24] Item an other grayell withoute any lettre of gold, prise 26s.

[25] Item a manuell which begynnyth *omnibus dominicis per annum*, prise 18s.

[26] Item a collatarie whiche begynnyth *dominica primis adventus domini* lymned with a lettre of gold, prise 20s.

[27] Item iij processionaries, prise in all 20s.

[28] Item a processionarye in Sir John Sender kepyng, prise 40d.

[29] Item a processionary of Sir John Penty yift, 6s. 8d.

[30] Item an organboke in parchemyn bounde and prikked with keryes, gloria in excelsis, patrem, sanctus and agnus of divers menys makyng in the begynnyng Ridlygton kyrie, prise 26s. 8d.

[31] Item iij other organbokes prikkid in paupier, prise 40d.

[32] Item a bible in Frenssh and cheyned, prise 40d.

[33] Item an oþer boke of holy wrÿte compiled in Frenshe also cheyned, prise 20s.

[34] Item an ordinall þat Sir Henry Bourne and John Tirlowe made, prise 100s.

[35] Item an antiphoner on þe parsons side of Portyngdons yift with a capitall lettre of gold florisshed, prise 100s.

[36] Item a processionary of the gift of Sir Thomas Code, prise 3s. 4d.

[37] Item a prikkid song boke covered with rede begynnyng with iij great lettres of .K. of asure, prise 20s.

Summa £154 11s. 4d.

Early Music History (2000) Volume 19. © Cambridge University Press
Printed in the United Kingdom

ELIZABETH EVA LEACH

FORTUNE'S DEMESNE: THE INTERRELATION OF TEXT AND MUSIC IN MACHAUT'S *IL MEST AVIS* (B22), *DE FORTUNE* (B23) AND TWO RELATED ANONYMOUS BALADES*

Machaut's balades *Il mest avis* (hereafter B22) and *De fortune* (hereafter B23), adjacent in the music section of the Machaut manuscripts, form a diptych on the theme of Fortune.[1] In relation to each other, their poetic texts offer complementary perspectives on the power of Fortune: B22 is static, detached in tone, a clerk commentating in a public sententious statement upon the political manifestations of Fortune; conversely, B23 is personal and dynamic, a spurned lady's personal testimony to the power of Fortune to change happiness into sorrow. Despite these contrasts, the two poems share a diction markedly different from that of the twenty-one balades that precede them in the music section.

Since B22 articulates the break with what has gone before, and stands out amongst the first twenty-four musical balades (the number contained in the earliest source) on account of its sententious and impersonal tone, I shall begin with an account of *Il mest avis* (B22), before preceding to show how, as a pair, it and *De fortune* (B23) generate further meanings from being read against one another, as is invited by their adjacency, their shared vocabulary

* A shorter version of the first half of this essay was read at the Sixteenth Congress of the International Musicological Society (London, 1997). I should like to thank Margaret Bent, Bonnie Blackburn, Kevin Brownlee, Terence Cave, Charles Heppleston, Stephen Lovell and Anne Stone for valuable help at various stages of this essay's protracted genesis.

[1] In MS **C** they occur separately in the disordered section which Ursula Günther has termed **CII**; see the information given in L. Earp, *Guillaume de Machaut: A Guide to Research* (New York and London, 1995), p. 78. They are also non-adjacent in MS **E**. The manuscript sigla used here are the standard sigla as detailed in Earp, *Guillaume de Machaut*.

and similar theme.[2] The role of music in the creation of meaning within the individual lyrics and the role that their musical setting plays in furthering their interrelationship will be considered. Using two anonymous songs, each based on one of these two Machaut balades, the situation with respect to B22 and B23 will be contrasted with that outside the Machaut sources. In conclusion I will consider the part that poetic and musical elements play, both separately and together, in terms of allusion, quotation, modelling and intertextuality.

A POETIC PAIR: *IL MEST AVIS* (B22) AND *DE FORTUNE* (B23)

The poetic text of *Il mest avis* (B22) describes the public domain of Fortune. The authorial voice is that of a detached, sententious narrator, a clerk who pronounces Nature's gifts to be worthless until they are coloured by Fortune's dark light. In a traditional way, drawn ultimately from Boethius' *Consolation of Philosophy*, he describes Fortune herself as a collection of paradoxes: her light is dark, lying is her greatest honour, her outside offers happiness, her inside only misery. Her world is a topsy-turvy one, in which the virtues are discomfited and the vices reign.[3] The text is as follows:

[2] MS **C** contains twenty-four balades in total which correspond to the first twenty-four in the modern numbering. The authorial ordering for these, however, is contained in the prescriptive index to MS **A**. The main departure from the modern order (based on a different source, **Vg**) is that the canonic balade *Sans cuer / Amis / Dame* (B17) is placed ninth. Further evidence for Machaut's interest in order can be found in the *Prologue* (contained in *Guillaume de Machaut: poésies lyriques*, ed. V. Chichmaref (Paris, [1909]), I, pp. 1–13) and is manifest in his work, especially as contained in those manuscripts which he is thought to have overseen; see S. Huot, *From Song to Book: The Poetics of Writing in Old French Lyric and Lyrical Narrative Poetry* (Ithaca, 1987), pp. 211–301.

[3] The topic of the actions of Fortune, and her personification, are traditional and had a long history by the fourteenth century; see H. R. Patch, 'Fortuna in Old French Literature', *Smith College Studies in Modern Languages*, 4/4 (1923), pp. 1–45 and *idem*, *The Goddess Fortuna in Medieval Literature* (Cambridge, Mass., 1927).

B22		Musical form	Verse structure	
			Syllables	Rhyme
1.1	Il mest avis quil nest don de nature	A1	10′	a
	com bon quil soit que nulz prise a ce jour	(ouvert)	10	b
1.3	Se la clarte tenebreuse et obscure	A2	10′	a
	de fortune ne li donne coulour	(clos)	10	b
1.5	Ja soit ce que seurte	B	7	c
	ne soit en li amour ne loyaute		10	c
1.7	mais je ne voy homme ame ne chieri		10	d
R	Se fortune ne le tient a ami	R	10	D

2.1 Si bien ne sont fors vent et aventure
donne a faute et tolu par irour
2.3 On la doit croire ou elle se parjure
Car de mentir est sa plus grant honnour
2.5 Cest .i. monstre envolope
De bon eur plein de maleurte
2.7 Car nulz na pris tant ait De bien en li
R Se fortune [ne le tient a ami]

3.1 Si me merveil comment raisons endure
si longuement a durer ceste errour
3.3 Car les vertus sont a desconfiture
Par les vices qui regnent com signour
3.5 Et qui vuet avoir le gre
De ceulz qui sont et estre en haut degre
3.7 Il pert son temps et puet bien Dire ai mi
R Se fortune [ne le tient a ami]

Translation: In my opinion there is no gift of Nature, no matter how good it may be, that anyone would value today if the shadowy and dark light of Fortune did not give it colour, no matter how much certainty may be in it, or love, or loyalty. And I see no man loved or cherished, *if Fortune does not hold him a friend.*

Thus there is nothing except wind and chance, wrongly bestowed and withdrawn out of anger; one should believe her when she perjures herself, for lying is her greatest honour. She is a monster, clothed outside with happiness, [yet] filled with misery; for no one has any worth, no matter how much good is in him, *if Fortune does not hold him a friend.*

Therefore I am amazed that Reason bears this error for so long, because the virtues are discomfited by the vices who rule as lords. And whosoever wants to have the favour of those of high degree (or to gain high degree for himself) is wasting his time and might as well say, 'woe is me' *if Fortune does not hold him a friend.*[4]

[4] The Machaut texts are transcribed from the music section of the earliest source, MS **C**. I am very grateful to Kevin Brownlee for helping me with this translation in the early stages of this study.

The preponderance of learned terms emphasises the authority of the speaker. The Latinate rhetorical term 'colour' has a first meaning of 'to give colour to', but is overlaid with the sense of 'to misrepresent the truth of', that is, 'to lie'. Fortune's paradoxically dark and shadowy light colours or misrepresents nature's gifts so that they become like her, a monster – seemingly good on the outside but evil within. The speaker establishes his detached stance at the outset by the opening phrase, 'Il mest avis', which epitomises the admonitory tone of the whole. This is reinforced by the subjunctive 'soit', as the scholarly speaker produces his hypothetical exemplum. The poem's 'je' is only once the subject of a verb, in the penultimate line of the first stanza (line 7), where the author introduces the refrain as his own personal (and therefore, given his uninvolved status, authoritative) observation of the world. All other verbs are impersonal or have a generalised or personified subject ('nulz', 'qui', 'homme', 'Fortune', 'Raison', 'les vertus', 'les vices').

Leonard Johnson discusses B22 as the first of five poems exemplifying Machaut's treatment of the theme of Fortune.[5] He interprets it as 'rather flat' with 'no real development throughout the poem', the impersonal first person presence serving 'to generalise rather than to particularise the reflection'. It is 'a moral reflection on Fortune and the state of the world, entirely traditional'.[6] However, I will argue that the interplay in which this poem engages with B23 makes it part of a more complex lyric expression than it could articulate as an individual item.[7]

De fortune (B23) is set in the internal, erotic and private world of Fortune. Its text is as follows:

[5] L. W. Johnson, *Poets as Players: Theme and Variation in Late Medieval French Poetry* (Stanford, Calif., 1990), pp. 41–54. Of the musical balades he also discusses *De fortune* (B23) and *De toutes flours* (B31).

[6] *Ibid.*, p. 43.

[7] C. Heppleston's unpublished paper 'The *Louange des Dames*: Misreading a Poem and Reading the Collection' makes a similar point against Johnson's view, although Heppleston is arguing from the point of view of B22's place in the *Louange* (hereafter Lo and a standard number taken from Earp, *Guillaume de Machaut*), where it appears as Lo188, and its connections with *Douce dame savoir de puis noir* (Lo187) and *Helas pour ce que fortune mest dure* (Lo189). I am grateful to Charles Heppleston for allowing me access to this material.

B23		Musical form	Verse structure	
			Syllables	Rhyme
1.1	De fortune me doy plaindre et loer	A1	10	a
	ce mest avis. plus quautre creature	(ouvert)	10′	b
1.3	Car quant premiers [en]commancai lamer	A2	10	a
	mon cuer mamour ma pensee ma cure	(clos)	10′	b
1.5	Mis si bien a mon plaisir	B	7	c
	qua ssouhaidier peusse je faillir		10	c
1.7	nen ce monde ne fust mie trouvee		10	d
R	Dame qui fust si tres bien assenee	R	10	D

2.1 Car je ne puis penser. nymaginer
ne dedens moy trouver conques nature
2.3 De quanquon puet bel et bon apeler
Peust faire plus parfaite figure
2.5 De celui ou mi desir
sont et seront A tousjours sans partir
2.7 Et pour ce croy quonques mes ne fut nee
R Dame qui fust [si tres bien assenee]

3.1 Lasse or ne puis en ce point demorer
car fortune qui onques nest seure
3.3 Sa roe vuet encontre moy tourner
Pour mon las cuer metre a desconfiture
3.5 Mais en foy jusques au mourir
Mon doulz ami vueil amer et chierir
3.7 Quonques ne dust Avoir fausse pensee
R Dame qui fust Si tres bien assenee

Fortune I should blame and praise, in my opinion, more than any other creature;[8] for when I first began to love him, my heart, my love, my thought, my care, I placed so well in the service of my pleasure [*or*, as I wished] that I could not have failed to wish that in this world there would have been found *a lady so well provided for*.

For I cannot think, imagine or find within myself that Nature, out of whatever is called beautiful or good, would have ever been able to fashion a more perfect figure of him, in whom my desires are and shall be forever, without leaving; and because of this I believe that there never was born *a lady so well provided for*.

Alas! now I can no longer stay in this condition, because Fortune, in whom there is no certainty, wants to turn her wheel against me so as to discomfit my

[8] Charles Heppleston (personal communication) has pointed out that 'The 1st line is ambiguous; syntactically it could read either "je doy me plaindre de F. et je doy me loer" which would mean "I must blame F. *and rely on her*" or "je doy plaindre de F. et je doy la loer" – "I must blame F. and praise her"'.

weary heart. But, in good faith, I want to love and cherish my sweet friend unto death for never should *a lady so well provided for* have a false thought.[9]

The contrast between B23 and B22 is sharp. As Johnson remarks, B23 displays a very much more personalised treatment of Fortune. Instead of the detached male authority figure of B22, the narrator of B23 is a woman, who is involved as a lover-protagonist. Her gender is only confirmed by the refrain where she is the 'dame' who is 'si tres bien assenee'; the male direct object pronoun in line 3 is elided ('quant premiers encommancai lamer') and therefore effectively gender neutral. B23 is much more ambiguous than B22, in part because it is emotionally dynamic, as encapsulated in the shifting nuances of its refrain. In B22 the refrain is a self-contained gnomic statement, reiterated to bring home the moral point. In contrast, B23's refrain is embedded so that it has a slightly different force and meaning in each stanza. The opening line promises both blame and praise of Fortune. The praise of the first two stanzas is thus coloured from the outset by the expectation of blame, which is eventually signalled by 'Lasse' at the opening of the third stanza. The narrator's praise of Fortune is effectively cast in Fortune's 'shadowy and dark light'. Reading the sense of B22 into B23 in this way is invited by the parallel situation and specifically by Nature's personification in both poems. B22's conventionality as a poem is transcended by the way in which its meanings are not restricted to its own boundaries as an individual lyric. Instead it informs, complements, and is informed by the following balade, B23.

In addition to a shared topos the complementary nature of balades 22 and 23 is flagged more formally by shared words and, in particular, by shared rhyme-words and the fact that each quotes the incipit text of the other within the body of its text. The '-ure' a-rhyme of B22 is B23's b-rhyme and two rhyme-words are common to both balades, significantly, 'Nature' and 'desconfiture', both part of the pair's differentiated diction in the context of the first

9 Again I am grateful to Kevin Brownlee, and also to Charles Heppleston, for assistance in the initial translation and interpretation of this text.

twenty-four musical balades.[10] In the public world of B22 it is the virtues which are discomfited (by the vices). In B23 it is the narrator's own weary heart (by Fortune), implicitly paralleling the heart with virtue and Fortune with vice.

Each poem quotes words from the other's opening in their first quatrains (see Figure 1). Although ostensibly common stock, these phrases too are part of the differentiated diction of this pair in the notated balades. Fortune is first mentioned only in B22 and the phrase 'Il mest avis' is not common in the preceding twenty-one balades.[11] In addition these phrases represent the incipit tags which would designate the song, or label a tenor or contratenor as belonging to it, in a musical repertory manuscript index.

Much of the diction common to both poems signifies equally well but differently in the political sphere of B22 and the erotic one of B23. For example, 'ami', 'amour' and 'loyaute' in B22 refer to political friendship. In B23 these qualities refer instead to erotic love. Retrospectively, the two worlds of Fortune become fused through this common vocabulary. Fortune's deceit and inconstancy in the political sphere mirror her behaviour towards the woman in B23. This in turn re-informs Fortune's political self, making her seem more like a fickle lover – no man succeeds unless he is Fortune's 'amis', or darling.

The woman of B23 describes her lover as the most perfect figure Nature could fashion out of whatever is called good or beautiful, clearly establishing him, by reference back to B22, as just such a gift. As the narrator of B22 advises, all such gifts will be coloured by Fortune. Specifically B22 assures us that not only would no one value such a gift however much good was in it (line 2.7), but that unless Fortune holds the man to be her darling there *will be* neither love nor loyalty in the gift (line 1.6). In saying that Fortune wishes to turn her wheel against her, the lady of B23 indirectly implies that she believes her lover to be unfaithful because

[10] Nature does not feature in the notated balades preceding B22. 'Desconfiture' previously appears only in *De desconfort* (B8). That 'desconfiture' is a word of some significance for Machaut is shown by the extremely dissonant treatment of it at the end of Motet 15; see M. Bent, 'Deception, Exegesis and Sounding Number in Machaut's Motet 15', *Early Music History*, 10 (1991), pp. 15–27.

[11] Of the musical balades preceding B22, the sententious announcement of opinion occurs (in a slightly different form) only in *Amours ne fait* (B1), *Pour ce que tous* (B12), *Esperance* (B13) and *De petit po* (B18).

B22

Il mest avis quil nest don de *nature*
com bon quil soit que nulz prise a ce jour
Se la clarte tenebreuse et obscure
de fortune ne li donne coulour
    Ja soit ce que seurte
ne soit en li amour ne loyaute
mais je ne voy homme *ame ne chieri*
Se fortune ne le tient a ami

Si bien ne sont fors vent et aventure
donne a faute et tolu par irour
On la doit croire ou elle se parjure
Car de mentir est sa plus grant honnour
    Cest .i. monstre envolope
De bon eur plein de maleurte
Car nulz na pris tant ait De bien en li
Se fortune ne le tient a ami

Si me merveil comment raisons endure
si longuement a durer ceste errour
Car les vertus sont *a desconfiture*
Par les vices qui regnent com signour
    Et qui vuet avoir le gre
De ceulz qui sont et estre en haut degre
Il pert son temps et puet bien Dire ai mi
Se fortune ne le tient a ami

B23

De fortune me doy plaindre et loer
ce mest avis plus quautre creature
Car quant premiers encommancai lamer
mon cuer mamour ma pensee ma cure
    Mis si bien a mon plaisir
qua *souhaidier* peusse je faillir
nen ce monde ne fust mie trouvee
Dame qui fust si tres bien assenee

Car je ne puis penser nymaginer
ne dedens moy trouver conques *nature*
De quanquon puet bel et bon apeler
Peust faire plus parfaite figure
    De celui ou mi desir
sont et seront A tousjours sans partir
Et pour ce croy quonques mes ne fut nee
Dame qui fust si tres bien assenee

Lasse or ne puis en ce point demorer
car fortune qui onques nest seure
Sa roe vuet encontre moy tourner
Pour mon las cuer metre *a desconfiture*
    Mais en foy jusques au mourir
Mon doulz ami vueil *amer et chierir*
Quonques ne dust Avoir fausse pensee
Dame qui fust Si tres bien assenee

Anon. **PR**, fol. 83^{r}

Dame qui fust si tres bien assenee
come je sui a mon tamps vrayement
Onques ne fu de nulle feme nee
qua droit *sohayt* je sui certainement
    Mais fortune ma partie
soudainement a de mi departie
si mest avis qua droit considerer
De fortune me doy plaindre et loer

Figure 1 The texts of B22, B23 and Anon. **PR**, fol. 56^{v}

even as the best Nature can do, unless one is held to be Fortune's friend, 'ne soit en li amour ne loyaute' (there is in him [as the gift of Nature] neither love nor loyalty).[12] At the end of the poem, however, she berates herself for the unworthiness of this implicit thought, re-avowing to carry on loving and cherishing her sweet friend even unto death ('Mon doulz ami vueil *amer et chierir*', line 3.6) because a lady so well provided for (or, as Johnson also translates it, 'so *fortunate*')[13] ought not to have false thoughts ('ne dust avoir fausse pensee', line 3.7). This provides another verbal link to B22, in which the authorial voice saw no man loved or cherished ('je ne voy homme *ame ne chieri*', line 1.7) unless Fortune held him a friend. This was significantly the only 'je' subject in B22, and although 'homme' (man) is general in the context of B22, it is personalised through its connection with the 'ami' of the lady in B23, whom she wishes to love and cherish. In B22 it is the holder of Nature's gift who must be the 'ami' of Fortune. In B23 it is the 'ami' who is the gift. Since gift ('don') in B22 is a masculine noun, the gift is masculine; it therefore makes sense for B23's 'je' to be a woman lamenting the spoiling of her gift (that is, her male lover) by Fortune's wheel-turning antics. That the lady is on the point of thinking false thoughts about her lover, however, risks an equation between her potential changeability and that of Fortune. This reading is supported by the overlap of key phrases in the two poems. Just as the lady of B23 wishes to 'amer et chierir' her 'ami', so no man is 'ame ne chieri' unless Fortune holds him an 'ami'. Significantly the lady of B23 *must* ('doy') blame and praise Fortune and yet she *wishes* ('vueil') to love and cherish her 'doulz ami'. This reflects the certainty that Fortune will make love uncertain. The idea of security or certainty is also shared verbally between the balades. In B22, Fortune's colouring of Nature's gifts occurs regardless of how much security ('seurte') may be in them. In B23 it is Fortune herself in whom nothing is certain ('seure'). In equating Fortune's uncertainty with the gift's uncertainty, this gift,

[12] Johnson comments that 'we are not told exactly what her "desconfiture"' is, but one can only assume that it is some amorous *mis*fortune, perhaps her lover's absence' (45). That it is more than this is, I think, connoted by the relationship between the two texts, which implies a change (reported, if not real) in the man's love.

[13] Johnson, *Poets as Players*, p. 44 (emphasis added).

usually the lady or her favours when not the political advancement of B22, could be equated with Fortune.

Both poems also occur as Lo188 and Lo195, several items apart, in the unnotated lyric section the *Loange de Dames*, where they form the twin poles of a larger sequence of balades (Lo187–95) interrelated formally by shared rhymes and key words and thematically by their treatment of Fortune and rumour, or gossip, about infidelity (the *mesdisans*) from various different subject positions.[14] B22 and B23 are the only two of that lyric group to receive a musical setting and therefore to be textually duplicated in the Machaut manuscripts.[15] Although it is not possible to give a full analysis here it should suffice to say that, as a result of this *Loange* sequence, Fortune becomes paradigmatic of a false woman. If a woman either believes the gossip about her lover, or is herself unfaithful, she is as unfaithful as Fortune.[16] In blaming Fortune, the lady of B23 is effectively berating herself, which she does in the penultimate line of the poem, for having false thoughts, for being inconstant. The sensible solution, it seems, is to continue in loyalty so as to put oneself above the blame that accrues to those who are inconstant.

[14] The viewpoints of Lo187–95 include a man who has heard that he is refused but does not wish to believe it (*Douce dame savoir ne puis noir*; Lo187), a man abandoned by his lady and his friends (the rondeau *Helas pour ce que fortune mest dure*; Lo189), a balade which vents anger on 'tongue', a synecdochal (but feminine) personification which enables a depersonalised invective (*Langue poignant aspre amere et ague*; Lo190), a man who suffers nobly, is of good cheer and pledges loyalty, come what may (*La grant doucour de vostre biaute fine*; Lo191), a man who councils that one ought not to believe lightly the false reports, especially that his lady should not credit those circulating about him, with the implication that if she were to do so she would be unworthy (*On ne puet riens savoir si proprement*; Lo192), a man who laments his lady's perfidy in a poem very similar in terms of rhyme words and diction to both B22 and B23 (*Il ne mest pas tant dou mal que jendure*; Lo193), and a woman suffering because she is far from her sweet loyal lover to whom she pledges loyalty and to put aside all other men (*Il nest dolour desconfors ne tristece*; Lo194).

[15] MS **G** lacks the larger sequence from the *Loange* within which B22 and B23 normally occur. MS **E** transmits the sequence but omits B22 and B23 from the *Loange*. This posthumous source also has its own particular version of order within all the music sections in which B22 and B23 are no longer adjacent.

[16] This comparison is made by Machaut more directly in the *Voir Dit*, where he compares his lady to Fortune, and is then himself compared to a different ('pagan') type of Fortune by a messenger who berates him for believing gossip too readily ('tout par legierement croire'). The refrain in the *Voir Dit* 'Et tout par legierement croire' is similar to that of Lo192, 'De legier croire encontre son ami'. See Machaut, *Le Livre dou Voir Dit*, trans. and ed. D. Leech-Wilkinson and R. B. Palmer (New York and London, 1998), pp. 564–617 and also the extended discussion of both the 'feminisation of Machaut' as Fortune, and the equation of Fortune with 'fame' (i.e. both 'woman' and 'renoun') in Jacqueline Cerquiglini, *"Un engin si soutil": Guillaume de Machaut et l'écriture au XIV*[e] *siècle* (Geneva and Paris, 1985), pp. 139–55.

THE POEMS AS SONGS

It is now time to examine the role that the musical setting plays in the creation of meaning in B22 and B23 as sung lyrics. I will start by considering B22.

Johnson argues that because of its conventionality and flatness, B22's lyricism is purely a result of its musical setting. I would disagree because of the supra-lyrical meanings that B22 takes on in conjunction with its contexts in the music section and the *Loange*. Johnson reports that this musical setting 'underlines the structure of the strophe' by dividing it in two parts after line 4.[17] This is true, but merely describes the large-scale bipartite form of all balades: first, an A section comprising A1 with an ouvert cadence and A2 its repeat with a clos cadence, and secondly a section comprising B and R, the refrain. In terms of its segmentation of the lines of text *within* those two large sections, the musical setting of B22 is actually unconventional and adds its own 'textual' gloss by reading the poem *against* its versification.

B22 exemplifies one of Machaut's most popular verse forms – eight lines, rhymed ababccdD, seven of ten syllables and the fifth *vers coupé* with seven – which it shares with both *De fortune* (B23) and with *De toutes flours* (B31), a balade occurring later in the music section also dealing with the theme of Fortune.[18] Whilst as an individual lyric Johnson considers B22 conventional, at the level of musical setting it is very similar to *De toutes flours* (B31), which he treats as the culmination of his discussion of Fortune in Machaut lyrics, admirably bringing out its manifold subtleties as a poem.[19] I would argue that neither is conventional as a song. On the contrary, in each song the musical setting serves the same similarly executed subversive purpose.[20] Strong musical cadences – usually

[17] Johnson, *Poets as Players*, p. 43.

[18] I have considered *De toutes flours* in a paper read at the 24th Medieval and Renaissance Music Conference, York, 1998, entitled 'Counterpoint, Norms and Semitone Placement in Machaut's Ballades'. See also S. Fuller, 'Guillaume de Machaut: *De toutes flours*', in M. Everist (ed.), *Music before 1600* (Models of Musical Analysis; Oxford, 1992), pp. 41–65.

[19] See Johnson, *Poets as Players*, pp. 51–4.

[20] The most reliable modern edition for the Machaut balades is Guillaume de Machaut, *Musikalische Werke: Balladen, Rondeaux und Virelais*, ed. F. Ludwig, i (Publikationen älterer Musik; Leipzig, 1926). The edition by L. Schrade, *The Works of Guillaume de Machaut* (Polyphonic Music of the Fourteenth Century, 2–3; Monaco, 1956), in which the balades are in vol. iv, is probably more widely available, for which sole reason its bar numbers will be used here. Readers are strongly advised to refer back to the original sources

indicated by at least two of the following elements: a directed progression, a rest in texted voice, a held note in one or more voices – are placed at the caesuras of all lines.[21] Conversely, poetic line endings are not always marked by musical cadences. In the A section the rhyme words at the end of lines 1 and 3 occur in the middle of a musical phrase, with short note values on an unstable imperfect sonority. The three musical phrases of the A section thus set (i) the first four syllables, (ii) the ten syllables from caesura of line 1 to the caesura of line 2, and (iii) the final six syllables of line 2. Although the ouvert cadence is a breve in length it is imperfect in sonority and thus not a true point of rest. This means that the rhyme word at the end of line 4 is the first in each stanza to coincide with a musically emphasised phrase-end cadence ('coulour', 'honnour', 'signour'). Line 4 occurs at the end of the A section with the clos cadence. In the B section, this plan continues: the only line ends which coincide with a musical phrase-end cadence are lines 7 and 8, the end of sections B and R respectively. Table 1 summarises the first stanza as segmented by musical cadences (rhyme words are shown in bold and cadence words are underlined).

In a more traditional balade setting (of which even Machaut's works possess plenty of examples) rhyme words coincide with musical phrase ends. The offsetting of musical and poetic structures in B22 brings certain words into prominence by treating them as if they were rhyme words. Two of these words in B22's first stanza anticipate the poem's own later rhymes. The end of the first musical phrase in A2 sets 'clarte', which anticipates the c-rhyme, and the end of the first phrase of the B section sets 'li', which anticipates the d-rhyme.[22] This serves to create aural confusion, removing any musical security as to the structure of the poem, reflecting the disruptive actions of Fortune herself. This deceptiveness is

wherever feasible and at least to take note of the corrections to Schrade proposed by various authors and summarised in Earp, *Guillaume de Machaut*, p. 588.

[21] In my usage, 'cadence' is not coterminous with 'directed progression', a term adopted from Fuller. I reserve the former term specifically for closural protocols which are often, but not always, effected by directed progressions. Directed progressions, conversely, often mark the opening of phrases and are not therefore always cadential in the modern sense. For further clarification see E. E. Leach, 'Counterpoint and Analysis in Fourteenth-Century Song', *Journal of Music Theory*, 43 (2000), forthcoming.

[22] The anticipation of rhymes in the first stanza is also found in *De toutes flours* (B31).

Table 1 *The musical segmentation of the poetic text (B22, first stanza)*

Section	*Suppressed rhyme*	*Emphasised pseudo-rhyme*	*Emphasised rhyme*
[A1]		Il mest <u>avis</u>	
	quil nest dons de **nature**	Com bons quil <u>soit</u>	
	que nulz prise a ce **jour**		
[A2]		Se la <u>clarte</u>	
	tenebreuse et **obscure**	De <u>fortune</u>	ne li donne **<u>coulour</u>**
[B]	Ja soit ce que **seurte**	Ne soit en <u>li</u>	
	amour ne **loyaute**	Mais je ne <u>voy</u>	home ame ne **<u>chieri</u>**
[R]		Se <u>Fortune</u>	ne le tient a **<u>ami</u>**

increased by the proportions of the A section. The third phrase is as long (roughly in A1, exactly in A2) as the preceding two phrases added together, so that the expectation of a normal bipartite A section setting two poetic lines in two poetic phrases is deceptively met by the cadence at bars 15–16, which appears to represent the end of the first poetic line. It is at this same musical point in the first stanza of B22 that the words 'de Fortune' occur, providing a link to the opening words of B23.

The musical setting's effects include such formal play with sounds and rhymes but also affect issues of meaning. The setting of the pre-caesural incipit to the opening musical phrase emphasises the clerkish nature of the balade that is to follow, 'Il mest avis'. Because every time Fortune is named, her name is followed by a lyric caesura,[23] the musical structure places 'Fortune' first at the cadence at the mid-point of A2 (the end of the second musical phrase, bar 15) in the first stanza, and subsequently in all stanzas at the first cadence in the refrain (bars 45–6). The former has been mentioned above; the naming of Fortune in the refrain makes

[23] Johnson, *Poets as Players*, p. 53 comments on the caesural placement of 'Fortune' in *De toutes flours* (B31), saying that 'by its position, followed in each case . . . by a lyric caesura . . . it becomes the epicenter of the poem'. This is also true of B22, which he thinks conventional. In both balades *Fortune* is emphasised by the musical disruption of the verse structure.

a musical rhyme with the clos, a feature usual for a final cadence, perpetrating a deceit that this is indeed the end. In both places the cadence at 'Fortune' is immediately followed by a melisma on the negative particle 'ne' – reiterating the final syllable of Fortune and linking her with the negativity which she represents. Obviously this feature is inherent in the poetic text as read but is brought out using a melisma's ability to prolong a text syllable. Also, Fortune is notably far more prominent aurally in the first stanza than Nature, whose name forms the first rhyme word. Caesural Fortune is contrapuntally stable and Nature's a-rhyme is hidden away in a mid-phrase imperfect sonority, its status as a line end only articulated by a minim rest. However, here, as in the refrain, Fortune's stability is chimerical. Fortune deceives, and is not as she seems, nor as she sounds.

The musical setting of B22 thus seems to add much to the meaning of the whole. Is the same similarly achieved in B23, and how is the intertextual relationship between the two poems reflected in, or further formed by, their musical setting? From Schrade's edition both might seem four-part works. In reality only B22 is in four parts. However, in its earliest source only the cantus part is entered and the copy has staves labelled for tenor and contratenor, suggesting that a three-part version with contratenor preceded the addition of a triplum (making it the only balade in the vocal combination tenor, contratenor, cantus in MS **C**).[24] *De fortune* (B23) survives in three parts with triplum in most Machaut sources – perhaps the original intention was that B22's low-voice three-part combination would contrast with B23's high-voice three-part one.[25]

[24] For B22 all the sources which transmit the work in a performable version do so with all four parts, the counterpoint of which confirms that the triplum (Tr) cannot be performed without the contratenor (Ct). The triplum assumes a discant relationship with the lowest voice at places where the contratenor supports a tenor–cantus (T–Ca) progression by falling below the tenor; the tenor–triplum (T–Tr) discant relationship is briefly abandoned (although the T–Ca and T–Ct relationships are retained). The manuscript copy of B22 in **PR** has a contratenor which does not take on tenor function at these places. I have argued elsewhere that the version of the song in **PR** works in the combination T–Ct–Ca but not in the combination T–Ct–Ca–Tr, transmitting the earliest surviving version of the contratenor that should have appeared in **C**; see E. E. Leach, 'Machaut's Balades with Four Voices', *Plainsong and Medieval Music*, 9 (2000), forthcoming.

[25] Although no copy transmits a three-part version with contratenor, examination of the counterpoint of those later sources with four parts copied (**Ch**, **PR** and **E**) reveals that a T–Ct–Ca performance of B23 is possible, whereas a four-part one is not. Any single source in which all four parts are transmitted together represents, therefore, a compendium of three possible performance versions, one two-part and two different three-

Just as the vocal scoring in B23 is dissimilar to that in B22, the way in which the musical setting works with the poetic text is also very different. In B22 the relatively conventional poetry is set subversively and with great complexity by the music, which provides another layer of meaning. B23's dynamic and shifting poetry is conversely set to musical phrases which correspond to the lines of the poetic text, generating a different form of disruption from that in B22. Most notably, musical breaks occur at places where there is no corresponding syntactical or sense break in the poem, for example at the end of line 4 in the first two stanzas. The A section consists of three twelve-breve phrases and one of fourteen breves. The first, third and fourth (clos) phrases terminate in a T–Ca directed progression to *d*8, the final sonority; the second phrase (ouvert) cadences to *e*8 (with *c*′-mi in the triplum). The reuse of not only the clos ending (at the end of the balade as a whole), but also the ouvert ending at the end of the B section, creates musical identity between the rhymes of lines 2 and 7 and lines 4 and 8. Line 6 also ends with a *d* cadence. Thus the song is tonally homogeneous in accordance with the ouvert–clos protocol (*d* and *e*), reflecting its melodic homogeneity.[26] Only line 5 is not cadentially end-stopped, connecting instead into the start of line 6 with a contrasting cadence to *f*8 in bar 36. This creates another twelve-breve phrase, which makes particular sense in the second stanza, where line 5 is enjambed. The only caesural words which are emphasised are those which occur in the middle of the second musical phrase (lines 2 and 4) and are set, not to the clear held resolutions of the caesuras in B22, but to a held imperfect

part combinations. That the contratenor and triplum are alternatives is exemplified by their readings of the tenor ouvert note *e*. In the ouvert cadence the triplum takes *c*′-mi above the tenor *e*, and below the cantus *e*′. This relates the open and closed endings as an imperfect sonority and its perfect resolution respectively (an unusual feature shared with B22). The contratenor reads the ouvert ending more normatively, effecting a T–Ct directed progression simultaneously with the T–Ca progression, giving a perfect resolution to *e*5/8. Like the triplum, the contratenor recognises the repeat of ouvert material at the end of the B section so that this cadence is replicated there in bars 49–50. The contratenor version thus takes away one of the few musical parallels with B22 – an imperfect sonority in the ouvert. This fact and its source situation combine to support those commentators who have denied that the contratenor is by Machaut.

[26] See also C. Berger, 'Tonsystem und Textvortrag: Ein Vergleich zweier Balladen des 14. Jahrhunderts', in *Alte Musik als ästhetische Gegenwart* (Internationaler musikwissenschaftlicher Kongress 1985, Stuttgart; Kassel, 1987), ii, pp. 202–11, esp. music example 2.

sonority. In stanzas 1 and 3, the second line has at this point 'Ce mest avis' and 'Car fortune', respectively encapsulating the two incipits of B22 and B23.

Any musical parallel between B22 and B23 serves to emphasise their pre-existing poetic contrasts and verbal connections. It would arguably be difficult to identify these balades as a specific pair without their poetic texts. They are in contrasting mensurations – exploring the major and minor prolation of imperfect time respectively. They are different in terms of the proportions they allot to major sections: B22 has very long A sections and very short B and R sections, whereas B23's second half (section BR) is longer than either A section (either A1 with ouvert ending or A2 with clos ending). They are in contrasting vocal arrangements. They have different tonal emphases. The melodic contour of each is different, as are the ways in which basic directed progressions are ornamented and spun out. Whilst they do share common rhythmic figures, especially variously contoured four-minim ornamental figures, these are of a pervasive and conventional type. Nevertheless, the fact of their poetic pairing lends on one hand a certain emphasis to the sharing of these otherwise conventional and widespread features, and, on the other hand, enables their differences to be perceived (like those of the poems) as significant complementarities rather than mere dissimilarities. Whereas the contrasting poetic texts could nevertheless be perceived as related *per se* because of shared diction (different from all preceding music-section balades), shared subject matter, formal verse structuring, and diptych complementarity, their musical contrasts alone cannot undeniably relate these songs. Where music alone is responsible for making a connection, similarity, usually a significant quotation, is usually required because there is no semantic level upon which to signal a connection in contrast. For both music and text, a quotation great enough in extent (at least a line or a phrase, respectively), is often enough for an intentional link to be perceived. However, words have levels of meaning and nuance due to their semantic content that music does not. A poetic pair such as B22 and B23, complementary in voice, tone and situation, can be nevertheless fairly clearly linked by their texts, since different meanings can be forced into dialogue without the need for simple similarity or extensive clear quotation. For contrasting musical pieces, a lack of relationship is assumed unless a textual auxiliary allows it to be perceived as intentionally linked contrast.[27]

MACHAUT ABROAD: B23 AND *DAME QUI FUST*, AND B22 AND *SE JE NE SUY*

Two anonymous balades exist which are each built on one of the pair B22 and B23. In this section I shall examine these pieces for how each alludes to its model in terms of music, poetry and musico-poetic features, and compare the findings with the way in which the mutual reference of the balades of the Machaut manuscripts has been shown to operate.

Outside Machaut's direct purview in the Machaut manuscripts the transmission of his poems and music seems to be sharply divided. On one hand some of his lyrics continue to be copied without their music in anthologies right up to their inclusion in the *Jardin de Plaisance* at the beginning of the sixteenth century.[28] On the other hand, interest in the poetic texts of balades with music seems to diminish so that, as copied in non-Machaut music sources, his songs frequently have very corrupt texts, often lacking syllables, or entire stanzas, of text. This sharp dichotomy may be illusory since the later text-only copying of Machaut songs often featured those which were set elsewhere to music, and there is some evidence that they were made from notated exemplars.[29] In

[27] Arguably musical links within the balade section actually cut across the paired nature of B22 and B23, reaching out to de-isolate them from their lonely pairing and ensconce them in the heart of the closing of the sequence of twenty-four musical balades in MS **C**. B22, for example, is musically more linked to *Se quanque amours* (B21) since they are jointly the only two four-part balades in the first twenty-four, sharing the same mensuration and the rhythmic patterns that accompany it. In this case the musical similarities, in combination with manuscript order, can forge comparisons which at the level of text alone might be overlooked. In the dark and shadowy light of Fortune, the happiness of B21's lover appears as hubris.

[28] *Le Jardin de Plaisance et Fleur de Rethoricque* (Paris: Ant. Vérard, [1501]). Later editions were also made until *c.* 1527; see Earp, *Guillaume de Machaut*, pp. 114–15, sect. 3.5 [49]. All the Machaut works included are those that also have a musical setting, including B23 (which appears in a male-voiced version; see C. Berger, 'Tonsystem und Textvortrag', p. 208, n. 25).

[29] MS **Pa** copies from MS **E**; see Earp, *Guillaume de Machaut*, pp. 115–18. On this issue see also Y. Plumley, 'Lyrics for Reading and Lyrics for Singing: The Relationship between the Chanson and Lyric Poetry Repertories in the Late Fourteenth Century', unpubl. paper read at the annual meeting of the American Musicological Society, Boston, 1998. I am grateful to Yolanda Plumley for allowing me access to this paper. I have also noticed similarities between the copies of some of the lyrics in MSS **I** and **E**. **I** copies the balade

what follows I shall first consider the contratenors of B22 and B23 specific to the Reina Codex (**PR**). I shall then examine two anonymous balades, unica from the same manuscript, which seem to be related, in different ways, to B23 and B22 respectively. *Dame qui fust* presents an obvious case of text and music quotation, taking B23's refrain as its opening line and B23's opening line as its refrain (see Figure 1), in both cases using the melody line and the tenor.[30] By contrast, *Se je ne suy*'s dependence on B22 has not been previously noted.[31] This is perhaps because it involves musical quotation which is neither accompanied by textual quotation, nor used at the beginning or in the refrain of the balade. Ultimately this essay will consider the variety of modelling that may occur in the mixed medium of song, how much and of what type are enough to identify deliberate allusion to another source, and what information we may glean from links between lyrics.

PR also transmits both B22 and B23. Although they not adjacent, the link between them is arguably not lost, but is made more dependent on musical factors. Both balades have cantus, tenor, triplum and contratenor entered, even though B23 can only be performed in two three-part versions. For B22, the relationship of the contratenor in **PR** to that in the Machaut manuscripts is one of prototype to finished object.[32] For B23, three-part with triplum in most Machaut manuscripts, the contratenor of **PR** is virtually identical, even to the extent of sharing ligature patterns, with one found in the posthumous Machaut source, **E**, except for one important variant occurring at the start of the B section. As the source situation is difficult to appreciate from Schrade's edition, it is shown in Example 1a.

texts of B18, B25, B29 (Ca 1, complete and first seven lines of Ca 2), B32, B34 (both texts), B39 and B42. Of these all but the *Voir Dit* balades B32 and B34 show evidence of **I** copying from **E**'s music section (which lacks the *Voir Dit* balades).

[30] This relationship has been previously noted by several scholars; see U. Günther, 'Zitate in französichen Liedsätzen der Ars Nova und Ars Subtilior', *Musica disciplina*, 26 (1972), pp. 53–68. The tenor of the opening of B23 in the refrain of *Dame qui fust* is changed fairly significantly in its detail. The underlying counterpoint remains similar, however. The relationship between these balades has been examined by C. Berger, 'Tonsystem und Textvortrag', pp. 202–11.

[31] *Dame qui fust* and *Se je ne suy* can be found in *French Secular Compositions of the Fourteenth Century*, ed. W. Apel, ii (Anonymous Ballades) (Corpus mensurabilis musicae, 53; American Institute of Musicology, 1971), as numbers 131 and 174, respectively. They can also be found in *A Fourteenth-Century Repertory from the Codex Reina*, ed. N. Wilkins (Corpus mensurabilis musicae, 36; American Institute of Musicology, 1966).

[32] As I have argued in Leach, 'Machaut's Balades with Four Voices'.

Example 1 Figure *z* in (a) B22 (B section opening); (b) B23 (A section opening); and (c) *Dame qui fust* (B section opening)

At the opening of the B section of B23 in **PR**, a four-minim turning figure followed by a downward leap (labelled *z* in Example 1) occurs in the contratenor. The turn starts on *d′*, turning around the note *c′* and is followed by a repeated semibreve *c*. The whole two-bar phrase is itself immediately and exactly repeated. Figure *z* is otherwise entirely absent from B23, although it is common in B22, opening the whole song in the contratenor part (see Example 1b). B23 in the Machaut sources does not have a contratenor, except in the late MS **E**. It also has a contratenor in the anthology sources **PR** and **Ch**. For the most part the contratenors of **E** and **PR** are identical in their detail; the **Ch** contratenor differs significantly. However, at the point shown in Example 1a the contratenors of **E** and **Ch** are the same and **PR** is briefly different from **E**.[33] That the **PR** contratenor is individuated here and that the figure *z* is one lacking in B23 but prevalent in B22, is arguably a musical recognition of the relationship between these two balades. If so, it has perhaps been preserved as a unique trait in **PR**, which has linked them, or has been copied from a tradition which has linked them.

Although the poetic relationship with Machaut's B23 is clear from its poetic text alone, in both cases the text citation is supported by a musical quotation of the tenor–cantus core. The text is as follows:

	Anon., **PR** fol. 56v	Musical form	Verse structure: Syllables	Rhyme
1	[D]ame qui fust si tres bien assenee	A1	10′	a
	come je suy a mon tamps vrayement	(ouvert)	9 [10]	b
3	Onques ne fu de nulle feme nee	A2	10′	a
	qua droit sohayt je suy certainement	(clos)	10′	b
5	Mais fortune ma partie	B	7′	c
	soudainement a de mi departie		10′	c
7	si mest avis qua droit considerer		10	d
R	De fortune me doy plaindre et loer	R	10	D

[33] The contratenors of **E** and **PR** re-converge in bar 35, as can be seen in Example 1a.

A lady who was as well provided for as I was in my time, truly, never was born of any woman [. . .].[34] But Fortune has suddenly taken my companion from me and yet it seems to me that, to consider [the case] properly *I should both complain about Fortune and praise her.*

As with B23, the speaker of *Dame qui fust* is a woman. The first stanza has the content of Machaut's last (the woman losing the favour of Fortune) and the two halves of this content are reversed (see Figure 1).[35]

Dame qui fust and B23 are in the same mensuration and deploy broadly the same vocal ranges for their voices. Both balades reuse their open and closed endings for lines 7 and 8 respectively. Christian Berger has shown how the melodic material from B23's cantus, lines 2 and 5–6 are used in the same lines in *Dame qui fust*.[36] In addition, the underlying simple counterpoint of the cantus and tenor lines is remarkably similar between the two pieces. The counterpoint of lines 2–7 in *Dame qui fust* corresponds directly to the same lines in B23. This is most clear in the T–Ca discant progressions of the two pieces in which each poetic line in *Dame qui fust* has the same cadence tone as its equivalent in B23.[37]

[34] There are several problems with the first quatrain. Line 2 is a syllable short and probably corrupt and I do not see how line 4 follows from lines 1–3; I have therefore left it untranslated. The overall sense is, in the first half of the stanza, that the woman has been very fortunate and, in the second half, that (good) Fortune has now abandoned her.

[35] It is possible that, were the rest of the poem preserved, this technique would continue – the third strophe returning to the praise of Fortune and possibly the lover's success. Certainly the verb 'loer' only makes sense if some comparison to a formerly happy fortunate state were made in later stanzas, unless it here means (as 'me loer') that the lady must complain of Fortune and yet rely on her (see n. 8 above). This remains speculative: as with many other texts – B22 and B23 amongst them – **PR** does not transmit the second and third stanzas of the poem.

[36] See Berger, 'Tonsystem und Textvortrag', pp. 210–11, esp. examples 1b and 4.

[37] Line 1 is the same as B23, line 8 (bars 1–14 based on B23, bars 51–64). Line 2 in each starts with *d*12 (bar 15; cf. B23, bar 13) and proceeds through a descending chain of sixths to the interval *e*6, held for an entire long and resolved by directed progression to *d*8 (bars 17–20; cf. B23, bars 14–17). In both songs the ouvert cadence has the T–Ca duet resolving to *e*8, and the clos cadence to *d*8, preceded by three descending sixths. The clos ending in each is longer than the ouvert. The B section of both balades opens with the perfect sonority *a–e'*, which is then imperfected and resolves – to *f*8 in *Dame qui fust* and *g*8 in B23. The passage from the *f*8 sonority of bar 39 to the *d*8 resolution of bar 44 in *Dame qui fust* resembles the outline of line 6 (bars 36–42) in B23 (perhaps suggesting that the text underlay of lines 5–6 in the former should be adjusted). Line 7 in each resembles the ouvert cadence and both resolve to *e*8. The refrain, bars 54–65, quotes the T–Ca duet from the opening of B23 (bars 1–12) but with ornamentation in the tenor.

Despite the similarity of the underlying tenor–cantus progressions in each balade, their contratenors are dissimilar. From this it might seem likely that the version of B23 known to the composer of *Dame qui fust* was in two parts.[38] However, one element of the contratenor in *Dame qui fust* brings such an assumption into question – the opening of the B section. Since section A of *Dame qui fust* uses B23's Refrain section and its Refrain uses the opening of section A, the reversal pivots around the B section. Logically therefore, the B section of *Dame qui fust* might resemble the B section of B23. Indeed, the first two bars in *Dame qui fust* have the same tenor line and the same initial sonority between the tenor and the cantus as B23's B section. The most noticeable connection, however, is in the otherwise contrasting contratenor, which has the figure that opens B23's B section in the contratenor of **PR**: figure *z* starting on *d′* with four minims – dissonant, consonant, dissonant, consonant. This is exactly the same pattern as in B23, at the opening of the B section, and at the very opening of B22 (see Example 1c and cf. Examples 1a and 1b). This figure appears nowhere else in B23 and is *only* present in the version of the contratenor transmitted in **PR** (despite this contratenor being in other respects identical to that in manuscript **E**). This makes it likely that it was specifically **PR**'s version of B23 which the composer of *Dame qui fust* knew (which does not, of course, mean that he knew the Reina codex itself). It may also show some awareness on the part of *Dame qui fust*'s composer that B23 was itself linked to B22.

That B22 is the model for the anonymous balade *Se je ne suy* is, from its text alone, far less obvious than was the case for B23 and *Dame qui fust*. Two stanzas survive in **PR**, which are as follows:

Anon. **PR**, fol. 83r		Musical form	Verse structure	
			Syllables	Rhyme
1.1	[S]e je ne suy si gay com ie soloie	A1	10′	a
	il mest avis quil i a bien rayson	(ouv)	10	b
1.3	Car fortune du tout si me desvoie	A2	10′	a
	si que mon cuer na se tristece non	(clos)	10	b
1.5	Et dautre part de mes mals garison	B	10	b

[38] The fifteenth-century manuscript copy New York, Pierpont Morgan Library, MS M.396 (**Pm**) does indeed transmit the song in only two parts.

	avoir ne puis de vous dame hunoree	10′	c
R	Que jaim de cuer de corps et de pensee R	10′	C

2.1 Mais non pour tant partout ou que je soie
vous ameray sans male entencion
2.3 Ne vous laray pour riens qui venir doie
Et lait mie fortune voile ou non
2.5 Coment quen ay mon petit gerer don
si estes vous celle sur toutes nee
R Que jaim de cuer [de corps et de pensee]

If I am not as merry as usual, it is my opinion that there is a good reason for it; for Fortune has so much misled me in everything that my heart has nothing but sadness. And on the other hand I cannot [hope to] have my ills cured by you, honoured lady, *that I love with my heart, body and thoughts.*

But nevertheless, wherever I may be, I will totally love you without ill intent and I will not abandon you whatever might happen. And whether Fortune wishes it or not, however little my reward may be, you are still the one above all women born *that I love with my heart, body and thoughts.*

Although *Se je ne suy* contains B22's incipit text, 'Il mest avis', at the start of its second line and is a poem lamenting the action of Fortune, it seems initially as though this stock phrase has merely been used coincidentally, since, unlike the quotation of B23 in *Dame qui fust*, the shared phrase is not flagged by musical quotation.

The music of *Se je ne suy* is in three parts (T–Ct–Ca) in broadly the same ranges as B22 and the two balades share large-scale similarities like those present between B23 and *Dame qui fust*. *Se je ne suy* opens with the same T–Ca sonority as B22, *f–c′*, and has the same tonal hierarchy, with primary terminal endings on *c*, secondary ones on *d*, and important tertiary sonorities on *f* (which serves as a surrogate for *c* linked by the common semitone progression *b*–mi to *c′*). Both *Se je ne suy* and B22 have the same use of musical rhyme between the clos and final cadences – in the former the passage duplicated is extensive (13 breves) – but not between the ouvert and the end of the B section (although in *Se je ne suy* these have the same sonority). These are quite general similarities and would not be enough to argue for an intentional modelling without some sort of textual or musical quotation of the kind present between B23 and *Dame qui fust*. In this case the quotation is purely musical, unaccompanied by the text of its model, seemingly ungenerated by textual cues, and is hidden away in the B section of the balade.

The entire B section of *Se je ne suy* is comprised of a mosaic of quotations from B22, each accompanied by a triple grouping of semibreves (achieved through harmonic rhythm), which is unfortunately obscured in the notation of the modern editions. The harmonic rhythm of *Se je ne suy* in these places works against its mensuration so as to group the units into iambic triple bars against the prevailing duple time. Triple time is the mensuration of B22, which organises its cadences to *c*8 in a characteristically iambic way (bars 7–8, 21–2, 31–2, 36–7, 45–6 and 52–3). The main musical links between *Se je ne suy* and B22 can be seen in Example 2. The opening of the B section in *Se je ne suy* (bars 29–35; Example 2a) resembles both the end of the opening phrase of B22's B section (bars 35–7, Example 2b) and, more closely, the cadence in bars 18–22 (Example 2c). The T–Ca directed progression to unison *g* in *Se je ne suy*, bars 36–42, although weakened by a rest in the tenor, is contrapuntally similar to the important unison *g* cadence in bars 14–15 of B22 (the mid-point of A2; see Example 2d). The cadence at the mid-point of *Se je ne suy*'s B section (bars 41–2) is similar to that at the end of its B section (bars 55–6). Both these cadences resemble that at the end of B22's B section (bars 42–3; see Example 2e).

The most striking and analytically decisive quotation, however, is directly before the end of *Se je ne suy*'s B section, in bars 48–51, which quotes the end of B22's refrain (see Example 2f). This is made more complex by internal similarities within *Se je ne suy*. The opening of line 6 (bar 44) in *Se je ne suy* resembles the balade's own opening – a rising line *c′ d′ e′ f′*, with the *f′* achieved by directed progression (cf. bars 44–7 and Example 2g, bars 1–6). Although *f′* is the contrapuntally important note of bar 6, it is ornamented such that it resembles the first part of the refrain of B22, bars 44–5 (see Example 2h).

The quotation of openings (incipits) and refrains are two principal ways of signalling deliberate reference in medieval poetry and, by extension, music.[39] On the other hand, the importance of

[39] Cerquiglini, *"Un engin si soutil"*, pp. 23–32 proposes a typology of insertions of lyrics into narrative. Her first type is that which works by *collage*, using refrains and incipits from lyrics by other authors which are incorporated in a fragmentary way into the narrative. For musical balades, although it is the insertion into another *lyric* frame of other lyric fragments, it remains the use of incipits and refrains which enable the reader's 'plaisir de la reconnaissance, plaisir de classe, comme souligne Jean Renart, "que vilains nel porroit savoir"' (p. 28).

Example 2 Quotations from B22 in *Se je ne suy*'s B section: (a) *Se je ne suy* (B section); (b) B22, bars 35–7; (c) B22, bars 18–22; (d) B22, bars 13–15; (e) B22, end of line 7; (f) B22, final cadence; (g) *Se je ne suy*, opening compared with B22, bars 44–6 (Refrain)

Example 2 *Continued*

mid-points for the signalling of authority has its own model in the *Roman de la Rose*.[40] Here, *Se je ne suy* quotes its model's refrain *music* and its opening *text* but places the refrain music in its middle section and the incipit text in the middle of the opening section, separating each of the refrain's text and music components from their other half in the song medium. It may be no coincidence, then, that the incipit text of B22 quoted in *Se je ne suy* is not just the pre-caesural 'Il mest avis' but five syllables 'Il mest avis quil'. Although the setting of the first four of these syllables is different in the two balades *Se je ne suy*'s bar 17 setting 'quil' uses the same pitches in the same rhythm as B22's 'quil' in bar 10 (see Figure 2 and Example 3).

Example 3 Shared text and music in
(a) *Se je ne suy* and (b) *Il mest avis*

In the light of the musical links between *Se je ne suy* and B22, the textual links acquire significance they would not have borne alone.[41] Although unclear in its details, the poetic voice is that of a man explaining why he does not seem as merry as he usually is. There are a few textual links to B22 (see Figure 2). Line 1.2, 'Il mest avis', is B22's incipit and, as in B22, 'rayson' is invoked

[40] See K. Brownlee, 'Authorial Self-Representation and Literary Models in the *Roman de Fauvel*' in M. Bent and A. Wathey (eds), *Fauvel Studies: Allegory, Chronicle, Music, and Image in Paris, Bibliothèque Nationale de France, MS français 146* (Oxford, 1998), pp. 73–103 for a discussion of the use of the *Rose* as a model for authorial self-naming at the mid-point of a text. See also a similar argument about the mid-point as a site of musical citation in M. Bent, 'Polyphony of Texts and Music in the Fourteenth-Century Motet: *Tribum que non abhorruit / Quoniam secta latronum / Merito hec patimur* and Its "Quotations"', in Dolores Pesce (ed.), *Hearing the Motet: Essays on the Motet of the Middle Ages and Renaissance* (New York and Oxford, 1997), pp. 82–103.

[41] Nevertheless, my own suspicions about *Se je ne suy*'s use of B22 as a model were initially awakened by the textual links. The quotation of an incipit text is usually significant in this repertoire. Once the text had directed my attention to the music I found the putative link more than adequately confirmed.

B22

Il mest avis quil nest dons de *nature*
com bon quil soit que nulz prise a
Se la clarte tenebreuse et obscure
de fortune ne li donne coulour
Ja soit ce que seurte
ne soit en li amour ne loyaute
mais je ne voy homme *ame ne chieri*
Se fortune ne le tient a ami

Si bien ne sont fors vent et aventure
donne a faute et tolu par irour
On la doit croire ou elle se parjure
Car de mentir est sa plus grant honnour
Cest .i. monstre envolope
De bon eur plein de maleurte
Car nulz na pris tant ait De bien en li
Se fortune ne le tient a ami

Si me merveil comment raisons endure
si longuement a durer ceste errour
Car les vertus sont *a desconfiture*
Par les vices qui regnent com signour
Et qui vuet avoir le gre
De ceulz qui sont et estre en haut degre
Il pert son temps et puet bien Dire ai mi
Se fortune ne le tient a ami

B23

De fortune me doy plaindre et loer
ce jour *ce mest avis* plus quautre creature
Car quant premiers encommancai lamer
mon cuer mamour ma pensee ma cure
Mis si bien a mon plaisir
qua *souhaidier* peusse je faillir
nen ce monde ne fust mie trouvee
Dame qui fust si tres bien assenee

Car je ne puis penser nymaginer
ne dedens moy trouver conques *nature*
De quanquon puet bel et bon apeler
Peust faire plus parfaite figure
De celui ou mi desir
sont et seront A tousjours sans partir
Et pour ce croy *quonques mes ne fut nee*
Dame qui fust si tres bien assenee

Lasse or ne puis en ce point demorer
car fortune qui onques nest seure
Sa roe vuet encontre moy tourner
Pour mon las cuer metre *a desconfiture*
Mais en foy jusques au mourir
Mon doulz ami vueil *amer et chierir*
Quonques ne dust Avoir fausse pensee
Dame qui fust Si tres bien assenee

Anon. **PR**, fol. 83r

[S]e je ne suy si gay com je soloie
il mest avis quil i a bien *rayson*
Car fortune du tout si me desvoie
si que mon cuer na se tristece non
Et dautre part de mes mals garison
avoir ne puis de vous dame hunoree
Que jaim de cuer de corps et de pensee

Mais non pour tant partout ou que je soie
vous ameray sans male entencion
Ne vous laray pour riens qui venir doie
Et lait mie fortune voile ou non
Coment quen ay mon petit gerer don
si estes vous *celle sur toutes nee*
Que jaim de cuer de corps et de pensee

Figure 2 The texts of B22, B23 and Anon. **PR**, fol. 83r

(although not, here, personified). Line 1.3, 'Car fortune', places Fortune caesurally as she is in both Machaut balades and directly quotes B23, line 3.2. In fact textual links to B23 are almost as common as to B22. The text 'Il mest avis', as well as being B22's incipit, is identically placed (to open the second line of first stanza) as 'Ce mest avis' is in B23. The refrain rhyme of *Se je ne suy* is the same as B23's ('-ée') and the two balades share one rhyme word 'nee', and also share the word 'pensee', not a rhyme in B23's list of attributes the lady places in the service of her love ('mon cuer mamour ma pensee ma cure'), but arguably resonant with *Se je ne suy*'s refrain: 'Que iaim de cuer de corps et de pensee'. These features might not in themselves be sufficient either to establish a strong intentional link between *Se je ne suy* and B22 or B23, even though the incipits of each are quoted, but the musical link between *Se je ne suy* and B22 in combination with a pre-existing relationship between B22 and B23 is suggestive. **PR** transmits one balade based on B22 (*Se je ne suy*) and one based on B23 (*Dame qui fust*). The contratenor for B23 in **PR** introduces a melodic-rhythmic figure (*z*) which is common in B22 and in *Dame qui fust*. *Se je ne suy*'s most decisive reference to B22 is to quote the final phrase of the refrain which has figure *z* transposed a fourth higher. In the light of this it is not impossible that the two anonymous balades, whilst each based on only one of the Machaut balades B22 and B23, make acknowledgement of the paired status of these two songs.

CONCLUSION

In one of his contributions to a colloquium entitled 'Intertextuality in Fourteenth- and Fifteenth-Century Song', Kevin Brownlee outlined a spectrum of intertextualities ranging from that 'most highly marked by a visible authorial or textual intentionality, coupled with extreme specificity with regard to the model texts or texts' to that in which the 'model is not a textually specific one' and 'intentionality is much less clearly visible'.[42] As Wulf Arlt pointed out in the introduction to that colloquium, the idea that a textual reference or a musical one may act as a keyhole through

[42] K. Brownlee, 'Literary Intertextualities in 14th-Century French Song', in *Musik als Text: Bericht über den Internationalen Kongreß der Gesellschaft für Musikforschung Freiburg im Breisgau 1993* (Kassel, 1998), pp. 295–9, at p. 295.

which reference to a whole range of different meanings may be imported to a text from another source is not new to musicology but has already been a very fruitful area of enquiry, especially for motets.[43] Although the possibility exists for the attribution of 'guilt' to a text which may be 'innocent' of intertextual reference, it seems that authorial intention can, in the end, only be subjectively assessed, and must stand or fall against the index of the plausibility and richness of the reading which the intertext produces. As Sylvia Huot has shown, relational meaning between texts *not* intended by their authors to be read against one another can be made by scribes exercising control over their manuscript placement.[44] Machaut famously wears the hats not just of poet and composer but also of poet and scribe, such that he is able to create collections of individual items which are meant to be read in conjunction with one another. His means of signalling the relatedness of poems, even those set to music, are primarily textual. In addition to adjacency and duplication in other sections of the manuscript, textual quotations are used, often self-quotation, but occasionally imported from other sources.[45]

The three song pairs adduced in this article exemplify three different approaches to creating intertextual meaning: B22 and B23 are related through poetic text and work by contrast; *Dame qui fust* quotes B23's music with its text; *Se je ne suy* quotes B22's music only. Machaut's balades B22 and B23 exhibit an intertextual relationship driven by the meaning of their individual texts, in combination with their shared lexis, and assisted by their adjacent manuscript placement. Their musical settings serve to underline the contrast that they articulate. There is no musical modelling or quotation between them, and the issue of compositional priority does not arise (although the manuscript situation makes it

[43] W. Arlt, 'Einführung' in *Musik als Text*, pp. 287–90, at p. 287.

[44] See S. Huot, *From Song to Book*.

[45] The work of Jacques Boogaart has shown that the Machaut motets are peppered with quotations from trouvère poets (see J. Boogaart, 'Love's Unstable Balance', *Muziek & Wetenschap*, 3 (1993), pp. 1–33). Whilst many refrains are known and catalogued from the thirteenth century, the song repertory in the fourteenth century is yet to be fully investigated in this regard; Machaut's songs have turned up textual and text–music quotations (see the notes to *Nen fait nen dit* (B11) and *Pour ce que tous* (B12) respectively in Earp, *Guillaume de Machaut* for a summary). The refrain of *Esperance* (B13), long suspected to be a quotation, is found in Rondeau 139 from Oxford, Bodleian Library, MS Douce 308.

likely that B23 was written before B22). If the use of figure *z* is an attempt to reflect their textual link musically in **PR**, this could show a more international (that is, not exclusively francophone) musical culture's unease with the idea of linking songs by text alone, and a desire to provide a music link in an environment where poetic texts are incompletely transmitted.[46] In *Dame qui fust* the reference to a model is clearly audible and was long ago recognised by modern musicology. In *Se je ne suy* the reference is slightly more hidden as far as we are concerned because of our lack of aural and performerly familiarity with the work, especially in its manuscript version.

Several issues arise from these different types of example. First, as music operating alone, without textual cue, can only allude to another work by quotation, how much is sufficient to be convincing? How long and how exact should a quotation of a melody be? Would the quotation of a tenor line be less convincing because such lines are often less individuated? How much similarity in tonal plan, rhythmic organisation, or sectional proportions would be enough to differentiate between mere coincidental similarities lent by a shared vocabulary, musical style, or starting point and deliberate modelling? Susan Rankin has cited as a 'major hurdle' the 'tension between intuitive, common-sense, observations of musical-textual connection between songs and the wish to ground such analysis in appropriate historical modes of thought'.[47] I agree with Rankin that the only way to proceed is in detail and though example, since every case seems to be different and any kind of generalisation is hard to support.

Secondly, can we establish compositional priority or clarify issues of chronology by assuming certain things about the use of models? This is certainly tempting because of the very few fixed points that exist for the composition of songs in the fourteenth century. For the pairs offered here it seems likely that the Machaut balades provided the model for both anonymous ones (and I have framed my discussions as if this were indeed the case). However,

[46] **PR**'s contratenor for B22 lacks figure *z* at the very opening although the figure still pervades the balade as a whole, especially in the cantus refrain.

[47] S. Rankin, 'Observations on Senleches' "En attendant esperance"', in *Musik als Text*, pp. 314–18, at p. 318.

it is not always possible to tell. A putative assessment of comparative quality is not necessarily a good measure, since in the shifting sands between emulation, competition and homage it is as possible for an admirer's dependent balade to be less competent than its model, as it is for a competitor's one to better it. It is not even necessarily the case that material quoted will be placed at the beginning of a piece (as *Se je ne suy* attests), and the material quoted can be taken from an incipit, a refrain, or a mid-point, as in the contratenor of *Dame qui fust*. Again individual assessment in line with what is known about the source situation for each member of any two related pairs is necessary.[48]

Thirdly and most importantly, what does the reuse of these models mean? With notable exceptions, the tendency so far in songs has been to index quotations without offering much by way of interpretation. Interpreting text allusions is easier since the intertextual context carries its own semantic content. Quotation of purely musical material is more problematic. Does the music 'silently' carry its literary component as well? And what might the semiotic content of any purely 'musical intertext' be? In embedding segments of the contrapuntal core of B22 in *Se je ne suy* is the composer casting doubt on the ability of the lady, loved totally in the refrain, to live up to the speaker's expectations? He cannot hope that Fortune's ills will be cured by his lady's gift, 'don' (of herself), and B22 advises the exercise of caution with respect to all gifts which will inevitably be worthless when coloured by Fortune. The aptness of reading B22's text into *Se je ne suy* seems to argue in this case for the musical quotation carrying its textual content with it and acting as an intertextual cue. On a purely musical level, although it seems plausible that the composer of *Dame qui fust* knew a contratenor version of B23, the quotation in *Dame qui fust* takes only the tenor and cantus; the contratenor is different. In writing a different contratenor to essentially the same dyadic progressions, the composer of *Dame qui fust* at once displays

[48] For recent examples treating related fourteenth-century songs see W. Arlt, 'Machaut, Senleches and der anonyme Liedsatz "Esperance qui en mon cuer s'embat"', in *Musik als Text*, pp. 300–310; S. Rankin, 'Observations on Senleches' "En attendant esperance"', *ibid.*, pp. 314–18; L. Welker, 'Weitere Beobachtungen zu "Esperance"', *ibid.*, pp. 319–21; *idem*, '"Soit tart tempre" und seine Familie', *ibid.*, pp. 322–34; C. Berger, 'Modus und Intertextualität', *ibid.*, pp. 335–6; and Y. Plumley, 'Citation and Allusion in the Late *Ars nova:* The Case of *Esperance* and the *En attendant* Songs', *Early Music History*, 18 (1999), pp. 287–363.

his own skill in counterpoint, whilst, at the same time, paying tribute to the richness of the core of Machaut's conception. This reification of music might be seen as a musical parallel to the literary (and music-theoretical) recourse to *auctoritas* – using an accepted authority and reinterpreting it so as to claim it for the author who can both recognise and use it. It does not necessarily attest to a master/pupil relationship, since Machaut's songs are fairly widely distributed. All that remains is for each case to be provided with as much of the contextual information we can obtain so that it can be decided on its own merits. Whilst these intertextualities may not necessarily help with questions of chronology or biography, they may enable us to form a more complete picture of the musical horizons of fourteenth-century composers and listeners.

University of Bristol

Early Music History (2000) Volume 19.
Printed in the United Kingdom

KENNETH LEVY

A NEW LOOK AT OLD ROMAN CHANT

Historians of plainchant continue to puzzle over the existence of two monophonic repertories, each with claims to Roman origin. The 'Gregorian' chant (GREG)[1] is spread throughout Europe: there are thousands of manuscripts and printed editions; the earliest, lacking neumatic notation, reach back to the late eighth century; with notation they date from the late ninth century; the repertory has remained in continuous use. The 'Old Roman' chant (ROM) is found in fewer than half a dozen complete manuscripts and a handful of fragments; they date between the eleventh and early thirteenth centuries, and nearly all are from the region of Rome.[2] GREG and ROM are very similar in their verbal texts and liturgical provisions. But ROM has the more archaic Roman traits and clearly represents the city's usage, while there is little trace of GREG's use at Rome before the thirteenth century. As for the music, where there are corresponding liturgical texts, they tend to share some underlying musical substance. But the nature and

[1] Before all else, I owe profound thanks to Susan Rankin for many improvements, great and small. The following abbreviations are used for recensions, dates and certain related bibliography: ROM = Old Roman; GREG = Gregorian; GALL = Gallican; OLD HISP = Old Hispanic; MOZ = Mozarabic; MED = Milanese or 'Ambrosian'; BEN = Old Beneventan. Numerals refer to a particular century or range of centuries: GREG-8/10 = 'Gregorian recension, text-witnesses of the late eighth century (as documented by R.-J. Hesbert, *Antiphonale missarum sextuplex* (Brussels, 1935), [hereafter *AMS*]), and first musical witnesses of the tenth century (as in *Graduale triplex*, ed. M.-C. Billecocq and R. Fischer (Solesmes, 1979) [hereafter *GT*])'; or ROM-8 = 'Old Roman states of the eighth century'; ROM-9/11 = 'Old Roman states of the ninth through eleventh centuries', that of the eleventh century as in *Monumenta monodica medii aevi*, ii (Kassel, 1970): *Die Gesänge des altrömischen Graduale Vat. lat. 5319*, ed. B. Stäblein and M. Landwehr-Melnicki [hereafter *MM-2*].

[2] M. Huglo, 'Le Chant "vieux-romain": liste des manuscrits et témoins indirects', *Sacris erudiri*, 6 (1954), pp. 96–124; J. Boe, 'Music Notation in Archivio San Pietro C 105 and in the Farfa Breviary, Chigi C. VI.177', *Early Music History*, 18 (1999), pp. 1–45.

patterns of the musical sharings are not clear, and how the relationships came about has not been satisfactorily explained.

Example 1[3] shows a case of musical relationship. The ROM and GREG versions of the Offertory *Vir erat in terra* have some modal–melodic matter in common, but there are surface differences in style and substance. Did both develop from a common source, or was one a remodelling of the other; and if so, which was the model? The issues were broached by Dom André Mocquereau in 1891, but at the time the priority and authority of GREG could scarcely be questioned, and ROM's possibilities were consigned to a footnote.[4] Two decades later Dom Raphael Andoyer advanced arguments for the priority of ROM.[5] But there was no substantial discussion until the 1950s, when a run of speculation began that continues today. Bruno Stäblein (1950) saw both musical repertories as originating at Rome, with ROM refashioned into GREG during the later seventh century.[6] Perspectives were broadened with the description of the Trastevere Gradual of 1071 by Jacques Hourlier and Michel Huglo (1952), and the comprehensive inventory of ROM sources by Huglo (1954).[7] The basis for a more durable theory was actually laid in a paper of 1933 by Theodor Klauser dealing with the liturgical consequences of Pope Stephen II's journey to the Frankish kingdom in 754;[8] this distinguished

[3] GREG: C. Ott, *Offertoriale sive versus offertoriorum* (Tournai, 1935 [hereafter *Ott*]), p. 122; ROM: *MM-2*, p. 255; transposed by a fourth.

[4] *Paléographie musicale: les principaux manuscrits de chant grégorien, ambrosien, mozarabe, gallican*, 1st ser. [hereafter *PalMus*], ii (1891), pp. 6–9: '. . . attendant qu'on soit à même de rechercher avec plus de maturité les origines de cette dernière version et d'analyser la nature des singularités qu'elle présente' (p. 6, note).

[5] 'Le Chant romain antégregorien', *Revue du chant grégorien*, 20 (1911–12), pp. 69–75, 107–14.

[6] B. Stäblein, 'Zur Frühgeschichte des römischen Chorals', in *Atti del Congresso internazionale di musica sacra*, ed. H. Anglès (Rome, 1950; repr. Tournai, 1952), pp. 271–5. There were variants of this 'two Roman chants' theory from J. Smits van Waesberghe, 'L'État actuel des recherches scientifiques dans la domaine du chant grégorien', *3e Congrès international de musique sacrée* (Paris 1957), pp. 206–17; and from S. J. P. van Dijk, 'The Urban and Papal Rites in Seventh- and Eighth-Century Rome', *Sacris erudiri*, 12 (1961), pp. 411–87; *idem*, 'Papal Schola versus Charlemagne', in *Organicae voces: Festschrift Joseph Smits van Waesberghe* (Amsterdam, 1963), pp. 23–30.

[7] J. Hourlier and M. Huglo, 'Un important témoin du chant "vieux-romain": le graduel de Ste. Cécile du Transtévère', *Revue grégorienne*, 31 (1952), pp. 26–37; Huglo, 'Le Chant "vieux-romain"'.

[8] T. Klauser, 'Die liturgischen Austauschbeziehungen zwischen der römischen und der fränkisch-deutschen Kirche vom achten bis zum elften Jahrhundert', *Historisches Jahrbuch der Görres-Gesellschaft*, 53 (1933), pp. 169–89.

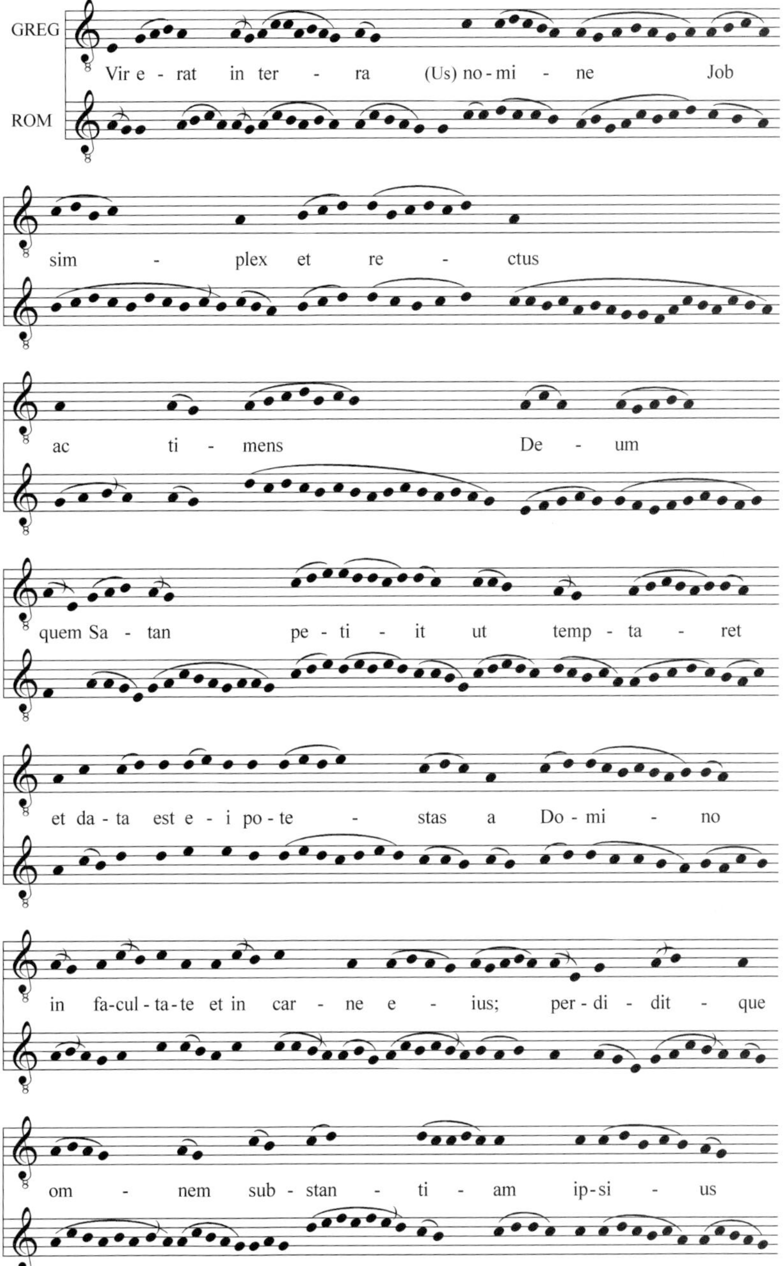

Example 1 Offertory, *Vir erat in terra*

between Roman and Frankish elements in the Sacramentary and Lectionary, and that distinction was extended to the music by Walter Lipphardt in 1950,[9] and more systematically by Helmut Hucke in 1954–5.[10] ROM music was seen as having Roman origin, while GREG music was a late eighth-century version, shaped in the Frankish north in response to Pippin's and Charlemagne's call for liturgical–musical unity. Today, that formulation still seems sound, and it provides a working basis for what follows.

The theories about the ROM–GREG musical relationship are diverse, yet there is one notion that runs through practically all of them: it is the ROM-to-GREG flow. Where modal–melodic substance is shared (as in Example 1), the source music was that of ROM-8, which was then elaborated by GREG-8/10. This fits with Rome's stature; John the Deacon and the monk of St Gall even say it was so.[11] It is so well lodged in the universal mindset that it often can go without saying, though it is generally made explicit.[12] The difficulty is that it leaves much about the actual music unexplained.

In this essay, I will suggest a different picture. Based primarily on a comparative examination of musical behaviour among the ROM and GREG offertories, it questions the ROM-8 to

[9] 'Gregor der Grosse und sein Anteil am römischen Antiphonar', *Atti del Congresso internazionale di musica sacra, Roma, 1950*, pp. 248–54: GREG is the 'fränkische Einheitsfassung' (p. 248; 'Frankish centralised version'); the 'fränkische Tradition' (p. 249).

[10] 'Die Einführung des Gregorianischen Gesangs im Frankenreich', *Römische Quartalschrift*, 49 (1954), pp. 172–87; 'Gregorianischer Gesang in altrömischer und fränkischer Überlieferung', *Archiv für Musikwissenschaft*, 12 (1955), pp. 74–87, translated and with extensive commentary by E. Nowacki, 'Chant Research at the Turn of the Century and the Analytical Programme of Helmut Hucke', *Plainsong and Medieval Music*, 7 (1998), pp. 47–71.

[11] John Hymmonides (John the Deacon), ninth-century biography of Gregory the Great: 'again and again the Germans and Gauls were given the opportunity to learn [Roman] chant . . .'; the St Gall anonymous: 'Charlemagne, deploring the widespread variety of the chanted liturgy, got some experienced singers from Pope Stephen . . .'; the statements are reviewed by T. Karp, *Aspects of Orality and Formularity in Gregorian Chant* (Evanston, Ill., 1998), p. 32; extensive citations in *MM-2*, pp. 142* ff.

[12] D. Hiley, *Western Plainchant: A Handbook* (Oxford, 1993); cf. pp. 561–2. P. Bernard, *Du chant romain au chant grégorien (IVe–XIIIe siècle)* (Paris, 1996); reviewed by Dom D. Saulnier, *Études grégoriennes*, 25 (1997), pp. 169–74, and P. Jeffery, *Speculum*, 74 (1999), pp. 122–4. M. Haas, *Mündliche Überlieferung und altrömische Choral: Historische und analytische computergestützte Untersuchungen* (Bern, 1997); pp. 117 ff., 169 ff. T. Karp, *Aspects of Orality and Formularity*, pp. 31 ff., 365 ff. J. Dyer, 'Tropis semper variantibus: Compositional Strategies in the Offertories of Old Roman Chant', *Early Music History*, 17 (1998), p. 8 on the Roman offertories' two standard formulae, 'all evidence of which has been eradicated in the "Frankish" revision of the music'.

GREG-8/10 flow, at least for the offertories. Instead, it sees GREG-8 as a major contributor of musical substance to ROM-11. This may seem surprising, but it fits the meagre array of facts, and supplies plausible answers to some of the thornier outstanding questions.

The main players are ROM and GREG, but some other musical liturgies also have significant roles, and my point of departure is a line of argument that I first developed in 1984, involving the offertories of the Hispanic-'Mozarabic' rite.[13] These are called Sacrificia in MOZ-10,[14] and they are preserved only in staffless neumes, so that full melodic versions are not possible. In 1967, however, Giacomo Baroffio pointed to some striking correspondences between MOZ-10 sacrificia and identically texted offertories of GREG-8/10. There was *Oravi Deum*, whose 'versions correspond in an astonishing way' ('Fassungen in erstaunliche Weise entsprechen'); also the sacrificium–offertory *Sanctificavit*; and another, *Stetit angelus*, which connected Spain with Milan (MED); Baroffio saw this as 'repeatedly suggesting a very close melodic relationship' ('mehrfach eine sehr enge melodische Verwandtschaft . . . spürbar').[15] In 1984 I addressed these correspondences, adding a further MOZ–GREG item to the list, *Erit (hic) vobis*, and attempting to develop a larger historical framework.[16] To begin, it seemed striking that all the texts were 'non-psalmic' – based on other sources than the Psalter. Psalmic texts tend to be devotional, but these had more of a story to tell. Among the MOZ offertories, non-psalmic texts were a great majority, assigned to nearly all important feasts, while the psalmic ones were a small minority. However, in GREG and ROM (the two rites are largely identical in their texts and calendar assignments) that situation is reversed: psalmic offertories are a majority (roughly four out of every five pieces) and they have most of the major liturgi-

[13] K. Levy, 'Toledo, Rome, and the Legacy of Gaul', *Early Music History*, 4 (1984), pp. 49–99; reprinted in Levy, *Gregorian Chant and the Carolingians* (Princeton, 1998), pp. 31–81.

[14] D. M. Randel, *An Index to the Chants of the Mozarabic Rite* (Princeton, 1973), pp. 457–71, provides the inventory.

[15] G. B. Baroffio, 'Die Offertorien der ambrosianischen Kirche' (diss. Köln, 1964), pp. 29, 64; *idem*, 'Die mailändische Überlieferung des Offertoriums Sanctificavit', in M. Ruhnke (ed.), *Festschrift Bruno Stäblein* (Kassel, 1967), pp. 1–8, at p. 1.

[16] The parallel neumations are seen in 'Toledo, Rome', pp. 59–64. The relationships would be of the kind I have called 'close multiples'; 'On Gregorian Orality', *Journal of the American Musicological Society*, 42 (1990), pp. 185–227.

cal assignments, while the non-psalmic minority are at feasts of lesser importance (Sunday cycles, etc.) and of apparent later entry to the calendar. The non-psalmic texts can therefore be seen in some sense as 'at home' in MOZ and peripheral in GREG–ROM; and it is the other way around for the psalmic texts.

One noteworthy aspect of the non-psalmic texts is the relation to their literary source – generally some other biblical book than the Psalter. Often, the chant texts are radically altered and compressed, something evidently done to make 'librettos' suitable for musical setting; the verbal economies suggest the texts were shaped with melismatic music in mind. And melismatic music is what they have in both the MOZ sacrificia and their GREG–ROM offertory counterparts.

The distinctive literary formulations of the non-psalmic offertories make something else clear: the textual correspondences between MOZ and GREG and/or MED were not the result of different places accidentally hitting on the same formulation. The librettos were distinctive literary entities that must have travelled from one usage to another. And since textual–liturgical considerations show the non-psalmic offertories to be at home in MOZ, the likely direction of transfer was from MOZ (or better, its ancestor, OLD HISP) to GREG–ROM. That would also apply to the music. The close correspondences between MOZ neumed versions and GREG and MED pitched versions involve largely fixed, memorised melodies that were wedded to particular non-psalmic texts and taken from MOZ into GREG (and/or MED).

The three offertories common to MOZ and GREG (*Oravi Deum*, *Erit hic vobis*, and *Sanctificavit*) doubtless were attached to GREG-8 by the middle to late eighth century, when that repertory was definitively formulated; they are documented by the end of that century in the Blandiniensis.[17] With regard to MOZ there is a classic argument by Dom Louis Brou, based on the Orationale of Verona: that many of the MOZ chanted texts were established in the OLD HISP liturgy before *c.* 700.[18] This is likely to apply as well

[17] *AMS* 189b, 85, 193.

[18] 'L'Antiphonaire wisigothique et l'Antiphonaire grégorien au début du VIIIe siècle', *Anuario musical*, 5 (1950), pp. 3–10; the Verona Orationale is a MOZ prayer book where many of the standard pieces of the eventual MOZ repertory are cued; before *c.* 730 it was taken from its Tarragonese home to a refuge in northern Italy, escaping the Muslim invasions that began in 711.

to the MOZ melodies which surface in GREG just a half century later.

So far this has been about three pieces in GREG with textual–musical counterparts in MOZ. For most of the twenty or so non-psalmic offertories in GREG-8, however, MOZ has no counterparts, and that suggests the GREG editors were working from some other source. There were liturgical overlappings between seventh- and eighth-century OLD HISP and GALL rites, and a likelier direct source for the GREG-8 pieces would be a GALL liturgical–musical usage that flourished precisely in the Frankish heartland where GREG-8 was formulated. Almost all the chants of GALL-7/8 are supposed to have disappeared. Yet now it looks as if one might reckon with a carryover from GALL to GREG-8 of some or even most of the twenty offertories with non-psalmic 'libretto' texts in GREG-8/10 – and as the MOZ–GREG links show, not just their texts, but also their music.

There was an even farther-reaching conjecture in my paper of 1984, but my proposals at the time were already so likely to prove controversial that it seemed better not to emphasise it. Linked with the theory of GALL origin for the GREG non-psalmic offertories was an obvious corollary concerning the GREG pieces with psalmic texts. The GREG offertories have often been singled out for their distinctive stylistic traits: prominent skips, extensive melismas, modal ambiguities, etc.[19] The point is that there are no major differences in musical style between the one-fifth minority of GREG offertories with non-psalmic texts and the four-fifths majority with psalmic texts.[20] This can be established by extensive

[19] H. Sidler described them as 'Eigengewächs': *Studien zu den alten Offertorien mit ihren Versen* (Veröffentlichungen der Gregorianischen Akademie zu Freiburg, Schweiz, 1939), p. 7; W. Apel wrote of 'a veritable mine of bold formations not encountered anywhere else in the repertory'; *Gregorian Chant* (Bloomington, Ind., 1958), p. 512; R. Steiner and G. B. Baroffio in *The New Grove Dictionary of Music and Musicians* [hereafter *NGD*], ed. S. Sadie (London, 1980), xiii, p. 516a, s.v. 'Offertory': 'Many of the offertory melodies have a wide range, sometimes involving a daring use of modulation. The chants are difficult to perform; the musical style is distinctive and virtuoso. Unusual intervals such as octaves and sevenths covered in two leaps are found . . ., and a melodic tritone occurs . . .'.

[20] I ventured this in passing in 'Toledo, Rome', pp. 95–6; Hiley has picked it up: 'Levy's hypothesis is that these [non-psalmic offertories] are the descendents of the Gallican chant repertory. It is . . . difficult to see much musical difference between them and other [psalmic] offertories' (*Western Plainchant*, p. 122); as has R. Steiner, 'Holocausta medullata: An Offertory for St. Saturninus', in P. Cahn and A.-K. Heimer (eds), *De musica et cantu: Studien zur Geschichte der Kirchenmusik und der Oper. Helmut Hucke zum 60. Geburtstag* (Hildesheim, 1993) [hereafter *Hucke Festschrift*], pp. 263–74; cf. p. 268.

comparisons. It is also apparent from the occasional assignment of the same music to both text-types, as happens with the non-psalmic *Angelus Domini* and the psalmic *Posuisti*.[21] Now that stylistic identity would have a major consequence. If the music of the GREG non-psalmic offertories had (MOZ)–GALL antecedents, then so as well must the music of the psalmic offertories. This would mean that a very considerable amount of GREG music – nearly all the offertories – was carried over from GALL: with their florid verses these represent more than a third of all the music for the GREG mass propers. All this might be seen as having come, with relatively little change, from GALL music.

The argument to this point has focused on aspects of GREG, MOZ and GALL. Yet Rome is also fundamentally involved. Example 1 showed a case of a ROM-11 offertory (*Vir erat*) that shared considerable modal–melodic substance with a GREG-8/10 analogue. In the vast majority of offertories, however, little or no music is shared. ROM and GREG even seem to have different approaches that rule out substantial sharing. The GREG offertories have fixed melodies; they are remembered entities, with distinctive, memorable contours, capable of being transported from one liturgical environment to another and of being applied to different texts (*Angelus Domini* and *Posuisti*). In Byzantine use, such melodies are called *idiomela* ('with their own melody'), and the musical stance of the MOZ–(GALL) and GREG offertories might be described as 'idiomelic'. With ROM, it is different. ROM-11 offertory style has been charted by Joseph Dyer in his dissertation of 1971, and again in a recent article.[22] Dyer's in-depth analysis of ROM needs to be dealt with in a manner appropriate to its wealth of musical detail. Yet for present purposes that might be reduced to just three factors: a general process or style, and two collections of formulaic bits.

[21] The original may be the non-psalmic *Angelus*, with paschal assignments; the psalmic *Posuisti*'s most notable assignment is the 'gallican' St Gorgonius of Metz. Other offertories with text–music accommodations include the group *Viri Galilei*, *Stetit angelus* and *Justorum animae* (*NGD*, xiii, p. 516b, art. 'Offertory'; R. Steiner, 'Holocausta medullata', pp. 270–1).

[22] J. H. Dyer, Jr, 'The Offertories of Old-Roman Chant: A Musico-Liturgical Investigation' (Ph.D. diss., Boston University, 1971), table I, pp. 138–41; *idem*, 'Tropis semper variantibus'.

The process/style is apparent from even a casual reading of the ROM-11 repertory in *MM-2*: melodic twists and turns; explorations of narrow ranges with stepwise motion; elegant variations; there is little longer-term directionality, little form-building repetition.

Dyer's first collection of formulaic bits, FormA, is shown in Example 2a.[23] Example 2b shows the verse *Misericordias tuas, Domine* of the offertory *Confitebuntur caeli* in ROM. FormA accounts for nearly all the music. In contrast, Example 2c shows the music of GREG, a distinctive melody which lacks any elements of the repetitions that are so prominent in the way ROM is made.

Dyer's other formulaic collection is shown in Example 3a.[24] Examples 3b and 3c contrast the ROM and GREG versions of the Dedication offertory *Domine Deus in simplicitate*. ROM draws almost exclusively on FormB (with supplemental *alpha*, *m* and *n*); the GREG melody has a distinctive, idiomelic profile. The approaches are different; except perhaps at the beginning of Verse 1, there is at most between them a modal connection.

Specialists in ROM-11 have often pointed to the presence of improvisational symptoms in the noted versions; these are features that might reach well back in time. Lipphardt in 1950 spoke of 'the South's lively improvisatory art' ('die lebendige Improvisationskunst des Südens').[25] Thomas Connolly devoted a serious discussion to this with the introits; Dyer remarked recently about the offertories: 'the notated versions . . . particularly in their use of the resources mentioned above [i.e. the twists and formula-sets A and B] hint strongly at their oral, improvisational antecedents . . .'.[26]

23 Example 2a after Dyer, 'Tropis semper variantibus', p. 9; FormA also operates in a transposition from a modal centre on C to one on F. Example 2b is from R. Snow, 'The Old-Roman Chant', in Apel, *Gregorian Chant*, p. 491. Example 2c is from *Ott*, p. 139.

24 Example 3a, after Dyer, 'Tropis semper variantibus', p. 21; with the same alternative transposition as FormA; Example 3b, GREG: *Ott*, p. 159, transposed by a fourth; Example 3c, ROM: *MM-2*, p. 341.

25 Also of melodies that show 'in ihrer formlosigkeit typische Auflösungstendenzen, gegenüber der sicher geformten plastischen Weisen der gregorianisch-fränkischen Einheitsfassung'; 'Gregor der Grosse und sein Anteil am römischen Antiphonar', p. 249. Hiley remarks about the offertory *Benedic anima mea*: 'The Gregorian version is set out with the same line divisions as the Old Roman, but . . . the vocabulary as well as the form is different'; *Western Plainchant*, p. 536.

26 T. H. Connolly, 'Introits and Archetypes: Some Archaisms of the Old Roman Chant', *Journal of the American Musicological Society*, 25 (1972), pp. 157–74; Dyer, 'Tropis semper variantibus', p. 7.

Example 2a ROM FormA (Dyer)

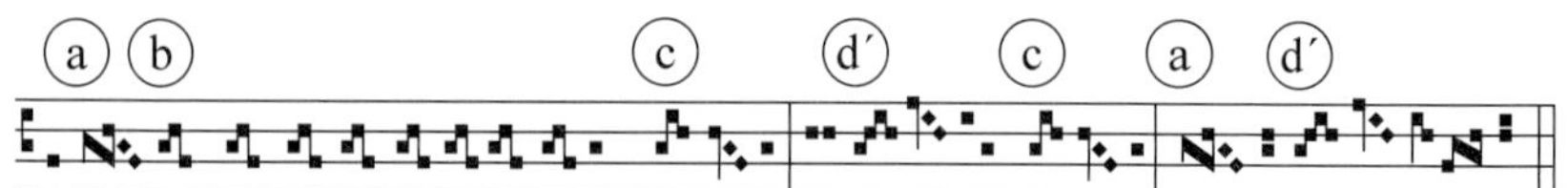

1. Mi - se - ri-cor-di-as tu-as, Do-mi - ne,
2. in ae - ter-num can - ta - bo:
3. in ge - ne - ra - ti - o - ne et pro - ge-ni - te
4. pro-nun - ti - a - bo ve-ri-ta-tem in o-re me-o.

Example 2b ROM Verse, *Misericordias tuas* (Snow)

V. 2. Mi-se - ri -

cór - di - as tu - as, Dó-mi-ne,

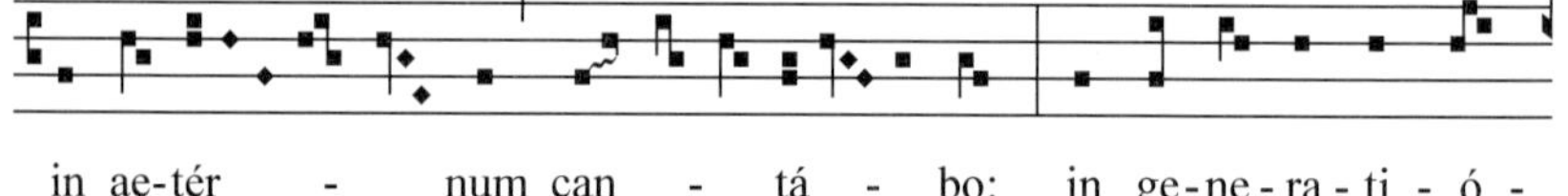

in ae-tér - num can - tá - bo: in ge-ne - ra - ti - ó -

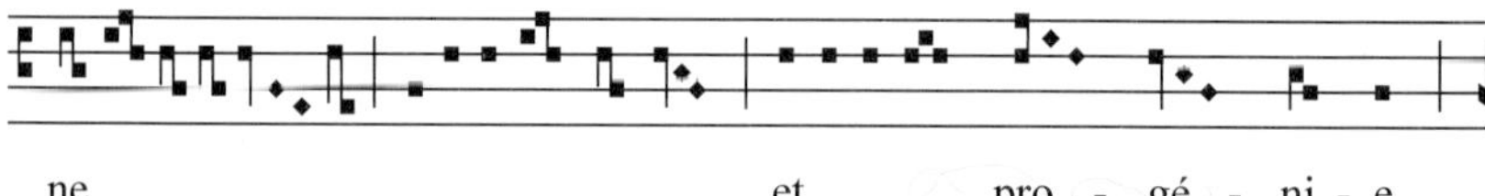

ne et pro - gé - ni - e

ad-nun - ti - á - bo ve-ri - tá - tem tu - am in

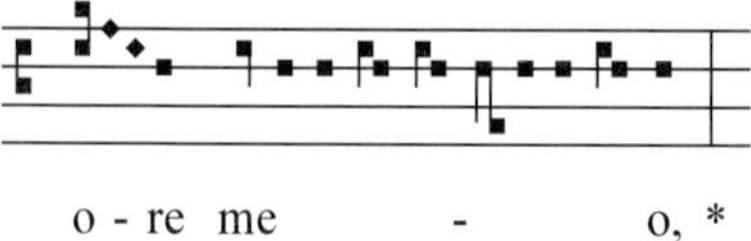

o - re me - o, *

Example 2c GREG Verse, *Misericordias tuas* (Ott)

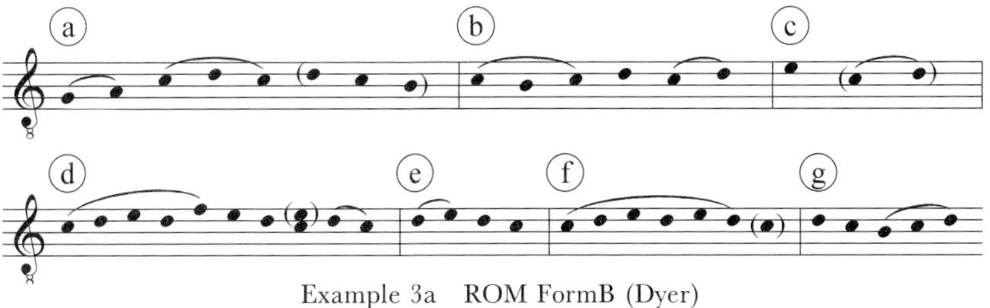

Example 3a ROM FormB (Dyer)

b. GREG

Do-mi-ne De - us in sim-pli - ci-ta - te cor-dis me - i

α m n α m n d e e

c. Form B: ROM

le - tus ob - tu - li u - ni - ver - sa

f m n d f e

et po - pu - lum tu - um qui re - per - tus est

f m d g

vi - di cum in - gen - ti gau - di - o

m n d e

Example 3b and c Offertory, *Domine Deus in simplicitate*

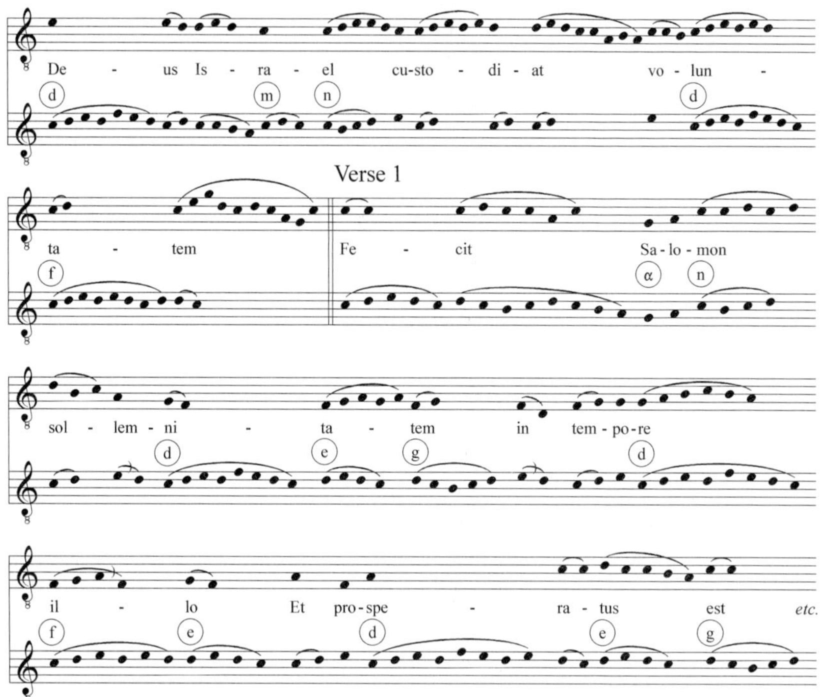

Example 3b and c *continued*

Thus in ROM-11 and GREG-8/10 there seem to be two different principles at work: ROM music, improvisational–formulaic; GREG music, more distinctive–idiomelic. In most cases that rules out melodic relationships between the corresponding offertories. Yet there are cases, like that of *Vir erat* in Example 1, where musical relationships are substantial. How have these two principles come to coexist? Where there is a substantial musical relationship (as in Example 1), various explanations seem possible. One would suppose a proto-Roman state (ROM-6/7) from which GREG-8/10 and ROM-11 music independently derive; an original ROM melos that would erode considerably on the way before reaching ROM-11. The trouble with that is it places the non-psalmic idiomelic offertories at Rome at a very early stage; not only is there is no evidence for doing so, but there are reasons for just the contrary

– connecting such pieces to ultimate Hispanic/Gallican origins. Another explanation would be the common one: a musical infusion from ROM-8 to GREG-8/10 – the GREG stylisation drawing on a Roman melodic basis. That remains plausible enough wherever the musical relationship is close; but it will not do where the corresponding chants are musically diverse.

Now there would also be my third explanation, which reverses the flow and sees GREG-8 music as exercising a decisive influence on ROM-9/10. Already in its favour there are the circumstances of the MOZ–GALL–GREG relationships: the offertories with non-psalmic librettos, native to MOZ–GALL, filling secondary liturgical assignments in ROM. There are also certain details of the verbal texts. The psalmic offertory texts that are shared by GREG-8/10 and ROM-11 are often faithfully excerpted from the Psalter; as a result they may be traceable to a particular translation – Old Roman, Old Latin, Gallican, etc.[27] Where a source can be identified, a Roman psalter reading should generally point to a chant text's Roman origin, and a Gallican psalter reading to Gallican origin.[28] What is striking about the ROM-11 psalmic offertories is that many of them have what are apparently Gallican psalter readings. Dyer has listed variants among psalmic offertory texts, where there are dozens of cases of ROM and GREG agreeing with one another but disagreeing with the Roman Psalter.[29] Roughly four times out of five, the ROM–GREG text agrees with a Gallican or Mozarabic psalter reading.

In the offertory *Constitues*, where the Roman psalter reads *omni generatione et progenie* (Ps. 44:18; *Weber*, p. 101), the ROM-11 offertory (*MM-2*, p. 366) agrees with GREG-8 (*AMS* 122b; *GT*, p. 434) as well as Gallican and Mozarabic psalters in the variant *omni progenie et generatione*. In the offertory *Eripe me . . . Domine*, the Roman psalter has *tu es Deus meus* (Ps. 142:10; *Weber*, p. 344), while ROM-11 (*MM-2*, p. 308) and GREG (*AMS* 74; *GT* p. 152) both

[27] The psalmic texts are not always continuous; like the non-psalmic offertories, they are often assembled from scattered verses, with rearrangements, tailorings, and minor compressions. They too can be seen as 'librettos', and with the same implications for ROM offertory style as the non-psalmic librettos have for the early style of GALL–GREG; such texts were compiled with melismatic music in mind.

[28] R. Weber, *Le Psautier romain et les autres anciens psautiers latins* (Collectanea Biblica Latina, 10; Rome: Abbaye Saint-Jérôme, 1953) [hereafter *Weber*].

[29] Dyer, 'The Offertories of Old-Roman Chant', table I, pp. 138–41.

read *Deus meus tu es* (or *es tu*), in agreement with the Gallican psalter. And in the offertory *Filiae regum*, the Roman Psalter has *circumamicta* (Ps. 44:10; *Weber*, p. 100) while ROM-11 (*MM-2*, p. 281) and GREG (*AMS* 23b; *GT*, p. 506) both have *circumdata*, which is in line with old Gallican psalters.

Having proposed this theory about text-variants, I must also say that they are not reliable witnesses. Chance played a large role in what sixth- through eighth-century psalters have survived, possibly distorting our view. And at any point in a transmission, it was the work of just a moment to replace a received reading with one that suited local practice.[30] Nevertheless, there is little reason for the ROM-11 offertory texts to transmit so many apparently GALL readings other than a considerable Gallo-Frankish exposure along the way.

The most persuasive indications that GREG-8 offertory music left a considerable imprint on ROM-8/11 music come from the music itself. The standard notion that ROM-8 was a melodic source for GREG-8 is based largely on such classes as the graduals, where the relationships are often close.[31] Yet even in those situations, as I have remarked about the offertory *Vir erat* (Example 1), the flow might have gone the other way. Among the offertories, furthermore, close relationships are rare. There is often little if any musical relationship, and that in turn may throw some welcome light on the historical development. Examples 2 and 3 have shown instances where there is no GREG–ROM musical relationship. No less common, and historically more suggestive, are the many cases where there is a musical relationship at the start which soon erodes so that ROM-11 and GREG-8/10 finish on independent musical tracks. Example 4[32] shows this in the psalmic offertory *Eripe me*. Some similarity may be claimed in Example 4a; but in the verse *Exaudi* (Example 4b) the ROM material is standard FormA with even some of FormB thrown in; the changes in level of musical correspondence often coincide with the division

[30] P. Bernard, 'Les Chants du propre de la messe dans les répertoires Grégorien et Romain Ancien: essai d'édition pratique des variantes textuelles', *Ephemerides liturgicae*, 110 (1996), pp. 210–51, with a useful list that may be appraised in this light.

[31] N. Van Deusen, 'An Historical and Stylistic Comparison of the Graduals of Gregorian and Old Roman Chant' (Ph.D. diss., Indiana University, 1972).

[32] GREG: *Ott*, p. 51; ROM: *MM-2*, p. 308.

Example 4a Offertory, *Eripe me . . . Domine*

Example 4b Verse, *Exaudi me*

between verses. Through it all, GREG maintains its customary independence of melodic profile.

A similar case is Example 5.[33] This is one of the MOZ-linked offertories of non-psalmic text-type with which this essay began. All the major musical families are here: the neumatic MOZ-10(–GALL) and its melodic analogue in GREG; MED-12, which, as often happens, appears to restylise music that came from GREG;[34] and ROM. The text suggests an important liturgical occasion. MOZ, GREG and ROM all assign the piece to Friday in Easter Week; but MED has it for Pentecost, and there was probably a similar use in early MED and/or GALL. As for its music, MOZ, GREG and MED appear to share common material, but ROM-11 has little if anything to do with that: perhaps some melodic relationship at the start, and at *progenies vestras*; but for the rest, ROM relies on FormB and has no connection with GREG or its analogues. Again, a formulaic, 'improvisational' ROM, and an idiomelic, memorable GREG–(MED–MOZ–[GALL]).

Situations where the musical relationship is irregular or declines offer a fresh key to the riddle of the ROM–GREG relationship. At least for the offertories, they make it hard to suppose that the ROM melos generated the distinctive idiomelic profiles of GREG. ROM-11's still simple, improvisational–formulaic stance suggests that between it and its ROM-8 forerunner there was little in the way of change; and if the ROM-8 offertories were close to the ROM-11 we know, they can scarcely have been the source for the GREG-8/10 music we know. Where underlying musical substance is shared, ROM represents it only in part, and often ignores it, offering instead its own formulaic twists and turns. If one influenced the other, it must be GREG, which throughout maintains a distinctive melodic profile, that was the source. That direction of flow fits with what is already suggested by the MOZ–GALL and GREG offertory links and the Gallican psalter readings among the ROM-11 offertory texts. The partial accommodations say that ROM was working with, reacting to, GREG melos.

33 GREG: *Ott*, p. 63; MED: *AMM*, p. 256; ROM: *MM-2*, p. 415.

34 The situation of MED, sampled in Example 5, calls for a full-dress study. MED and GREG sometimes relate in the way proposed here for ROM and GREG.

Example 5 Offertory, *Erit vobis*

One question remains. Why the pattern of partial accommodations? There are answers that may fit comfortably within the general framework of eighth- through twelfth-century musical developments set forth by Dom Cardine.[35] The GREG-8/10 music was given a definitive formulation between *c.* 755 and *c.* 785; this happened in the Frankish heartland, not unlikely at Metz.[36] GREG's liturgical and textual provisions came chiefly from Rome. But for its offertories (this is the first of my proposals), if any ROM-8 music accompanied the Roman verbal texts, the GREG-8 editors made no use of it. Perhaps this was because the GREG-8 repertory would need promptly to be memorised by all the realm's choirmasters, and the homogenous, curvaceous, improvisational Roman melodic style offered too little that was distinctive for memories readily to grasp. Furthermore, the Frankish choirmasters were already in control of distinctive, idiomelic offertory melodies (the likes of *Oravi*, *Erit*, and *Sanctificavit*), which could be transferred whole from MOZ–GALL into GREG. There remained the Roman psalmic offertory texts, needing memory-friendly music. My thought is, this came from applying the music of existing GALL offertories (non-psalmic or psalmic) to the Roman texts: the sort of contrafacting that may be seen in GREG's pairing of the non-psalmic *Angelus Domini* and the psalmic *Posuisti*: in all, a practical as well as congenial way of complying with the Carolingian mandate to Romanise.

Once GREG-8 was compiled, it was sent out to replace the local plainchants in Carolingian-controlled regions. Rome's prestige made it a prime target for installing GREG, which is unlikely to have arrived there much later than in the Beneventan zone to the south, where it apparently supplanted most of the local repertory before *c.* 838.[37] But at Rome (this is my next proposal) the musical establishment refused to let go of its music. Instead it accommodated GREG-8 music to traditional Roman style. We may get

[35] E. Cardine, 'Vue d'ensemble sur le chant grégorien', *Études grégoriennes*, 16 (1977), pp. 173–92, at pp. 173–4.

[36] On the role of Metz, C. Maître, *La Réforme cistercienne du plain-chant* (Brecht, 1995), pp. 42–5.

[37] *PM*, 14, pp. 450–1 (R.-J. Hesbert); K. Levy, 'The Italian Neophytes' Chants', *Journal of the American Musicological Society*, 23 (1970), pp. 181–227, at p. 221; T. F. Kelly, *The Beneventan Chant* (Cambridge, 1989), pp. 12–23; *Beneventanum troporum corpus*, ed. A. E. Planchart and J. Boe, i, ed. Planchart (Madison, Wis., 1994), pp. xii–xiv.

some notion of the process from the *Veterem hominem* antiphons for the octave of the Epiphany. These began as Byzantine hymns; at Charlemagne's request, they were translated from Greek into Latin during the early ninth century, and their music was turned into GREG style.[38] The pieces then made their way to Rome (and Charlemagne's role as prime mover suggests this was not delayed),[39] where a further musical transformation took place as the GREG versions were turned into a more rounded Roman style.

Something similar can be imagined for the offertories. The Carolingian-sanctioned GREG-8 appeared at Rome with its claim to primacy; the Romans reacted by naturalising the GREG-8 music, rounding off its craggier profiles, adapting it to their own traditional style. What sets the offertories apart from some other musical classes is that so little accommodation was done. *Vir erat* is almost alone as an offertory whose full music was turned to ROM style. Much commoner, as in Examples 2b and 3c, was for ROM to ignore the GALL–GREG melos and use just the archaic local style. And also common, as in Examples 4 and 5, was for the Romans to make initial gestures of accommodation but then fall back on that archaic style.

Why would the Romans do it that way? Perhaps it was a matter of local pride. Perhaps there was some animus: the Roman music was ignored by GREG-8's formulators, and here was a gesture of payback. Perhaps it was the great amount of labour: the offertories were a full third of the GREG music; to convert and then memorise all of them was a major undertaking. Whatever the reasons (and any or all of these might apply), the significance of the Romans' spotty accommodations lies in what they suggest about the history. In ways that only the music can, they say that the GREG music was not built with ROM musical input; rather, it was the other way around: the Romans accommodated GREG music to their own Roman style.

[38] O. Strunk, 'The Latin Antiphons for the Octave of the Epiphany', in *Essays on Music in the Byzantine World* (New York, 1977), pp. 208–19; Levy, 'Toledo, Rome', 93; an ample discusssion, with musical illustrations, in E. Nowacki, 'Constantinople–Aachen–Rome: The Transmission of *Veterem hominem*', in *De musica et cantu* (Hucke Festschrift) (1993), pp. 95–115.

[39] P. Bernard remarks on Charlemagne's general interest in the region: '[il] a proposé son aide pour réformer certains des plus grands monastères de Rome et certains des monastères proches de l'Urbs, comme celui de Farfa . . .'; *Du chant romain au chant grégorien*, p. 483.

While this much has been about the GREG–ROM offertories, inevitably questions are raised about other classes. Comprehensive answers must wait until many or even all GREG–ROM parallels are examined in detail, class by class, piece by piece, in the light of these perspectives. Random samplings already yield some noteworthy results. Traces of the ROM offertories' improvisational–formulaic materials in some other classes indicate a broader application of the developments described here. Dom Mocquereau's comparison of the Easter introit *Resurrexi et adhuc* in ROM and GREG showed a close musical relationship,[40] where the musical flow might have gone either way. With the introit *Justus ut palma* in Example 6,[41] there is little if any musical relationship. As with many offertories, the GREG music is idiomelic while ROM is made up of FormB elements and podatus declamation. Once again, the GREG-8 music seems likely to have journeyed to Rome, which ignored it while continuing with its own Roman style.

There also are traces of FormB in the ROM introit *Justi epulentur*, in the processional antiphon *Custodit Dominus animas sanctorum*, and some others.[42] Example 7[43] shows the GREG and ROM versions of the communion *Gustate et videte*. Ps. 33:9 is a fundamental communion text, which enjoys musical prominence in Byzantine and related rites as the ordinary communion for the Lenten Liturgy of the Presanctified.[44] In GREG, there is a recognisable modal–melodic type. In Rome, more than half the music is standard FormB, another mark of that material's authority.

There is something similar with the Requiem communion, *Lux eterna*. Requiem chants were not included in early states of the ROM–GREG mass antiphoner (the *Sextuplex* has none), and there tend to be oddities when they appear. The scribe of Vatican lat. 5319 entered two musical versions of *Lux eterna* in succession; each

[40] *PM*, 2 (1899), pp. 8 f.

[41] *GT*, p. 508; *MM-2*, pp. 64–5.

[42] *Custodit Dominus*: ROM: *MM-2*, p. 583; GREG: *AMS*, p. 210; Paris, lat. 903, fol. 138v; *PM*, 18 (Rome, Angelica 123), fol. 177v. Among the anomalous relationships involving introits, singled out by Connolly, 'Introits and Archetypes', p. 171, the ROM Introit *Confessio* has traces of FormA while *In virtute tua* and *Esto mihi* have traces of FormB.

[43] GREG: *GT*, p. 303; ROM: *MM-2*, p. 470.

[44] D. E. Conomos, *The Late Byzantine and Slavonic Communion Cycle* (Washington, 1985), pp. 50, 54–64; S. J. M. Harris, *The Communion Chants of the Thirteenth-Century Byzantine Asmatikon* (Amsterdam, 1999).

Example 6 Introit, *Justus ut palma*

has a claim to being 'Old Roman' (see Example 8).[45] ROM-1 (Example 8a) would be the more recent. Musically, it is close to the universal GREG melody whose Beneventan and Sarum readings are also shown.[46] But ROM's flourish on [*eter*]-*na* and its roundings-off on [*luce*]-*at eis do*-[*mine*] and *eternum* set it apart, suggesting a purposeful Roman retouching of GREG. ROM-II

[45] Example 8a: ROM-I: *MM-2*, p. 499; GREG–BEN: *PM*, 15 (Benevento VI.34), fol. 266v; GREG–SARUM: *Graduale Sarisburiense*, ed. W. H. Frere (London, 1895), p. 233. Example 8b: ROM-II: *MM-2*, p. 474.

[46] ROM-I also appears twice in Vatican, Arch. S. Pietro, F. 11, fols. 56v and 68v, with minor variants.

Example 7 Communion, *Gustate et videte*

(Example 8b; Vat. 5319 is its sole witness) would be the earlier one, and its music is purely Roman, deriving from FormB.

This essay has proposed a fresh perspective on the ROM-11 and GREG-10 offertories. The entrenched belief has been that ROM-8 modal–melodic substances were reworked in forming GREG-8. But that has not explained the actual musical relationships. My alternative is to see the GREG-8 offertories as drawing much of their musical substance from GALL, then making their way to Rome, which turned that GREG-8 music into ROM style. Not everything was converted. Perhaps because the job was so large, the Romans settled for doing less than all of it. They processed token amounts

Example 8a Communion, *Lux eterna*, ROM-I

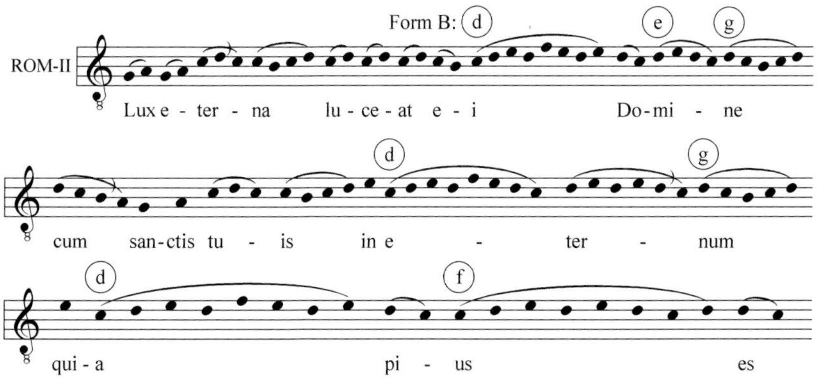

Example 8b Communion, *Lux eterna*, ROM-II

of GREG, while for most of the music perpetuating their own traditional style. That may open an extraordinary window on proto-Roman musical style. If one skims away from ROM-11 the melos attributable to GREG-8, what remains bids to be a more archaic state of ROM music than has ever been confidently accessed: a closeup view of eighth-century schola cantorum practice. The traces of the offertories' improvisational–formulaic materials among ROM introits, communions, etc., also suggest that those materials and practices once had even broader applications. How far it went can only be gauged when all the ROM–GREG parallels have been evaluated. That will take major efforts, which may now seem worthwhile.[47]

Princeton University

[47] For the introits, comparisons are readily made, thanks to A. Turco, *Les Antiennes d'introït du chant romain comparées a celles du grégorien et de l'ambrosien* (Subsidia Gregoriana, 3; Solesmes, 1993); the MED readings, included by Turco, are essential to a comprehensive picture. For the graduals, the ROM–GREG comparisons are easily made with the tabulations in van Deusen, 'An Historical and Stylistic Comparison'.

Early Music History (2000) Volume 19. © Cambridge University Press
Printed in the United Kingdom

BERNADETTE NELSON

RITUAL AND CEREMONY IN THE SPANISH ROYAL CHAPEL, *C.*1559–*C.*1561*

Day of St Matthias, on his birthday, His Majesty offers as many coins as years as he has attained, and [one] more for the year in which he has entered; the King Our Lord does the same on the twenty-first of May.[1]

On the abdication of his father Charles V from the Spanish throne in 1556, Philip II was to inherit probably the most important and prestigious court chapel in Europe.[2] Its history, structure and musical eminence were well established during the time of the Burgundian dukes in the fifteenth century, under whose patronage some of the most prominent musicians and composers found

* I wish to thank the following people for kindly commenting on an earlier version of this study and for making suggestions for improvements: Juan Carlos Asensio, Bonnie Blackburn, Barbara Haggh, Tess Knighton, Michael Noone and Luis Robledo, and Kirstin Kennedy for checking my transcriptions of the royal chapel documents in the Biblioteca da Ajuda in Lisbon.

The following abbreviations are used:

B-Agr	Brussels, Archives Générales du Royaume
E-Mn	Madrid, Biblioteca Nacional
E-Mpa	Madrid, Palacio Real
E-Sag	Simancas, Archivo General
F-Pn	Paris, Bibliothèque Nationale de France
GB-Ob	Oxford, Bodleian Library
P-La	Lisbon, Biblioteca da Ajuda
P-Ln	Lisbon, Biblioteca Nacional

1 'Dia de Sancto Mathia por su nascimento offrece Su Magestad tantos ducados quantos annos cumple, y más el anno en que entra; esto mismo haze El Rey Nuestro Señor a viente y vno del Mayo'; *La Orden que se tiene en los Officios en la Capilla de Su Magestad* (P-La 51-VI-37), fol. 68v. A full transcription of the document is included as Appendix 3.

2 Studies on Charles V's court chapel include chapters in E. Vander Straeten, *La Musique aux Pays-Bas avant le XIXe siècle*, 8 vols. (Brussels, 1867–88; repr. New York, 1969, ed. E. Lowinsky); H. Anglés, *La música en la Corte de Carlos V*, i (Barcelona, 1944, repr. 1984); J. Schmidt-Görg, *Nicolas Gombert, Kapellmeister Karls V: Leben und Werk* (Bonn, 1938); and B. Bouckaert, 'The *Capilla Flamenca*: The Composition and Duties of the Music Ensemble at the Court of Charles V, 1515–1558', in *The Empire Resounds: Music in the Days of Charles V*, ed. F. Maes (Leuven, 1999), pp. 37–45.

their livelihood; as an institution, it was also partly indebted to traditions and an infrastructure inherited from the Castilian court of Ferdinand and Isabella which was passed on to Charles V following the death of Ferdinand in 1516. When Philip II came to power, the amalgamation of his own court and chapel with that of the Emperor resulted in an organisation of unheard proportions, even though many officers of the Imperial court were to accompany Charles V on his retirement to the monastery in Yuste, in Spain, and others of Philip's own train were to return independently to their homeland on periods of extended leave. This was evidently a time of considerable upheaval, during which membership fluctuated and the structural organisation necessarily underwent a period of some adjustment. Before Philip II finally returned to Spain from the Netherlands in September 1559, and during the succeeding years embracing the establishment of the court in the royal Alcázar, Madrid, in May 1561, measures were taken to stabilise the institution during a period of almost relentless political and religious activity which marked the times: certainly in the royal chapel itself there is evidence that efforts were made to account for this changeover of sovereignty, and while no new statutes seem to have been drawn up at the beginning of Philip's reign, many statutes and other constitutional documents primarily dating from Charles V's time were redrafted and reinstated.[3]

[3] For a synopsis of the historical circumstances leading to Philip II's inheritance, and the impact these influences had on the court, see L. Robledo Estaire, 'La música en la corte Madrileña de los Austrias. Antecedentes: las Casas Reales hasta 1556', *Revista de musicología*, 10 (1987), pp. 753–96. A graph demonstrating 'la evolución de las Casas Reales' from the time of Ferdinand and Isabella to that of Philip II is included on pp. 794–5 (Table V). See also L. Robledo, 'La música en la corte de Felipe II', in *Felipe II y su Epoca, Actas del Simposium, San Lorenzo del Escorial, 1/5-IX-1998* (El Escorial, 1999), pp. 141–67. Concerning the Castilian royal chapel during the time of Ferdinand and Isabella, see T. Knighton, 'Ritual and Regulations: The Organization of the Castilian Royal Chapel during the Reign of the Catholic Monarchs', in E. Casares and C. Villanueva (eds), *De Musica Hispana et aliis: miscelánea en honor al Prof. Dr José López-Calo* (Santiago de Compostela, 1990), pp. 291–320. Several documents of the royal chapel were transcribed by the historian and archivist Francisco Asenjo Barbieri. These papers, now preserved in the Biblioteca Nacional in Madrid (E-Mn), have recently been edited (though not without error) as a two-volume collection by Emilio Casares: *Francisco Asenjo Barbieri: Documentos sobre música española y epistolario* (Madrid, 1986–8). The documents of the royal court are included in vol. 2. In the present study, this collection will henceforth be referred to as 'Barbieri papers 2', followed by the number of the document ('doc.') cited. See also below, 'Statutes of the royal chapel'. I would like to thank Michael Noone for making available to me the latter and numerous other books and articles for the preparation of this study.

This study centres on a newly discovered constitutional document of the *Capilla Real* which was drawn up for the Imperial chapel most probably in about 1550, but which was slightly adapted on Philip II's accession to the throne, and certainly after September 1559.[4] Entitled *La Orden que se tiene en los Officios en la Capilla de Su Magestad* ('The Order which is held in the Offices in the Chapel of His Majesty'), the text largely consists of a record of procedure, ceremony and matters of protocol in the Spanish royal chapel, the main body of which was apparently written by a certain Aguirre, who is identified as 'chaplain of His Majesty, and receiver of his Chapel' ('Capellan de Su Magestad, y Receptor de su Capilla').[5] Having been written by an active member of the chapel, the document often offers insight into practices and ceremonial traditions which have eluded the majority of formal statutory edicts. Woven into details of liturgical ritual of a more everyday nature – the lists of occasions for sermons, offerings and processions, for instance – are glimpses of what can only have been long-standing practices inherited from the Burgundian court of Philip the Fair, Charles V's immediate predecessor, as well as customs associated with important anniversaries dating from Charles V's time itself: these include the procession of knights holding lighted candles during mass at chapter meetings of the Order of the Golden Fleece, an allusion to ceremony on the feast day (29 September) of the Order of St Michael, when the robes of that order were worn,[6] the offering by the king of a gold coin and a lighted candle in which was embedded *un escudo* (a gold coin bearing the royal coat of arms) during mass for commemorations of members of the royal family such as the Empress Isabella, and the offering at mass on the anniversary of the Emperor's birthday

4 Among the amendments are clauses indicating Philip's status as monarch, as well as a reference to observances on each anniversary of the death of his father, the Emperor Charles V, which occurred on 21 September 1558.

5 *La Orden*, fol. 77.

6 This reference to the French Order of St Michael, which was founded by King Louis XI in 1469, is unusual within Burgundian-Habsburg court documents. Although the Order was only established at that time, a chapel dedicated to St Michael had been founded in the Sainte-Chapelle in Dijon in 1452, the court of the Burgundian dukes and of the Order of the Golden Fleece from 1432. There was a close association between these two Orders and the statutes of that of St Michael were in fact modelled on those of the Golden Fleece. See B. Haggh, 'The Archives of the Order of the Golden Fleece', *Journal of the Royal Musical Association*, 120 (1995), pp. 1–43, at pp. 36–7.

and coronation (again by the king) of a bag of gold coins. Only some of this more contextual evidence is clearly stated, however: it is often only through the process of the unmeshing of a series of oblique and dislocated references that the significance of some details in *La Orden* emerges more strongly, particularly when they can be linked with descriptions and accounts found in chronicles and other historical documents from the era. Further, *La Orden* provides insight into liturgical acts and ceremonies in which the choreography is sometimes intimately linked with the timing of musical items – an aspect which is unique among constitutional documents and which has considerable bearing on appropriate contexts for the performance of sacred vocal polyphony. It is also possibly the earliest royal chapel document to give evidence of the use of *violones* in the accompaniment of vocal music, and one of the few to give a reference to the interaction of organ music with polyphony.

LA ORDEN: CONTEXT AND DATING

A Miguel Pérez de Aguirre is clearly documented in Spanish archival sources as *receptor* in Charles V's chapel in 1548, 1550 and 1552,[7] which therefore provides a specific context for the origin of the document, if not an almost exact date. We learn of his probable authorship through the acknowledgement provided by an unknown recipient which in full reads, 'This account was given to me by Aguirre, Chaplain of His Majesty and receiver in his Chapel.'[8] Judging from Aguirre's final statement, it seems likely that the recipient had requested of him an account of procedures in the royal chapel and that this was made after the court had settled in Spain. Here, while saying that what he has written reflects present-day customs in the royal chapel, Aguirre also indicates that variations occur according to context and circumstance, and that therefore a number of 'diverse ceremonies' can be found in the

[7] I am most grateful to Luis Robledo for providing me with this important information about Aguirre's activities in Charles V's chapel. These dates correpond with a series of pay documents in Aguirre's name preserved in the Archivio de Simancas (Casas y Situos Reales, leg. 92). One made out to his heirs in 1561 indicates that Aguirre had died on 24 August the previous year.

[8] 'Esta rellacion me dió Aguirre, Capellan de Su Magestad y Receptor de su Capilla', *La Orden*, fol. 77.

royal chapel in Spain. It is possible that this particular statement may reflect more his long experiences as chaplain in the Imperial royal chapel; on the other hand, it does show his awareness of rituals and ceremonies peculiar to the royal institution:

This [the foregoing account] is that which is customary at present, and is observed in His Majesty's chapel; however, it [the order of things] has been varied in some way with the times and places where His Majesty travels, and thus we see that with the royal chapel in Spain there are some diverse ceremonies.[9]

Aguirre's position both as chaplain and *receptor* in the royal chapel would inevitably have some bearing on the bias of the document and the question of which issues receive more attention. His was an ancient and extremely responsible post, the origins of which lay in the Spanish royal chapel of the Catholic Monarchs.[10] According to this tradition, a *receptor*'s role was a high-ranking and all-embracing one which ranged from being responsible for organising mass rotas and for taking account of all absences among chapel members, to the collecting of fines and the distribution of fees and collections. In the portion of the document devoted to the various officers of the chapel and their duties, Aguirre outlines the responsibilities of a *receptor* much along the lines (though in less detail) of those found in the early fifteenth-century set of constitutions for the Castilian royal chapel:[11]

The receiver of the chapel receives and administers all the distributions offered as admission duty, offerings, legitimations or whatever else he has to distribute.

In the absence of the first chaplain (*capellan mayor*), or his deputy (*lugar teniente*), the receiver recommends which prelate and chaplains should go and take the Office.

On Sundays and [major] feasts, the receiver accompanies the prelates who are to offer the 'Gospel' and the *pax* to the celebrants [to be kissed].[12]

[9] 'Esto se acostumbra al prezente, y se guarda en la Capilla de Su Magestad, pero ha se variado en alguna manera con los tiempos, y lugares por dó Su Magestad anda, y ansy vemos que en España con la Capilla Real hay algunas ceremonias diversas'; *La Orden*, fols. 76^{v}–77.

[10] See Knighton, 'Ritual and Regulations', p. 300.

[11] *Constituciones de la Real Capilla de Don Henrique IV*, ed. Barbieri papers 2, doc. 124.

[12] This evidently refers to the custom of offering the Missal and the plaquette (the *pax*) to be kissed after the reading of the Gospel and after the Agnus Dei respectively. (See *La Orden*, fol. 63^{v}.)

The receiver is responsible for assigning the [occasions] for sermons, the weekly masses and other offices of the chapel [to the chaplains].[13]
The receiver is responsible for advising the chaplains; when there are any extraordinary offices in the chapel the receiver takes distributions for [the equivalent] of two chaplains.[14]

Aguirre is quite explicit about this question of distributions (*destribuciones*) and, at a later point and with specific reference to the singers of the chapel, he provides more detail on the relationship between the paying of an entrance fee and the receiving of distributions. He relates how all new chaplains admitted to His Majesty's services should pay the 'receiver' 3,000 *reis*[15] as entrance fee and how, like the chaplains, but excepting the *maestro de capilla*, the clerks and the boys, *all singers* of the chapel should also pay this fee.[16] In keeping with traditions of the Spanish chapel of the Catholic Monarchs, the *receptor* in Charles V's chapel witnessed the taking of an oath of allegiance of new chapel members before the *capellan mayor*, head of the chapel. If, in assessing this document, we take into account the role of Aguirre in the royal chapel as chaplain and receiver, then a more precise context can be given for its apparent emphasis on such issues as offerings, the allocation of gifts and distributions, occasions for preaching sermons, the ceremonies of the Gospel blessing and the kiss of the *pax*.

[13] In the section immediately following, which concerns the responsibilities of the chaplains, it is written: 'Unless there is a legitimate reason, no chaplains can excuse themselves from serving [at the Offices] of their week of duty and which were recommended to them by the *receptor*'; *La Orden*, fol. 74^{v}. This particular responsibility of the *receptor* was also stipulated in the *Constituciones* of Henry IV (*c.* 1436) and that of the Catholic Monarchs. See Barbieri papers 2, docs. 124 (item 9) and 126 (item 8). For further information on these specific duties, see below, p. 131.

[14] *La Orden*, fols. 73^{v}–74.

[15] A similar amount was also stipulated in the earlier *Constitutiones de la Capilla Real* (item 20). See Barbieri papers 2, doc. 126. A number of these stipulations, including the payment of an entrance fee, are also familiar in such institutions as the sixteenth-century papal chapel. See R. Sherr, 'A Curious Incident in the Institutional History of the Papal Choir', in R. Sherr (ed.), *Papal Music and Musicians in Late Medieval and Renaissance Rome* (Oxford, 1998), p. 192, where he refers to this occurrence in the 1545 *Constitution* of Pope Paul III. See also *ibid.*, p. 188, n. 5, for sources for modern transcriptions of this papal document.

[16] 'Entradas de Capellanes. Todos los Capellanes de Su Magestad primero que tomen sobrepellis ó le admitan en la Capilla, quando entran de nuevo han de hazer la solemnidad del Juramento ante el Capellan Mayor, y el Receptor, y pagan al Receptor tres mil reis de entrada para toda la Capilla. . . . Todos los Cantores y officiales de la Capilla, se quisieren ganar destribuciones han de pagar la entrada como vn Capellan excepto el Capellan Mayor, y los mozos y los niños'; *La Orden*, fols. 76 and 76^{v}.

As Aguirre died in August 1560, the document as a testimony of practices in Philip II's chapel *in Spain* (see quotation above) theoretically can only have passed hands sometime between late 1559 and the summer of 1560, a vital period when Philip and his court, though primarily stationed in Toledo at the royal Alcázar, were engaged in the numerous political and religious disturbances which shook Spain at the time. On Philip's arrival in Valladolid in September 1559 he immediately became involved in affairs of state and the drastic measures instigated by the Inquisition, presiding over his first *auto da fe* in Valladolid in early October. It was also during this period of unrest that Philip married Elizabeth de Valois (on 31 January 1560) and began to make plans for the building of the royal Jeronymite monastery of El Escorial and also to look for an alternative royal residence for his court; the court eventually moved from Toledo to the royal Alcázar in Madrid in May 1561.[17] It is possible therefore that the recipient had recently assumed new responsibilities in the chapel (perhaps even as *receptor* himself), thus coinciding with Philip's return to Spain, and was anxious to become acquainted with details of ceremony and procedure; he certainly shows his awareness of the possible implications of the changeover of sovereignty.[18] For instance, after stating that he had received the account from Aguirre, he notes that there is another *Relacion* in the hands of the *contralor*, written in French, which recounts how to serve the chapel 'in the Burgundian manner' ('al uzo de Borgoña');[19] then immediately following this statement is what appears to be a direct copy of a paragraph from the set of statutes originally issued by Charles V for the Spanish royal chapel in *c.* 1518 (see below) which lists a number of feast days on which sermons should be preached in the chapel, preceded by the rider that these are the occasions for sermons 'if one keeps

[17] For an outline of events during this period, see H. Kamen, *Philip of Spain* (New Haven and London, 1998), pp. 79–81 and 179–82. For an account of the history of El Escorial, see M. J. Noone, *Music and Musicians in the Escorial Liturgy under the Habsburgs, 1563–1700* (Rochester, NY, 1998).

[18] The names of the *receptors* during this period have not been traced, though one is mentioned in a document dating from 1562 (see Barbieri papers 2, doc. 156).

[19] *La Orden*, fol. 77. The office of the 'contralor' ('controller' or 'inspector') was as general mediator in the section of the royal court administered by the 'House of Burgundy'. See Robledo, 'La música en la corte de Felipe II', p. 142.

[the customs in the chapel] of his father'.[20] The remainder of the addendum to Aguirre's text appears to have been added over a relatively short period between the feast of the Purification and Ash Wednesday, being largely concerned with the procession and other rituals on both these days, mentioning that it was usual for the king to celebrate the feast of the Purification at a monastery. In this section, his concern about the correct days for sermons during the Lenten season again indicates his responsibility in this regard: 'On passing Septuagesima Sunday one should consult with His Majesty regarding the Order that he requires for all the sermons during Lent so as to inform the preachers.'[21]

From the contextual point of view, one of the most significant details in the addendum occurs after the description of the distribution of the ashes on Ash Wednesday. In connection with the question of the ritual of the Gospel blessing and the kiss of the *pax*, the text mentions five living members of the royal family: the King, the Queen, the Princess, the Prince and, by name, Philip's half-brother Don Juan de Austria. Curiously, this passage implies that Don Juan may have been excluded from certain royal privileges. The text relates that the Gospel and the *pax* were to be offered to the King, the Queen, the Princess, and the Prince; however, they were *not* to be offered to Don Juan even though he was apparently present in the King's canopy: 'The *pax* and the Gospel are offered to the King, the Queen, Prince and Princess; nothing is served to Don Juan de Austria even though he occupies just a small textiled chair without a cushion within the canopy.'[22] The precise implications of this passage are at present obscure, yet it does help towards dating this particular section of the document. The prince referred to here could either have been Don Carlos, who died in 1568, or Alessandro Farnese, son of Margaret of Parma (Philip's half-sister) who was at court with Don Carlos and Don

[20] 'Ver Capitulo zerca de los sermones que ha de haver en la Capilla de Su Magestad, si se guarda lo que en la de su padre'; *La Orden*, fol. 77. The clause listing the sermons was copied directly from Charles V's *Estatutos de la Capilla del Emperador Carlos quinto al vzo de la Caza de Borgoña* (clause [10]), a copy of which immediately succeeds *La Orden que se tiene* in P-La 51-VI-37, fols. 79^{v}–83^{v}. The text is edited below in Appendix 4. I am most grateful to Kirstin Kennedy for deciphering this phrase, which has thrown very important light on the circumstances of the transmission of *La Orden* in *c.* 1560.

[21] *La Orden*, fol. 78^{r-v}.

[22] *Ibid.*, fol. 79.

Juan during this period, first in Toledo and then in Madrid.[23] Don Juan was only infrequently at court after the mid-1560s, and so it is likely that the Queen was Elizabeth de Valois (who also died in 1568), and the Princess the King's sister Juana, who spent much time at court following the termination of her regency in 1559. (She died in 1573, Don Juan in 1578.) The identity of the Prince, however, is difficult to determine, but Don Carlos began to have troubles with his health in *c.* 1561–2, which makes it less likely that he would have been regularly in chapel with his family after this time. It seems reasonable to propose, therefore, that the addendum was written more or less at the time the document reached the hands of Aguirre's recipient in *c.* 1560 and that the period covered here, from the feast of the Purification (2 February) to the beginning of Lent on Ash Wednesday, actually reflects specific occasions either in early 1560 or, most probably, in early 1561. In all events, it was certainly penned before the mid-1560s.

Unfortunately, like so many other royal chapel documents,[24] the original version of *La Orden* is not known to have survived. The copy which comes down to us dates only from about the mid-seventeenth century, and is one of a series of documents apparently originating in Spanish and Portuguese courtly circles which were copied around the same time and bound together in a single volume with consecutive foliation.[25] As it is written in a uniform hand, there is some difficulty in deciphering the different layers and assessing their precise historical chronology. Significantly, *La Orden* is immediately succeeded in this volume by a copy of the previously untraced set of statutes drawn up by Charles V in Spain towards the beginning of his reign in *c.* 1518 entitled *Estatutos de*

23 See Kamen, *Philip of Spain*, pp. 89 and 134 ff.

24 The copies of royal chapel documents made by Barbieri, for instance, and which now form the basis of the so-called Barbieri papers (see above, n. 3), are in most cases all that we have of this important series. When taking these documents into consideration, one cannot always be certain as to which passages constituted part of an original document, which passages or phrases may have been lifted from others, and which may have been edited and transformed or even miscopied. This of course poses problems for their dating and chronology.

25 P-La 51-VI-37. The volume as a whole includes copies of a number of official court documents, including notices, letters, regulations, and also copies of Wills of members of the Spanish royal family. It was probably copied in Portugal (a number of orthographical details indicate that the copyist was Portuguese), and is one of several such volumes now preserved in the Biblioteca da Ajuda.

la Capilla del Emperador Carlos quinto al vzo de la Caza de Borgoña ('Statutes of the chapel of the Emperor Charles V according to the use of the House of Burgundy'), and a further mandate issued by the Emperor concerning the ways in which his court was to be organised.[26] The statutes were to become the model for a document also drawn up shortly after Philip II's return to Spain (see below); it is possible, therefore, that at least *La Orden* and a copy of the *Estatutos* were kept together, serving as reference to the *receptor* and other members of the royal chapel in the 1550s and 1560s.

STATUTES OF THE ROYAL CHAPEL

The familiarity of the Spanish royal court with Burgundian ceremonial and etiquette since about 1548, when it was officially adopted during Prince Philip's regency (though not without some resistance by the Castilians), and Philip's personal agreement to follow his father's ideas on courtly procedure, were factors which contributed to the already 'Burgundian mode' which flavoured the court prior to his accession to the throne.[27] Further, just before Charles's abdication, Philip promised to maintain the structure of the Imperial chapel completely[28] and, certainly as regards structure and ceremony, there is every evidence to suggest that Philip's chapel was indeed modelled on that of his father. This would explain the context for at least one other important document dating from the first years of Philip's return to Spain which is clearly derived from the *Estatutos*. It is likewise headed *Constituciones o estatutos de la Real Capilla de S. M. el Emperador Carlos V al uso de la Casa de Borgoña*, but, as an indication of its new function and status,

[26] *Ordem e firma que o Emperador Carlos 5° teve em o servico da sua Camara*, P-La 51-VI-37, fols. 85–93.

[27] See Robledo, 'La música en la corte Madrileña', pp. 771 ff., where he discusses the implications for Philip's court of the *Etiquetas de Palacio de 1545* of Charles V and the new set of instructions drawn up in August 1548 regarding the change of etiquette. From that time, Philip's royal household increased greatly in size and was divided into five parts, of which one was the chapel, each headed by its own administration. For details of the chapel ordinances of 1545, see Appendix 2. See also Kamen, *Philip of Spain*, pp. 34–5 and 194–5.

[28] See M. J. Noone, 'Philip II and Music: A Fourth Centenary Reassessment', *Revista de musicología*, 21 (1988), pp. 431–51, at p. 446. For further indications of the influence of Charles V on his son, see *idem*, *Music and Musicians in the Escorial Liturgy*, pp. 26–31.

it is subtitled *Estatutos que hasta agora se han guardado en la Capilla Imperial y se han de observar en la Real Capilla de su S.M. conforme al uso de Borgoña* ('Statutes which were observed in the Imperial chapel *until now*, and which *should be observed* in His Majesty's Royal Chapel according to the Burgundian manner').[29] In this text, the directives originally issued by the monarch are refashioned so as to read in the third person, and details of some of the issues are slightly expanded. Further, we find that the term for the Flemish chapel, *capilla flamenca*, had originally been described as 'Our Chapel of our States of Flanders' ('Nuestra Capilla de Nuestros Estados de Flandes'), and that the titles of a few chapel officers were adapted.

The recovery of a copy of one of the original versions of Charles V's *Estatutos* means, for the first time, that those reissued during Philip II's time can be placed in a more specific historical context and that a more thorough investigation into their content and contextural significance is now possible. Also, some attempt can be made in tracing their lineage through earlier constitutional texts. The very fact that the essence of the text remains the same, about forty years after the original drafting of the document, does imply the intended continuance of ceremonial practice and chapel regulations, in keeping with Philip's desire to respect long-established traditions. In outline, Charles V's *Estatutos* classify the hierarchy of chapel members under the headship of the *limosnero mayor* (first almoner). It specifies that, from thenceforth, offices were to be celebrated according to 'Roman custom and usage', and it gives important details such as the times of sung mass and the occasions when sermons were to be preached. It also indicates procedural and disciplinary matters for the chaplains, singers and other officers of the chapel as well as information about the care and schooling of the *cantorçicos* (choirboys). The only reference to musical performance is somewhat cryptically given, and concerns the singing of the Alleluia during mass. (It is possible that it was made at the behest of the *maestro de capilla* in order to clarify certain misunderstandings among choir members at the time this clause was formulated.)[30]

[29] The document is included in Barbieri papers 2, doc. 136.

[30] For more details, and an interpretation of this passage, see below, pp. 140–41, where it is also posited that this clause predated Charles V's arrival in Spain and originated in practices in the chapel of the Catholic Monarchs.

A survey of about the first half of Charles V's *Estatutos* reveals that they were heavily modelled on the French Burgundian statutes issued by himself in Brussels in 1516, which in turn were derived from a standard set of issues forming the basis of ordinances issued by the Burgundian dukes in the fifteenth century. In this regard, Charles V's 1516 *Statutz et ordennances* is pivotal. This fact provides a very important context for the apparent legislative structure of the royal chapel, its enormous debt to tradition, and the origin of a few statements or terms which, in other respects, perhaps fall outside normal terms of reference in Iberian liturgical history and can best be understood in terms of their Franco-Burgundian heritage. Analysis of the Spanish *Estatutos* shows that the first nine items were directly modelled on a selection of ten of the twelve items forming the 1516 *Statutz*, and that these can be traced back at least to the ordinances issued during the time of Charles the Bold: the 1469 *Ordennances de L'Hostel*, in the section 'Ordennances touchant la chapelle', and the *Statutz et ordennances* reisssued by Philip the Fair in 1500.[31] For instance, the former (1469) stipulation that mass should be celebrated (as was traditional) according to the Use of Paris – 'le tout en observant et gardant l'usage de l'eglise de Paris', though omitted in the 1516 *Statutz*, evidently inspired the direction in Charles V's Spanish statutes that all offices in the royal chapel should, from henceforth, be celebrated according to the Use of Rome and therefore be distinguished from those of Parisian Usage: 'Mandamos que de aqui adelante el Officio Divino se celebre en Nuestra Capilla conforme al Vzo, y Costumbre de la Iglesia Romana' (clause 2), a mandate which was preserved in the copy reissued during Philip II's time.[32] Further, in referring to the Temporale, and the changes

[31] Observations about the connections between the various court chapel statutes have also been made by Robledo in 'La música en la corte de Felipe II', p. 148. For transcriptions of these documents, see D. Fallows, 'Specific Information on the Ensembles for Composed Polyphony, 1400–1474', in S. Boorman (ed.), *Studies in the Performance of Late Mediaeval Music* (Cambridge, 1983), pp. 109–59, at pp. 146–59, G. van Doorslaer, 'La Chapelle musicale de Philippe le Beau', *Revue belge d'archéologie et d'histoire d'art*, 4 (1934), pp. 21–57, at pp. 45–6, Vander Straeten, *La Musique aux Pays-Bas*, vii, pp. 278–81, and Schmidt-Görg, *Nicolas Gombert*, pp. 340–2.

[32] Whether or not this took effect immediately in Charles V's reign is at present difficult to gauge. In the Castilian court chapel of Ferdinand and Isabella both the Roman and the Toledan Rites had been followed. See T. W. Knighton, 'Music and Musicians at the Court of Fernando of Aragon, 1474–1516' (Ph.D. diss., University of Cambridge, 1983), p. 129. It is therefore of some interest that a document issued by Philip II in 1584, the

of mass times in the 'winter' and 'summer' seasons (clause 3), it is intriguing that in the *Estatutos* (but not in the Burgundian statutes consulted, however) the beginning of the first season is associated with the feast of St Remigius (1 October) when morning mass was to begin at 9 a.m., as opposed to 8 a.m. for the second season beginning at Easter. The custom of marking the feast of St Remigius with a change of mass time was one evidently derived from practices in northern Europe (as, for instance, at the French royal court), where this saint had an important association.[33] Reference to this date in both versions of the *Estatutos* was made solely in connection with the saint's feast day, and not by calendar day, and the spelling of the saint's name in the original *Estatutos* of Charles V (Remis) was derived from the French Saint Rémy, or Remis; in the later version of these statutes, the name was hispanicised to 'San Remegio'.[34] Table 1 comprises a summary of the statutes from the Burgundian court chapel and those issued by Charles V, first in Brussels and then in Spain.[35] Here it can be seen how a combination of items from the ordinances of Charles the Bold resulted in the formation of Charles V's French *Statutz*, and how all these relate to the two sets of Spanish statutes, where the French term *bureau* for the governing body of the Burgundian House is retained (clause 9).[36]

The precise origins of the remainder of the Spanish *Estatutos* (clauses 10–24) have not been traced, though there is the possi-

Advertencias de como se ha de ganar y repartir las distribuciones, specifies that chant of Toledan Usage should be used in the royal chapel: 'El canto llano de la capilla sea conforme al toledano . . . que así lo disponen las bulas de la Real Capilla' (Barbieri papers 2, doc. 161). See Robledo, 'La música en la corte de Felipe II', pp. 151–2.

33 St Remigius was Bishop of Reims in the early sixth century. There was a special chapel dedicated to this local saint in Notre-Dame; see C. Wright, *Music and Ceremony at Notre Dame of Paris, 500–1550* (Cambridge, 1989), pp. 133–4.

34 During the course of the sixteenth century, the saint's name began to be dropped in Spanish documents in favour of just the date. By the late sixteenth century, some royal chapel documents merely refer to these two seasons as 'winter' ('invierno') and 'summer' ('verano'). This was only loosely related, therefore, with the Temporale. In the *Advertencias* dating from 1584, however, while specifying 1 October for a change of mass time, it is stated that the next season was to begin on the first day of Lent ('el primero día de cuaresma'). See Barbieri papers 2, doc. 161, item 3.

35 For sources and transcriptions of these and other royal chapel documents see Appendix 2.

36 In the later, and slightly abbreviated, copy of the *Estatutos*, the word is translated as *Bureo*. See Barbieri papers 2, doc. 135[b].

Table 1 *The origins and formation of Charles V's* Estatutos *(summary)*

Charles the Bold *Ordonnances touchant la chapelle*[a] (1469)	**Charles the Bold** *Statutz et ordonnances pour ladite chapelle* (reissued in 1500 by Philip the Fair)	**Charles V** *Statutz et ordonnances sur le faict de nostre grande chapelle* (Brussels *c.* 1516)	**Charles V** *Estatutos de la capilla . . . al vzo de la Caza de Borgoña* (Spain, *c.* 1518)	**Charles V & Philip II** *Constituciones o estatutos de la Real Capilla . . . al vzo de Borgoña* (Spain, *c.* 1560)
2. Chapel officers to be subject to the first chaplain		1. Chapel officers to be subject to the first chaplain	1. Chapel officers to be subject to the major almoner [limosnero mayor]	1. Chapel officers to be subject to the major almoner [limosnero mayor]
3. Sung daily mass celebrated according to the Use of Paris	1. Sung daily Mass, Vespers and Compline, at the stipulated hour and place where [the duke] is;	2. Sung daily mass [omits Use of Paris]	2. Mass and other offices celebrated according to the Use of Rome	2. Mass and other offices celebrated according to the Use of Rome
4. Sung daily Vespers and Compline		3. Sung daily Vespers and Compline	3. Sung daily mass: 9 a.m. from the feast of S. Remis to Easter; 8 a.m. from Easter to S. Remis.	3. Sung daily mass: 9 a.m. from the feast of S. Remigio to Easter ('Pascha de flores'); 8 a.m. from Easter to S. Remigio. Vespers at 3 p.m.
5. Matins and Little Hours to be celebrated on major feast days listed		4. Matins and Little Hours to be celebrated on major feast days listed 5. Officers of the chapel to celebrate the divine office wherever [the duke] is;	Offices to be celebrated in nearby church when there is no chapel in the [Emperor's] palace; sung daily Vespers and Compline according to the Use of Rome	Offices to be celebrated in nearby church when there is no chapel in the [king's] palace; 4. Sung daily Vespers and Compline according to the Use of Rome
12–14: Robing and appearance of chapel officers	robing and appearance of chapel officers	robing and appearance of chapel offices	4. Robing and appearance of chapel officers	5. Robing and appearance of chapel officers
	2. Officers to kneel on entering the chapel and pay homage to the Lord,	6. Officers to kneel on entering the chapel and pay homage to the Lord,	5. Officers to kneel on entering the chapel and pray	6. Officers to kneel on entering the chapel and pay homage to the Lord

	the Virgin Mary and the chapel patron	the Virgin Mary and the chapel patron		and the chapel patron
	3. Officers to stand during listed items of the mass and the offices[b]	7. Officers to stand during listed items of the mass and the offices	6. Officers to stand during listed items of the mass and the offices	7. Officers to stand during listed items of the mass and the offices
19. Officers to maintain silence (etc.) during the offices	4. Officers to maintain silence during the offices	8. Officers to maintain silence during the offices	7. Officers to maintain silence during the offices	8. Officers to maintain silence during the offices
	5. Officers to undertake their assigned duties	9. Officers to undertake their assigned duties		
24. Officers to attend chapter meetings every Monday on disciplinary matters, led by the first chaplain or another official [25–6: further details of meetings]	6. Officers to attend chapter meetings at least once a week on disciplinary matters, and to obey the first chaplain	10. Officers to attend chapter meeting at least once a week on discipli-nary matters, and to obey the first chaplain	8. Major almoner to hold chapter meetings of officers of the [Flemish] chapel every Friday on disciplinary matters	9. Major almoner to hold chapter meetings of officers of the Flemish chapel every Friday on disciplinary matters
	7. If the first chaplain fails to impose punish-ments, this task should be undertaken by the [duke's] confessor, M. de Salubrye	11. If the first chaplain fails to impose punish-ments, this task should be undertaken by the [duke's] confessor		
27. No absences to be taken without permis-sion of the first chaplain	8. First chaplain to report presences and absences to the *bureau* on a daily basis	12. First chaplain to report presences and absences to the *bureau* on a daily basis	9. Absences taken without the major almoner's permission to be reported to the *bureau* by the *furrier*	10. Absences taken without the major almoner's permission to be reported to the *bureau* by the *furrier*
	9. Chaplains and officers to follow the statutes and ordinances of Duke Charles of Burgundy			
	[end of document]	[end of document]	[continued below]	[continued below]

[a] Only the clauses which relate to the succeeding sets of statutes on this table are entered in this column.

[b] For details, see n. 65. This and the succeeding clause about behaviour in chapel are also covered under clause 7 in Enrique IV's *Constituciones de la Real Capilla* of *c.* 1436. See Barbieri papers 2, doc. 124, p. 23.

bility that some of the clauses were inspired by constitutional texts inherited from the courts of the Catholic Monarchs, despite the fact that some of the issues raised are of a general nature and could therefore obtain in any number of European court chapels. It is only in this portion that isolated musical references are made and indications given as to the care and schooling of the choirboys – matters which were to be expanded in Philip II's *Constituciones para el Real Colegio de Cantores de la Real Capilla* of about the 1580s.[37] That the whole of this document was recopied in *c.* 1560, shortly after Philip II's return to Spain, gives further indication of Philip II's apparent respect for tradition regarding liturgical observances, ceremonial practice and chapel regulations, and even dress as it was 'in former times'. (See Table 2.)

One other important constitutional document of the Spanish royal chapel which was apparently reinstated at the beginning of Philip II's reign is the Latin *Leges et constitutiones* originating sometime in the early sixteenth century, if not before. As the only version of this text recovered to date was recopied in the late sixteenth century, and thus well after its initial conception and subsequent revisions, scholars have expressed some disagreement as to its origin and function.[38] While Vander Straeten contended that it was formulated during the time of Philip the Fair, and that subsequent additions were made up to 1568 in order to account for a number of royal anniversaries, Bouckaert has dated it to 1556, and Robledo has placed it firmly in the reign of Philip II while (similar to Bouckaert) acknowledging its origins in 'the Burgundian tradition' ('la tradición borgoñona').[39] In contrast to the *Estatutos*, which is more concerned with procedure and etiquette, this document is more informative about musico-liturgical matters, listing several occasions for the performance of items in

[37] The document is included in Barbieri papers 2, doc. 157.

[38] This text was first edited by Vander Straeten in *La Musique aux Pays-Bas*, vii, pp. 183–6, and has subsequently been discussed in Schmidt-Görg, *Nicolas Gombert*; H. Rudolf, 'The Life and Works of Cornelius Canis' (Ph.D. diss., University of Illinois, 1977); L. Robledo, 'La música en la corte de Felipe II', pp. 146–8; and Bouckaert, 'The *Capilla Flamenca*', pp. 39–40. The full title of the document preserved in the Palacio Real in Madrid (E-Mpa, Administrativa, leg. 1133) reads: *Leges et constitutiones capellae Catholicae Maiestatis, à maioribus institutae, à Car. Quinto studiosè custoditae, hodierno die, mandato Regis Catholicae, singulis sanctissimè servandae.*

[39] Bouckaert, 'The *Capilla Flamenca*', p. 39, and Robledo, 'La música en la corte de Felipe II', p. 146.

Table 2 *Charles V's* Estatutos *(summary of clauses 10–24)*

Charles V: ***Estatutos*** (cont.)	**Charles V and Philip II:** ***Constituciones o Estatutos*** (cont.)
10. List of Sundays and selected feast days throughout the year for sermons	11. List of Sundays and selected feast days throughout the year for sermons
11. Positioning of celebrant before the altar at the beginning of Matins, Vespers, Compline and Vigils, and of those reciting the Gospel, the Epistle and the Lessons of Matins	12. Positioning of celebrant before the altar at the beginning of Matins, Vespers, Compline and Vigils, and of those reciting the Gospel, the Epistle, and the Lessons of Matins
12. Obligation for singers to sing a duo or trio when ordered by the chapel master	13. Obligation to sing a duo or trio 'in front of the book' [i.e. *super librum*] when ordered by the chapel master
13. From henceforth, the Alleluia to be sung (in polyphony) every day, as on major feast days, and the chapel master should order the singers to take turns in singing (the Alleluias)	14. From henceforth, the Alleluia to be sung (in polyphony) every day, as on major feast days, and that the master of the choirboys [= chapel master] should designate the voice parts to the singers, and that no one should refuse to sing the duo or trio, or whatever else was deemed suitable
14–16. From henceforth, the chapel master must accompany the choirboys to and from the chapel; other details of care and schooling of the choirboys	15–17. The chapel master must accompany the choirboys to and from the chapel; other details of care and schooling of the choirboys
17. Details of annual allowance of robing of chapel officers and choir-boys, and order that they should be dressed as in former times[a]	18. Details of annual allowance of robing of chapel officers and choir-boys, and order that they should be dressed as in former times
18. From henceforth, all admitted to the Flemish chapel to take an oath of allegiance in the presence of the major almoner[b]	19. That all admitted to the Flemish chapel to take an oath of allegiance in the presence of the major almoner
19. No books of chant or of polyphony to be taken out of the chapel	20. No books of chant or of polyphony to be taken out of the chapel, not even for the purposes of teaching or any other singing

Table 2 *Continued*

Charles V: Estatutos (cont.)	**Charles V and Philip II:** Constituciones o Estatutos (cont.)
20. From henceforth, no one should play [music] in mass or Vespers without first advising the major almoner or, in his absence, the chapel master, and that the offices should be according to the Use of Rome	21. No one should order for the bells to be rung before mass or Vespers without first advising the major almoner or, in his absence, the chapel master, nor begin the services without his permission, and that the offices should be according to the Use of Rome
21. Positioning of the chapel master behind the choirboys	23. Positioning of the chapel master behind the choirboys
22. The chapel master to be responsible for looking after the music books and for choosing music for the divine offices	22. The chapel master to take care of the music in the offices, and all should obey him
23. The above [i.e. the statutes] should be declared publicly to all chapel members (by the major almoner)	24. All contents [of this document] should be declared publicly to all chapel members (by the major almoner)
24. The chapel steward (*furrier*) should be in the chapel before each service to ensure that the chapel officers perform their duty on entering [see item 5]	25. The porter and the housing master (*aposentador*) should be in chapel every day before each service to ensure that all perform their duty regarding the above

[a] For details of the allowances made in 1559, and a description of the dress of the choirboys, see Vander Straeten, *La Musique aux Pays-Bas*, viii, pp. 25–7.

[b] This also constitutes the third clause in the *Constituciones de la Real Capilla* of *c*. 1436, 'Que los capellanes juren a su entrada en manos del capellan mayor o de su lugarteniente'. Barbieri papers 2, doc. 124.

fabordón, for example, as well as a few occasions for the singing of polyphonic motets. It also outlines procedures in offices for commemorations of the dead – a section undoubtedly updated in the early years of Philip II's reign as, in the lines of *La Orden*, it refers specifically to the exequies of the Emperor and members of the House of Austria and here there are clear indications of practices stemming from Parisian Usage (see below).[40] Significantly, it also

[40] See below, 'Royal anniversaries and commemorations'.

provides information about performing traditions, in particular about the positions of members of the choir around the music stand, and it is in these clauses especially that perhaps the origins of the document may be most closely considered. Here, instead of referring to a four-part adult choir and choirboys, such as characterised the chapels of Charles V and Philip II, the document refers to arrangements of first a three-part adult choir with a group of choirboys (for the top line), and then a three-part adult choir on its own, with the voice parts designated as contratenors, tenors and basses.[41] There is thus no mention of the *tiples* which formed a regular part of the Spanish royal chapel in the sixteenth century. The origin of this particular positioning of a choral group cannot at present be verified. David Fallows's discussion about performing ensembles in the fifteenth-century Burgundian court chapel and similar institutions, in which he concludes that the normal four-part distribution of voices in polyphonic performance in at least the 1469 chapel of Charles the Bold (according to the pay records) involved *adult* singers only, despite the probable use of boys in the chapel, unfortunately throws little light on the implications of these passages, therefore.[42]

PHILIP II'S CHAPEL

The complexity of the organisation of the Philip II's royal court and chapel, with its dual bureaucratic structure represented by the 'House of Burgundy' and the 'House of Castile', has recently formed the basis of a series of important studies by Luis Robledo.[43] His findings are founded on the interpretation of a wide selection

[41] 'XXVII. In supplicationibus, pueri medium, tenores sinistrum, contratenores dextrum, gravi toni novissimum locum occupando', and 'XLII. Unusquisque suum locum occupet, nimirum contratenores lateris dextri, tenores sinistri, bassi vero (ut vocuntur) postremi'; *Leges et constitutiones*, clauses 37 and 42.

[42] See Fallows, 'Specific Information', pp. 110–14, 117, 125 and 143–4, and H. M. Brown, 'Music and Ritual at Charles the Bold's Court: The Function of Liturgical Music by Busnoys and his Contemporaries', in P. Higgins (ed.), *Antoine Busnoys: Method, Meaning and Context in Late Medieval Music* (Oxford, 1999), pp. 53–70, at pp. 54–8. I would like to thank Bonnie Blackburn for drawing the latter reference to my attention.

[43] Robledo's work on the history and formation of the Castilian royal court and chapel (particularly that of Philip II) is of extreme importance, enabling me to evaluate the significance of *La Orden* among other royal constitutional documents. References to his studies are cited throughout this article.

of documentary material, including a number of statutes and other constitutional texts, and he is the first to clarify that, musically, Philip II's so-called *Capilla flamenca* and *Capilla española* were in fact sections of a unified institution directed by one *maestro de capilla*;[44] the *maestro de capilla* was traditionally a member of the House of Burgundy, and hence always Flemish.[45] The singers, choirboys, organists and other musicians of the *capilla flamenca* and *española* are therefore listed separately in the documents, even though members from both institutions combined forces during the celebration of the liturgical offices. While the head of the chapel during Charles V's time was the first almoner (the equivalent of the first chaplain in the Burgundian court chapel), it was the *capellan mayor* who was instated as official head of the chapel on Philip's accession to the throne, this post having originally been inherited from the *Casa de Castilla* of Charles V.[46] In practice, however, the *limosnero mayor* (there was usually more than one of these) enjoyed equal status with him, and substituted for him in his absence from court.[47] Other members inherited from Charles V's *capilla española* included the first sacristan (*sacristan mayor*) and the *receptor*. These four high-ranking officers, with the chamberlains of the king's oratory (*sumilleres del oratorio*), head the list of the 'Officers of the chapel' (*Officiales de la Capilla*) in *La Orden*, seemingly the only royal chapel document from the time to list their various duties in that hierarchical order, though it is not clear from other documents whether these latter two maintained exactly the same roles after

[44] This corrects the previously held notion that the two chapels existed independently, despite the fact that only one *maestro de capilla* is recorded in the documents. For further details and a clarification of the organisation of the royal institution, see Robledo, 'La música en la corte Madrileña', p. 790, and *idem*, 'Sobre la capilla real de Felipe II', *Nassarre*, 4 (1988), pp. 245–8. See also Robledo, 'La música en la corte de Felipe II', pp. 143–4.

[45] This situation persisted until 1637 when a Spaniard, Carlos Patiño, was appointed *maestro de capilla*.

[46] See Robledo, 'La música en la corte de Felipe II', p. 143.

[47] The absence of the *capellan mayor* was evidently quite common, particularly during the early years of Philip II's reign. For instance, neither of the two *capellanes* officially forming part of Philip's Spanish chapel in *c.* 1556–9 – Pedro de Castro, bishop of Cuenca, and Gaspar de Zúñiga y Avellaneda, archbishop of Santiago, who was appointed on 1 May 1558 – formed part of his train on the voyage to Flanders and England. Avellaneda was, however, present at court from 1561. See H. Anglés, *La música en la Corte de Carlos V*, i, p. 137, and Barbieri papers 2, doc. 156[a]. See also Appendix 5.

Philip's accession to the throne.[48] Other officers of the chapel included the chaplains, officially designated as 'chaplains of the bench' (*capellanes de banco*) and 'chaplains of the altar' (*capellanes de altar*) according to whether they were members of the Spanish or Flemish chapels respectively, the clerks of the oratory and of the chapel (*mozos de oratorio* and *de capilla*); and the chapel steward (*furrier*, or sometimes called the *portero* or *aposentator*). There was also the first almoner's personal clerk called the *mozo de limosna*.

The upheaval in the Imperial court around the time of Charles V's abdication from October 1555 must have been quite considerable. Judging from the available lists of chapel officers at this time, and comparing the names and numbers of those from his Flemish chapel who 'survived' the transition to Philip's own Capilla on his accession to the throne, and then to Spain (travelling after the beginning of August 1559), this period of adjustment only gradually achieved stabilisation: see Appendix 5.[49] Further, a few officers from Charles's chapel accompanied the Emperor to Spain in 1556 to serve him in his chapel and monastery at Yuste;[50] at least one of these returned to Flanders following the Emperor's death in order to take up service in Philip's chapel and follow him to Spain.[51] Only a portion of the original group of seventeen Flemish singers and eight chaplains from Charles's chapel in 1556

[48] The list of chapel officers and their duties forms the last section of the document originally compiled by Aguirre (*La Orden*, fols. 71^{v}–76^{v}). For a summary of the duties and responsibilities of the various officers of the royal chapel as described in *La Orden* and the 1545 *Estriquete y Relascion*, see Appendix 1.

[49] The information presented in this table has been collated from the documents transcribed in Anglés, *La música en la Corte*; Vander Straeten, *La Musique aux Pay-Bas*, viii (Brussels, 1888); M. A. Virgili Blanquet, 'La capilla musical de Felipe II en 1562', *Nassarre*, 4 (1988), pp. 271–80; and Robledo, 'La música en la corte Madrileña'. Unfortunately, there are a few discrepancies in the available documents, and the extent of, for example, a chapel member's period of leave is not always clear. However, the juxtaposition of the available information about membership in the Flemish and Spanish chapels during this period (the end of Charles V's sovereignty and the first six of Philip II's) does give some indication of the membership, and the extent of fluctuation during the final years of Nicolas Payen's tenure as chapel master, and the first three of Manchicourt's. According to Vander Straeten, Manchicourt was responsible for a certain degree of reform (see below, n. 52).

[50] The choir at his Jeronymite monastery at Yuste was also formed by singers coming from various Jeronymite convents in Spain. For a list of members, see Vander Straeten, *La Musique aux Pays-Bas*, vii, pp. 361–3.

[51] The chaplain George Nepotis is recorded as having left Flanders in 1556, with the Emperor, returning in 1559 to serve Philip; Vander Straeten, *ibid.*, vii, p. 365, and viii, p. 45.

apparently followed Philip to Spain, while a few more were recruited between late 1558 and August 1559, thus making a total number of about fifteen officers and a dozen choirboys who joined Philip's chapel; among these was the organist Michel Boch,[52] who was to remain in the royal chapel in Spain along with Antonio and Juan de Cabezón for many years.

This period of transition was probably complicated further by the numbers of chapel members from Philip's own chapel, including several musicians, who asked for leave of absence to return to Spain in 1556; many never returned to the Netherlands.[53] These included a number of key singers and choirboys,[54] instrumentalists,[55] as well as the organist and keyboard player Antonio de Cabezón, who was given a year's leave in January 1556.[56] His brother Juan de Cabezón and Cristóbal de León (organist and organ tuner), however, remained in Philip's service throughout this period in the company of the Flemish organist Michel Boch. There were always about twelve choirboys in Charles V's chapel, the number specified in *La Orden*;[57] by 1562, the total number of twenty-two in Philip's chapel comprised seventeen Flemish and five Spanish choirboys. Nicolas Payen, who had served in the Imperial chapel since his term as choirboy from 1526, was Charles V's

[52] Michel Boch played a large role in recruiting new officers and choristers in 1561/2, involving considerable time and expense. We also learn of fifteen 'chantres' from the Flemish chapel retiring at this time and being replaced by fourteen new ones. See Vander Straeten, *La Musique aux Pays-Bas*, viii, pp. 39–43, and Appendix 5.

[53] Some musicians went to serve in the chapel of Don Carlos, Philip's son. See Anglés, *La música en la Corte*, p. 139. A number of Philip's court musicians, including his *maestro de capilla* Pedro de Pastrana, remained in Spain during this period and went to serve his sister María, who was married to Maximilian of Austria. Anglés, *ibid.*, p. 106.

[54] A few choirboys (whose voices had presumably broken at that stage), such as Bernaldo Monje, Agustín de Cabezón and Francisco de Torres, were given leave of absence for longer periods in order to study (with scholarships from the King) at the University of Alcalá de Henares. See Anglés, *La música en la Corte*, pp. 137–8. The choirboys were normally sent off for a three-year training with the aim of returning as singers when they had regained their voices. See *Estriquete y Relascion*, ed. Schmidt-Görg, in *Nicolas Gombert*, p. 339.

[55] For the names of the group of instrumentalists see Anglés, *La música en la Corte*, pp. 139–40.

[56] Following Queen Isabella's death in 1539, Cabezón spent much of his time in the household of Prince Philip, as well as that of his sisters, but after 1548 he was officially employed in Philip's chapel. After returning to the Netherlands from leave, he accompanied Philip to England on the occasion of the prince's marriage to Mary Tudor in July 1557.

[57] 'Los niños suelen ser ordinariamente doze'; *La Orden*, fol. 76^{v}.

chapel master at the time of the Emperor's abdication, and continued as Philip's *maestro de capilla* until his death in February 1559. He was succeeded by Pierre de Manchicourt the following April, who remained in this post until his own death in 1564, thus directing the chapel choir for about the first five years after Philip's return to Spain. By July 1562 there were about thirty-five singers in the royal chapel, of which twenty were Flemish. Of the fifteen Spanish singers, all but three were listed as members of Philip's Spanish chapel in 1556, thus showing some degree of stabilisation there, though about half a dozen of these had returned to Spain during the intervening period. The documents show that the voice parts of the Spanish singers were divided more or less evenly into four groups comprising *tiples*, *contraaltos*, *tenores* and *contrabaxos*, though only three *tiples* are ever listed at one time. While the changeover of sovereignty instigated certain readjustments in the two chapels between *c*. 1556 and *c*. 1560, and the two musical forces only officially amalgamated at this time, it is probably true that members of both Charles's and Philip's musical chapels had already performed together on a great number of other occasions following Philip's arrival in northern Europe in the spring of 1549.[58]

LITURGICAL OFFICES IN THE ROYAL CHAPEL

Central to the run of liturgical offices in the royal chapel was the daily celebration of High Mass, or the 'Missa cantata', which normally took place at 8 a.m. in the 'summer' season, or 9 a.m. in the 'winter' season.[59] In addition, the most commonly celebrated liturgical offices were Vespers and Compline, and vigils comprising first

[58] Philip and his court left Spain in November 1548, travelling first to Italy, then through Germany, arriving in the Low Countries in late March 1549. He met his father for the first time in six years, in Brussels, on 1 April. See Kamen, *Philip of Spain*, pp. 35–40. It was at about this time that Charles V's Spanish chaplain Miguel Pérez de Aguirre originally compiled his account of customs and rituals in the Emperor's chapel, and therefore a period when Philip and his court may well have been initiated into ceremonies and procedures peculiar to the Imperial chapel.

[59] These times are specified both in Charles V's *Estatutos* (clause 3) and in *La Orden* (fol. 63). The two seasons of the Temporale began at Easter and 1 October (the feast of St Remigius) respectively (see above). According to *La Orden* mass could start an hour later on Sundays and major feasts when the King was not present.

Vespers, Matins and Lauds on major and minor feasts, as well as on anniversaries and commemorations. *La Orden* specifies only the following days for Vespers: every Saturday and Sunday, feasts of the Virgin Mary, the Apostles and the Four Doctors of the Church, and Holy Days of Obligation ('fiestas de guardar'); Compline was always to be celebrated when Vespers was over on these days even when it was celebrated pontifically.[60] It also states that on Sundays during the Lenten period, Vespers and Compline were to take place in the afternoon.[61] The only other time specified in *La Orden* is for Matins on Christmas night, which was to begin at 10 p.m.[62] In the revised set of *Estatutos* issued for Philip II's chapel, a time for Vespers is given as 3 p.m.[63] In all events, and including when the chapel was obliged to use a neighbouring church for the offices during the king's travels, the same times were to be observed throughout the year and the degree of solemnity of the liturgy was to be commensurate with the rank of feast and celebrated in accordance with the Roman Use:

> And when His Majesty is accommodated in some part where there is no convenient place to celebrate and sing the divine office in [the] palace, it is ordered that [it] be celebrated at the normal hour, and this in the nearest church or chapel to the palace . . . Also, that on all solemn feasts, major and minor, that are observed in the village where His Majesty is [residing], Vespers and Compline are sung, and it is [to be] understood that the major solemn feasts be said differently from the minor [ones], as obtains in every feast in the ceremonies and all the rest according to the Roman Use.[64]

That the major musical items in the offices were sung in polyphony (particularly on major feast days) is thus generally understood merely by implication in the statutes, though there is ample evidence of music once forming the core of repertories performed by the royal chapel choir in the set of inventories compiled at the end of the sixteenth century (see below). In another clause in Charles V's *Estatutos*, and in line with all statutory texts dating

[60] *La Orden*, fol. 64. In this section of *La Orden*, Aguirre also provides a few details concerning the positioning of the *semanero* officiating and of his robing.

[61] *Ibid.*, fol. 65.

[62] *Ibid.*, fol. 67.

[63] 'Las vísperas se digan a las tres horas de la tarde'. See Barbieri papers 2, doc. 136, clause 3.

[64] These details from clauses 3 and 4 in the revised set of *Estatutos* slightly expand on the information provided in clause 3 of the earlier set.

from the time of the Burgundian dukes and the fifteenth-century Castilian court, for instance, a selected number of items of the mass and of Vespers and Compline is listed during which the chaplains and singers were obliged 'to stand'; no other instructions are given.[65] The instruction regarding a polyphonic Alleluia at mass in the *Estatutos* is an exception.[66] However, more information on musico-liturgical practice is provided both in *La Orden* and in the *Leges et constitutiones*, with the latter indicating the extent to which *fabordón* was practised in the psalms, hymns and responses, and how a motet was to be sung during the procession at Corpus Christi. *La Orden* gives important insight into the performance in polyphony at Vespers and Compline: the singers were to begin the first verse of the first Vespers psalm – presumably as one group in an alternatim performing scheme, and on major feast days to sing either a Marian antiphon after Compline (on Saturdays) or a motet (on other days). It also specifically states that the Marian antiphon sung on Saturdays should be the *Salve regina*, but that from Easter to the feast of the Ascension the *Regina caeli* was to be sung with the organ responding.[67]

In addition, *La Orden* is particularly notable for providing some insight into ways in which musical performance was integrated with liturgical ceremony at mass and how this was evidently very carefully staged and choreographed. This is witnessed especially with the description of the sprinkling of hyssop during the performance of the antiphon *Asperges me* and the procession with the monstrance on Corpus Christi accompanied by verses of the hymn *Pange lingua* (see below). Despite the fact that these are among the few specific references to musical performance, the ways in which these rituals are described here is clearly indicative of the care taken over timing and procedure in other parts of the mass, all of which would presumably have been matched by appropriate musical elaboration as occasion demanded.

[65] These invariably comprise the Introit, the Kyrie and Gloria, the Gospel, Credo, Sanctus, Pater Noster and the Agnus Dei of the mass, and the opening items and canticles (Magnificat and Nunc dimittis) of Vespers and Compline. See *Estatutos*, clause 7, and related passages in the statutes summarised in Table 1. A similar directive is divided between clauses 6, 10 and 38 in the *Leges et constitutiones*.

[66] See above, p. 115, and below, pp. 140–41.

[67] See *La Orden*, fols. 64^{v}–65.

High Mass at the royal chapel

Judging from *La Orden*, and other constitutional documents and accounts in chronicles dating from the time of both Charles V and Philip II, preparations for High Mass, particularly on Sundays, major feast days and pontifical occasions, were evidently quite considerable, with no expense spared. The tone of important occasions such as the celebration of the feasts of the Purification, Easter, Corpus Christi and Christmas, and royal anniversaries and commemorations such as the Emperor's birthday and meetings of the Order of the Golden Fleece, was invariably set by elaborate and colourful processions both on the vigils and on the day itself. These processions usually involved the king, his immediate court and other officials, clerics, and a band of musicians (sometimes singers), the size and extent varying as occasion demanded, with everyone processing in prescribed order (see below). The chronicles also provide vivid descriptions of the colour of the dress and the accoutrements of those involved.

Preparation of the chapel or church (depending on the lieu of the court at the time) itself was an extremely important part of the proceedings, and here also everyone was assigned a particular seating place according to rank. On pontifical and other important occasions, the walls may have been hung with special tapestries, the King's oratory draped with curtains appropriate to the occasion, and the benches and seats furnished with special fabrics and cushions. Henrique Cock, for instance, describes how for the pontifical mass on the occasion of the presentation of the Order of the Golden Fleece to three noblemen during Philip II's sojourn in Zaragoza in 1585, the King's oratory inside the *iglesia mayor* (presumably the cathedral) was draped with gold curtains.[68] Similarly, in the royal chapel document *El Etiqueta* dating from 1545, for pontifical masses the wall facing the King's oratory was hung with a piece of tapestry of the same height, on top of which was fixed a length of scarlet velvet with gold trimmings; other details are specified for the decoration and furnishing in the vicinity.[69] Much of

[68] 'En la iglesia mayor estaba adreçado el oratorio del Rey con cortinas de oro . . .'. For a description of this event, see H. Cock, *Relación del viaje hecho por Felipe II en 1585, a Zaragoza, Barcelona y Valencia*, ed. A. Morel Fatio and A. Rodríguez Villa (Madrid, 1876), p. 80.

[69] See Vander Straeten, *La Musique aux Pays-Bas*, vii, pp. 401–2, and Barbieri papers 2, doc. 135[c].

this preparation would have been the responsibility of the *mozos del oratorio*, while the *mozos de capilla* would have ensured that the correct silver and other ornaments were displayed and ready for liturgical use. Likewise, the *furrier* and the 'candle boy' (*mozo de la zereria*) would have prepared the appropriate numbers of torches and candles according to the different occasions.

Preparation for the liturgical ceremony itself inevitably involved the interaction of several of the leading officers in the royal chapel, in particular the *capellan mayor* (when he was present at court), the *limosnero mayor*, the *sacristan mayor*, the *receptor* and the *maestro de capilla*. The degree of preparation depended on the category of office, and whether it was a pontifical occasion, a Sunday or a major feast, or an ordinary weekday. The *limosnero mayor*, for instance, regularly conferred with the *maestro de capilla* to ensure that the musical elaboration suited the particular occasion (especially when it was to be pontifical), while the *receptor* was frequently responsible for orchestrating the duties of various of the chaplains. Every chapel officer had his prescribed place, and the smooth running of this daily celebration was very much dependent on each taking responsibilty of his allocated duty – from the correct staging and rituals of the celebrants and the precise timing of the entry of the page-boys (*pajes*) with their torches, to the tuning of the organ. Of the ministers normally designated to perform the ritual of mass, the appointed deacon and subdeacon only performed their duties on Sundays and on special feast days, including days during Advent and Lent when a sermon was to be preached, while the bishop (possibly even the *capellan mayor*) would celebrate on pontifical occasions. Otherwise, the chaplains took it in turns to substitute for these officers on a rota basis for weekday masses along the lines established in the court chapels of the Burgundian dukes and the Catholic Monarchs: the chaplain appointed as celebrant on one week, and therefore called the 'semanero', would on the following week perform the role of deacon, and on the third that of the subdeacon.[70] In all events, the Epistle was to be sung by the subdeacon (or acting subdeacon), and the Gospel by the deacon (or acting deacon), and none was allowed to excuse himself from

[70] See *La Orden*, fol. 61^{r-v}. In the Burgundian court chapel the celebrant of the week was called the *sepmainier*. See Fallows, 'Specific Information', p. 148 (item 7); see also Knighton, 'Ritual and Organization', p. 302.

his week of duties.[71] In the absence of the *capellan mayor*, or his deputy, this rota was organised by the *receptor*, and it is thus that Aguirre provides an almost exact choreography of movements surrounding the reciting of the Epistle and the Gospel, and how the missal (placed on its cushion) was passed from one lectern to the other by a *mozo de capilla*.[72]

Other ritualistic duties such as the administration of the hyssop, the giving of the missal to the king to kiss after the reading of the Gospel, the offering of the *pax*, and the holding of the salver or communion plate were all assigned to particular officers (especially the *limosnero mayor*), with the *sacristan mayor* and the *receptor* described as accompanying the groups of officers as they administered these rituals. *La Orden* also provides a precise record of the number of torches to be held by the page-boys at various points of the mass, which ranged from between two and six according to festal category and function – whether held during the reciting of the Gospel or at the consecration – and how these were only handed to the page-boys at the moment they were required. At the Gospel, torches were only held on important days: these varied between four on major feasts on the liturgical calendar, feasts of the Apostles and the Virgin Mary, and two on Sundays and other feast days when the deacon and subdeacon were officiating. After the Gospel, the page-boys (who normally stood on either side of the lectern) with their torches would then accompany those administering the Gospel blessing. Torches were always held by the page-boys at the consecration: six on major feasts, and four on all other occasions, including masses for the dead. Aguirre also describes how the page-boys entered with their torches at the beginning of the Sanctus.[73]

Aguirre's intimate acquaintance with the timing of the movements of the chapel officers in such rituals, especially where music was involved, informs his detailed description of the administra-

[71] 'Los capellanes han de tener cuenta con no faltar en sus semanas en los Officios que les toca'; *La Orden*, fol. 74^{v}.

[72] *Ibid*., fol. 61$^{r–v}$.

[73] Information about the use of torches at High Mass ('Missas cantatas') is found in various parts of *La Orden*: principally fols. 61^{v}–62, 66 and 71^{v} (*La orden de servir las hachas en la Capilla*).

tion of hyssop accompanied by the singing of the *Asperges me*.[74] It shows how the performance structure of the antiphon, the sequence of verses followed by the doxology, provided cues to the ministers for their movements and subsequent resumption of the liturgy of the Word. The antiphon is 'begun' (presumably intoned) by the priest at the foot of the altar steps, who then gives the hyssop to the deacon, and both go to serve water to the King.[75] When the priest returns to his position at the foot of the altar, the *sacristan mayor* takes the hyssop and goes with a *mozo de capilla* (who carries the water) to administer to the apostolic delegate (if one is present), then the prelates, the chaplains and the singers, and afterwards the ambassadors and grandees and everyone else. As the singers finish singing the verses of the *Asperges* antiphon, the priest ascends to the altar alone to begin the prayers. When the 'ministers' (the deacon and the *sacristan mayor*) have completed their task, they also ascend to the altar, and the three of them stand at the middle of the altar until the singers begin the 'Gloria patri'. At that point, the priest dons his chasuble, which lies at one corner of the altar (on the Gospel side), and begins the Confession. Aguirre adds that on pontifical occasions the *Asperges* and the prayers are recited by the deacon.

The Offertory

A focal point of the mass proceedings was the Offertory and the accompanying procession which, particularly on major festal occasions and funeral services, was characterised by an elaborate array of lighted candles and torches involving large numbers of chapel officers, knights and court dignitaries. Sometimes the candles were embedded with a gold coin (*un escudo*) bearing the royal coat of arms or perhaps emblazoned with insignia and other heraldic devices appropriate to those attending the ceremony.[76] There was

[74] *La Orden*, fols. 62–3.

[75] Aguirre adds that if there is no priest, the deacon performs this task (alone) and then returns to his place at the foot of the altar.

[76] In *La Orden* references are made to the offering of candles embedded with *un escudo* during masses for the dead: in particular, mass on the feast of All Souls and the Requiem on the day after St Andrew's day (on the occasion of meetings of the Order of the Golden Fleece). An *escudo* was a term used both for arms and a gold coin bearing the royal coat of arms. It is possible also that the custom of emblazoning a candle with insignia such as is referred to in various chronicles and, indeed, in the fifteenth-century statutes of

evidently much ritual and etiquette to be observed on these occasions, many of the customs no doubt emanating from those enjoyed in the Burgundian court chapel. *La Orden* is about the only royal chapel document to place some emphasis on this part of the mass, no doubt because of Aguirre's close involvement with the preparations of many of the gifts, several of which had specific monetary value. In addition to the list of occasions when there were special Offertory processions (*Offrendas*),[77] other references to gifts are found scattered throughout the text, and some of these appear to reflect customs unique to the royal chapel. The numbers of people involved is not specifically stated, though this must have varied from occasion to occasion. Certainly on the feasts of St Michael and St Andrew, the days traditionally associated with the Orders of St Michael and the Golden Fleece respectively, the knights fully participated wearing their special robes of fifteenth-century Franco-Burgundian origin.[78] We are also given clear indications of the King's integral part on many of these occasions, particularly on the feast of the Epiphany, the anniversary of Charles V's birthday and coronation on the feast of St Matthias (24 February), the anniversaries of the deaths of Queen Isabella (1 May) and Charles V (21 September), and Philip II's own birthday on 21 May. Details provided in *La Orden* of the gifts themselves give us fascinating insight into traditions and enactments which have otherwise escaped historical accounts, though sometimes contemporary chronicles provide corroborative evidence.

the Order of the Golden Fleece in connection with the Requiem mass on the day after St Andrew's Day was followed on these occasions: 'a l'offerture de la quelle Messe le Souverain & chacun des dits Chevaliers presents & procureurs des absens offriront chacun ung chierge de cire armoyé des armes d'icelluy pour qui offert sera' (G. G. Leibnitz, *Mantissa: Codicis duris Genitium Diplomatici* [part ii] (Hanover, 1700), p. 25). See also below, n. 87.

[77] *La Orden*, fols. 68^{v}–69.

[78] The dress of the knights of these Orders on their respective feast days were different: that of St Michael consisted of long white robes and ermine fur capes, and that of the Golden Fleece of scarlet robes. A copy of the statutes of the Order of St Michael is preserved in the Bodleian Library, Oxford, MS Ashmole 775 (the dress is described on fols. 18^{v}–22). For a description of the dress of the knights of the Order of the Golden Fleece, see W. Prizer, 'Music and Ceremonial in the Low Countries: Philip the Fair and the Order of the Golden Fleece', *Early Music History*, 5 (1985), pp. 113–53, at p. 119, where he refers to an original source for the statutes of this order. See also Leibnitz, *Mantissa* [part ii], 'III. Ordenances & statuts de l'Ordre de la Thoison d'Or', p. 25.

Many of these offerings apparently involved a gold coin, or coins, from the tradition of offering a single gold coin (*ducado*) as well as the candle embedded with a gold coin during masses for the dead, such as made by the King on the anniversaries of his parents,[79] to the offering of a bag containing a set number of gold coins both on the Emperor's birthday (and coronation) and that of Philip II. Also, one may surmise that, in keeping with traditions of the Burgundian court, the offerings made by the knights of the Orders of St Michael and of the Golden Fleece on their respective feast days comprised gold coins and lighted candles.[80] Further, on the feast of the Epiphany, and in imitation of the three Magi, the King made offerings of gold, incense and myrrh, which were afterwards given to poorly endowed churches and monasteries.[81]

It is interesting that for the offering made by 'His Majesty' on the feast of St Matthias, the Emperor's birthday, Aguirre makes no reference to the anniversary of the coronation as such, which could suggest that parts of *La Orden* were sketched out some twenty years before he compiled his own version. The juxtaposition of this reference to the Emperor's birthday with one to his son Philip's *as King* is therefore intriguing in the light of the possible chronological layers of this document: 'Day of St Matthias, on his birthday, His Majesty offers as many coins as years he has attained, and [one] more for the year in which he has entered; the King Our Lord does the same on the twenty-first of May.'[82] It is possible,

[79] For more details, see below, 'Royal anniversaries and Offices for the dead'.

[80] It is clearly stated in the statutes both of the Order of St Michael and of the Golden Fleece that all knights (whether present or absent) should make an offering of a gold coin; see GB-Ob MS Ashmole 775, fol. 20v and Leibnitz, *Mantissa*, [part ii], p. 25. It is, however, curious that while Olivier de la Marche's eyewitness account of ceremonies at the Burgundian court in the mid-fifteenth century includes a detailed description of the ritual of the candle ceremony which took place at the Offertory at mass at chapter meetings of the Order of the Golden Fleece, no reference is made to the offering of gold coins. See *Olivier de la Marche: Mémoires [1474]*, ed. H. Beaune and J. D'Arbaumont, ii (Paris, 1884), pp. 90–2, and iv (Paris, 1888), pp. 179–80.

[81] This ritual is described both in *La Orden* and in Charles V's 1545 *El Etiqueta*, but with a few discrepancies in detail between them. In the 1545 document, it is written that *on each day of the Holy Kings*, the King offers three cups made of gold (with the total value of about 100 ducados). In the first he offers a gold coin, in the second, incense, and in the third, wax (*cera*). In *La Orden*, as an offering on the day of Epiphany (no other occasions are mentioned), the three cups (valued at thirty ducados each) are again filled with a gold coin, incense and myrrh (*mira*). It is only in the 1545 document that we are told that these offerings are then appropriately distributed. See Vander Straeten, *La Musique aux Pays-Bas*, vii, pp. 402–3 and Barbieri papers 2, doc. 135[c].

[82] *La Orden*, fol. 68v. (See also above, n. 1.)

therefore, that this ritual originated in the custom of Charles V making an annual offering of coins, the number being commensurate with his age. The date of his coronation in Bologna in 1530 was specifically chosen to coincide with his thirtieth birthday, and it is therefore fascinating to find in an eyewitness account of the coronation firm evidence that, at the Offertory during mass, the Emperor actually carried a bag containing thirty coins to the altar.[83] That this commemoration of the Emperor's coronation was kept very much alive during Philip II's reign is witnessed both by accounts of traditions at El Escorial[84] and in Henrique Cock's *Relación* of 1585, though Cock's vivid description of the colour and sounds of the processions involved does not include details of the mass celebration itself.[85] Other days singled out in *La Orden* for 'offerings' include Christmas Day, the feast of the Purification (2 February), Easter, the feast of the Ascension, Corpus Christi and the feast of the Assumption (15 August), which is referred to merely by the popular Spanish festal designation *Nuestra Señora de Agosto*.

Processions

Lighted candles and torches also characterised the types of processions preceding and concluding mass, both in the immediate vicinity of the church or chapel and also in the streets, depending on the location of the royal court.[86] As during the Offertory processions, these candles would often have been embedded with sil-

[83] This is in Ugo Boncompagni's letter describing the coronation dated 18 March 1530 which reads: 'e anco quando il prefato Cardinale volse fare l'offertorio S.M. andò all'altare, ed offerse una bolsa con trenta doppioni da dieci ducati l'uno; e poi tornò alla sua sedia . . .'. See *Lettera inedita del bolognese Ugo Boncompagni, poscia con nome immortale Gregorio XIII sommo Pontifice Romano, nella quale si descrive La Incoronazione di Carlo V Imperatore, seguita il 24 Febbraio 1530 in Bologna* (Bologna, 1841), p. 8. A full description of both coronation days in February 1530 (the date of the Emperor's coronation on 24 February was in fact the second of the two) is given in P. de Sandoval, *Historia de la vida y hechos del Emperador Carlos V*, ii, ed. C. Seco Serrano (Biblioteca de Autores Españoles; Madrid, 1956), pp. 367–73. The Emperor offered a bag of coins at mass on both these days. I should like to thank Bonnie Blackburn and Leofranc Holford-Strevens for providing me with a lead for the interpretation of this clause in *La Orden*.

[84] At El Escorial, special commemoration services for Charles V took place on 24 February, and a Requiem mass was sung in his honour on the following day. See Noone, *Music and Musicians*, p. 41 (Table 2.1).

[85] Cock, *Relación*, pp. 32–5.

[86] Numerous references to such processions are in the historical accounts of Sandoval and Cock. See, for example, the description in Cock's *Relación* (p. 250) of a procession for mass during Philip II's visit to Valencia in January 1586.

ver plates embossed with appropriate insignia or embedded with a gold coin bearing the royal coat of arms.[87] In a short section in *La Orden* headed *Processiones*, which immediately follows a description of ceremonies and music on Corpus Christi and its Octave, information is provided about the role of the King, his courtiers, and members of the clergy and other chapel officers. For the three feasts listed under this heading – Palm Sunday, Corpus Christi and the feast of the Purification – the court and clergy were to process in the following order: immediately behind the prelate officiating that day was to follow the King, while the ambassadors, princes, and grandees were to proceed in front of the prelate along with the bishops, the chaplains and the singers. This group was to be followed by the knights and all the rest 'in sequence', with the *sacristan mayor* and the *receptor* being responsible for seeing that the correct order was observed. In processions involving the Holy Sacrament (Corpus Christi), the King, the princes and other dignitaries held white candles.[88] A full description of the procession following the blessing of the candles at High Mass on the feast of the Purification when the King went to a monastery, as was customary on this feast, is provided in the addendum to *La Orden*. The processing order tallies to a great extent with the general order just described, but on this occasion, besides the King, his chapel officers and courtiers, a large number of other court officials and church dignitaries are listed, including the majordomos, bishops and the delegate; further, the whole procession is led by two acolytes, a friar with a cross, and the entire community of friars. A detail is provided that the King was only presented with his candle once all his chaplains had joined the procession. Once the procession was over, the prelate (with his assistants and ministers) went to the high altar (*Altar Mayor*) and gave his blessing, and the singers provided the response.[89]

[87] This was of course a characteristic feature of processions in many other European courts and religious communities, and was a particular feature of funeral services. An eyewitness account of the exequies for Charles V in Brussels, for instance, refers to citizens carrying white candles bearing the Emperor's coat of arms: 'docientos pobres con lobas y capirotes con hachas de cera blanca con las armas del Emperador . . .'. See L. Cabrera de Córdoba, *Filipe Segundo, Rey de España* (Madrid, 1876), p. 246.

[88] *La Orden*, fol. 68. See also below.

[89] This is presumably the verse and response, 'Dominus vobiscum: et cum spiritu tuo'. See *La Orden*, fols. 77v–78.

Music at mass

There is no doubt that music – vocal polyphony especially – formed an extremely important and integral part of the proceedings, much of which was of course designed to accompany and correspond with specific liturgical ceremonies and rituals. The richness of the polyphonic repertories performed in the Spanish royal chapel can be measured by the series of inventories made of the musical collection at the end of the sixteenth century.[90] Here are numerous choirbooks and part-books containing polyphonic mass settings, motets, Magnificats, hymns and psalms by a wide range of primarily Franco-Flemish composers, some of whom, such as Pierre de La Rue, Agricola, Gombert, Cornelius Canis and Crecquillon, had direct associations with the royal chapel from the time of Philip the Fair onwards.[91] In addition, much of this repertory would have dated from the periods when Payen and Manchicourt were chapel masters. In 1602 Géry de Ghersem, lieutenant of the royal chapel, somewhat enthusiatically decided to empty the chapel library's collection of choirbooks, many of which he considered too old to be of any use or whose repertories were 'outmoded', which gives some indication of changing fashions in the royal chapel at that time.[92]

It is difficult in retrospect to judge exactly which of the items listed here would have been used regularly in the early years of Philip II's reign, but it is probable that this repertory would have

[90] The inventories were compiled in 1597 as part of a larger project entitled *Cargo del Officio de Guardajoyas de S.M.* For further information and transcriptions of the inventories, see A. Andrés, 'Libros de canto de la Capilla de Felipe II', *Música Sacro-Hispana*, 10 (1917), pp. 92–5, 109–11, 123–6, 154–7 and 189–90; Vander Straeten, *La Musique aux Pays-Bas*, viii, pp. 352–83; and Barbieri papers 2, doc. 178.

[91] La Rue entered the chapel of Philip the Fair in 1493; after Philip's death (in Spain) in 1506, he remained there in the chapel of Juana the Mad, Philip's widow, only returning to the Netherlands in *c.* 1508 (M. Staehelin, 'La Rue, Pierre de', *The New Grove Dictionary of Music and Musicians*, ed. S. Sadie (London, 1980), x, pp. 473–4). Agricola joined Philip the Fair's chapel in 1500, remaining there until his death in 1506 (E. R. Lerner, 'Agricola, Alexander', *ibid.*, i, p. 162). Gombert became a singer in Charles V's chapel in 1526, and *maître des enfants* in 1529, and was succeeded in 1547 by Canis. He was a contemporary of Adrian Picart (= Thibault) who was *maestro de capilla* from 1526 to 1540. In the 1540s the royal chapel included Canis, Crecquillon and Nicolas Payen. Canis left shortly after Charles V's abdication (see G. Nugent, 'Gombert, Nicolas', *ibid.*, vii, p. 512; L. F. Bernstein, 'Canis, Cornelius', *ibid.*, iii, p. 684; and H. M. Brown, 'Crecquillon, Thomas', *ibid.*, v, p. 26).

[92] Ghersem valued the entire collection for the paltry sum of just one thousand ducados. See Vander Straeten, *La Musique aux Pays-Bas*, viii, p. 353.

included the masses of Josquin, Pierre de La Rue, Mouton, Gombert and Crecquillon, and other music acquired or copied during Charles V's reign. For example, there is almost conclusive evidence that the bulk of the collection of choirbooks now preserved in Montserrat was either passed over from Charles V's chapel following his abdication, or acquired shortly after Philip II's return to Spain in 1559 – these manuscripts having once formed part of the chapel collection of his aunt Mary of Hungary.[93] This repertory includes a large collection of fifty-five complete mass settings by Lupus Hellinck, Benedictus Appenzeller, Manchicourt, Pierre de La Rue and others, and several motets, with one of the books being entirely devoted to twelve mass settings by Manchicourt (Montserrat 768). All of these choirbooks have been identified in Ghersem's inventory, and one of them, a book of four masses and eleven motets by Manchicourt himself (Montserrat 772), was copied by the *maestro de capilla* in *c.* 1560.[94] It is no doubt significant that three of the four masses in this manuscript consist of a mass to the Holy Spirit, a Marian mass and a Requiem mass – the three masses traditionally celebrated at royal exequies and in the series of commemorations surrounding the feast of St Andrew which was normally associated with chapter meetings of the Order of the Golden Fleece.[95] Unlike the majority of Manchicourt's masses, which are written for four voice parts, these three masses are scored for five or six voice parts, which probably gives some indication of the type and richness of polyphonic repertories performed in the royal chapel in the early 1560s, at least on pontifical occasions, and Manchicourt's taste in music. The fact of Manchicourt's active involvement in music of the royal chapel at this time no doubt would have ensured a steady run of Franco-Flemish repertories such as would have accompanied his profes-

93 For details, see entries for MontsM 765, 766, 768, 772, 773 and 776 in *Census-Catalogue of Manuscript Sources of Polyphonic Music, 1400–1550* (Renaissance Manuscript Studies, 1; Neuhausen-Stuttgart, 1982), iii. This collection of manuscripts also includes a book of twenty-five Magnificats by Benedictus Appenzeller, Clemens non Papa, La Rue and others (MontsM 769).

94 The volume is inscribed 'Liber quatuor missarum musicalium nec non aliquot carminum ecclesiaticorum; A Pedro de Manchicourt regie cappelle magistro conscriptus et compositus'.

95 See below. The three masses by Manchicourt are *Missa Veni Sancte Spiritus*, *Missa de domina virgine Maria*, and *Missa de requiem*. The fourth mass is his *Missa Reges terre*. See also below, n. 97.

sional career in northern French cathedrals[96] right up to his employment as royal *maestro de capilla*, starting in Brussels in April 1559.[97]

The information provided by both the set of inventories and the *Leges et constitutiones* would suggest that mass propers and responses were frequently sung in polyphony, particularly on Sundays, major feasts and pontifical days. These may have been settings in imitative counterpoint, improvised elaborations of the chants in *contrapunto*, or settings in *fabordón* for four or more voices, as witnessed especially by the series of entries in the *Leges*, for example at mass (and on the vigils) on the birthday of the king, the queen or the prince.[98] Within the series of inventories of music books of the royal chapel are just two entries for books containing Introits (usually only the first item of a book is listed in the inventory), and a similar number containing mass responses – in particular a set of *fabordones de la Missa* included in a book of polyphonic masses and motets.[99] There are also two books of *fabordones* by Manchicourt on these lists, which were almost certainly copied when he was in Spain; however, whether these included mass responses is not specified.[100]

A clause in Charles V's *Estatutos* suggests that the practice of singing the Alleluia in polyphony at every Mass, and not just on major feasts, was instigated during his reign, though this probably originated in slightly earlier practices in the Spanish royal

[96] Previous to his term at the royal chapel, Manchicourt had spent time at the cathedrals of Tours, Tournai and Arras. See J. D. Wicks, 'Manchicourt, Pierre de' in *The New Grove Dictionary*, x, p. 598.

[97] It is therefore probable that this background would have influenced his choice of music for at least three important events which occurred during his first months in this post while the court was still stationed in the Netherlands: the proxy wedding of Philip to Elizabeth de Valois in the cathedral of Notre-Dame in Paris on 15 June; the funeral rites (in Ghent) for Henry II of France on 24 July, and the chapter meeting of the Order of the Golden Fleece in Ghent beginning on 29 July. See Kamen, *Philip of Spain*, pp. 74–5.

[98] 'In die nativitatis Regis, Reginae, Principis aut prolis regiae, in primis vesperis, completis, missa in omnibus versiculis et responsoriis fabordon canunto'; *Leges et constitutiones*, clause 16.

[99] See Vander Straeten, *La Musique aux Pays-Bas*, viii, p. 382. As these responses were usually improvised in performance, very few examples are to be found in surviving polyphonic manuscripts.

[100] The inventory entry indicates that the royal coat of arms is included on the first folio of these two books: 'Dos libros de un tamaño, enquadernados em papelon y cuero negro, y las armas reales en la primera hoja, de fabordón, de Manchicourt'; *ibid.*

chapel. This stipulation is preceded by the dictum that the singers are obliged to sing a duo or a trio, if ordered by the *maestro de capilla*; the way these clauses are expanded in the version of the *Estatutos* issued during Philip II's time is strongly indicative that the Alleluia and its verse were sung in improvised polyphony *super librum*, which could be interpreted as *contrapunto*, a practice which was common at the time.[101] A large number of Alleluia settings (but no other Proper items) survive in a series of manuscripts with strong associations with the 'court repertory' of the Catholic Monarchs.[102] The majority of these Alleluias are anonymous, but at least two may be attributed to Escobar, who was associated with the royal court.[103] All are written for either three or four voices, and it seems likely that these were originally conceived as elaborations on a chant, normally being placed in these settings as a cantus firmus in long notes in one of the voices (including the lowest voice) in keeping with the practice of *contrapunto*. Of those included in Tarazona 2/3, all receive major festal designations.

The feast of Corpus Christi

La Orden provides quite a detailed account of the special rituals and procedures which took place in the royal chapel on the feast

[101] The version of the *Estatutos* issued during Philip II's reign most clearly expresses this: 'Cuando el Maestro de Capilla . . . mandare cantar algún dúo o trío a los dichos, que les fuere mandado, sean obligados de ponerse *delante el libro* y hacer lo que les fuere mandado, so pena de castigo y ser mutados'; 'Que el verso y Alleluya se digan de aqui adelante cada día como se ha acostumbrada los días solemnes . . . y que ninguno . . . rehúse de cantar el dicho dúo o trío'. See Barbieri papers 2, doc. 136, items 13–14.

This contrapuntal idiom complements the type published in the Lyons *Contrapunctus* (1528), a cycle of polyphonic settings of chant mass propers. See *The Lyons Contrapunctus (1528)*, ed. D. A. Sutherland (Recent Researches in the Music of the Renaissance, 21; Madison, 1976).

[102] Barcelona, Biblioteca Central, MS 454; Tarazona, Archivo Capitular de la Catedral, MS 2/3; Segovia, Cathedral, Archivo Musical, MS s.s.; and Coimbra, Biblioteca Geral da Universidade, MS 12. See Knighton, 'Music and Musicians', pp. 175–7. Several Alleluia settings are also included in Porto, Biblioteca Pública Municipal, MS 40. I would like to thank Owen Rees and Michael Ryan for providing me with transcriptions of selected Alleluia settings found in Portuguese manuscripts.

[103] See R. Stevenson, 'Escobar, Pedro de' and 'Peñalosa, Francisco de', in *The New Grove Dictionary*, vi, p. 243 and xiv, p. 347. Tarazona 2/3 also includes six Alleluia settings attributed to an Alonso de Alva. For the possible identity of Alva, who was either sacristan at the Castilian royal chapel in the early sixteenth century or *maestro de capilla* at Seville Cathedral (d. 1504), see Knighton, 'Music and Musicians', pp. 249–50.

of Corpus Christi, beginning with the vigils on Wednesday.[104] It is evident that this feast and its Octave were marked by considerable musical elaboration, and this description once again underlines Aguirre's awareness of the close correlation between liturgical acts and the timing of musical items, particularly with regard to the structure of the texts (or verses) being sung. At sung mass ('Missa cantata')[105] on the vigils, the celebrant consecrates one more host ('forma') than is needed, and after mass places it in the monstrance which he will use to bless the people. Although an exact choreography of ensuing events is not given in the text, the rituals surrounding what must have been a splendid procession of the monstrance to the place reserved for it, perhaps a special side altar, may be interpreted as follows. While the priest, followed by the king and other members of the court holding white candles, processes, blessing the people with the monstrance, the singers sing *Tantum ergo* and *Genitori genitoque*, the final two verses of the Corpus Christi hymn *Pange lingua*. When the phrase 'Sit et benedictio' (in the verse *Genitori genitoque*) is reached, the priest carries the monstrance to its resting place. During this ceremony there are 'many torches, incense and bells' (presumably small hand bells), and the monstrance is incensed three times every time it is raised or lowered by the priest. Aguirre then describes how at Vespers, which is attended by the king, the same ceremony takes place but in reverse order. After Vespers, the host is once more taken to its place of repose 'with the same solemnity' where it remains until the following day at Matins when it is taken up again.[106] The same ritual takes place during the course of the week (the precise number of occasions is not stated), and on the Friday after the Octave, the host is finally consumed by the priest celebrating sung mass that day.

[104] *La Orden*, fol. 67r–v. According to *La Orden*, all the divine Offices were celebrated during the Octave of Corpus Christi, beginning at dawn each day, with the psalms sung alternatim.

[105] It seems likely that Josquin's *Missa Pange lingua* would frequently have been performed on the feast of Corpus Christi, as also Hotinet Barra's *Missa Ecce panis angelorum*. Both masses were included in a choirbook in the royal chapel collections, and Barra's mass headed yet another choirbook. See Vander Straeten, *La Musique aux Pays-Bas*, viii, p. 357.

[106] 'y acavadas las Visperas le buelven con la misma solemnidad, hasta otro dia a la mañana, que le sacan a los Maytines . . .'; *La Orden*, fol. 67v. There is the implication here that Matins took place in the morning.

This is one of the most vividly described ceremonies in *La Orden* and was one of the high spots on the royal chapel's calendar. The practice of singing verses in honour of the Holy Sacrament during the procession on Corpus Christi and on Maundy Thursday was of course a time-honoured tradition found in churches all over Europe,[107] though the ceremonies in the Habsburg royal chapel probably had far-reaching symbolic intent.[108] Although the feast of Corpus Christi was first adopted in the Christian Church only from 1317, and soon developed its own ritual and ceremony which spread throughout Catholic Europe, the elaborate ceremonies exercised in the Spanish royal chapel, and then at El Escorial, probably owed much of their origin to the special services venerating the Sacrament which took place in the Burgundian chapel from about the mid-1430s. In 1433 a relic of the miraculous bleeding host was presented by Pope Eugenius IV to Philip the Good, and brought to the Sainte-Chapelle in Dijon.[109] Barbara Haggh relates that an Office (which unfortunately does not survive) was created for the relic and its veneration, and that 'a sequence for the relic was sung at Masses and processions'.[110] Such liturgies, including sequences, were once contained in a number of books belonging to the dukes of Burgundy,[111] and it seems likely that these were absorbed into the rituals of Charles V's royal chapel on his inheritance. According to Tanner, Charles also adopted 'new forms of eucharistic devotion' and even 'established that in pro-

[107] For a full account of Corpus Christi processions in Spain from as early as 1280 (in Toledo), and their very elaborate nature in Barcelona in particular, see K. Kreitner, 'Music in the Corpus Christi Procession of Fifteenth-Century Barcelona', *Early Music History*, 14 (1995), pp. 153–204.

[108] See M. Tanner, *The Last Descendant of Aeneas: The Hapsburgs and the Mythic Image of the Emperor* (New Haven and London, 1993), chapter 11, 'The Hapsburg cult of the eucharist', pp. 207–22, for an overview of the history of the Habsburgs' strong devotion to the eucharist which had largely been adopted through the Burgundian–Habsburg dynastic ties.

[109] The Sainte-Chapelle in Dijon was both the chapel of the Burgundian dukes since its foundation, and of the Order of the Golden Fleece from 1432. See B. Haggh, 'The Archives of the Order of the Golden Fleece', *Journal of the Royal Musical Association*, 120 (1985), pp. 1–43, at pp. 24–5.

[110] Haggh, *ibid.*, p. 25 and n. 112. She also says that in 1436 a daily Mass was founded for the relic by King René of Anjou.

[111] See Haggh, 'The Archives', p. 25, n. 113, where she also makes reference to C. Wright, *Music at the Court of Burgundy* (1979), pp. 141, 144–5 and 147. Haggh suggests that a precedent for this may have existed in the Sainte-Chapelle in Paris and its founder King Louis IX (St Louis); *ibid.*, p. 26.

cessions celebrating his military triumphs, the Eucharist would be displayed in a monstrance carried by the archbishop'.[112] After 1530 Charles V made the feast of Corpus Christi the focus of eucharistic devotion in the Imperial chapel,[113] a devotion which continued unabated with Philip II. The description of the 1530 Corpus Christi procession in Augsburg led by the archbishop carrying the monstrance, and followed by Charles V and other royalty carrying white candles, certainly tallies with the account in *La Orden*,[114] and has much in common with the ceremony created for another relic of a bleeding host at El Escorial in the seventeenth century.[115]

Although a 'sequence' as such is consistently recorded in the fifteenth-century Burgundian documents, it is not without possibility that the music most frequently sung on these occasions was the hymn *Pange lingua* adapted by Thomas Aquinas[116] from the earlier Passiontide hymn of the same name by Venantius Fortunatus. (The verses of the *Pange lingua* were originally written by Aquinas for the Feast of Corpus Christi when it was instituted by Pope Urban IV in 1264.) In the *Leges et constitutiones*, which probably has its origins in the Burgundian court chapel of Philip the Fair, it is specifically stated that on occasions of veneration of the Holy Sacrament, the hymn *Pange lingua* was to be performed in polyphony.[117] Further, there is evidence dating from the seventeenth century that on the feast of Corpus Christi at El Escorial at least the verse *Tantum ergo* was sung during the procession.[118] No mention is made of the organ's role in either *La Orden* or the *Leges*, but

[112] Tanner, *The Last Descendant*, p. 214.

[113] *Ibid.*, p. 215. For a vivid description of the 1530 ceremony and procession which took place in Augsburg, including indications of the participation of musicians, see Sandoval, *Historia*, ii, pp. 396–8.

[114] See *La Orden*, fol. 68.

[115] For an account of the origin of the special ceremony created for the sacred relic of a bleeding host ('sagrada forma') at El Escorial in the late seventeenth century, a relic which had been in the possession of Philip II since 1594, see E. J. Sullivan, 'Politics and Propaganda in the *Sagrada Forma* by Claudio Coello', *Art Bulletin*, 68 (1985), pp. 243–59, at pp. 251–4, and Noone, *Music and Musicians*, pp. 160 ff., where several other bibliographical references are given.

[116] Aquinas was a friend of St Louis, founder of the Sainte-Chapelle in Paris (see above).

[117] The whole passage reads: 'In supplicationibus Venerabilis Sacramenti, hymnum *Pa(n)gelingua* musicae, et statio ante altare motetum in honorem Venerabilis Corporis Christi, et si non sit statio, illud motetum in ecclesia in quam defertur Venerabile Sacramentum et responsoria et versiculos, cantores in fabordon canunto' (*Leges et constitutiones*, clause 29).

[118] See Noone, *Music and Musicians*, pp. 171–7.

evidence again of customs enacted at El Escorial would suggest that Charles V's famous portative organ made of silver was frequently used on such occasions, and would have been played perhaps in alternation with the choir or solo to accompany the protracted procession and ceremony.[119] It is likely that in Philip II's chapel the settings attributed to Antonio de Cabezón would have been used on these occasions.[120]

Holy Week

The sequence of rituals and ceremonies characterising Holy Week, one of the most highly charged and solemn seasons of the liturgical year, was evidently undertaken with extreme care and precision at the royal court and chapel; it was also a period when the monarch almost invariably retired to the peaceful environment of a monastery, with members of his court and chapel in train.[121] It is striking how on these and other important festal occasions in the year both Charles V and Philip II frequently chose the seclusion of monasteries of the Jeronymite order, a religious house for which the Spanish royal family had strong affection.[122] The account of Philip II's sojourn at El Escorial during Holy Week in 1587, for instance, provides ample evidence of the King's participation in the ceremonies, and even his involvement in the choice of musical elaboration; but it also indicates his assumption of a more humble and pious role appropriate to the monastic environment.[123] Inevitably the whole of the Lenten season was marked by special practices and rituals in the royal chapel, and *La Orden* gives some

[119] See Sullivan, 'Politics and Propaganda', p. 245, and Noone, *Music and Musicians*, p. 171.

[120] Evidence for the the organ's role in providing renderings of the Corpus Christi hymn *Pange lingua* is widespread in Iberian sources, and the version of the hymn tune used at the Castilian court would certainly have been the one commonly identified as 'more hispano'; it is a matter of some interest whether this tune was familiar in the Imperial chapel and whether indeed the famous setting by Juan de Ureda (Johannes Wreede) was regularly sung there.

[121] See Kamen, *Philip of Spain*, pp. 89 and 102.

[122] In the mid-sixteenth century, these orders were chosen for the foundation of the royal monasteries at Yuste and El Escorial, and a decade or so earlier in Valencia following the obit request made by Queen Germana, consort of the Duke of Calabria, and formerly of King Ferdinand. See B. Nelson, 'A Choirbook for Don Fernando de Aragón, Duke of Calabria: The Sacred Repertory in Barcelona M.1166/1967', in *Actas del Coloquio internacional: fuentes musicales en la Península Ibérica, ca. 1250 – ca. 1550* (Lleida, 1999) (forthcoming).

[123] See Noone, *Music and Musicians*, pp. 91–2.

indication of the distinctions to be made between this season and others in the liturgical year: these include changes in times for celebrating Vespers and Compline on Sundays during Lent, and how this might affect whether a motet was to be sung at Vespers, and the apparent increase in the number of days in which sermons were to be preached. Table 3 comprises a summary of the information provided about the season of Lent, up to and including Easter.

Characteristically, information about the liturgy of Holy Week, rituals and the timing of various of the offices in *La Orden* may be found in a number of different places in the document, in addition to the main section headed '*Tenieblas*' (Tenebrae).[124] In this section, Aguirre provides one of the most significant details about musico-liturgical practice in the Spanish royal chapel concerning the performance of the Lamentations (presumably referring to those of Matins for Maundy Thursday). Here he writes, 'The Lamentations are normally "said" with four *biolones* and four voices: *tiple*, *contralto*, *tenor* and *contravajo*;[125] and the lessons [are said] by the chaplains', the latter indication very probably referring to the practice of chanting the lessons on a reciting tone.[126] In the light of Robledo's study on the use of bowed stringed instruments at the royal court, this reference is clearly important, and may even be the earliest such record.[127] According to Robledo, the first documented use of the *violones* during Holy Week at the royal chapel dates from as late as 1601, although the earliest use of the word *violon* occurs in the 1559 inventory of Mary of Hungary.[128] However, it is probably pertinent that the term became more frequent in documents after the arrival of Elizabeth de Valois at court in the

[124] For the section concerned with Holy Week practices beginning with Tenebrae on the Wednesday, see *La Orden*, fol. 70^{r-v}. It begins by stating that Tenebrae only began at the moment the king made his appearance.

[125] Information about which sets of Lamentations formed part of the royal chapel repertories is wanting; these may have included those composed by Pierre de La Rue in 1509, for instance, and later those by Morales (see also below).

[126] *La Orden*, fol. 70^{v}. The practice of reciting the lessons in chant was common practice in important foundations; similar indications of performance in the lessons of Matins are also described in the documents in connection with Matins on vigils for the dead; see below, pp. 155–8.

[127] See L. Robledo, 'Vihuelas de arco y violones en la corte de Filipe III', *Actas del Congreso Internacional celebrado en Salamanca, 29 de octubre–5 de noviembre de 1985* (Madrid, 1987), pp. 63–76.

[128] *Ibid.*, p. 64.

Table 3 *Liturgical customs during the season of Lent, up to Easter*

Ash Wednesday (*La Orden*, fols. 78v–79)
The ashes are blessed at low mass in the morning.
The King is blessed with the ashes as the prelate circulates wearing his rochet, then the ashes are administered to all those who wish to receive them, beginning with the nobility.
The King, Queen, Prince and Princess are offered the Gospel blessing and kiss of peace; Don Juan de Austria is excluded from this ceremony.

Sundays during Lent (*ibid.*, fols. 65, 70, 79)
Sermon at mass.
Vespers and Compline to take place in the afternoon.
No motet at Vespers if this is celebrated prior to dining.

Every day during Lent (*ibid.*, fol. 70)
Sermon at mass when sufficient number of preachers are available.

Palm Sunday (*ibid.*, fols. 67v, 68)
Processsion.
Episcopal blessing of the palms. (Prelate does not say mass this day.)
[St Matthew Passion]
(Sermon at mass)
(Torches at the Gospel and the Elevation)

Wednesday of Holy Week (*ibid.*, fol. 70)
Tenebrae commmences when the King makes his appearance.
Low mass in the morning (with sermon)

Maundy Thursday (*ibid.*, fol. 70v)
Mandatum normally preached at mass at the time of the sermon. (*Advertencia*, Barbieri papers 2 doc. 135[c])
Ceremony of the washing of the feet of 13 'pobres' (poor people) by the King, and their feeding and clothing.

[Maundy Thursday to Holy Saturday] (*La Orden*, fol. 70v)
Lamentations: normally performed by 4 singers (*tiple*, *contralto*, *tenor*, *contravajo*) and 4 *violines*.
Lessons recited by the chaplains.

Good Friday (*ibid.*, fols. 69r–v, 70v)
[St John] Passion to begin at 7 p.m.
Adoration of the Cross beginning with the priest, the deacon and subdeacon, the apostolic delegate, and then the rest of the chapel officers, the King and his court.
When there is a relic of the True Cross in the palace, this is always to be used for the adoration ceremony.

Easter Day ('Primer dia de Pascua de Resurreción') (*ibid.*, fols. 65, 68v)
Pontifical mass (only the King is incensed)
(Torches at the Gospel and the Elevation)
Offerings.

Easter Monday ('Segundo dia de Pascua de Resurreción') (*ibid.*, fol. 70)
Sermon at mass.

beginning of 1560, even though the instruments did not apparently feature in the lists of salaried musicians.[129] At what point this performance record was entered into the main body of *La Orden* is impossible to gauge, though it is possible that the four players of the *vihuela de arco* recorded in Charles V's court chapel in at least 1556 played in the chapel services.[130]

No other details of observances on Maundy Thursday are provided in *La Orden* itself, but in the late copy of the descriptive *Advertencia de lo que se executaba en la Capilla* found in the Barbieri papers, which is clearly derived from a portion of the 1545 *El Etiqueta* (see above),[131] is included a description of the Mandatum ceremony enacted by both the Emperor and Philip II. Headed *Lavatorio de Jueves Santo*, the passage describes how the king (Charles V) 'when he was in good health and residing in Spain' performed a ceremony which was both a symbolic re-enactment of Christ's actions at the Last Supper and an act of charity. According to this account the king washed the feet of thirteen poor people ('pobres'), and fed them, serving each of them with a plate of food and a goblet of wine which he poured himself. The text relates how during Charles V's time the thirteenth person, representing Judas, was set at a table apart from the other twelve, who sat together on one side of the other table. (During Philip II's time, all thirteen sat at the same table.) After they had finished eating, the king gave them woollen cloth and linen with which to garb themselves and a gold sovereign inside a small bag.[132] Such

[129] *Ibid.*, p. 65. Robledo omits a further reference to the use of *violones* in sixteenth-century Spain: in her Memoirs, Marguerite de Valois refers to a mass she attended while she was in Madrid in 1577, even calling it 'une messe à la façon d'Espagne avec musique, *violons et cornets*'. R. Stevenson, *Spanish Cathedral Music in the Golden Age* (Los Angeles, 1961), p. 341, n. 152.

[130] See Vander Straeten, *La Musique aux Pays-Bas*, vii, p. 360, and Robledo, 'La música en la corte Madrileña', p. 787.

[131] These documents are edited in Barbieri papers 2 (doc. 135[c]) and in Vander Straeten, *La Musique aux Pays-Bas*, vii, pp. 401–3, where they are headed 'Oficios del culto divino'. For details of these documents, see Appendix 2.

[132] 'Lavatorio de Jueves Santo. Cuando S.M. tenía salud y se hallaba en España, daba de comer el Jueves Santo a 13 pobres, y les lavaba los pies y servía él mismo a cada uno trece platos de vianda, sin la fruta de principio y postre, y echaba vino en sus copas; el treceno pobre se ponía en una mesa aparte, representando el lugar de Judas y los otros doce pobres se ponían juntos al mismo lado en otra mesa, y después que habían acabado de comer, Su Majestad les daba a cada uno paño y lienzo para vestirse y un escudo en un bolsillo, pero el Rey nuestro señor D. Felipe Segundo, (Dios lo guarde), sienta todos trece a una mesa.' Barbieri papers 2, doc. 135[c].

distributions to the poor also apparently took place on 'Pascuas' (i.e. Easter, Pentecost and Christmas) and other great feasts during the time of Charles V 'in memory' of the the plate of food which was offered to the poor by the dukes of Burgundy on similar occasions.[133] The custom of the King perfoming the Mandatum ceremony on Maundy Thursday was retained on his attendance at Holy Week services at El Escorial, but no other symbolic actions such as the feeding of the thirteen poor seem to be recorded.[134]

Good Friday and the veneration of the Holy Cross

La Orden appears to be the only constitutional document dating from the time of the Habsburg monarchs to bear witness to the special rituals focusing on the veneration of the Cross both on Good Friday and on 3 May, the feast of the Invention of the Holy Cross. (No mention, however, is made of the feast of the Exaltation of the Cross on 14 September.) The significance of these feasts at the royal court was intimately bound up with the Habsburg faith in the Holy Cross to ward off the infidel and as a symbol of their mission as world leaders.[135] Both monarchs had significant collections of crucifixes, including relics of the True Cross, and *La Orden* tells us that such a relic was always to be taken out for the Good Friday service whenever possible, as also on the feast of the Invention of the Holy Cross.[136] In time-honoured tradition, the veneration of the Holy Cross on Good Friday took place after the recitation of the Passion which, as stipulated in *La Orden*, was to begin at 7 p.m.[137] The text lists the prescribed order in which members of the clergy should worship the cross as follows: behind the priest officating, and the deacon and subdeacon, should follow the apostolic delegate (if he is present), then the bishops, the chap-

[133] This is described in the passage outlining the duties of the *mozo de limosna* (almoner's assistant) in the 1545 *El Etiqueta*. See Vander Straeten, *La Musique aux Pays-Bas*, vii, pp. 400–1.

[134] See Noone, *Music and Musicians*, p. 92.

[135] See Tanner, *The Last Descendant*, ch. 10, '*Fidecrucem*: The Hapsburg Veneration of the Cross', pp. 183–206.

[136] 'Siempre que hay palo de la vera Cruz en Palacio le ponen este dia para la adoracion. En la fiesta de la Cruz que se celebra a tres de Mayo sacan al altar la Cruz con el vero palo'; *La Orden*, fol. 69ᵛ.

[137] 'La Passion el viernes a las siete, y acavada se comienza el Officio'; *La Orden*, fol. 70ᵛ. This instruction occurs outside the description of the ceremonies on Good Friday.

lains, the singers and other chapel officers. This group should be followed by the king, then the ambassadors, the grandees and the knights.[138]

There are no references in the documents to the music which might have been performed on these days. However, judging from the number of extant choirbooks copied at El Escorial in the early seventeenth century, repertories which one may assume owed much of their origins to those of the royal chapel (at least from the last few decades of the sixteenth century), polyphonic music performed a vital role in the elaboration of the liturgy and the liturgical Word during Holy Week: as many as seven of the fifteen choirbooks identified by Noone as having been copied in the early seventeenth century for El Escorial comprise, or include, music for the Lenten season and Holy Week.[139] Among these repertories are eight sets of Lamentations and a large series of Passions, or parts of Passions (*turbae*), though some of this music was newly composed at El Escorial in the late sixteenth century. Needless to say, this royal monastery was an inevitable home for the choral repertory from about the mid-1560s, which may partially explain why Holy Week music is apparently only scantily represented in the royal chapel inventories.[140] It is almost impossible to tell which of these pieces would have been performed regularly by Philip II's *capilla* in the middle decades of the sixteenth century, but among the earlier repertories copied at El Escorial are Jan Nasco's setting of the St Matthew Passion[141] and a set of Lamentations by Morales. A search for more details of Holy Week music in the mid-sixteenth century royal chapel, however, will remain inconclusive until more precise data comes to light.

[138] 'Adoracion de la Cruz en el Viernes Sancto', *La Orden*, fol. 69^{r-v}.

[139] For inventories and descriptions of these manuscripts, see Noone, *Music and Musicians*, pp. 191–245. The seven choirbooks are EscSL 1, EscSL 4, EscSL 5, MontsM 750, MontsM 751, NYorkH 278 and NYorkH 288.

[140] None of the Holy Week items listed on the royal chapel inventories provides any indication that these were polyphonic repertories; rather, the 'Libros passionarios' and other Holy Week 'offices' would appear to be books of chant, many of which were printed. Among the manuscript items were included an unspecified number of 'Libros passionarios de canto' copied by the royal scribe Pompeyo de Russi, who had earlier been employed as scribe at the court and royal Jeronymite monastery (San Miguel de los Reyes) of Fernando de Aragón, Duke of Calabria, in Valencia. See Nelson, 'A Choirbook for the Chapel of Don Fernando de Aragón'. See also Appendix 5.

[141] The Passion is copied anonymously into the Escorial manuscripts (e.g. NYorkH 288), but was identified by Greta Olson in her paper 'Some Clues to the Transmission of an Unusual Passion Setting' given at the Sixth Biennial Conference on Baroque Music,

Royal anniversaries and commemorations

In addition to the major feasts on the liturgical calendar, probably the most important events celebrated in the royal chapel were the royal anniversaries and commemorations. These took place at regular intervals throughout the calendar year, and *La Orden* gives clear references to at least four significant anniversaries associated with Philip II and his parents: the commemorations of the deaths of Empress Queen Isabella on 1 May and Charles V on 21 September, the anniversary of the birthday and coronation of Charles V on the feast of St Matthias (24 February), and Philip II's own birthday on 21 May. By *c.* 1560, the anniversaries of Maria of Portugal, Philip's first wife who died on 12 July 1545, Mary Tudor and Mary of Hungary, both of whom died in November 1558, would have been added as these were absorbed into the yearly run of commemorations at El Escorial a few years later.[142] The Spanish royal court also had a history of observing exequies and funeral rites over a protracted period of time. For instance, Philip II's request in his Will that the day of his death should be succeeded by a period of nine days during which a daily mass was to to be offered for the repose of his soul had a precedent in the observances surrounding the deaths of his fifteenth-century predecessors.[143] *La Orden* also stipulates that the Empress was to be remembered in a said or low mass ('Missa resada') *each day* of the year, as one of the two low masses which were apparently celebrated on a daily basis:

Each day two low masses are said: one in the palace for the Empress, and the other for the saint of the day in accordance with the rule of the Old Roman

University of Edinburgh, 9 July 1994. It was previously known and performed at the court of the duke of Calabria in Valencia before 1550. See Nelson, 'A Choirbook for the Chapel of Fernando de Aragón'.

142 See Noone, *Music and Musicians*, p. 41 (Table 2.1). At El Escorial, Empress Isabella was also commemorated on 24–5 October.

143 'Item mando que el dia de my falecimiento, y los nueve dias sequientes diga Missa por mi alma . . .'; *Testamento de Philippe 2°*, P-La 51-VI-35, fol. 3. Enrique IV's funeral in 1474 was characterised by a nine-day period, and Juan II's funeral in 1479 by one of eleven days; see G. Wagstaff, 'Music for the Dead: Polyphonic Settings of the Officium and Missa pro defunctis by Spanish and Latin American Composers before 1630' (Ph.D., University of Texas, 1995), p. 112.

Calendar. But on Thursdays, Fridays and Saturdays, when the saint has no particular office, [mass] should be said of the Holy Sacrament, of the Cross, and of Our Lady.[144]

The choice of commemorations for the last three days of the week here has many similarities with the series frequently found in royal foundations in the fifteenth and sixteenth centuries both in Spain and in the Burgundian court.[145] Again, it is probable that this list was augmented by *c.* 1560, with prayers added for other deceased members of the royal family; a similar procedure of low masses characterised commmemorations at El Escorial.[146]

Funeral rites and ceremonies were almost invariably preceded by elaborate preparations and marked by considerable pomp and ritual. Seemingly both the Burgundians and the Spanish had a tradition at royal funerals of erecting vast catafalques and 'chapelles ardentes' which formed a spectacular theatrical backdrop to the splendid but solemn processions involving hundreds of lighted candles and torches, and the rituals and ceremonies integrated into celebrations of the vigil offices and the Requiem mass the following day.[147] Further, the church or chapel would have been completely draped with black velvet, much in the style depicted in a surviving sketch of the Portuguese royal chapel interior in 1649.[148] Elaborate exequies were not necessarily confined to the place where the body itself lay in state, but may also have taken place in various parts of the kingdom.[149] In November and December

[144] *La Orden*, fol. 63ᵛ. According to the *Constituciones para el Real Colegio de Cantores de la Real Capilla* (Barbieri papers 2, doc. 157), these would have taken place shortly before High Mass.

[145] An example is the weekly series of masses instituted by Philip the Good at the Sainte-Chapelle in Dijon. In this case, the masses on the last three days of the week were of the Holy Ghost, the Holy Cross and Our Lady. See Prizer, 'Music and Ceremonial'. p. 116. For her obit, Queen Germana, consort of the Duke of Calabria, specifically requested masses for the Virgin, the Holy Name of Jesus and the Passion. See Nelson, 'A Choirbook for the Chapel of Fernando de Aragón'.

[146] Noone, *Music and Musicians*, p. 41 (Table 2.1).

[147] For example, see J. Anderson, '"Le roi ne meurt jamais": Charles V's Obsequies in Italy', in *El Cardenal Albornoz y el Colegio de España* (Studia Albornotiana, 36; Bologna, 1979), pp. 379–99.

[148] See B. Nelson, 'A Plan of the *Capella Real*, Lisbon, in 1649', *Revista Portuguesa de musicologia*, 8 (1998) (in press).

[149] See C. M. N. Eire, *From Madrid to Purgatory* (Cambridge, 1995), p. 287.

1558, for instance, Philip II organised a series of ceremonies in Brussels in honour of Mary Tudor and Mary of Hungary, and, on a separate occasion, of his father,[150] and several exequies took place all over Spain following the death of Philip II in October 1598.[151] There is little doubt that many of the ritualistic elements of these special events were re-enacted at each anniversary. We have already alluded to the tradition of the king presenting a bag of gold coins at the Offertory on the anniversary of the Emperor's birthday and that of Philip II himself; likewise, *La Orden* is singular for giving us insight into a ritual enacted by the king during the Offertory of commemoration masses for the Empress Isabella and the Emperor on the anniversaries of their respective deaths (1 May and 21 September). On these occasions the king (and possibly other members of the court) made an offering of a gold coin, at the same time carrying a candle in which was probably embedded a gold coin bearing the royal insignia, comparable to the custom enacted during the Requiem mass at meetings of the Order of the Golden Fleece (see below).[152] In the summary of procedures for the commemoration of the Empress on the anniversary of her death Aguirre relates: 'At mass, His Majesty offers a gold coin and a wax candle in which [the arms] is embedded; after mass [there is] a sung response. The same [at mass] for the Emperor on the twenty-first of September'.[153] During the obsequies for Philip II at Zaragoza in October 1598, a similar ritual took place at mass: on this occasion twenty-four citizens came forward at the Offertory

[150] For an account of the exequies for Charles V on 29 December 1559 which took place in Sainte-Gudule, Brussels, see Anderson, '"Le roi ne meurt jamais"', pp. 383–4.

[151] For an account of the ceremony for Philip II which took place in Madrid in October 1598, see Eire, *From Madrid to Purgatory*, p. 291, and L. Robledo, 'Questions of Performance Practice in Philip III's Chapel', *Early Music*, 20 (1994), pp. 199–218, at pp. 204 and 209–12. For that which took place in Zaragoza, see Juan Martínez, *Relación de las exequias* (Zaragoza, 1599); a study of this document is currently in preparation by the present author.

[152] It would seem that the scribe of the Ajuda Library document *La Orden* inadvertently omitted the words *un escudo* in this clause, such as characterises the entries describing the offerings made at mass on the feast of All Souls and at the Requiem mass during meetings of the Order of the Golden Fleece (see also above, 'The Offertory').

[153] The original passage in *La Orden* referred only to the vigils and mass to be celebrated on the anniversary of Queen Isabella: 'Cabo de Anno por la Emperatriz Nuestra Señora' (*La Orden*, fol. 71).

holding black lighted torches, each containing a gold coin as was 'customary in similar acts'.[154]

From the liturgical point of view, the focus in funerals and commemorations held in the royal chapel was on the vigils, comprising first Vespers, Matins and Lauds, and on the mass for the Dead the following day; but, within that framework, we learn that there was considerable variation according to the category of commemoration. The documents are quite specific about this even though they are lacking in more detailed prescriptions, and there is some correlation between information provided at various junctures in *La Orden* and the series of clauses relating to commemorations in the *Leges*. However, discrepancies regarding the structure of Matins on the various occasions make it difficult to gauge which was the norm. The principal differences to be found concern the number of Nocturns to be said (or sung): either the standard three, comprising nine lessons therefore, or just one Nocturn (probably the first), with three lessons. In the section 'Obequies for the death of kings, princes, or infantes' *La Orden* describes how, while Vespers and 'vigils' (no further details are provided) are to be conducted by a prelate, as many as three pontifical masses were to be celebrated on the day itself ('otro dia'), provided that there were bishops and abbots available: the first mass of the Holy Spirit, the second of the Blessed Virgin Mary, and the third of the dead (a Requiem mass) for which the king made his appearance (the first two masses were celebrated prior to his arrival).[155] The tradition of celebrating these particular three masses on such occasions was long established in a number of European courts and confraternities from at least the fifteenth century, and indeed obtained for the funerals of Charles V in 1558 and Philip II in 1598.[156] The

[154] 'Al tiempo de ofrecer, aviendose sentado, en medio del Altar, en su silla, el Arçobispo, se levantaron veynte y quatro ciudadanos, y llevando cada vno vna hacha negra encendida, y en cada vna, vna pieça de a quatro de oro, ofrecieron, como es costumbre en semejantes actos . . .'; Martínez, *Relación de las exequias*, p. 176.

[155] *La Orden*, fols. 66v–67. This indication of the king's appearance only at the Requiem mass tallies with Wagstaff's findings of procedures in other sixteenth-century exequies: 'the dignitaries arrived only for the last of the three; it was then that the candles were lighted, and the lavish ceremony began'. See Wagstaff, 'Music for the Dead', p. 92, n. 32.

[156] See Haggh, 'The Archives', p. 10. Haggh also lists such observances for the funeral rites of King Francis I in 1547 and Charles V in 1558 (*ibid.*, n. 47). For Philip II's funeral rites see Robledo, 'Questions of Performance Practice', p. 211.

same stipulation is made in the *Leges* for deaths of the king, the queen, or other members of the Austrian royal family, and here it is indicated that the third should be a *solemn* sung mass for the Dead. This text also gives an indication of a performing pattern of the nine lessons of Matins on these occasions in which the first lesson (in each Nocturn) was to be sung by a solo choirboy, and the rest by the chaplains.[157]

For the offices in honour of the Empress on the anniversary of her death on 1 May, a slightly different scenario is outlined. Here, *La Orden* states that the vigils, which began after Vespers for Saints Philip and James (whose feast coincided with her anniversary), were to include three Nocturns (i.e. a full-length Matins) and Lauds, but just one mass is indicated for the following day (presumably the Requiem mass) during which a coin and a candle were offered; the only specific reference to music concerns the singing of a responsory after mass. The same structure obtained for the Emperor's anniversary on 21 September.[158] In the *Leges*, conversely, exequies for the Emperor, the Empress, and other members of the royal family were to comprise Vespers, but Matins with only one Nocturn, and again a solemn mass concluding with a sung responsory. Here a more specific performing performing pattern for the three lessons is provided: as indicated on other occasions, the first was to be sung by a solo choirboy, but the second was to be sung in *fabordón*,[159] and the third by 'the priests'.[160]

For vigils for the dead in a more general sense, both documents specify a Matins comprising three Nocturns and nine lessons, also

[157] 'Quando Rex aut Regina, aut quisquam ex familia Austriaca vita fungitur, vigilias mortuorum ix lectionibus quarum, primam puer alius, reliquas capellani, cum laudibus solemniter canunto. Quando Rex aut Regina, aut quisquam ex familia Austriaca vita fungitur, tres missae, prima S. Spiritus, secunda Divae Virginis, solemnitur tercia defunctorum canunto'; *Leges et constitutiones*, clauses 35–6.

[158] *La Orden*, fol. 71.

[159] This direction clearly evinces a widespread tradition for performing the second lesson of the first Nocturn on vigils for the dead. In Victoria's *Officium defunctorum* written for the funeral rites of the Dowager Empress Maria in 1603, the second lesson only is set polyphonically and in *fabordón* style. A much earlier *fabordón* setting of this responsory survives in Coimbra, Biblioteca Geral da Universidade, MS 12. See O. L. Rees, *Polyphony in Portugal, c.1530–c.1620: Sources from the Monastery of Santa Cruz, Coimbra* (New York and London, 1995), p. 190.

[160] 'In exequiis Imperatoris, Imperatricis, Regis, Reginae, Principis, dominorum nostrorum defunctorum, vesperas cum uno nocturno et laudes, primam lectionem puer unus, secundam in fabordon, tertiam sacerdos, missam solemniter et deinde responsorium musicae canunto'; *Leges et constitutiones*, clause 32.

indicating a pattern in which the sequence of lessons was to be led by a solo choirboy.[161] The only occasion when *La Orden* specifies just one Nocturn on vigils for the dead occurs in the passage describing procedures for All Saints and for commemorations at meetings of the Order of the Golden Fleece on the feast of St Andrew, also mentioning that 'His Majesty' frequently called for no more than one Nocturn. This particular passage also states that despite the shortening of the office of Matins, Lauds was still to be celebrated: 'On these vigils for the dead, Lauds is always said, even though not more than one Nocturn is said, in the way that His Majesty often requests that not more than one Nocturn is said.'[162] This recommendation for Matins with one Nocturn on the occasion of exequies for knights of the Order of the Golden Fleece, as well as Lauds, also occurs in the *Leges*.[163] Information about the different categories of commemorations and the varying structures of Matins found in the royal chapel documents is summarised in Table 4; for liturgical offices for meetings of the Order of the Golden Fleece on St Andrew's day see below, Table 5.

While these royal chapel documents do not expound on the office of Vespers on vigils for commemorations, considerable emphasis is placed on Matins which, as outlined above, was frequently coupled with Lauds. Like the majority of other offices celebrated in the Spanish royal chapel, the ceremonial aspect and format of these particular services during the time of Charles V and Philip II had features in common with traditions of royal commemorations in various European courts and churches with royal foundations. Bearing in mind the probable origin of the *Leges et constitutiones* in the court of Philip the Fair or even earlier, it is notable that the two structures of Matins were usually referred to by the number of *lessons* involved, this calling to mind the designations of 'feasts of nine lessons' and 'feasts of three lessons' found in the liturgical calendar at Notre-Dame in Paris.[164] Further, the practice of differentiation in the 'performance' of the successive lessons comprising a Nocturn, which characterises their descrip-

[161] *La Orden*, fol. 70^{v}, and *Leges et constitutiones*, clause 34.

[162] *La Orden*, fol. 66.

[163] 'In exequiis equitum Aurei Velleris, tres lectiones et laudes canuntur'; *Leges et constitutiones*, clause 33.

[164] See Wright, *Music and Ceremony*, p. 74 and *passim*.

Table 4 *Patterns in vigils, Matins and mass for the Dead*

I *LA ORDEN*

Funeral rites for kings, princes or infantes (fols. 66ᵛ–67)

Vespers and vigils celebrated by one prelate (no other details given)

Three pontifical masses (the next day), provided there are bishops and abbots:

1. Holy Spirit
2. Blessed Virgin Mary
3. Of the dead, for which the king makes his appearance

Anniversary of Empress Isabella, 1 May (fol. 71)

Vigils after Vespers of SS Philip and James (30 April):

Matins with three nocturns and Lauds

Mass (the next day), during which the king offers a gold coin and a candle embedded [with arms or a coin ('un escudo')]

Sung responsory [*Ne recorderis*] after mass

Anniversary of Emperor Charles V, 21 September

(the same observances)[a]

Vigils for the dead (fol. 70ᵛ)

Matins [with three Nocturns and nine lessons]:

the first lesson [of each Nocturn] sung by a solo choirboy; the rest by the Chaplains 'de este arte'; the last three lessons [i.e. of each Nocturn] said by the *semanero*, the subdeacon, the deacon and the celebrant

II *LEGES ET CONSTITUTIONES*

Funerals of the king, the queen, or deceased members of the Austrian royal family (items 35–6)

Vigils: Matins with three Nocturns & nine lessons:

the first Lesson sung by a choirboy, the rest by the chaplains

Sung Lauds

Three masses (the next day):

1. Holy Spirit
2. Blessed Virgin Mary
3. Solemn sung mass for the dead

Exequies of the emperor, the empress, kings, queens, princes (item 32)

Vigils: Vespers; Matins with one Nocturn and three Lessons:

1. [*Parce mihi*] solo choirboy
2. [*Taedet animam meam*] *fabordón*
3. [*Manus tuae*] recited by the priests

Lauds

Solemn mass (the next day), concluding with responsory sung 'in music' [*Ne recorderis*]

Vigils for the dead (item 34)

Matins with three Nocturns and nine lessons:

the first three [i.e. the first of each set of three] sung by choirboy(s)

[a] The indication 'lo mismo por el Emperador, al veinte y vno de Septiembre' occurs in the same clause as the description for mass on the anniversary of the Empress (*La Orden*, fol. 71).

tion in both *La Orden* and the *Leges*, can certainly be linked with services going back to at least the twelfth century in the royal abbey of Saint-Denis in Paris, as also in Notre-Dame. Here, there was a clear correlation between the numbers of officers required to sing certain items and the category or hierarchical importance of the occasion; the increase in numbers of performers required being commensurate with the importance given to the succession of lessons in the Nocturns.[165] In the Spanish royal chapel the progression through the lessons was marked by contrasting musical forces with, as found in Parisian practice, the sequence of three lessons comprising a Nocturn (in whichever context) invariably beginning with a solo choirboy. It is by no means certain whether these distinctions were invariably upheld in the sixteenth century, and there is already some discrepancy between the patterns recommended on the various occasions in these two documents, particularly for Matins. For Philip II's funeral rites which took place in Madrid and Zaragoza in October 1598, for instance, both occasions entailed a Matins with three Nocturns and Lauds,[166] which contrasts with the stipulations apparently outlined in the *Leges* for the funeral rites of kings. Nevertheless, for the Madrid sequence, there is evidence that the lessons in each of these Nocturns were indeed performed first by a solo choirboy, then by four singers in polyphony (presumably *fabordón*), and third by an honorary chaplain.[167]

In other respects the documents are relatively silent about musical elaborations of offices for the dead, but that these were occasions for considerable participation on the part of the chapel singers is certainly understood by implication. There is a long history of musical performance at commemorations, and Wagstaff puts forward the hypothesis that Spanish royal funerals even took

[165] See A. W. Robertson, *The Service-Books of the Royal Abbey of Saint-Denis: Images of Ritual and Music in the Middle Ages* (Oxford, 1991), esp. pp. 86–9, and Wright, *Music and Ceremony*, p. 111. Given that the Burgundian court adhered to the Use of Paris, and in view of the dependency of the legislative structure of the Spanish royal chapel on that of the Burgundian court, it is not surprising that these particular musico-liturgical practices would have been retained.

[166] See Robledo, 'Questions of Performance', p. 209, and Martínez, *Relación de las exequias*, p. 163.

[167] Robledo, *ibid.*

the lead in elaborating the services with polyphony.[168] This was apparently well established by the early sixteenth century, and the ceremonies accompanying the commemoration offices on the anniversary of Philip the Fair's death in 1506 were enacted 'according to the custom of Spain', comprising sung solemn Vespers on the vigil, and a sung Requiem mass celebrated 'with great solemnity' on the day itself.[169] Nevertheless, the visit of Charles V to Barcelona in 1519 when he both presided over a chapter meeting of the Order of the Golden Fleece and held an elaborate funeral service for Emperor Maximilian, for which music was led by members of his Flemish chapel, was indicative of long traditions likewise enjoyed in the Burgundian court and which would have doubtlessly continued for the succeeding decades of the sixteenth century.[170] How and when the standard repertories used for funeral rites in the Spanish royal chapel of the Catholic Kings might have merged with those of the Burgundian or Imperial chapel is an issue which begs closer investigation, though it is outside the scope of this study to pursue this in any detail.

[168] Wagstaff, 'Music for the Dead', p. 100, notes that 'there is no documented use of polyphonic music at French or Burgundian funeral services before 1500'. He also cites the instance of Juan II's funeral in 1479 when ceremonial music was sung in 'cant dorgue e contrapunct' (*ibid.*, p. 84 and *passim*). Bonnie Blackburn, in 'Did Ockeghem Listen to Tinctoris', in *Johannes Ockeghem. Actes du XL*[e] *Colloque international d'études humanistes, Tours, 3–8 février 1998*, ed. P. Vendrix (Paris, 1998), pp. 597–640, pp. 623–4, provides important evidence for requests for polyphonic masses in Bruges being made by Spaniards which may, therefore, account for the origin of Ockeghem's setting: 'Ockeghem's Requiem may have originated in a private commission, perhaps a Spanish one. The only requests for polyphonic masses that I know of were made by Spanish merchants and their families in Bruges; if such Requiems came into use in the Low Countries, as we know they did from surviving settings, it was perhaps because of Spanish influence.' I would like to thank the author for bringing this information to my attention.

[169] 'A veinte é cinco dias del mes de Setiembre deste año se cumplio un año que el Rey don Phelipe muerto habia; é seguiendo la Reina la costumbre Despaña cerca desto, mando decir solemnemente visperas cantadas por el ánima de su marido, y en el seguiente dia con gran solemnidad mandó que se cantase misa y oficios de requiem . . .'; passage from an anonymous chronicle, *Continuación de la Crónica de Pulgar*, cited by Wagstaff, 'Music for the Dead', pp. 288–9 and n. 64. See also Knighton, 'Music and Musicians', pp. 178–9.

[170] See E. Ros-Fábregas, 'Music and Ceremony during Charles V's 1519 Visit to Barcelona', *Early Music*, 23 (1995), pp. 375–91, at pp. 378–82. His report that the 'official act of the Order of the Golden Fleece stated that funerals as magnificent as that of Maximilian had never been seen in the Spanish kingdom' is intriguing in view of Wagstaff's hypothesis. See *ibid.*, p. 388, n. 16, and above, n. 168.

There is little doubt that the Requiem mass, the third of the three masses celebrated on royal obsequies, was sung in polyphony. However, only two polyphonic masses from the time of the Catholic Kings and the early sixteenth century are known – the settings by Escobar and Basurto – and these survive as *unica* in sources preserved in Tarazona.[171] Wagstaff proposes that these formed part of a long-standing tradition of four-part polyphonic *pro defunctis* masses peculiar to Spain and the Spanish court, which enjoyed a different or independent line of development from the slightly earlier settings by Dufay and Ockeghem, the first known settings by Franco-Flemish composers. Intriguingly, two items of the proper of the mass composed by Ockeghem and Brumel were copied with the Basurto setting in Tarazona 5, along with other propers by Pastrana and Peñalosa,[172] and it has been suggested that this composite mass may even have been compiled for the funeral rites of Empress Isabella.[173] Both Escobar's and Pastrana's *pro defunctis* masses are found with settings of the responsories *Ne recorderis* and the *Libera me* attributed to Franciso de la Torre and Anchieta (two composers attached to the court of the Catholic Monarchs) and, judging from other Iberian sources containing Requiem masses, it would seem that these responsories were almost invariably associated with any commemoration, right up to the seventeenth century. One of these sources was copied in El Escorial in 1604 and may well, therefore, be indicative of traditions in the *capilla real* itself.[174]

It is notable that no complete Requiem masses by composers such as Pierre de La Rue who were associated with the Burgundian or Imperial court chapels have yet been located in Iberian sources, and whether Dufay's (now lost) three-voice setting travelled to

[171] Escobar's setting is in Tarazona 2/3, and that by Basurto in Tarazona 5.

[172] The portion of the manuscript beginning with Basurto's mass includes settings of the Tract (*Sicut cervus*) by Pastrana and Ockeghem, the Communion (*Luceat eis*) by Brumel, the latter probably having been copied from his 1516 publication, and a further settings of the Offertory (*Domine Jesu Christe*) by Peñalosa. Ockeghem and Brumel are unidentified in the source. See Wagstaff, 'Music for the Dead', pp. 229–50.

[173] This has been proposed by Eleanor Russell, in 'The *Missa in Agendis Mortuorum* of Juan García de Basurto: Johannes Ockeghem, Antoine Brumel, and an Early Spanish Polyphonic Requiem Mass', *Tijdschrift van de Vereniging voor Nederlandse Muziekgeschiedenis*, 29 (1979), pp. 1–37, at p. 13. See also Wagstaff, 'Music for the Dead', pp. 230 and 277.

[174] For an inventory and description of this manuscript see Noone, *Music and Musicians*, pp. 228–31.

Spain with or after the Emperor's investiture as head of the Order of the Golden Fleece may always remain a matter for speculation.[175] This lack of knowledge of the polyphonic Requiem masses which may have been regularly performed in the Imperial royal chapel therefore makes it difficult to ascertain which repertories may have been absorbed into the royal chapel on Philip II's accession to the throne, when much of the choice of music in liturgical services would probably have been led by the Flemish *maestro de capilla* Pierre de Manchicourt and built on the experience of his predecessor Nicolas Payen. Manchicourt copied his *Missa de requiem* into Montserrat 772 in *c*. 1560, and there is a reference to 'some' Requiem masses forming part of a choirbook listed in the royal chapel inventories.[176] We therefore have no knowledge of the extent to which offices for the dead by Basurto, Pastrana, Escobar or Peñalosa might have been used at royal exequies, though it seems likely that the responsory to be sung after mass on the anniversaries of Empress Isabella and Charles V in *La Orden*[177] would have been the *Ne recorderis* setting attributed to La Torre, as also the responsory specified in the *Leges et constitutiones* to be sung 'in music' after mass on these and similar occasions.[178]

The feast of St Andrew and the Order of the Golden Fleece

One of the most important institutions associated with the Spanish royal chapel was the Order of the Golden Fleece, of which Philip II assumed headship following the abdication of his father as sovereign of the Netherlands and duke of Burgundy in October

[175] Dufay's mass was apparently still performed in the sixteenth century, and was requested in endowments at Cambrai in 1517 and as late as 1550. See Craig Wright, 'Dufay at Cambrai: Discoveries and Revisions', *Journal of the American Musicological Society*, 28 (1975), pp. 175–229, at pp. 219–20, and Wagstaff, 'Music for the Dead', pp. 260–2.

[176] This is a book of nine masses headed by the *Missa surrexit pastor bonus*, presumably by Lupus Hellinck (only the title is given). See Andrés, 'Libros de canto', p. 156 (item 180), and Vander Straeten, *La Musique aux Pays-Bas*, viii, p. 380, where the entry is mistranscribed. This is the second of two books containing this mass by Hellinck, the other now identified as MontsM 776 (see above, n. 93).

[177] 'Acavada la Missa se dize un Responso Cantado'; *La Orden*, fol. 71.

[178] See above, n. 160. In fact on another occasion, *La Orden* specifies that the responsory *Ne recorderis* should indeed be 'said' (i.e., probably sung) after a Requiem mass: 'Acavando de dizir [*sic*] la Missa de Requien, dizen un responso Ne recorderis'; *La Orden*, fol. 63^{v}.

1555.[179] With Charles V, the system of election of knights to the Order had expanded to include noblemen of Spain and Portugal, as well as other parts of Europe, though this had initially met with some opposition: many Spaniards preferred allegiance to the more ancient Orders of Santiago, Calatrava and Alcántara, and knights of these Orders formed a regular part of the entourage of the Catholic Kings. The chapter in Barcelona in 1519 was the first and only one to take place outside the immediate vicinity of the Burgundian realms, and at the first of this double session, the ten knights named were all Spanish.[180] In total, of the eighty-two Knights elected at the four official chapters during Charles's term of office between 1517 and 1545, two were Portuguese kings, and just under one-third were Spanish; his son, prince Philip, was elected in 1531 at the age of four.[181] Philip presided over the last two official meetings, which took place in the Netherlands in 1556 and 1559 before his ultimate return to Spain. However, through chronicles and other contemporary documents we learn that at least investiture ceremonies of newly elected knights continued unabated throughout his reign, one of the last having taken place in Madrid in 1593.[182]

Although the core of *La Orden* was evidently established during Charles V's reign, it is indicative that in time-honoured custom annual commemorations centred on the feast day of St Andrew (30 November), patron of the Order, complete with solemn vigils, a pontifical mass on the feast day itself, followed by a Requiem mass the succeeding day.[183] In this sense *La Orden* is rare among

[179] For a discussion about the Order of the Golden Fleece and its history, see Prizer, 'Music and Ceremonial', and Haggh, 'The Archives of the Order of the Golden Fleece'. Concerning the Golden Fleece and its significance for the Burgundian–Habsburg dynasty, see Tanner, *The Last Descendant*, ch. 8, 'The Order of the Golden Fleece', pp. 146–61.

[180] It was for the Barcelona session that Charles V's motto *Plus ultra* was written in Latin for the first time, thus making it more universal; however it was some time before it was adopted globally. See E. Rosenthal, '*Plus Ultra, Non Plus Ultra*, and the Columnar Device of Emperor Charles V', *Journal of the Warburg and Courtauld Institutes*, 36 (1973), pp. 204–28, at pp. 223–4. For details of this meeting, see Ros-Fábregas, 'Music and Ceremony', pp. 375–91.

[181] See Sandoval, *Historia*, iii, pp. 172–4, which includes a list of all the knights elected by Charles V between 1517 and 1545.

[182] See Kamen, *Philip of Spain*, p. 202.

[183] Saint Andrew was also patron saint of the dukes of Burgundy and of the House of Valois. In the fifteenth century, the feast of St Andrew was frequently celebrated on days earlier in the year when the weather was more clement. See Prizer, 'Music and Ceremonial', p. 115.

royal chapel documents, also providing information about the procession and offerings during the Requiem mass of lighted candles embedded with coins, or possibly heraldic devices such as obtained in the Burgundian court (see above). As already suggested, it is likely that the offerings on St Andrew's Day itself consisted of lighted candles and gold coins; no other details about rituals during mass on St Andrew's Day, however, are given. That the 1593 commemoration took place on St Andrew's Day gives some indication that this was at least one Burgundian tradition that Philip II maintained throughout his reign even though he no longer apparently organised a 'grand chapitre' as such. The only other reference to the Order of the Golden Fleece in a royal chapel document occurs in the *Leges et constitutiones* in connection with funeral rites held for the knights.

The section in *La Orden* most concerned with the series of liturgical ceremonies associated with the Order of the Golden Fleece on St Andrew's Day is particularly convoluted, and is almost entirely concerned with vigils and the mass for the Dead on the succeeding day.[184] This was traditionally celebrated in honour of deceased members of the Order of the Golden Fleece, the vigils comprising pontifical first Vespers, Matins with only one Nocturn, and Lauds.[185] Reference to this mass is made through its association with St Andrew's Day, using the expression 'otro dia' ('otro dia de Sant Andres, y de Diffuntos'). The passage also makes an oblique reference to pontifical vigils and Vespers on the feast of All Saints which, like that on St Andrew's Day itself, was a preparation for the ensuing day's (All Souls) commemoration mass. In his summary concerning these liturgical ceremonies Aguirre shows great concern for correct procedure, and the distinctions to be made with regard to aspects of ritual, liturgy and music, stating how it was the responsibility of the *limosnero mayor*, the *sacristan mayor* and the *maestro de capilla* to ensure that all reflected the pontifical nature of the occasion. Here, reference is made to the sung response after the Requiem mass (though without specifying which

184 *La Orden*, fols. 65^{v}–66^{v}. Details of offerings for these ceremonies are included in the section *Offrendas* (fols. 68^{v}–69).

185 Both *La Orden* and the *Leges et constitutiones* concur on the format of Matins, with the *Leges* also indicating that the three lessons should be sung.

one)[186] and to the number of torches (four) to be held at the elevation. At the beginning of the section Aguirre gives one significant instruction regarding the response *De profundis* which, he says, should only be 'said' in connection with a chapter meeting.[187] According to the original statutes of the Order of the Golden Fleece and other fifteenth-century Burgundian documents, the psalm *De profundis* was sung at the conclusion of the Offertory procession, the central event in the mass during which 'every knight and participant had a prescribed place and function, with the knights processing with lighted candles'.[188] It is only further on in *La Orden*, under the section 'Offerings' (*Offrendas*), that one learns of the offering of an *escudo* embedded in a candle in this particular mass: 'Otro dia de Sant Andres con vna vela encendida offrece el escudo hincado en la vela'.[189]

The description of the vigil offices in *La Orden* is largely made in relation to the celebrant's donning of his cope at various junctures at Vespers, Matins and Lauds, which appear to be defined by the sequence of specific liturgical items – in particular the canticles of Vespers and Lauds, and the Lessons of Matins, all of which were presumably sung. Here another reference to a responsory is made (again unspecified), seemingly at the conclusion of Lauds. Aguirre states that it was only to be said when there was a corpse in the chapel which was to remain there until the conclusion of mass the next day.[190]

Information about the liturgical ceremonies associated with St Andrew's Day found in *La Orden* is presented in Table 5.[191] Much of the procedure resembles that indicated for commemoration masses

[186] It is likely that this was the *Ne recorderis*, the response traditionally said after Requiem masses as stated earlier by Aguirre (see above).

[187] This instruction follows immediately on from the first reference to a response after the mass as if by association: 'dize el Responso acabada la Missa, y no se dize De Profundis sinó en el Capitulo del Tuson'; *La Orden*, fol. 65^{v}.

[188] See Haggh, 'The Archives', p. 12.

[189] *La Orden*, fol. 69. To date, the only other references to this custom of offering a candle with a coin have been encountered in Iberian documents describing royal exequies. These include an account of ceremonies at the ducal palace of the Braganzas in Vila Viçosa, Portugal, of 1600. See J. A. Alegria, *História da capela e colégio dos Santos Reis de Vila Viçosa* (Lisbon, 1983), p. 33. I would like to thank Michael Ryan for drawing this reference to my attention.

[190] *La Orden*, fol. 66$^{r–v}$.

[191] This information has been compiled from various parts of *La Orden*: fols. 65^{v}–66^{v}, 69 and 70, as well as item 33 in the *Leges et constitutiones* (see above, n. 163).

Table 5 *Liturgical offices and customs for meetings of the Order of the Golden Fleece on St Andrew's Day*

St Andrew's Day (30 Nov.)
Pontifical mass.
Sermon.
All the knights of the Order of the Golden Fleece to make offerings on this day.
Only the king is administered incense, and no one else, even though the prince is present.
Pontifical first Vespers and vigils for the dead.
Matins, with only one Nocturn [the 3 lessons to be sung], and Lauds.
Response at Lauds only when corpse present in the chapel until the end of mass the next day.

The day after St Andrew's Day ('Otro dia de Sant Andres, y de Diffuntos') (1 Dec.)
[Requiem] mass
No Gospel blessing or kiss of the *pax* unless the mass is pontifical.
Offerings: a coin [or arms] embedded in a [lighted] candle.
De profundis is only to be [sung] at the chapter of the Golden Fleece [at the end of the Offertory].
Four torches held at the elevation.
Sung Responsory [*Ne recorderis*] after mass. No torches are held during the response if there are candles.

for royalty, and Haggh's comment that 'it seems more useful to view the votive masses, and the ceremonies of the Order's meetings, as extensions of the burial or commemorative liturgy typical of funerals of the nobility' is certainly apt, even if based on an earlier context.[192] However, *La Orden* provides no evidence for a third or fourth day in this cycle which, in accordance with practices established in the Burgundian court, would have been dedicated to the Virgin Mary and the Holy Ghost respectively, though there is evidence for the celebration of a Marian mass at the 1519 meeting.[193]

Both Prizer and Haggh have successfully demonstrated how the meetings of the Order of the Golden Fleece were occasions of ostentatious display with, by way of long tradition, liturgical ceremonies adorned with vocal polyphony. Chronicles dating from

192 Haggh, 'The Archives', p. 36.

193 See Wright, 'Music and Ceremonial', p. 120, and Ros-Fábregas, 'Music and Ceremony', p. 384. Wright indicates that these observances continued in Philip II's time, though he provides no references (*ibid*., p. 120).

Philip II's time certainly bear witness to the extent to which these occasions called for the participation of the whole court, no doubt involving considerable expense and painstaking preparation. In Cock's 1585 *Relación*, for instance, we have evidence of two election ceremonies taking place within a few months of each other (in Zaragoza and Barcelona), and each accompanied by elaborate pomp and ceremony, feasting and general celebration which occupied the court and invited officials and guests for the greater part of the day. Cock describes the dressing of the king's oratory in the church with gold curtains, and the procession to mass of the newly elected knights holding their 'toisones' (special ceremonial collars) in their left hands, with the King bringing up the rear.[194] The walls of the church were also hung with tapestries and other fabrics in traditional fashion, and the knights would probably have changed their dress each day as appropriate to each liturgical ceremony.[195] For the meeting on St Andrew's Day in 1593, Kamen refers to how the royal alcázar in Madrid was 'illuminated and decorated for the brilliant ceremony'.[196]

Clearly polyphonic masses and other vocal settings held a special place in these commemorations, even though the documents both from the Burgundian court and the Spanish royal court provide us with relatively little information. As already indicated, the question of whether or not Dufay's polyphonic Requiem remained in the repertory in sixteenth-century Spain, or any other of the possible commmisions to such composers as Josquin and Agricola for these celebrations,[197] as yet remains unproven, though music by the latter two composers once formed part of the royal chapel repertories. Similarly, we can only speculate whether Busnoys's *L'homme armé* mass, or any of the other *L'homme armé* masses, were regularly performed on St Andrew's Day.[198] With time, and with

[194] Cock, *Relación del viaje*, p. 81.

[195] See Prizer, 'Music and Ceremonial', p. 119.

[196] Kamen, *Philip of Spain*, p. 202.

[197] See Prizer, 'Music and Ceremonial', pp. 129, 133 and *passim*.

[198] The presence of Busnoys's *L'homme armé* mass in Barcelona 454B (copied some time before 1520) has prompted speculation about its use at the 1519 meeting. See Ros-Fábregas, 'Music and Ceremony', pp. 385–6. For further discussions about the possible connections between masses in the *L'homme armé* tradition and meetings of the Order of the Golden Fleece, see L. Perkins, 'The *L'Homme armé* Masses of Busnoys and Ockeghem: A Comparison', *Journal of Musicology*, 3 (1984), pp. 363–96; Prizer, 'Music and Ceremonial', pp. 128–9, and R. Taruskin, 'Antoine Busnoys and the *L'Homme armé* Tradition', *Journal of the American Musicological Society*, 39 (1986), pp. 255–93.

more archival research, it is possible that the original function of polyphonic masses composed by musicians associated with the court in the early and mid-sixteenth century will be revealed. Listed in the inventory of music books in the royal chapel, for example, is a folio manuscript of just a single six-voice mass by Canis, a member of Charles V's chapel between 1542 and 1555. Though no title is given to this work, the inventory describes how the front cover of the volume portrays two royal coats of arms, one of which includes 'the Fleece' ('el Tusón').[199]

To conclude, *La Orden* appears to be the first document encountered which provides relatively elaborate detail about a number of rituals and ceremonies in the Spanish royal chapel of around the mid-sixteenth century, about which little was known previously. Its significance also lies in the fact that it shows how the origin of many of these as well as a few musico-liturgical practices evidently lay in the fifteenth-century Burgundian court chapel and therefore Parisian Usage.[200] It was written and recopied at a strategic time when the royal court and chapel were in a period of transition, and at the time when when the joint institutions of the *capillas flamenca* and *española* really began. It must therefore directly reflect the customs in the royal chapel when Pierre de Manchicourt was elected *maestro de capilla* in succession to Nicolas Payen, both of whom would therefore have organised the style of musical elaboration to accompany the liturgical and ceremonial acts described here. Though by no means a complete account of proceedings in the royal chapel, it is also unique for having been compiled by a participant of the chapel whose concern for the coordination between the various celebrants and the chapel officers, and notably for that between certain rituals and their accompanying musical items, informs and frequently has a bearing on the way the docu-

199 'Otro quaderno . . . de una missa de música de Cornelio Canis a seis vozes, con dos escudos de las armas reales, el uno con el Tusón y el otro sin él, con un pliego de papel por cuvierta.' See Vander Straeten, *La Musique aux Pays-Bas*, viii, p. 371 (item 51). There are only two masses extant by Canis, and both are written for six voices. The title of one of these, *Missa super 'Salve celeberrima'*, is suggestive of Marian devotion. See also n. 94 for Manchicourt's masses in MontsM 772.

200 For information on musico-liturgical practices in the Burgundian and Habsburg-Burgundian courts, see M. J. Bloxam, 'A Survey of Late Medieval Service Books from the Low Countries: Implications for Sacred Polyphony 1460–1520' (Ph.D. diss., Yale University, 1987), pp. 67–88.

ment is presented. It is one of a number of constitutional documents apparently revived at this time and, like the *Leges et constitutiones* and Charles V's *Estatutos*, may well have served as a basis for procedure in the royal chapel for several decades to come; no other statutory documents seem to have been issued until the *Advertencias* of 1584. It is likely that liturgical ceremony remained unchanged for at least the early years of Philip II's reign, though we learn of his active intervention in liturgical matters after the Council of Trent in *c.* 1565.[201] In all events, despite the establishment of the court in Madrid in May 1561, Philip was continually moving between royal residences, and Aguirre's remark that ceremonies may vary 'with the times and places where His Majesty travels' no doubt held true throughout his reign. Nevertheless, there is little doubt that the 'diverse ceremonies' described in *La Orden* were extremely elaborate and protracted affairs in which ritual, ceremony and musical performance were linked within a coherent and highly programmed structure.

University of Hong Kong

[201] See Kamen, *Philip of Spain*, p. 105.

APPENDIX 1

Duties and Responsibilities of the Officers of the *Capilla Real*[1]

Capellan Mayor (First Chaplain)
Always conducts the Office when he is present in the chapel, unless, for the sake of politeness, another prelate is recommended. In his absence, another prelate resident in the court is to be nominated. He is to appoint a judge amongst members of the chapel when necessary. He is responsible for the governing and administration of the chapel, and once a month (or more, if necessary) he may hold meetings in his lodgings; with the *Receptor* he is to conduct ceremonies for new chaplains when they take an oath of allegiance.

He receives distributions for the value of two chaplains.

(Lugar teniente) (Second Chaplain)
The lieutenant, or second-in-command, performs his duties in his absence.

Limosnero Mayor (Major Almoner)
Apart from his job as almoner, he is to assist at all Offices in the chapel, and, in the absence of either a prelate or the deacon, he is to administer the Gospel blessing and the *pax*. He is responsible for the chaplains, singers and other officers who obey him as if he were *Capellan Mayor*. He is responsible for knowing at what time and in what manner His Majesty would like the Offices to be celebrated. He is to say the *Benedicite* and thanksgiving at the King's table.[2]

(Segundo Limosnero) (Second Almoner)
There is to be a second almoner in the chapel to substitute for the first in the latter's absence. (See also *Sumilleres del Oratorio*.)

Sacristan Mayor (First Sacristan)
He is responsible for preparing the altar. He accompanies the prelate, the *Limosnero*, deacon or whoever else performs a ceremony. He carries the salver bearing the [missal after the reading of the] Gospel, and the

[1] This information is largely taken from *La Orden*, 'Officiales de la Capilla', fols. 71^{v}–76 and other parts of the document. It is augmented by a few details from the 1545 *Estriquete y Relascion*, the only other royal chapel document to outline the duties of chapel officers. Details of wages found in the *Estriquete* are omitted on this table.

[2] This particular clause lifted from the 1545 *Estriquete* corresponds with a passage describing the Major Almoner's duties in Olivier de la Marche's *Mémoires* of the mid-fifteenth-century Burgundian court. See *Olivier de la Marche*, ed. Beaune and D'Arbaumont, iv, p. 3.

pax; he also accompanies the preachers to and from the pulpit, and the chaplains and singers to and from their places when they go to recite the Lessons.

Sumilleres del Oratorio (Chamberlains of the [Royal] Oratory)
There are two who serve on alternate weeks. Their task is to register the missal and the hours, or whatever other book His Majesty must pray from, and to know the hour when the King wants to hear mass. The Oratory chamberlain assists at the canopy, opening it when His Majesty wishes to enter, and then closing it, taking account of the King's wishes. He makes sure that the *Mozos del Oratorio* are cleanly dressed.

The eldest *Sumiller* assumes the office of the *Limosnero Mayor* in his absence.

Receptor (Receiver)
The receiver of the chapel receives and administers all the distributions offered as admission duty, offerings, legitimations, etc. In the absence of the *Capellan Mayor* or his deputy, the receiver recommends which prelate and chaplains should take the Office. On Sundays and [major] feasts, the receiver accompanies the prelates who are to offer the 'Gospel' and the *pax* to the celebrants [to be kissed]. He is responsible for assigning the days for sermons, the weekly masses and other offices of the chapel [to the chaplains]. The receiver is responsible for advising the chaplains; when there are any extraordinary offices in the chapel the receiver takes distributions for [the equivalent] of two chaplains.

He is to attend ceremonies for new chaplains when they take an oath of allegiance, and collect the entrance fee of 3,000 *reis*.

Capellanes (Chaplains)
The chaplains are subject to the *Capellan Mayor* or his *Lugar teniente*, or whoever has been appointed as judge by the *Capellan Mayor*. Unless there is a legitimate excuse, they must never excuse themselves from their week of duty which was assigned to them by the receiver, not must they ever miss offices in their week of duty. They must be in the chapel on Sundays and major feast days especially.

Maestro de Capilla y Cantores (Chapel master and singers)
They must never miss the hours of Office; when a singer fails to appear at the offices, the *Maestro de Capilla* reproves him and, when pertinent, asks the *Limosnero Mayor* to admonish him.

The *Maestro de Capilla* is in charge of the choristers; he feeds and clothes them and collects their wages. He also teaches them music and the liturgical offices. He arranges the mode of transport for the boys when the king leaves the court.

Cantorciços (Boy choristers)
When their voices break, they are sent off to study for three years at the King's expense; if they recover their voices they should normally return to the royal chapel as singers.

They have a Latin tutor.

Mozos de Capilla (Altar servers)
There are normally four: two to serve at sung masses, and two at low masses. Those serving at sung mass are responsible for preparing the altar in time so that everything is there for the mass.

Mozos de Oratorio (Boy servers of the King's Oratory)
The other two must help at low masses, and prepare the *Citial* and the canopy in such a way that it is clean and ready when His Majesty appears. After low mass, they must take off the altar cloths and put them in their coffers. This is because it is assumed that the *Mozos* of sung mass have already completed their task, and collected that which appertains to them.

Mozo de Limosna (Almoner's assistant)
His duty to visit the poor, widows and others, and report their needs to the *Limosnero Mayor*. He must attend the King's table when he dines in public, and he receives any leftover bread to distribute to the poor.

Furrier de la Capilla (Chapel steward)
His job is to find lodgings for the chaplains, the singers and other officers of the chapel. He must attend all services and, when it is time for them to begin, ring the chapel bell in the corridors or so that those (the chaplains and the singers) wandering in the courtyard can hear and attend the Office. His task is also to assist the chaplains and singers, and fetch a bench from the *Furrieria* when necessary. Candles and torches are prepared in the *Furrieria*.

Organista (Organist)
The organist and the organ tuner must be present at the offices when the organ is to be played. Any absences are to be reproved by the *Limosnero*.

APPENDIX 2
Statutes and Other Constitutional Documents[1]

Burgundian court – Charles V

Ordennances touchant la chapelle (Charles the Bold, 1469). GB-Ob Hatton 13, fols. 10^{v}–47: ed. Fallows, 'Specific Information', pp. 146–59

Statutz et ordennances pour ladite chapelle (Charles the Bold; reissued in 1500 by Philip the Fair). B-Agr, Fonds: Papiers d'État et de l'Audience, reg. 22, fol. 104: ed. Doorslaer, 'La Chapelle musicale', pp. 45–6

Statutz et ordennances sur le faict de nostre grande chapelle (Charles V, 1515). B-Agr, Fonds: Papiers d'État et de l'Audience, reg. 23, II, fols. 10^{v} ff. [seventeenth-century copy]: ed. Schmidt-Görg, *Nicolas Gombert*, pp. 340–2, and Vander Straeten, *La Musique aux Pays-Bas*, vii, pp. 278–81

Castilian court

Constituciones de la Real Capilla de Don Henrique IV (*c.* 1436). E-Mn MS 14.018/4 (Barbieri papers copied from E-Sag, Archivo de la Real Capilla, Leg. 1, no. 12): ed. Barbieri papers 2, doc. 124

Constituciones de la Capilla Real de Spaña (late fifteenth century: reign of the Catholic Monarchs). E-Mn MS 14.075/12 (Barbieri papers copied from E-Sag Patronato Real, Leg. 25-1): ed. Barbieri papers 2, doc. 126

Charles V

Estatutos de la Capilla del Emperador Carlos quinto al vzo de la Caza de Borgoña (*c.* 1518). P-La 51-VI-37, fols. 79^{v}–84 (mid-seventeenth-century copy): ed. below, Appendix 4

Estriquete y Relascion de la orden de seruir q(ue) se tenia en la Casa del Emperador don Carlos n(uest)ro señor el anno 1545. F-Pn, Section des manuscrits, Esp. 364, fols. 2–5: ed. Schmidt-Görg, *Nicolas Gombert*, pp. 338–40 (= first section of the following documents)

= *El Etiqueta. Relacion de la forma de servir, que se tenia en la casa del Emperador Don Carlos, nuestro s(eñ)or, que aya gloria, el año de 1545 y se havia tenido algunos años antes.* E-Mpa [n.s.]: ed. Vander Straeten, *La Musique aux Pay-Bas*, vii, pp. 398–403

[1] With the exception of documents found in Lisbon archives, all source references have been taken from the secondary literature cited here or from Robledo's 'La música en la corte de Felipe II'

= *Constituciones que se guardaban en la Real Capilla del Señor Emperador D. Carlos Nuestro Señor, el año 1545. Y se habían observado algunos años antes . . ..* E-Mn MS 1013 (*olim* cod. E. 76); E-Mn MS 14.018/1 (Barbieri papers copied from 1792 document): ed. Barbieri papers, doc. 135[a–c]

incl.: *Ordenanzas pertenecientes a las ceremonias que se mandaron guardar en dicha Real Capilla en lo tocante al culto divino* (abbreviated version of *Estatutos que hasta agora . . .* copied in 1792). Ed. Barbieri papers 2, doc. 135[b]

Charles V and Philip II

Leges et Constitutiones Capellae Catholicae Maiestatis a maioribus institutae, a Car. Quinto studiosè custodite, hodierno die, mandato Regis Catholici . . . (? originated in reign of Philip the Fair (d. 1506); adapted (before 1568) during the reign of Philip II). E-Mpa Administrativa, Leg. 1133: ed. Vander Straeten, *La Musique aux Pays-Bas*, vii, pp. 183–6; Schmidt-Görg, *Nicolas Gombert*, pp. 340–2

La Orden que se tiene en los Officios en la Capilla de Su Magestad (drawn up in *c.* 1550 by Aguirre, chaplain and receiver in the royal chapel; revised and updated in early 1560s). P-La 51-VI-37, fols. 61–79 (mid-seventeenth-century copy): ed. below, Appendix 3

Constituciones o estatutos de la Real Capilla de S.M. el Emperador Carlos V al uso de la Casa de Borgoña. Estatutos que hasta agora se han guardado en la Capilla Imperial y se han de observar en la Real Capilla de S.M. conforme al uso de Borgoña (copied early 1560s). E-Mn MS 14.018/6 (Barbieri papers, possibly copied from original sixteenth-century document): ed. Barbieri papers 2, doc. 136, and Vander Straeten, *La Musique aux Pays-Bas*, viii, pp. 178–82 (from Barbieri papers)

Philip II

Estatuto de la Real Capilla, año 1562 y representaciones de los capellanes del Banco de Castillo al limosnero mayor de S.M. D. Luis Manrique, año de 1567 y 1569. Estatuto formado por el arzobispo de Santiago, D. Gaspar de Zúñiga, primer capellan mayor del Rey D. Felipe II, acerca del servicio que deben hacer los capellanes de su Real Capilla. Año de 1562. E-Mpa, Real Capilla, caja 66/6 (*olim* leg. 1, no. 9]; E-Mn MS 14.018/2 (Barbieri papers): ed. Barbieri papers 2, doc. 156[a–c]

Advertencias de cómo se ha de ganar y repartir las distribuciones que Su Magestad Católica ha mandado poner en la capilla de cantores de su capilla real y capellanes de altar desde primero de o[c]tubre de 1584. E-Mpa Real Capilla, caja 76, *olim* Leg. 5, no. 1; E-Mn Ms 14.018/3 (Barbieri papers copied from 1791 document: *Constitutiones de la Real Capilla para repartir las distribuciones . . . 1584)*: ed. Barbieri papers 2, doc. 161

Constituciones para el Real Colegio de Cantores de la Real Capilla del Rey nuestro señor. Hechas en tiempo de Felipe II. Visita 3 de octubre de 1672. E-Mpa, Administrativa, leg. 1116; E-Mpa Real Capilla, caja 105; E-Mn MS 14.017/9 (Barbieri papers copied from 1672 document): ed. Barbieri papers 2, doc. 157

Regimento da Capella Real [*Lisboa*] . . . *1592* (drawn up in 1592 by Jorge de Ataide, first chaplain of the Portuguese royal chapel, and revised in 1608). P-Ln cod. 10981 (late copy); P-La cod. 50-V-26, fols. 1–11^{v} (late copy); partial transcription of MS in Madrid: ed. Barbieri papers 2, doc. 176 (E-Mn MS 14018/12)

APPENDIX 3

La Orden que se tiene en los Officios en la Capilla de su Magestad[1]

[Sung masses on weekdays and Sundays]

Cada dia se dize en la Capilla vna Missa Cantada sin Diacono, ni Subdiacono, los quales no sirven sinó en solos los dias de Domingos y fiestas de guardar, y otros dias que hay sermones como en la Quaresma y Adviento.

Tiene esta Orden para el Servicio de los Capellanes en las Missas Cantadas: que siempre el que dise la Missa una semana la que se sigue ha de hazer el Officio de Diacono, y luego la otra Tercera de Subdiacono, de manera que conforme al numero de los Capellanes de que les viene su turno, siempre comiença por la Missa, despues sirven de Evangelio, y Epistola.

El Subdiacono entre semana se halla a la Missa para cantar la Epistola, la qual (fol. 61[v]) se a costumbre siempre deçirse en atril con vn Missal pequeño teniendole el Subdiacono en las manos en el mismo lugar que se halla; quando acaba el Preste la Oracion, en aquel tiempo le dâ el Moço de Capilla el Missal en que ha de decir la Epistola, y acavada se le torna a tomar, y se sube al altar y passa el Missal con su Cojin, o atril a la parte del Evangelio.

El Evangelio canta el Diacono quando sirve en el altar, y al tiempo que se canta está el Sacerdote en pie arrimado al Altar el Rostro puesto hacia el Evangelio, y el Subdiacono vna grada en vajo.

Al Evangelio destas Missas Cantadas no acostumbran traer los pajes achas, sinó solamente en los dias de Domingo, o fiestas, quando se sirve la Missa con Diacono, y Subdiacono; (fol. 62) pero para la Consagracion siempre las sirven hasta que consume.

En los dias de Domingo o fiestas no principales sirven con dós achas al Evangelio, y a la Consagracion con quatro: quando son fiestas Principales, como Pascuas, y Apostoles, y dias de Nuestra Señora sirven quatro hachas al Evangelio, y seis a la Consagracion; tienesse por costumbre entrar los pajes con las achas al tiempo que comiençan los Sanctus.

Quando se acava el Evangelio van dos pajes con sus hachas acompañando a los que van a servir al Evangelio.

[1] P-La 51-VI-37, fols. 61–79; a mid-seventeenth-century copy of the ceremonial drawn up in *c.* 1550 by Aguirre, chaplain and receiver in the royal chapel; revised and updated in the early 1560s.

No se acostumbra en la Capilla a tomar Vendicion al Diacono del Prelado ni vendicir el insienso sinó en dias de fiestas principales que ay vendicion Episcopal.

El Asperges comiença el Preste vajo (fol. 62v) de las gradas del altar, y luego vuelve el isopo al Diacono el qual vá con el Prelado a servir el agua a Su Magestad y sinó ay Prelado el le dâ el agua, y vuelto a su puesto delante el altar le toma el Sancristan Mayor el Isopo y vá con vn Mozo de Capilla que lleva el agua, y comienza por el Legado o Nuncio si le ay, despues a los Prelados y a los Capellanes, Cantores, luego a los Embaxadores, y grandes, y a los demas pero quando los Embaxadores estan en vn banco con el Nuncio como es costumbre les dan el agua juntamente con el Nuncio. En este medio, el Sacerdote como acaban los Cantores los Versos del Asperges, se sube solo al Altar, y dize la Oracion, y acabada los Menistros suben tambien al Altar, y se ponen todos tres en medio hasta que comiencen el Gloria patri, y entonces le ponen la Casula que está en vn cuerno (fol. 63) del Altar a la parte del Evangelio, y comiença su Confession.

Estas Missas Cantadas de entre semana se comiençan en punto a las ocho desde Pascua de Ressurreccion hasta primera de Octubre, y dende en adelante, hasta Pascua, a las nueve; pero en los dias de Domingos, y fiestas principales, quando no sale Su Magestad vna hora mas tarde porque tengan lugar los que quisieren venir al officio.

Quando ay Pontifical, el Asperjes y la Oracion dize el Diacono, y el Prelado está asientado en su silla con los Menistros.

Sinó es Prelado el que dize la Missa no se acostumbra en la Capilla incensar la Oblacion.

En las Missas se sirve a su Ma- (fol. 63v) gestad, la pax, y el Evangelio y a las Visperas, a la Magnifica el incienso.

[Low masses]

Missas Rezadas.

Cada dia se dizen dos Missas rezadas en Palacio por la Emperatriz la vna, y la Otra del dia del Sancto que fuere segun la Regla del Calendario Viejo, y Romano, pero en los Jueves, Viernes, y Sabbados, quando el Sancto no tiene officio proprio dizen del Sancto Sacramento de la Cruz, y de Nuestra Señora.

[Requiem mass]

Acavando de dizir la Missa de Requien, dizen vn responso Ne recorderis, con solo la Oracion: Quaesumus Domine pro tua pietate.

Y en la Missa no se acostumbra a dezir mas desta Oracion. (fol. 64)

[Vespers]

Visperas.

Dicense en la Capilla Visperas todos los Sabbados, y Domingos, y fiestas de Nuestra Señora, y Apostoles, y Quatro Doctores, y fiestas de guardar; y las Visperas destas fiestas, comiençalas el Semanero en medio del altar solo con la Capa, començando los Cantores el primer verso del Psalmo le quita la Capa el Mozo de Capilla, y la pone en el Altar a la parte del Evangelio y el se vá a sientar en la cavecera del Vanco de los Capellanes hasta la Capitula que vuelve a tomar la Capa para dezirla, y se está en pie con ella hasta que se acavan las Visperas; y no se está acompañando a los lados ningun Capellan.

En estas fiestas Principales a la Missa y Visperas hay Vendicion Episcopal del Prelado, y en estos dias se toma del Obispo la Vendicion del Evangelio, y del incienso, (fol. 64^{v}) y el Subdiacono acavada la Epistola va a besar la Mano al Prelado, poniendose el Libro en las rodillas.

[Compline]

Completas.

Acavadas las Visperas siempre se dizen Completas avnque haya Visperas de Pontifical, y comienzalas en medio del Altar el Semanero como costumbra a las Visperas, y siempre con capa.

[When to sing the Salve and motets]

Salve, y motetes, quando.

Acavadas Completas siempre se dize vn motete en Canto de Organo, y los Sabbados Salve, quando son Visperas de fiestas principales, que quando lo son acavan las Completas con vn motete con sus versos y oracion; pero desde Pascua a la Ascencion en lugar de Salve (fol. 65) diçen Regina Caeli laetare, y responde el Organo, y al cavo la Oracion del tiempo.

[Compline]

Completas no se dizen en Visperas feriales quando se dizen acavada la Missa como en Quaresma; pero en este tiempo los Domingos se dizen Visperas y Completas a la tarde.

[Calendar of pontifical masses]

Missas de Pontifical.

Hay en la Capilla ordinariamente Missas de Pontifical.
Itten primer dia de Navidad.
Itten Dia de la Epiphania.
Itten a Veinte y vno de Mayo por el nascimiento de Su Alteza.
Itten dia de Pascua de Ressurreccion.
Itten dia de la Ascencion
Dia de Pascua de Pentecostes.
Dia de Corpus Christi.
Dia de Nuestra Señora de Agosto. (fol. 65[v])
Dia de todos los Sanctos.
Dia de los Defuntos.
Dia de Sant Andres.

Solo se inciensa a El Rey y no a otro, avnque este prezente el Princepe.

Otro dia de Sant Andres, y de Diffuntos no ay paz ni Evangelio solo siempre que hay Missa de Pontificial se dizen primeras Visperas de Pontifical, dize el Responso acabada la Missa, y no se dize De Profundis, sinó en el Capitulo del Tuson.

El Diacono y subdiacono que son semaneros se visten con el Prelado, los Assistentes y otros Menistros, no estando el Capellan Mayor presente los nombra el Receptor, danse Capas a los dos Assistentes, y al vaculo, y a la mitra.

Para todo se vea el Pontifical, y se siga tratandolo el Limosnero Mayor (fol. 66) con el Sancristan Mayor, y Maestro de Capilla.

[Vigils for commemorations]

Quando se dicen Visperas, y Vigilias de Pontifical como el dia de todos los Sanctos, y Sant Andres se tiene esta orden: dichas las Visperas del dia si Su Magestad no está presente aguardan a que salga, y dizen Visperas y Vigilias de difuntos y otro [dia] la Missa, y acavada la Missa se dize vn Responso Cantado.

No hay hachas quando hay velas al responso, y al alzar llevanse quatro hachas los pajes.

En estas Vigilias de Diffuntos siempre se dizen Laudes avnque no se diga mas de vn Nocturno, como acontece muchas vezes mandar Su Magestad que no se diga mas que vn Nocturno.

Dize el Semanero la Antiphona de las (fol. 66[v]) Visperas, con capa en medio del altar, y quitasela luego hasta que buelva a decir la antiphona del Magnifica: y la Magnifica y Oracion todo lo dize con capa y en la Vigilia los Pater Nostres antes de empezar las Liciones dize con capa paso entono, y canta Et ne nos, y dexa la capa a la postrera Liccion dize en el Altar con su capa, y la dexa en acavandola, y nó la toma mas hasta que buelva a dezir la antiphona del Benedictus; y el Benedictus y Oracion, y no se dize Responso si no hay Cuerpo presente hasta en fin de la Missa de otro dia.

[Obsequies for the death of kings, princes or infantes]

Obsequias por Muerte de Reyes, o Princepes, o Infantes.

Quando se hazen honrras por Muerte de Reyes Princepes ó Infantes dize las Visperas, y Vigilias vn Prelado, y otro dia se dizen tres Missas de Pontifical haviendo Obispos (fol. 67) ó Abbades que las digan: la primera del Spirito Sancto, la segunda de Nuestra Señora, la tercera de Diffuntos a la qual sale Su Magestad, porque las otras dos se dizen antes que salga.

[Time of Matins on Christmas night]

Maytines.

Dizense Maytines la Noche de Navidad suelense comenzar a las diez.

[Corpus Christi and Octave]

Dia de Corpus Christi con todo su Octavario, y comiençan en amaneciendo, y dizen todas las horas alternando los Psalmos sin que los Capellanes le ayuden.

La Orden que se tiene en esta fiesta de Corpus Christi es que el Miercoles de la Vigilia el que dize la Missa Cantada consagra vna forma de mas de la que ha de consumir y acavada la Missa la ponen en su Custodia, y cantando los Cantores Tantum ergo (fol. 67^{v}) Sacramentum, vendiciendo el Pueblo con la Custodia, al tiempo que llegan aquel passo Sit et benedi-tio, con muchas achas, y ensienso y campanilla le llevan al lugar que está aparejado para ponerle.

Siempre que el Sacerdote le toma ó le dexa le insiensa tres vezes.

Despues a las Visperas, venido Su Magestad, le sacan como le llevaron, y acavadas las Visperas le buelven con la misma solemnidad, hasta otro dia a la mañana, que le sacan a los Maytines; y lo mismo hazen entre semana el Viernes despues de la Octava le consume el Sacerdote que dize la Missa Cantada.

[Processions]

Processiones.

Dia de Ramos.
Dia de Corpus Christi.
Dia de la Purificacion. (fol. 68)
En las processiones se tiene esta orden: Su Magestad vá detras del Prelado que haze el Officio con los Embaxadores, y Princepes, y Embaxadores y Grandes; delante del Prelado y de los Menistros que le assisten, van los Obispos, y Capellanes, y los Cantores; luego los Cavalleros, y los demas todo en orden, el Sancristan Mayor y el Rec[ep]tor tienen cargo de Ordenallos.

Quando se lleva el Sacramento, lleva Su Magestad vna hacha blanca delante, y tambien los Princepes, y Señores que se hallan en la procession.

[Episcopal blessings: Palms and Candles]

Benediciones Episcopales de Ramos, y Candelas.

Dia de la Purificacion, las Candelas.
Dia de Ramos, los Ramos, y no dize la Missa estos dos dias el Prelado. (fol. 68v)

[Offerings]

Offrendas.

Primer dia de Navidad.
Dia de la Circuncizion.
Dia de la Purificacion.
Dia de la Epiphania. Este dia offrece Su Magestad tres copas de plata doradas con sus sobrecopas de valor de treinta ducados cada vna; en la primera offrece vn ducado y en la segunda encienso, y en la tercera Mirra.
Dia de Sancto Mathia por su nascimento offrece Su Magestad tantos ducados quantos annos cumple, y más el anno en que entra; esto mismo haze El Rey Nuestro Señor a viente y vno del Mayo.
Primer dia de Pascua de Resurreccion.
Dia de la Ascencion.
Primer dia de Pentecostes.
Dia de Corpus Christi.
Dia de Nuestra Señora de Agosto.
Dia de Todos Sanctos.
Dia de los finados, con vn escudo en vna vela (fol. 69) encendida.
Dia de San Miguel quando sale con habito de la Orden de Francia no hay Pontifical.
Dia de Sant Andres con todos los Cavalleros de la Orden del Tuson.
Otro dia de Sant Andres con vna vela encendida offrece el escudo hincado en la vela.

[Adoration of the Cross on Good Friday and on the feast of the Invention of the Cross on 3 May]

Adoracion de la Cruz en el Viernes Sancto.

En el Viernes Sancto se offrece a la adoracion de la Cruz, guardasse esta orden: acavado el Sacerdote, que haze el Officio de adorar con el Diacono, y Subdiacono, vá a adorar el Legado Nuncio Apostolico si está en la Capilla, despues los Obispos, los Capellanes, los Cantores, y officiales Clerigos de la Capilla; acavando estos sale Su Magestad, luego los Embaxadores (fol. 69ᵛ) los grandes, y los Cavalleros.

Porque no impidan al officio, acavando de adorar los Cavalleros, apartan la Cruz con el Coxin y estrado a vn lado, y acavado el Officio van addorar todos los que quieren.

Siempre que hay palo de la vera Cruz en Palacio le ponen este dia para la adoracion.

En la fiesta de la Cruz que se zelebra a tres de Mayo sacan al altar la Cruz con el vero palo, y acavada la Missa el Sacerdote o Prelado, si le hay con su Estola la dá a besar a Su Magestad delante del Altar; este dia no acostumbra Su Magestad a oir Missa Cantada.

[Calendar of days for sermons]

Sermones ordinarios.

En la Septuagessima, sexagessima, y quinquagessima. (fol. 70)
En la quaresma cada dia haviendo copia de Predicadores.
En el Adviento cada dia haviendo Predicadores.
Segundo dia de Pascua de Ressurreccion.
Dia de la Annunciacion de Nuestra Señora.
La Domin[ic]a infra Octava de la Ascencion.
Segundo dia de Pentecostes.
Domingo de la Trinidad.
La Dominica infra Octava Corporis Christi.
El dia de Santiago.
Dia de Sant Andres.
En Flandes, en Hespaña, primero Domingo de Adviento.

[Holy Week: Tenebrae]

Tenieblas.

Comienzan las Tenieblas el Miercoles de la Semana Sancta a la hora que Su (fol. 70ᵛ) Magestad sale.

[Lamentations]

Las Lamentaciones se dizen ordinariamente con biolones y quatro vozes: Tiple, Contralto, Tenor, y Contravajo; y las Lecciones los Capellanes.

[Mandatum on Maundy Thursday and Passion on Good Friday]

Mandato, y passion.

El Mandato se predica ordinariamente en la Missa a la hora de los otros sermones.

La passion el viernes a las siete, y acavada se comienza el Officio.

En la Capilla de Su Magestad, Jueves, Viernes, y Sabbado Sancto no se acostumbra hazer el Officio Prelado.

[Matins on Vigils for the dead]

Quando hay Maytines ó Vigilias de difuntos, la primera leccion suele dezir vn niño de los Cantores, y las demás los Capellanes (fol. 71) de este arte, y las tres postreras, dizen el Semanero, Subdiacono, y el Diacono, y el que haze el Officio.

[Vigils and mass for the Empress on 1 May, and for the Emperor on 21 September]

Cabo de Anno por la Emperatriz Nuestra Senora.

Cabo de anno se haze por la Emperatriz Nuestra Señora cada anno en la Capilla dizense Visperas, y Vigilias.

Primer dia de Mayo despues de las Visperas de San Philippe y Santiago, y otro dia la Missa, las Vigilias se dizen con tres Nocturnos y Laudes.

En la Missa offrece Su Magestad vn ducado, y vna vela de cera en que vá hincado [vn escudo][2] acavada la Missa se dize vn Responso Cantado, lo mismo por el Emperador, a veinte y vno de Septiembre. (fol. 71^{v})

[Order for preparing torches in the chapel]

La Orden de servir las hachas en la Capilla.

A todas las Missas Cantadas se hallan todos los pajes de Su Magestad, y sirven siempre las hachas de las quales tiene Cargo el furriel de la Capilla de tenellas encendidas, al punto que son necessarias; y despues del Servicio tomallas a los pajes y tambien tiene Cargo de hazer este officio vn mozo de la zereria.

Al Evangelio de las Missas Cantadas entre semana no se sirven hachas sinó es dia que se haga el officio con Diacono y Subdiacono.

[2] This word is omitted in the document.

[Officers of the chapel]

Officiales de la Capilla

[Capellan Mayor]

Capellan Mayor siempre que está en la Capilla haçe el officio, sinó lo (fol. 72) quiere por comedimiento encomendar a otro Prelado.

El Capellan Mayor quando está auzente suele nombrar por su substituto vn Prelado de los que residen en la Corte a quien dá sus vezes.

El Capellan Mayor nombra vn Juez en la Capilla de los mesmos Capellanes el qual conoce de todas sus cauzas y differencias sin que otro Juez intervenga entre ellas.

El Capellan Mayor manda y veda en la Capilla lo que le pareze que conviene al buen govierno y administracion de ella.

El Capellan Mayor o su Lugar Teniente en su auzencia acostumbra ajuntar Capilla en sus possadas adonde le parece en el mez vna vez, y más (fol. 72v) se se offrece necessidad.

El Capellan mayor, lleva destribuiciones por dós Capellanes.

Limosnero Mayor.

El Limosnero Mayor demás de hazer su officio de la Limosna assiste a todos los officios de la Capilla, y quando no ay Prelado ó Diacono, el sirve el Evangelio, y la paz.

El Limosnero Mayor en la Capilla de Su Magestad, govierna los Cantores a quien obedecen como a Capellan Mayor, y lo mismo los officiales de ella.

El Limosnero Mayor tiene cuenta con saber de Su Magestad a la hora, el como y quando quiere los Officios. (fol. 73)

Hay de contino en la Capilla de Su Magestad, segundo Limosnero, el qual en auzencia del Limosnero Mayor haze el Officio.

Sacristan Mayor.

El Sacristan Mayor probee todo lo que tocca al adrezo, y servicio del Altar.

El Sacristan Mayor acompaña al Prelado Limosnero, o Diacono, o qualquiera otro que vsa de alguna ceremonia en la Capilla. Y le toca el hazer la salva del Evangelio, y paz ansy mismo acompaña a los Predicadores allevarlos, y bolverlos del pulpito, y tambien a los Capellanes y Cantores que salen a dezir Licciones, y buelve con ellos a sus assientos y lugares. (fol. 73v)

Sumilleres del Oratorio.

Los Sumilleres del Oratorio son dos, y sirven a semanas, su Officio es registrar el Missal, y las horas ó a qualquiera otro Libro en que Su Magestad haya de rezar; el Sumiller assiste junto a la Cortina, y quando Su Magestad quiere entrar la abre, y despues la cierra, tiene cuenta con lo que Su Magestad mande.

Al Sumiller tocca advertir a los mozos del Oratorio que le tengan limpiamente aderezado.

Quando faltan los Limosneros, el sumiller mas antiguo haze el Officio.

Receptor.

El Receptor de la Capilla recive y reparte todas las destribuiciones que se offrecen (fol. 74) como de entradas, offrendas, legitimaciones o qualquier otra cosa que se haya de destribuhir.

El Receptor en auzencia del Capellan Mayor, o su Lugar teniente encomienda el Prelado y Capellanes que han de salir a hazer el officio.

Suele acompañar el Receptor en los Domingos, y fiestas a los Prelados que van a servir el Evangelio, y la paz a los prestes.

El Receptor tiene Cargo de encomendar los Sermones, y semanas de Missas y otros Officios de la Capilla.

El Receptor tiene Cargo de avisar los Capellanes; quando hay algun Officio extraordinario en la Capilla lleva el Receptor destribuiciones por dós Capellanes. (fol. 74^{v})

Capellanes.

Los Capellanes reconozen por su Superior al Capellan Mayor ó a su Lugar teniente, y por Juez al que constituyere el Capellan Mayor.

Los Capellanes han de tener cuenta con no faltar en sus semanas en los Officios que les toca.

Los Capellanes sino fuere con causa legitima no se pueden escusar de tomar la semana que les tocare, y les fuere encomendada por el Receptor.

Los Capellanes han de hallarse en la Capilla especialmente Domingos y fiestas.

Maestro de Capilla y Cantores.

El Maestro de Capilla y Cantores han (fol. 75) de tener quenta con no faltar a las horas de los Officios, y quando algun Cantor falta de nó venir a las horas, el Maestro de Capilla le reprehenda y quando es pertinaz, dizelo al Limosnero Mayor para que le corrija, y dicen todas las horas los Cantores.

Mozos de Capilla

Hay de ordinario quatro mozos que sirven: dós tienen cargo de servir en las Missas Cantadas, y dós en las rezadas.

Los de las Missas Cantadas tiene cargo de tener adereçado el Altar a su hora que no haya falta y ayudar a las Missas.

Mozos de Oratorio.

Los otros dos tienen cargo de ayudar a las (fol. 75[v]) Missas rezadas, y aderezar el Citial, y Cortina de manera que estê limpio todo, y aparejado para quando Su Alteza saliere. Estos han de cojer acavada la Missa rezada el adrezo del Altar, y metello en sus Cofres. Porque se presupone que los de las Missas Cantadas ya han hecho su officio, y recogido lo que les toca.

Furrier de la Capilla.

Hay Furrier de la Capilla el qual tiene Cargo de hazer el aposento de los Capellanes, y Cantores y officiales de la Capilla.

Este tiene Cargo de hallarse a todos los Officios, y al tiempo que quieren comenzar tañer la Campanilla de la Capilla, en los corredores, ó donde se oyga de los que andan en el patio, para que los Capellanes, y Cantores que estan en el patio acudan al officio. Más tiene Cargo de los (fol. 76) assientos de los Capellanes, y Cantores, y quando falta algun banco haze que lo traygan de la Furrieria.

Organista.

El Organista, y el que entona tiene de hallarse a la hora de los officios quando es necessario que se taña el Organo, quando haçen falta, el Limosnero los reprehende.

[Admission of chaplains and cantors to the chapel, and how to receive distributions]

Entradas de Capellanes.

Todos los Capellanes de Su Magestad primero que tomen sobrepellis ó le admitan en la Capilla, quando entran de nuevo han de hazer la solemnidad del juramento ante el Capellan Mayor, y el Receptor, y pagan al Receptor tres mil reis de entrada para toda la Capilla. (fol. 76[v])

En auzencia del Capellan Mayor o su Lugar teniente hazen la solemnidad del juramento ante dós Capellanes los mas antiguos, y el Receptor, el qual dâ fée a las espaldas de la Zedula de esto.

Todos los Cantores y officiales de la Capilla, se quisieren ganar destribuiciones han de pagar la entrada como vn Capellan excepto el Capellan Mayor, y los mozos y los niños.

Los quatro mozos de Capilla llevan dós destribuciones. Los niños suelen ser ordinariamente doze, y todos que hayan menos ó mas ganan por dós Capellanes, como los mozos de Capilla.

[Final statement]
Esto se acostumbra al prezente, y se guarda en la Capilla de Su Magestad, pero ha se variado en alguna manera con los tiempos, y lugares por dó Su Magestad anda, y ansy vemos que en España (fol. 77) con la Capilla Real hay algunas ceremonias diversas.

[Addendum]
Esta rellacion me dió Aguirre, Capellan de Su Magestad, y Receptor de su Capilla.

El Contralor tiene otra relacion en Frances, que le imbió el Limosnero Mayor, de la manera que se sirve la Capilla al vzo de Borgoña.

[Calendar of days for sermons]
Ver Capitulo zerca de los sermones que ha de haver en la Capilla de Su Magestad, si se guarda lo que en la de su padre.

Yten que los Domingos de la Septuagessima, o Sexagessima, o Quinquagessima, o Quadragessima, el dia de la Ceniza, los Domingos, Viernes, y fiestas de Quaresma, y del Adviento, (fol. 77^{v}) las fiestas de Nuestro Señor, y las de Nuestra Señora, los Lunes despues de Pascua y de Pentecostes, los dias de Sant Andres, Sam Pedro en Junio, Santiago, dias de todos los Santos, y de los finados habra Sermon en nuestra Capilla, si nó mandamos otra cosa.

Su Magestad, dia de todos los Santos y de difuntos, quiere Pontifical y no Sermon.

[Feast of the Purification when the King goes to a monastery]
Dia de la Purificacion, acostumbra Su Magestad hir a vn Monasterio; a la Vendicion de las Candelas, está vn flaire del mismo Monasterio, i a la Vendicion de las Candelas con la Cruz grande con su manga y dos acolitos con sus velas acavada la Vendicion vá el flaire con la Cruz, y los dos acolitos delante y todo el Convento le sigue; y luego los Cantores de Su Magestad, y luego los Officiales, y Capellanes de Su Magestad, y luego obispos, y despues (fol. 78) los mazeros, y Mayordomos, y luego el Prelado que dixo la Vendicion de las Candelas con sus assistentes, y Menistros, [y] luego Su Magestad, y vn poco mas atras el Nuncio y Embaxadores y Grandes, y los Cavalleros van adelante ó a los lados donde no estorben a la Capilla.

La Vela se le ha de dar a Su Magestad, quando ya acaban de hir sus Capellanes a la procession, y entonces acaba el Obispo a dezir la postrera Oracion.

Acavada la procession, va se el Prelado al Altar Mayor con sus assistentes y Menistros, y hecha la vendicion ordenaria, y respondenle los Cantores.

[Sermons during Lent]
En passando la Dominica de Septuagessima se trate con Su Magestad de la Orden que manda se tenga con (fol. 78[v]) todos los Sermones de la Quaresma para avisar a los Predicadores.

[Distribution of ashes on Ash Wednesday]
Miercoles de Zeniça vn Prelado dá siempre a Su Magestad la zeniza assi como anda con sola la roquete.

Por la mañana luego se dize una Missa Rezada, y se vendize la Zeniza, y otras vezes luego se vendize la zeniza, luego se dá a todos los que la quieren tomar, y despues antes que Su Magestad salga la toma toda la Capilla.

En saliendo Su Magestad se vá derecho a tomar la zeniza antes que entre en las Cortinas, despues la toman los Grandes, y Mayordomos, y Cavalleros de la Camara y nó mas, y luego se prosigue el Officio, y vn Capellan se pone a dar la zeniza a los otros Cavalleros porque no se impida el Officio a vn lado del Altar; y acavada la Missa, otro (fol. 79) Capellan dá la zeniza a todos los que quieren tomarla.

Yendosse Su Magestad fuera se junta toda la Capilla en el aposento de la Reyna y lo mesmo yendosse la Reyna en el aposento de El Rey.

Al Rey y Reyna, Princepe y Princeza se sirve paz y Evangelio, no se sirve nada a Don Juan de Austria, avnque le ponen sola una silla rasa pequeña dentro de la Cortina sin almohada.

[Vespers during Lent]
En las Visperas que se dizen en Quaresma antes de comer no se canta nunca motete, comienzanse las Visperas por el Diacono en alzandosse el Caliz.

APPENDIX 4

Estatutos de la Capilla del Emperador Carlos quinto al vzo de la Caza de Borgoña[1]

La Orden que mandamos que se tenga en Nuestra Capilla es la siguiente.

[1] Mandamos y ordenamos que todos los Cappellanes, Cantores y Officiales de Nuestra Capilla de Nuestros Estados de Flandes tengan por superior, y le tengan reverencia al nuestro Limosnero Mayor, obedeciendole en todo lo que el mandare, que fuere por el servicio de la dicha Capilla, sob pena, que quien no lo hiziere les pueden castigar por suspenciones de sus officios, rayar sus gajes o otra correccion que le pareciere porque en este le havemos dado, y damos la authoridad y poder que a el conviene.

[2] Mandamos que de aqui adelante el Officio Divino se celebre en Nuestra Capilla Conforme al Vzo, y Costumbre de la Iglesia Romana, tanto (fol. 80) a Maytines, Missas, Visperas, guardando las Ceremonias y Costumbres Romanas.

[3] Yten que cada dia la Missa se cante por nuestros Cantores, en la Capilla en Palacio, a las nueve horas encomenzando desde el dia de Santo Remis hasta el dia de Pascua de Ressurreccion, y desde el dicho dia de Pascua se dirá a las ocho hasta el dia de San Remís, y las Visperas en los dias que aqui seran nombrados, y entiendesse quando Nos estuvieremos presente, porque teniendo algunos negocios habran de esperar hasta la hora que havremos mandado a nuestro dicho Limosnero; y quando fuere que en Nuestro Palacio no obiere Capilla, ni lugar donde el officio no se pudiere celebrar, mandamos que se haga en la mas cercana Iglesia o Capilla de nuestro Palacio, conforme a lo que pareciere a nuestro dicho Limosnero, que en todos los dias de fiestas grandes y pequeñas y Vigilias dellas que se guardan en el pueblo donde estubieremos se diran Visperas y Completas conforme a la fiesta, y segun las Ceremonias, y Vso Romano. (fol. 80^{v})

[4] Yten que todos los Capellanes, Cantores, y Officiales de Nuestra dicha Capilla celebrando el Officio Divino seran obligados ser vestidos ropas largos bonetes, y habitos de Clerigos, la barba y corona rapada sob pena de ser rayado de sus gajes del dia que hicere falta.

[5] Yten q(ue) los Capellanes Cantores, y Officiales sean obligados

[1] P-La 51-VI-37, fols. 79^{v}–84, a mid-seventeenth-century copy of a document of *c.* 1518.

entrando en la dicha Capilla ponerse en rodillas, y hazer Oracion.

[6] Yten que los dichos Capellanes Cantores y Officiales haciendo el Officio Divino estaran en pie q(uan)do se cantare el Introito de la Missa, [Kyrie], Gloria in excelsis Deo, y el Evangelio, el Credo, Sanctus, Pater Noster, y Agnus Dei, y ansi mismo quando se encomienzan las Visperas, Completas, Magnificat, Nunc Dimitis, y las Oraciones teniendo las cavezas descubiertas, y en el Advento y Quaresma a las preces, y Oraciones se pondran de rodillas como es de costumbre.

[7] Yten zelebrando el Officio Divino se guardaran de hablar ni reir ni hazer cosas desconvenientes (fol. 81) para quitar la devoción a los assistentes sob pena de ser rayado de sus gajes.

[8] Yten que Nuestro dicho Limosnero mayor mandará venir a su posada, cada Viernes si no tienen occupacion legitima a todos los Capellanes, Cantores y officiales de Nuestra dicha Capilla donde terâ Capitulo, y corregirâ a los que habran errado para que se emienden, y se la pena del que huviere errado fuere pecuniaria el dicho Nuestro Limosnero la mandará executar, y recevirlo en que fuere el delinquente condemnado para que despues se reparta entre todos los otros.

[9] Yten si alguno de los dichos Capellanes, Cantores y officiales de la dicha Nuestra Capilla se auzentaren de la corte sin su licenzia el dicho Limosnero avisará por el furrier de la Capilla a los Mayordomos y los de Nuestro Bureau para que el dicho tal sea rayado de sus gajes durante su auzencia.

[10] Yten que los Domingos de la Septuagessima, Sexagessima, Quinquagessima, Quadragessima (fol. 81[v]) el dia de la zeniza, los Domingos, Viernes y fiestas de Quaresma, y del Adviento, las fiestas de Nuestro Señor, y las de Nuestra Señora, los Lunes despues de Pascua, y Pentecostes, los dias de Sant Andres, San Pedro en Junio, Santiago, Dias de todos los Sanctos, [y] de los finados abrá sermon en Nuestra dicha Capilla sinó mandamos otra cosa.

[11] Yten que el Capellan Semanero se estará delante del Altar vestido de vna sobrepelliz quando huviere de encomenzar los Maytines, Visperas, Completas, o Vigilias, assim mesmo el que huviere de cantar la Epistola estarâ em pie de la parte del Altar que conviene, y las Lecciones, que se han de cantar a los Maytines se cantaran en vn facistol delante del Altar, y el o ellos, que los huviere de cantar sera vestido de vna sobrepelliz.

[12] Yten quando el Maestro de la Capilla estando en ella mandare cantar vn duo (fol. 82) o trio, a algun Cantor seran obligados de hazerlo sob pena de haver la correpcion que mereciere.

[13] Yten que de aqui adelante las Aleluyas se cantaran cada dia como en las fiestas grandes, y mandarâ el Maestro de Capilla cantarla[s] a los

Cantores a cada vno su dia, y que los dichos Cantores se pongan donde han de estar sin se mesclar los vnos con los otros, y han de obedezer al dicho Maestro en lo que tocca al cantar sob pena como arriva esta dicho.

[14] Yten mandamos que de aqui adellante el dicho Maestro acompañe los Cantorcicos desde su possada a la Capilla, y desde allá a su possada, y se tiene occupacion legitima, comette a alguna persona que les acompañe, y les dê tiempo desde la vna hasta las tres despues de medio dia.

Y las Visperas de fiestas desde la vna hasta las dos para estudiaren gramatica y no permita a los dichos Cantorcicos hir cantar (fol. 82^{v}) de casa en casa sob pena de perder su Officio.

[15] Yten que el dicho Maestro tenga cuidado de los dichos muchachos que esten limpiamente y bien tratados, y les haga comer y bever acostar y llevantar a las horas acostumbradas, y que conviene para la salud de ellos.

[16] Yten que el Maestro que les ha de enseñar Latin será obligado a hir cada dia vna vez a darles leccion en la posada del Maestro de Capilla.

[17] Yten mandamos que todos los sobredichos Capellanes, Cantores, y officiales de Nuestra dicha Capilla sean vestidos vna ves al año de paño negro ó chamelote para ropas y sayos de terciopelo, y mandaran hazer sus vestidos todos de vna forma y los Cantorcicos seran vestidos como han sido en tiempos passados. (fol. 83)

[18] Yten mandamos que todos los que recevieremos de aqui adelante, de qualquier calidad que sean las personas para servicio de Nuestra Capilla, entiendesse de Nuestros Estados de Flandes y habran de jurar en manos de Nuestro dicho Limosnero Mayor.

[19] Yten mandamos que el Maestro de Capilla, si mandare a algunos muchachos sacar, y llevar algun libro de canto o musica fuera de la Capilla, y si lo hicieren, que los Mozos de Capilla avisen luego al Limosnero para remediarlo sob pena de ser castigado.

[20] Yten mandamos que de aqui adelante ninguno mande tañer a Missa ó a Visperas sin primero avisar al dicho Limosnero si estubiere presente ó en su auzencia al Maestro de Capilla, y que el officio se haga al vso Romano, si de otra manera, por algun buen respeto no se mandase (fol. 83^{v}) otra cosa por el dicho Maestro, o dicho Limosnero.

[21] Yten mandamos que el dicho Maestro se esté en el Coro detras de los muchachos, y que todo lo que huviere menester para la necessidad de ellos lo habrá de comunicar, y dar a entender al dicho Limosnero para que quando quisiere dar sus partidas que el dicho Limosnero abrá de firmar se acuerda de ellas.

[22] Yten mandamos que el dicho Maestro tenga cuidado de ver y ordenar los libros de musica, y lo que se ha de cantar en el Officio Divino, y que los Cantores le obedescan sob pena de ser castigados.

[23] Y mandamos que todo lo sobredicho se declare publicamente a todos los de la Nuestra dicha Capilla, para que despues no digan no lo havian entendido, y mandamos al dicho Limosnero que haga que (fol. 84) todos los susodichos prometan de guardar y cumplir nuestros dichos mandatos.

[24] Yten mandamos que el Furrier de la dicha Capilla, este en la dicha Capilla antes de la hora del Officio Divino, para ver si los dichos Capellanes, Cantores, y officiales hazen lo que les está mandado a la entrada de la dicha Capilla, y si estando en el servicio Divino hicieren alguna derision o falta será obligado a avisar dello al dicho Limosnero.

APPENDIX 5

Musicians and Other Members of the Royal Chapels, 1556–December 1562[1]

I FLEMISH CHAPEL[2]

Name	*Office*	*Year* 1556[3] (June)	*c.*1557–8[4]	1558[5] (May–Dec.)	1559[6] (before Apr.)	1559[7] (May–Aug.)	1562[8] (May–Aug.)	1562[9] (Sept.–Dec.)
Capilla								
Odart de Bersaques	Limosnero mayor	x	(x)	[x]	(x)	?		
Valeran Haugonart	Secundo limosnero	x	x	[x]	x	?		
Pedro Paçeco	Gran Limosnero mayor						x	[x]
François de Rosimbos	Sumiller de oratorio	x	x	x	x	?		
Maximilian de Bergues	Sumiller de oratorio	x	x	x	x	?		
M. de Latour (La Torre)	Sumiller de oratorio						x	x
Nicolas Payen (d. 1559)	Maestro de capilla x	x	x	x	x			
Pierre de Manchicourt	Maestro de capilla					x	x	x
Flemish chaplains		(8)	(7–8)	(6–9)	(7–10)	(8–9)	(10)	(11)
Jacques Pannier	(Missas cantatas)	x	x	[x]	x			
Pierre Lorier	(Missas cantatas)	x	x	x	x	x		
Odart Eyze	(Missas cantatas)	x	x	x	x	x	x	x
Noël Rou (de Roy)	(Missas cantatas)	x	x	x	x	x		

Jacques Alardi	(Missas rezadas)	x	x	[x]	x			
Gérard Tol	(Missas rezadas)	x	x	[x]	x			
George Nepotis	(Missas rezadas)	x	(x)	[x]	(x)	[x]	x	x
Jacques Hoemans	Confessor del comun	x	x	x	x	x	x	x
Fredrich Billot	(Missas cantatas)			x	[x]	x		
Johan Bulteau	(Missas cantatas)			x	[x]	x	x	x
Louys Souguenet	(Missas cantatas)					x	x	x
Johan de la Oultre	(Missas cantatas)					x	x	x
Philippe Hervin*	(Missas cantatas)						x	x
Jan Carlier*	(Missas cantatas)						x	x
Grégoire Haynault*	(Missas cantatas)						x	x
Franchois le Maître*	(Missas cantatas)						x	x
Jan Mofflin	(Missas rezadas)							x
Flemish singers		(17)	(17)	(16–18)	(17–18)	(19)	(18–21)	(18–20)
Joan Bleeker		x	x	x	x	x	(x)	
Pierre Clouvin		x	x	x	x	x	(x)	(x)
Robert de la Porte		x	x	x	x	x		
Hans Utenhoven		x	x	x	x	x		
Adrian Valmaeker		x	x	[x]	x			
Mathias Van Loo		x	x	x	x	x	x	x
Charles Boursse		x	x	x	x	x		
Pierre de Hot		x	x	x	x	x		
Noël Tonnecken		x	x	[x]	x			
Jean Gérard		x	x	x	x	x	x	x

Name	*Office*	*Year* 1556 (June)	*c*.1557–8	1558 (May–Dec.)	1559 (before Apr.)	1559 (May–Aug.)	1562 (May–Aug.)	1562 (Sept.–Dec.)
Martin de Malines (Cloot)		x	x	x	x	x	x	x
Guillen (van) Cutzen		x	x	x	x			
Bauldoyn Pernoys		x	x	x	x	x	x	x
Pierre Brabant		x	x	x	x	x		
Jean Bertoul		x	x	x	x	x		
Robert de Saint-Martin		x	x	x	x	x		
Adrian Couvenhouven (Cabo)		x	x	x	x	x	(x)	(x)
François Lochemberghe				x	[x]	x	x	x
Jan de Nalines (Nalmes)						x	x	x
Lambert de Fléru						x	x	x
Géry Marchand						x	x	x
Bertrand Nicolay						x		
Jan Caudron*							x	x
Jan Boonen*							x	x
Guido Godefroy*							x	x
Guillaume Gadifer*							x	x
George Bontefleur*							x	x
Nicaise Houssart*							x	x
Jan Morel*							x	x
Nicolas H/Sautoir*							x	x
Nicolas Buys*							x	x
Gilles de Clermortier*							x	x

Flemish choirboys		(10)	(11)	(11)	(11)	(12)	(14–17)	(17)
Johannes Flory						x	x	x
Michael de Camerette						x	[x]	x
Anthonius Miles						x		
Brix Gandy						x	[x]	x
Christien de Byner						x	[x]	x
Hansken Van Brabant						x		
Liévin Vanloo						x		
Gaspar Lochemberghe						x	x	x
Michael de Baneye						x	x	x
Charlos Renart						x	x	x
Paul Van Cauvenhoven						x	x	x
Louys Van Burcheleon						x		
Jan de Brabant							x	x
Jan le Mayre							x	x
George de la Heele							x	x
Antonie Deyst							x	x
Anthonie Pevernaige							x	x
Pierre Maillart							x	x
Jan de la Vallée							x	x
David Patbru							x	x
Melchior Lohemberghe							x	x
Other officers								
Adrian Loef	Master of boys/ Latin master	x	x	x	x	x		
[replaced by François Simon in 1562]								

Name	*Office*	*Year* 1556 (June)	*c*.1557–8	1558 (May–Dec.)	1559 (before Apr.)	1559 (May–Aug.)	1562 (May–Aug.)	1562 (Sept.–Dec.)
Michel Boch	Organist	x	x	x	x	x	x	x
Ludolf Volemont	Organ tuner	x	x	x	x			
Hendrich Van Voerste	Organ tuner and blower					x	x	x
Corneille Zuane	Furrier	x						
Gregorio le Pesquier	Furrier		x	x	x	x		
Henry Martin	Moço de capilla /Furrier	x	x	x	x	x	x	x
François Simon	Moço de capilla	x	x	x	x	x		
	/Latin master						x	x
Pasquier Regnart	Moço de capilla						x	x
Pierre de Bablincourt	Moço de capilla						x	x
Mathias Manort (Maneel)	Moço de oratorio	x	[x]	[x]	[x]	x	x	x
François Loquemberg	Moço de oratorio	x						
George Pesqueur	Moço de limosna	x						
Pompeyo de Rusy	Copyist						x	x

II SPANISH CHAPEL

Name	*Office*	*Year* 1556[10] (Jan.–Apr.)	1556[11] (Sept.–Dec.)	*c.* 1557–8[12]	1562[13] (*c.* July)
Capilla					
Pedro de Castro (Bishop of Cuenca)	Capellan mayor	(x)	[x]	[x]	
[Gaspar de Zúñiga y Avellaneda (Archbishop of Santiago)[14]	Capellan mayor		x	(x?)]	
Lupercio de Quiñones	Limosnero mayor			x	
[Antón Bravo[15]	Sacristan mayor				x]
Hernando Enríquez	Sumiller de oratorio			x	
Alonso de Castro	Franciscan preacher	x			
Bartolomé de Miranda	Dominican preacher	x			
[(unnamed)	Receptor[16]				x]
Spanish Chaplains		(4–5)	[5]	(10–14)	(3)
Francisco de Portugalete		x	[x]	x	
Francisco de Barrio		x	[x]	x	x
Joan de Angulo		x	[x]	x	x
Diego Suárez		(x)	[x]	x	
Pero Sánchez de Arellano		x	[x]	x	
Dr Goz Mediano				x	

Name	*Office*	*Year* 1556 (Jan.–Apr.)	1556 (Sept.–Dec.)	*c*.1557–8	1562 (*c*. July)
Dr Arnedo				x	
Dr Torres				(x)	
Dr Andréz Pérez				(x)	
Dr Gorrionero				(x)	
Juan Sarmiento				(x)	
Cristóbal Bezerra				x	
Bartolomé Pérez				x	
Juan Gómez de Salazar				x	
Francisco López					x
Spanish singers		(13–16)	(10–17)	(14–17)	(15)
Juan del Rincón	tiple/confesseur del comun	(x)	(x)	(x)	x
Jerónimo de Talamantes	tiple	x	x	x	x
Ginés López	tiple	x	x	x	x
Melchior de Valdés	contraalto	(x)	(x)	x	x
Ginés Laynes	contraalto	(x)	(x)	x	x
Luys López de Garabatea	contraalto	x	x	x	x
Francisco de Prado	[contraalto]	x	(x)	x	x
Miguel Garçó	tenor	x	x	x	
Francisco Rodríguez	tenor	x	x	x	
Doroteo de Guevara	tenor	x	x	x	x

Pedro Gelós	tenor	x	x	x	x
Antón Serrano	tenor	x	(x)	x	x
Pedro de Salazar	contrabaxo	x	(x)	(x)	x
Nofre de Queralte	contrabaxo	x	x	x	[x]
Lázaro Velázquez	contrabaxo	x	x	x	x
Hernán Pérez de Salamanca	contrabaxo	x	(x)	(x)	
Antonio de Acosta	contraalto		x	x	x
Francisco López	(?)				x
Cristóbal Serrano	[tenor]				x
Spanish choirboys		(2–4)	(2–5)	(5)	(5)
Agustín de Cabezón		(x)	(x)	x	
Mateo Fernández		x	x	x	x
Francisco de Torres		x	(x)	x	
Bernaldo Monje		(x)	(x)	x	x
Juan López de Garavate[a]			x	x	x
Gaspar de Arratia					x
Francisco de la Torre					x
Musicians					
Antonio de Cabezón	Organist	(x)	(x)	(x)	x
Juan de Cabezón	Organist	x	x	x	x
Cristóbal de León	Organ tuner		x	x	x
Francisco de Soto	Músico de cámera		x		

Name	*Office*	*Year* 1556 (Jan.–Apr.)	1556 (Sept.–Dec.)	*c.*1557–8	1562 (*c.* July)
Other officers					
[unnamed]	Moço de capilla	x			
[unnamed]	Moço de capilla	x			
Alonso de Almarez	Moço de capilla			x	x
Juan de Arce (Arze)	Moço de capilla			x	x
Simón Rodríguez	Moço de capilla			x	
Francisco de Almaraz	Moço de capilla			x	x
Cristóbal Ruiz	Moço de capilla			x	
Juan de Quizedo	Moço de limosna			x	
Iñigo de Santacruz	Furrier			x	

1 The spellings of the names on this table are usually derived from the first source listed here in which they appear; these may vary considerably in presentation between the sources. Unfortunately, there are *lacunae* in the surviving royal chapel documents, which explains why some years are not represented on this table. Only the names of instrumentalists of 1556 are available in the secondary sources; these have been omitted in this table. For details, and the names of the trumpeters, drummers and players of the *vihuelas de arco* in 1556, see Anglés, *La música en la Corte de Carlos V*, pp. 139–40; Robledo, 'La música en la corte Madrileña', pp. 786–7 and 789; and Vander Straeten, *La Musique aux Pays-Bas*, vii, pp. 359–60.

Indications of membership in round brackets (x) denote absences from court and in square brackets [x] where a name is omitted in a document (which might also indicate absence).

2 * = 'Chantres venutz nuvellement de Flandres' (1561); Vander Straeten, *La Musique aux Pays-Bas*, viii, pp. 42–3.

3 Robledo, 'La música en la corte Madrileña', pp. 786–7, and Vander Straeten, *La Musique aux Pays-Bas*, vii, pp. 359–60.

4 Vigili Blanquet, 'La capilla musical', pp. 275–6.

5 Vander Straeten, *La Musique aux Pays-Bas*, viii, p. 16.

6 *Ibid.*, p. 25.

7 *Ibid.*, pp. 30–1. See also Robledo, 'La música en la corte Madrileña', pp. 788–90.

8 *Ibid.*, pp. 40–1, and Vigili Blanquet, 'La capilla musical', pp. 276–9.

9 Vander Straeten, *La Musique aux Pays-Bas*, viii, pp. 41–2.

10 Anglés, *La música en la Corte*, p. 137.

11 *Ibid.*, pp. 138–40, and Robledo, 'La música en la corte Madrileña', pp. 787–8.

12 Vigili Blanquet, 'La capilla musical', pp. 273–5.

13 *Ibid.*, pp. 277–9.

14 See above, n. 47.

15 Antón Bravo entered the Spanish *Capilla* at an unspecified date in 1559, remaining until his death in 1576 (E-Sag, Casas y Situos Reales, leg. 82). I would like to thank Luis Robledo for providing me with this information.

16 A *receptor* is mentioned in a document dating from 1562. See Barbieri papers 2, doc. 156[a].

Early Music History (2000) Volume 19. © *Cambridge University Press*
Printed in the United Kingdom

Gretchen Peters

URBAN MINSTRELS IN LATE MEDIEVAL SOUTHERN FRANCE: OPPORTUNITIES, STATUS AND PROFESSIONAL RELATIONSHIPS*

By piecing together fragments of diverse archival evidence, it is possible to document a large minstrel population in urban settings in late medieval southern France that was able to support itself through a multiplicity of freelance activities and complex working relationships. Information concerning the urban minstrel in medieval Europe is usually drawn from city accounts and contracts providing details concerning the duties, function and wages of civic musicians. In order to create a multi-dimensional image of the urban minstrel, however, a wide variety of archival sources needs to be explored. Such sources – accounts of confraternities, university statutes, city statutes, tax records, property listings, private notarial contracts, among others – have offered glimpses into aspects of the minstrel community that have tended to remain elusive. This essay first establishes the nature of freelance activities, which were central to the urban minstrel's livelihood. Second, the socio-economic status of minstrels will be investigated, to determine how successful musicians were at supporting themselves in

* I should like to thank Larry Gushee and Keith Polk for reading earlier versions of this article and generously offering valuable and detailed suggestions.

The following abbreviations will be used throughout:

ADB	Archives Départementales des Bouches-du-Rhône
ADH	Archives Départementales de la Haute-Garonne
ADV	Archives Départementales de Vaucluse
AMA	Archives Municipales d'Avignon
AMMa	Archives Municipales de Marseille
AMMo	Archives Municipales de Montpellier
AMO	Archives Municipales d'Orange
AMT	Archives Municipales de Toulouse

the medieval urban environment. Finally, professional relationships among minstrels, ranging from the broad professional organisation of the guild to individual legal agreements between minstrels, will be discussed.

This study focuses upon cities in south-central France, with an eastern boundary of Marseilles, located on the coast of the Mediterranean, and a western boundary of Toulouse, located on the Garonne River in the foothills of the Pyrenees. This was a highly urbanised region during the late Middle Ages, tied closely to commerce and trade on the Mediterranean Sea. Montpellier and Toulouse were the leading cities, both with estimated populations at their peak of 30–40,000 and both with a history of early powerful and independent city councils. Avignon, another prominent city, gained importance with the arrival of the papacy in the fourteenth century, and the large entourage that followed the pope resulted in a population estimated as high as 45,000 by the mid-fourteenth century. For this study, evidence has also been drawn from the archives of Marseilles (20–25,000), Aix-en-Provence (6,000) and Orange. All of these urban centres in south-central France reached their demographic peak in the mid-fourteenth century, and then were devastated by recurring epidemics, natural disasters and bad harvests. While this was an important urban area in the late Middle Ages, with its principal cities among the leading cities in Europe, until now its urban musical history has by and large remained unexplored.[1]

FREELANCE OPPORTUNITIES

City governments in southern France, as elsewhere in Europe, became important and regular sources of employment for musi-

[1] A few exceptional studies for southern France exist: L. Barthélemy, *Notice historique sur l'industrie des ménétriers* (Marseilles, 1886); P. Pansier, 'Les Débuts du théâtre à Avignon à la fin du XVe siècle', *Annales d'Avignon et du Comtat-Venaissin*, 6 (1919), pp. 5–52. While Andrew Tomasello's study concentrates on music of the papal chapels, it does include a section on music in the urban setting of Avignon; see *Music and Ritual at Papal Avignon, 1309–1403* (Ann Arbor, Mich., 1983). A recent work that provides an interesting sociological study of minstrels in France is L. Charles-Dominique, *Les Ménétriers français sous l'ancien régime* (Toulouse, 1994).

cians during the second half of the fourteenth century.[2] In Montpellier, for example, the city council employed a civic wind band with as many as five members, two trumpeters who performed from the central bell-tower and a public crier who played the trumpet, as well as other musicians on important holidays. In Toulouse, a civic wind band and a pair of trumpeters were also regularly on the payroll of the city. This was a secure source of income for many musicians, as these were annually contracted positions that were commonly held by individuals for as long as twenty to thirty years and remained in families for generations. Even in the smaller cities, such as Aix-en-Provence, Orange or Apt, where civic positions were limited to trumpeters, musicians were hired quite extensively by the city on an ad hoc basis.

Yet, with few exceptions, civic employment offered musicians in south-central France only a portion of a full-time income. While the salaries of official trumpeters and tower-musicians were comparable to estimated incomes of modest artisans, such as cobblers and candle-makers, members of civic wind bands appear to have made approximately one-fourth this amount in annual civic wages. In addition, a large percentage of professional musicians in south-central France do not appear to have received any civic support. Of the approximately 125 musicians who have been identified in the records of Montpellier between 1350 and 1450, fewer than one-half are known to have been employed by the city. In Toulouse, it also appears that the majority of minstrels working in town did not benefit from civic funds. Statutes for a minstrel's guild, dating from 1492, survive from Toulouse.[3] Of the fourteen minstrels listed as members, only three appear in city accounts from this time. The first three on the list, Petrus Audram, Bartholomeus Serda and Guillermus Tanus, were the members of the official civic wind band in the late fifteenth century. It appears that many minstrels did not directly benefit from the increasing civic patron-

[2] For details on civic patronage in southern France see G. Peters, 'Civic Subsidy and Musicians in Southern France during the Fourteenth and Fifteenth Centuries: A Comparison of Montpellier, Toulouse and Avignon', in F. Kisby (ed.), *Music and Musicians in Renaissance Cities, c.1350–c.1650* (Cambridge, forthcoming) and Peters, 'Secular Urban Musical Culture in Provence and Languedoc During the Late Middle Ages' (Ph.D. diss., University of Illinois at Urbana-Champaign, 1994).

[3] AMT, HH 66, fols. 433–438v and ADH, E 1318.

age of music in the late Middle Ages. To determine how these musicians supported themselves, it is necessary to explore beyond city accounts.

Important and comparatively well-documented non-municipal sources of employment for musicians were the numerous professional and charitable organisations. In Avignon, for example, at least 140 different charitable organisations have been identified from the twelfth through the sixteenth centuries.[4] A well-documented example is the confraternity of Notre-Dame de la Major in Avignon, for which two registers containing the confraternity's receipt of revenues, expenditures and lists of membership survive from the fourteenth and fifteenth centuries.[5] The confraternity of Notre-Dame de la Major was formed in the early fourteenth century by Italian merchants who immigrated to Avignon following the arrival of the papacy, though it was open to all types of professions and nationalities. Each year in August, the confraternity celebrated the Assumption of the Virgin Mary, for which musicians were regularly hired. As early as two months prior to this celebration, the confraternity would customarily contract one or two minstrels to locate and employ the desired number of musicians. At this time, an agreement would be made concerning the wages, and 'down payment' was offered to the musicians. For example, on 28 June 1389, the confraternity promised to pay the minstrel Bertrand Bernard and 'his fellow minstrels', who were to be twelve in number, a total of 16½ florins for the upcoming festival, and at this time Bertrand received a small sum as 'down payment'.[6] On 13 August, two days before the festival, another small sum was given to Bertrand, and on 16 August, a day after the

4 P. Pansier, 'Les Confréries à Avignon au XIVe siècle', *Annales d'Avignon*, 20 (1934), pp. 5–48, at p. 5.

5 ADV, Archives hospitalières d'Avignon, Majour, E-4 and E-5. Large portions of both registers are very difficult to read due to deterioration of both the paper and the ink.

6 ADV, Arch. hospitalières d'Avignon, Majour, E-4, fol. 375[v]: 'Item die xxviii iunii Bertrando Bernard ministerio pro se et suis sociis ministeriis pro arris soluctione festi proxime futuri quo tempore debent xii ministrerii et debent habere integros omnes xvi florinos cum dimidio/ et bene servire more solito/ in dicto festo et ante ut est consuetum de quibus habuit ipse Bertrandus pro arris duos florinos cum dimidio . . .' ('June 28, to Bertrando Bernard, minstrel, for himself and his fellow minstrels for down payment for the next festival, at which time they owe 12 minstrels and owe to all 16½ fl. and to serve well in the usual manner, in the said festival and before as is the custom, of which Bertrand himself had for a down payment 2½ fl.').

festival, final full payment to the musicians was recorded.[7] Each musician received approximately 1 florin for his participation in the festivities, which was comparable to the wages of musicians paid by the city of Avignon for local processions. In addition to wages, the confraternity regularly provided wine for the musicians on these occasions, a customary practice throughout this area and elsewhere.

The number of minstrels hired for this festival, which included trumpeters and other wind instrumentalists, ranged from seventeen in 1365 to ten during the first half of the fifteenth century. Throughout the first half of the fifteenth century, a distinction between minstrels ('menestriers') and trumpeters ('trompetas') commonly appears in the payment receipts; and on one occasion, a further distinction was made between 'trompas' and 'trompetas', implying the use of trumpets of different sizes.[8] Six trumpeters were consistently employed from 1438 to 1457; earlier there were fewer, reflecting the growing popularity in the fifteenth century of large trumpet ensembles. The instruments of the 'menestriers' are never specifically identified, though the occasional use of the verb 'cornare' indicates the typical use of wind instruments for outdoor processions.[9] Among these musicians was a small number of minstrels, often referred to as the 'bons menestriers', whose function was to accompany a silver statue of the Virgin Mary, the confraternity's patron saint, in a procession. The expenses for the celebration in 1416, for example, include payments to the 'good minstrels who accompanied "Nostra Dona" in the procession'.[10] These minstrels appear to have been, at least at times, provided with livery, as the confraternity paid tailors to make coats and hats for two minstrels.[11] Evidently, to serve the important function of accompanying the silver statue of their patron saint in the procession, the confraternity wanted musicians who were highly skilled and wore official livery, thus reflecting the power and wealth of the confraternity.

7 *Ibid.*: 'Item dicto Bertrando die xiii mensis Augusti pro parte sui salarii fl. i s. xii. Item dicto Bertrando die xvi mensis Augusti pro integra solutione sui salarii de festo proximo fl. xii s. xii'.

8 ADV, Archives hospitalières d'Avignon, E-5, fol. 84.

9 *Ibid.* E-4, fol. 465.

10 *Ibid.* E-5, fol. 139^{v}: 'als bons menestriers que an compaunhat nostra dona ala prosession i fl'.

11 *Ibid.*, fol. 160, 1419; fol. 530, 1446; fol. 684^{v}, 1454.

In Marseilles, the charitable order of the 'Hôpital St. Jacques-des-epées' also employed musicians for an annual celebration in honour of its patron saint. This organisation was part of a larger charitable order founded in Spain in 1200 to construct shelters for poor pilgrims who were travelling to the Holy Land. Three registers with the organisation's annual dues and expenses from the mid-fourteenth to the mid-fifteenth centuries include regular payments to 'the minstrels who made "la festa de moseyer Sant Jacme"' and specifically for 'the cost of their wine'.[12] In 1351, three 'cornamuza' players (meaning bagpipes or, more generally, reed players), two trumpeters, and one nakers player performed in the celebration, and in 1353 all four musicians hired for this celebration were identified as 'cornamuza' players.[13] Fifteenth-century records provide only isolated references to specific instruments, but the purchase of four pennons for 'tronbas' in 1412 or the payment in 1455 to 'las trombas' indicate the appearance of the popular trumpet ensemble.[14] In the second half of the fifteenth century, 'taborin' (pipe and tabor) players appear in these festivities, as they did in celebrations throughout southern France at this time.

Other charitable organisations in this region, including confraternities of carpenters, butchers and masons, had similar practices of music patronage. In Avignon, the confraternity of carpenters employed musicians for the elaborate annual procession for Rogations, specifically to accompany their official banners and figure of the Virgin Mary.[15] In Montpellier, the charitable organisation of butchers was accompanied by its 'joculatores' on Ascension Day in 1365, as the members processed through the city streets with their charitable contribution.[16] The masons of Montpellier in 1367 commissioned banners, which were to be decorated with pictures of hammers, for two trumpets and two 'cornamusis', the same type of ensemble that the city council of Montpellier

[12] ADB, Archives hospitalières de Marseilles, II H/E 7, p. 49, 1351: 'pagat als menetries que fero la festa de mosenyer Sant Jacme entre lur pres del vin, ii ll. v s'.; p. 81, 1352: 'Item donem als menestriers antre vin et autras cauzas l s'.

[13] *Ibid.*, p. 42, 1351 and p. 96, 1353.

[14] *Ibid.* II H/E 1, fol. 125; II H/E 2, unfoliated.

[15] ADV, Archives hospitalières d'Avignon, Fusterie, E-10, fol. 209.

[16] AMMo, BB 8, fol. 10.

employed at this time.[17] Finally, in Toulouse, the statutes of the minstrels' guild identify confraternities as an important source of employment.

This practice of charitable and professional organisations hiring musicians bears considerable resemblance to the customs of civic patronage of music at this time. Like civic musicians, the musicians hired by these organisations customarily displayed pennons with official emblems on their musical instruments, and at least on occasion wore livery, to reflect and enhance the organisation's importance within the urban community. These organisations employed wind players and trumpeters for processions, just as the cities did. When the records are more specific concerning the instruments, they indicate ensembles similar to those employed by the cities, such as the combination of trumpets, 'coramusas' and nakers in the second half of the fourteenth century, and the pipe and tabor later in the fifteenth century. If only a portion of the large number of charitable and professional organisations in these cities employed musicians for annual celebrations, they would have been an important and regular source of employment for musicians.

Another type of institution that hired musicians periodically for special celebrations was the university. The graduation ceremony for doctoral students at the University of Montpellier in the early fifteenth century, for example, was quite elaborate and involved musicians, evidently to the displeasure of university officials. A university statute at this time insists that the graduation ceremony for doctoral students be more modest: the students were not to ride on horses to Notre Dame-des-Tables, where the ceremony was held, and were not to be accompanied by trumpeters.[18] Similarly, at the University of Toulouse in the late fifteenth century, minstrels performed for the graduation festivities of doctoral students,

[17] *Ibid.* BB 10, fol. 5: 'Item et duos penones [*sic*] magnos pro tubis et duos penos pro cornamusis cum pictura martelli et borladura tinctatura bene et sufficienter' ('Two large pennons for trumpets and two pennons for bagpipes with paintings of hammers and borders dyed well and sufficiently').

[18] Conseil général des facultés de Montpellier, *Cartulaire de l'Université de Montpellier* (Montpellier, 1890), p. 318. 'Baccalarius doctorandus, pedes semper et sine equis et simpliciter sine tubis . . . vadat ad Ecclesiam' ('Students receiving a doctorate go to the church always on foot and without horses and simply, without trumpets').

as well as bachelor students.[19] For this type of event, as well as others, including weddings and meals for engagements, the minstrels had to turn over three deniers tournois to the minstrels' guild.

The activities of musicians when employed by individuals or when working independently, rather than when employed by institutions, are the most difficult to document. Of these, performing at weddings appears to have been a central source of employment for minstrels. The city of Montpellier frequently reissued ordinances throughout the thirteenth century, apparently without success, prohibiting 'jotglars', 'jotglaressas' and 'trompas' from attending weddings day or night, indirectly providing evidence of the participation of minstrels at such events. These ordinances appear among other restrictions placed upon festivities at weddings, such as a ban on torches that were not in lanterns or a limit of twenty people at a wedding banquet. A restriction in 1253, for example, states: 'We establish that neither a "jotglar", nor "jotglars", nor "jotglaressas", nor "trompas" will go to weddings in the day or at night, nor will a man give them clothes or other things for the occasion of a wedding.'[20] Playing at weddings continued to be an important source of income for musicians in the area two centuries later. The professional activity of minstrels most commonly cited in the guild statutes in Toulouse is weddings, and it also lists meals of engagement as a professional opportunity for minstrels. Finally, in an apprenticeship agreement between two trumpet players in Aix-en-Provence from 1444 the apprentice promised to accompany his master at weddings, along with processions on festive days and sounding the watch.

An ordinance in Montpellier from 1255 sought to limit the participation of musicians at festivities outside the home of brides prior to a wedding, seeming to allude to the popular custom known as a 'charivari' or 'a noisy sneer upon newlyweds' at their home involving dancing, drinking, costumes, as well as violence and

[19] ADH, E 1318: 'ung cascun menestrier et confrayre de ladita confreyria, que aura sonat en festa de doctor licenciat ou bachelier qui se feran en tholosa . . . pague et sia tengut de pagar a la dita confreyria tres diniers de tournes'.

[20] *Le Petit Thalamus de Montpellier*, ed. F. Pégat, E. Thomas and Dezmases (Montpellier, 1840), p. 147: 'Encaras establem que jotglar, ni jotglars, ni jotglaressas, ni trompas non anon a novias de jorns ni de nuegs, ni que lur done hom per occayzon del novi o de la novia vestirs ni autra cauza . . .'.

revenge.[21] It states, 'We establish that no "jotglars" henceforward will come nor ought to come to a house with a woman who is to be married, when it is closed, nor at night, open or secretly, with or without instruments or in another form. During the day he is able to come there to sing and to bring instruments or not; on the condition that he will have no trumpets.'[22] Charivaris were frequently directed towards unpopular people and marriages in France during the last centuries of the Middle Ages, and in late medieval Montpellier specifically the remarriage of a widow or widower often led to a charivari.[23] They continued during the late Middle Ages 'in spite of indignant protests against their appalling excesses launched by secular and ecclesiastical authorities'.[24]

City ordinances also place special restrictions on performing in city streets, implying that normally this was an accepted means by which musicians could help support themselves. In Marseilles, for example, an ordinance dating from 1341 prohibits musicians from 'singing with or without instruments' at night in the city under 'the penalty of 50 sous and of losing a coat and instrument'.[25] In 1381, the city council of Marseilles issued a deliberation concerning the appropriate behaviour of citizens in the light of the misfortunes of Queen Jeanne of Sicily, who was being held prisoner by Charles of Durazzo, her rival in Provence, and who would finally be assassinated in 1382. The deliberation states that temporarily women were not to wear jewels, nobody was to celebrate day or night, and that 'menestrers' and 'jogularors' could not play their instruments.[26]

[21] R. Bernheimer, *Wild Men in the Middle Ages: A Study in Art, Sentiment, and Demonology* (1952; repr. New York, 1970), p. 166.

[22] *Le Petit Thalamus*, p. 142, 'Item establem, et establem vedam, que neguns jotglars dayssi enan non vengon ni auzon venir a mayzon de novia, pueys que sera fermada, ni esser de nuegs, a prezen ni a rescostz, ab estrumens ni ses estrumen ni en autra forma. De jorns empero i puescon venir et esser e cantar e de portar ab estrumens e ses estrumens; empero trompas noy iaia.'

[23] N. Z. Davis, 'The Reasons of Misrule: Youth Groups and Charivaris in Sixteenth-Century France', *Past and Present*, 50 (1971), pp. 41–75, at p. 52; J. Baumel, *Histoire d'une seigneurie du Midi de la France*, ii (Montpellier, 1969–71), p. 395.

[24] Bernheimer, *Wild Men*, p. 66.

[25] AMMa, FF 165, fol. 2: 'non audeat de nocte per villam superiorem seu ante diem cantando cum instrumentis vel sine instrumentis sub pena L solidorum pro qualibet persona et vice qualibet et amissionis raube et instrumentorum'.

[26] *Ibid.* BB 28, fol. 79.

In addition to performing on streets, musicians probably found audiences in places of entertainment, such as taverns, inns and bathhouses. A few musicians in Montpellier and Avignon have been noted who owned inns and bathhouses. Simon Requier, who was a minstrel, tower-trumpeter and public crier in early fifteenth-century Montpellier, owned an 'old' and a 'new' bathhouse, appropriately situated near the 'Rue des bains'.[27] In Avignon, a minstrel Poncius Blaconi, who performed in processions during the 1430s for both the city and the confraternity of Notre-Dame de la Major, owned a bathhouse.[28] Another musician in Avignon, Brocardus de Campanino de Pavia, who was identified as a 'player of musical instruments' ('tactor instrumentorum musicorum') in numerous fourteenth-century records, owned many pieces of property, including an inn with a tavern.[29] While some bathhouses only served a utilitarian function, others were centres of entertainment where a person could receive a meal, hire a prostitute, or listen to music. Referring to medieval bathhouses, Jean Larmat writes: 'Most often, in medieval literature, the bath is an enjoyable pastime, even voluptuous, that one offers to his guest, to a friend, a recreation taken willingly in company.'[30] Paintings from the fifteenth century commonly depict musicians performing in bathhouses for men and women bathing together.[31] Confirming these literary descriptions and paintings, the statutes of the minstrels' guild in Toulouse dating from 1532 state that minstrels were not 'to play instruments in the houses of prostitution and other places of debauchery' at the penalty of 5 l., suggesting that this was not an uncommon occurrence in the fifteenth century.[32] Perhaps these musicians who owned bathhouses and an inn performed for their

[27] AMMo, Inventory 6, No. 248 (CC 580), fol. 148^{r-v}.

[28] ADV, 3 E 5/717, fols. 303–4.

[29] Brocardus 'owned as many as eight hotels from 1336 until 1354 when he acquired an inn with a tavern'; Tomasello, *Music and Ritual*, p. 30.

[30] 'Le plus souvent, dans la littérature médiévale, le bain est un passe-temps agréable, même voluptueux, que l'on offre à son hôte, à un ami, un divertissement pris volontiers en compagnie'; J. Larmat, 'Les Bains dans la littérature française du moyen âge', in *Les Soins de beauté: Moyen Age–début des temps modernes. Actes du IIIe Colloque international, Grasse (26–28 avril 1985)*, ed. D. Menjot (Nice, 1987), pp. 195–210, at p. 204.

[31] An example of a painting of a bathhouse scene with a musician from Germany and dating from 1470 is provided in E. Bowles, *Musikleben im 15. Jahrhundert* (Musikgeschichte in Bildern, III/8; Leipzig, 1977), pp. 150–1.

[32] Charles-Dominique, *Les Ménétriers français*, p. 64.

customers or arranged for their friends and colleagues to provide musical entertainment.

For large celebrations in honour of visiting nobility or other important events, official civic musicians held prominent and central roles, though other minstrels participated as well. The city chronicle of Montpellier, for example, provides a general description of festivities in 1392 extending for more than a week in honour of the birth of a son to Charles VI, involving 'diverse instruments and songs and dances' and 'many minstrels'. During these festivities, 'students made a large celebration for the entire day in front of the consulate and throughout the whole city, with dancing with minstrels and with large decorations and singing rhymed couplets'.[33] Another such occasion was in Orange in 1438 when the entry of the Princess of Orange was honoured by the performance of the 'moresca', involving a dozen bells, probably attached to the dancers' costumes, and a minstrel and his 'compagnons' from Laudun.[34] Smaller cities, such as Orange, did not have the funds to employ an ensemble of minstrels regularly, so for these special events minstrels from the surrounding area were hired. This was the case in Apt for a celebration of Corpus Christi in 1370, when minstrels came from the nearby towns of Les Baux, Saignon and Viens.[35] In addition, it appears that on occasion minstrels were hired by local nobility. In the autumn of 1432, the city council of Montpellier employed five trumpeters for 'the celebration of the Miracles', an important local holiday, to replace the civic minstrels who were employed at this time by the Seigneur of Clermont.[36]

In addition to supporting themselves as performers, some musicians added to their income through teaching. Unusually direct and detailed evidence of this professional opportunity is a notar-

[33] *Petit Thalamus*, pp. 421–3, 'amb estrumens diverses et am cansos et am danssas' and 'am motz menestriers'; 'los estudians feron gran festa tot lo jorn al plan del cossolat e per tota la vila, danssans am menestriers et am grans paramens e cantan coblas rimadas'.

[34] AMO, CC 360, fol. 30 and CC 363, fols. 38^{v}–39.

[35] Abbé Rose, *Études historiques et religieuses sur le XIVe siècle, ou Tableau de l'Église d'Apt sous la Cour Papale d'Avignon* (Avignon, 1842), p. 638.

[36] AMMo, Inventory 9, No. 712 (CC 712), fol. 118: 'Item a ii setembre per v trompetas que loget per vegolar als myracles per default dels menestryers que eron anast a moss de clarmont' ('Payment on 2 September for five trumpeters who were hired for the vigil of the miracles for the lack of minstrels who had gone to Mr de Clermont').

ial contract from Avignon dating from 1449, which formalises an agreement for private music lessons between two musicians.[37] The teacher, identified as a Jewish cloth dyer, promises to teach the student, identified as a student at the University of Avignon, specified songs and dances on either the citara or harp. The fee was set at 5 florins, evidently regardless of the number of lessons the student required, which was a substantial fee in comparison with the wages of musicians when performing at civic processions and banquets in Avignon. Another notarial contract dated 21 September 1444 from Aix-en-Provence documents a five-year apprenticeship agreement between two trumpeters; and while the master does not specifically receive monetary compensation from his apprentice, he does benefit from his services.[38]

Some musicians, specifically wind players, appear to have built their own instruments or those of their colleagues, perhaps providing another source of revenue. A tower-trumpeter in Montpellier, Petrus Ayle, was one such musician, as his city contract includes a special stipulation that he was not to make trumpets while on duty.[39] Consistent with this stipulation, Petrus is identified in this contract as a turner ('tornyer') or someone who produced round shapes in wood or metal, particularly with a lathe. Three other minstrels in Montpellier, including Petrus' father, Johan Ayle, have also been identified as turners.[40]

Finally, professional urban musicians in southern France frequently supplemented their income through non-musical sources. The vast majority of musicians owned rural pieces of property, including vineyards, fields, olive groves, orchards and gardens, and evidently did some farming. A number of musicians also owned both urban and rural property that they let to tenants. Professional

[37] ADV, 3 E 8/714, fols. 135v–136r. A transcription and discussion of the document appears in Pansier, 'Les Débuts du théâtre', pp. 40–2. Also see Peters, 'Urban Musical Culture in Late Medieval Southern France: Evidence from Private Notarial Contracts', *Early Music*, 25 (1997), pp. 403–10, at pp. 408–9.

[38] ADB, Dépôt annexe d'Aix-en-Provence, 302 E 282, unfoliated.

[39] AMMo, BB 36, fol. 55v: 'recolligere aliquos fayditos nec tubicinatores docere seu ibi trompam facere' ('not to entertain others, nor to teach other trumpeters, nor to make a trumpet while there').

[40] AMMo, BB 36, fol. 55v; ADH, II E 95/446, fol. 12v; AMMo, Inventory 6, No. 269 (CC 597), fol. 164v. The construction of string instruments seems to have required a greater degree of specialisation than that of wind instruments, as makers of string instruments, particularly harps, have been identified in these cities during this period.

musicians have also been identified in these cities who owned and operated a stall for selling fish, and as previously noted, three bath-houses and an inn with a tavern.

Urban minstrels in southern France appear to have performed in a variety of settings to support themselves and their families, and did not rely solely upon the city or any other single source of income. The nature of their employment ranged from being contracted months in advance for specific duties and wages to playing on the streets in the hopes of drawing an audience and some remuneration. For example, Poncius Blaconi in Avignon was hired by the city and the confraternity of Notre-Dame de la Major, and in addition owned a bathhouse; Monnetus Monneri, a city trumpeter in Aix-en-Provence, 'sounded the watch' from a bell-tower, performed at festivals and weddings, and taught the trumpet.

SOCIO-ECONOMIC STATUS

Determining how freelance minstrels fared economically in the urban environment is a difficult task. The best-known image of the medieval minstrel, which has frequently appeared in literature from the past two centuries, is one of the itinerant social outcast without basic rights of citizenship, who barely pieced together a paltry existence. As John Southworth writes in his recent book, *The English Medieval Minstrel*, 'It is not just that the status of the minstrel was low; for very many of his contemporaries, he was altogether beyond the pale of social acceptance. In this respect, he was worse off than a serf; if the serf occupied the lowest place in the medieval hierarchy, the minstrel had no place at all.'[41] The diversity within this body of musicians in the Middle Ages, however, from itinerant outcasts to the wealthy and respected town musicians, demands that any discussion of the socio-economic status of medieval minstrels address specific sub-groups. In addition, the dramatic change of status within the profession of minstrelsy by the end of the Middle Ages, connected with the rise of civic patronage, demands that any discussion address specific time periods. In much of the literature considering the socio-economic

[41] J. Southworth, *The English Medieval Minstrel* (Woodbridge, 1989), pp. 4–5.

status of musicians, adequate consideration has not been given to the diversity within this population nor to any change in status throughout the period.[42]

Through tax records, property listings, and other private contracts, such as wills, it has been possible to determine how many urban musicians fared in southern France, particularly Montpellier, in the late fourteenth and fifteenth centuries. These types of civic records yield insight only into the permanent residents of the city and do not concern the minstrels who were passing through or residing in the city for a short period of time. In Montpellier a substantial percentage (20%) of the known minstrel population has been identified in either tax records and *compoix*, or property listings compiled for tax purposes.[43] Based on these records, musicians in Montpellier were generally members of the lower and middle classes, though significant variation existed. For example, in tax records of 1382, the tax bracket of eleven musicians, that is the percentage of taxpayers whose wealth was at or below that level, ranged from 22 to 90 per cent: while approximately one-half the musicians were in the bottom one-third tax bracket, three were in the top one-fifth. (The taxable wealth of each of these musicians and their tax bracket is provided in Table 1.) In the *compoix* dating from 1384 to 1449, manifests, or declarations of individuals' property, of twelve musicians have been identified which enumerate real estate piece by piece and estimate the personal estate in a lump sum.[44] The manifests of these musicians present a consistent economic picture with the earlier tax

[42] The following offer some of the most extensive and valuable discussions on the social position of professional musicians within medieval society: W. Salmen, *Der fahrende Musiker im europäischen Mittelalter* (Kassel, 1960); S. Zak, *Musik als "Ehr und Zier" im mittelalterlichen Reich* (Neuss, 1979); H. Schwab, 'The Social Status of the Town Musician', in *The Social Status of the Professional Musician from the Middle Ages to the Nineteenth Century* (Sociology of Music, ed. W. Salmen, 1; New York, 1983), pp. 31–59; R. Strohm, *Music in Late Medieval Bruges* (Oxford, 1985); Charles-Dominique, *Les Ménétriers français*.

[43] Unlike in German cities, civic musicians do not appear to have been exempt from paying taxes, even though certain members of the municipal personnel were exempt. The only evidence that has been located for this practice dates from significantly later; an official 'aulboys' of the city in 1574 was exempt from paying taxes specifically because of his employment. M. Oudot de Dainville, *Archives de Montpellier: inventaires et documents*, viii (Montpellier, 1943), p. 12.

[44] AMMo, Inv. 6, No. 240 (CC568), fols. 15 and 55^{v}–56; No. 244 (CC 573), fol. 84; No. 248 (CC580), fol. 148^{r-v}; No. 249 (CC 579), fols. 105^{r-v}, 133 and 163; No. 250 (CC 577), fol. 80; No. 252 (CC 581), fols. 66–7; No. 257 (CC 586), fols. 81^{v}–82; No. 262 (CC591), fols. 86^{v}, 105 and 139; No. 280, fol. 46^{r-v}.

Table 1 *Taxable wealth and tax bracket for musicians in tax records of 1382*

Musician	*Taxable wealth (livres)*	*Tax bracket (%)*
Duran Tacau	10	22
Miqualet	15	25
P. Floret	20	34
Posset	20	34
Carpin	20	34
Tibaut	50	58
Robert	60	62
Hugon la Crida	103	73
Mondo	235	84
Martin Malaret	300	87
Johan Mota	370	90

SOURCES: AMMo, Inv. 11, No. 4, fols. 46, 95^{v}, 96, 97^{v}, 98; No. 5, fols. 4, 5, 8, 104, 107; No. 6, fol. 107.

records; considerable variation in economic status continued to exist between musicians, though generally they were part of the lower and middle economic classes. While one-half the musicians could be classified as poor, one-third appear to have had quite comfortable lifestyles.[45] One of the wealthier musicians, a trumpeter who served as a civic minstrel in the mid-fourteenth century, even had a city block, or *irla*, named in his honour, the 'Irla de Peire Bonet trompaire', a privilege generally reserved for one of the wealthiest individuals of the block. The majority of musicians tended to be in the same economic bracket as labourers, servants, small artisans and minor civic employees, such as messengers and squires, while the wealthier musicians were among grocers, merchants of barley, butchers, fishmongers, retailers and notaries.

The types of property owned by musicians were typical of citizens in Montpellier at this time. (See Table 2 for the property listed in the manifests of three musicians.) The urban property owned by musicians consisted primarily of homes, with over 75 per

[45] Two recent socio-economic studies of late medieval Montpellier are based on the *compoix* and provide a context in which to interpret the wealth of the musicians: A.-C. Marin-Rambier, 'Montpellier à la fin du moyen âge d'après les compoix (1380–1450)', *École nationale des chartes, Positions des thèses* (1980), pp. 119–28 and M. Prieur, 'Le Quartier Sainte-Anne à Montpellier au XVème siècle à travers les compoix' (Mémoire de maîtrise d'histoire: Université Paul Valery, 1983).

Table 2 *Property of select musicians from Montpellier*

Musician	*Date*	*Property*	*Value (livres and sous)*
Peire Bonet	1384	home	8
		home	10
		home	12
		home	30
		field and vineyard (3 ca.)	34
		vineyard (5 cart.)	12
		vineyard (1 ca.)	16
		vineyard (1 ca.)	12
		vineyard (2 ca.)	12
		vineyard (5 cart.)	12
		vineyard	8
		vineyard	20
		vineyard	13
		field (9 cart.)	20
		field	20
		field (1 ca.)	8
		fallow field	4
		enclosure	2
		boat ('vaissel')	12
		2 fireplaces ('ares')	10
		?	52
		TOTAL	**327**
Simon Requier	1435	new bathhouse	200
		old bathhouse	100
		vineyard (2 ca.)	6
		vineyard (5 cart.)	4.5
		vineyard (5 cart.)	4.5
		vineyard (1 ca.)	3
		personal estate	25
		TOTAL	**342.10**
Durand de la Vinha	1435	home	65
		small farm or cottage	6
		young vineyard (10 cart.)	7.10
		young vineyard (3 cart.)	2.5
		vineyard (2 ca.)	6
		old vineyard (1 ca.)	3
		field (2 ca.)	6
		field (2 ca.)	6
		fallow field (1 ca.)	3
		orchard	10
		orchard	6
		personal estate	40
		TOTAL	**160.15**

ca.= cartayrada = 394 square metres; cart. = carton = 102 square metres

SOURCES: AMMo, Inv. 6, No. 240 (CC568), fols. 55^{v}–56; No. 248 (CC580), fol. 148^{r-v}; No. 252 (CC581), fols. 66–7.

cent of the musicians in the *compoix* owning at least one home. Other urban property of musicians included the two bathhouses mentioned earlier, and a commercial table for the purpose of selling fish. Rural land constituted a major portion of the wealth of citizens of Montpellier; all but one of the musicians owned land outside the city walls, with vineyards and fields being the most common, though other types include olive groves, orchards and gardens.

The economic diversity among musicians was not unusual, as such diversity of wealth has been noted within all the professions of Montpellier at this time. The wealthiest musicians in town tended to be those regularly employed by the city. The wages that a musician received from the city, however, do not account for the economic disparity between civic and non-civic musicians, as these wages, except for those of the tower-trumpeters, constituted only a small portion of a total annual income. The wages of the tower-trumpeters were comparable to those of modest artisans, such as cobblers, candle-makers, butchers, millers and weavers. The economic disparity between civic and non-civic musicians can most likely be explained either by the exposure and status of a civic position creating a greater number of professional opportunities for a musician, or by the city hiring the most highly skilled musicians, who would have naturally acquired more jobs. A civic position did not guarantee a musician a higher economic status, however, as some of the civic employees were among the poorest musicians in town. While elsewhere in Europe trumpeters enjoyed special privileges and higher pay, no consistent economic distinction between trumpeters and other types of instrumentalists is evident in civic salaries or tax records in Montpellier.

During the late fourteenth century in Montpellier, at least twelve musicians lived in the adjoining quarters of Ste Anne and St Paul, clustered on the street near the city wall or near the Rue St Guilhem, a main street of town separating these two quarters.[46]

[46] AMMo, Inv. 11, No. 4, fols. 46, 95^{v}, 96, 97^{v} and 98; No. 5, fols. 4, 5 and 8; Inv. 9, No. 852, fols. 76 and 107. ADH, II E 95/404, fols. 40–1; II E 95/440, fols. 16^{v}, 17, 18^{v}, 19^{v}.

(See Figure 1.)[47] In contrast to these quarters, the residences of only a few musicians have been noted at this time throughout the rest of the city. In the first half of the fifteenth century, the residences of musicians seem to have been more evenly distributed throughout the city, though the highest percentage of musicians continued to live in the quarters of St Paul and, particularly, Ste Anne. St Paul and Ste Anne were respectively third and fourth in overall wealth among the seven quarters of town. Within these two quarters, the musicians tended to live in the centre or back near the city walls, which were areas economically in the middle or slightly below. The three most common professions represented in these areas of the town were those of the butchers, the labourers and the minstrels themselves, with other frequently represented professions being those of other artisan trades: the tailors, bakers, cobblers and fishmongers.

The musicians of Montpellier were not unique in their tendency to live in one area of town near their colleagues. By the end of the twelfth century in Montpellier, as in other important cities in Languedoc, members of a profession tended to congregate in particular streets and quarters, and areas in Montpellier had become associated with specific professions.[48] The tendency for musicians to live in this one area of town might have been related to professional opportunities. First, this congregation of musicians would have provided a central location for a person to go who wished to hire a musician, perhaps serving a similar function as the 'Rue aus jongleurs' in late medieval Paris. In addition, various sources of employment might have been available in this area for musicians, including a high concentration of hotels located near the two main entrances into St Paul and Ste Anne, houses of prostitution situated outside the walls of St Paul, and numerous bathhouses along the 'Rue des Bains'. Finally, this area was relatively close to the consulate, the meeting place of the city council, and the central church of Notre-Dame-des-Tables, where the civic wind band and tower-trumpeters were frequently required to perform.

[47] The map has been drawn from L. Guiraud, *Recherches topographiques sur Montpellier au moyen âge: formation de la ville, ses enceintes successives, ses rues, ses monuments, etc.* (Montpellier, 1895); also published in *Mémoires de la Société archéologique de Montpellier*, 2nd ser., 1 (1899), pp. 89–335.

[48] A. Gouron, *La Réglementation des métiers en Languedoc au moyen âge* (Paris, 1958), pp. 69 and 115.

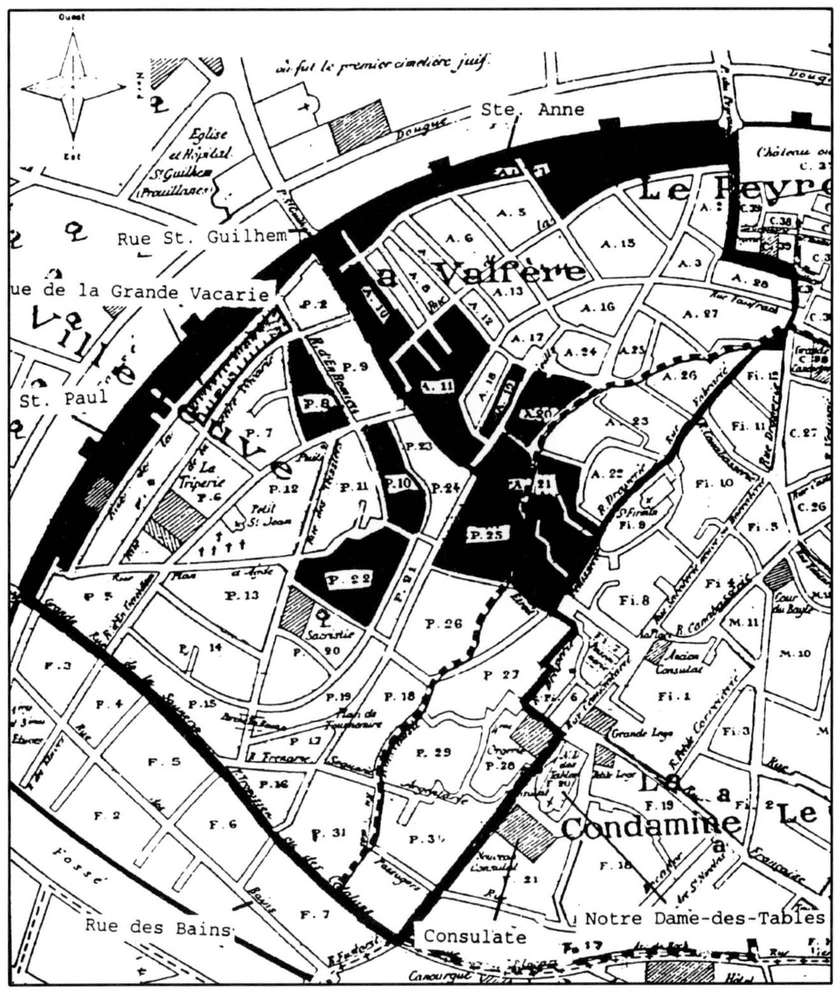

Figure 1 *Irlas* with musicians in the quarters of Ste Anne and St Paul (after Guiraud, *Recherches topographiques sur Montpellier*)

While it has been well established that the late medieval instrumental world was international in character, and specifically that by the beginning of the fifteenth century instrumentalists from the Low Countries and particularly Germany were prominent elsewhere in Europe, generally only a small number of musicians from outside this region have been identified. Many minstrels have been identified as stable, even life-long members of their communities with parents and other relatives, who tended to be modest artisans, including farmers, weavers, butchers, cloth-makers and musicians, also from the area. The talents of skilled foreigners, however, were sought on occasion. For example, in Montpellier in 1403, a 'menestrer' from Tournai was offered a tax exemption on his personal estate for five years for settling in Montpellier and later became a member of the civic wind band.[49] In 1453, the city council of Toulouse sent a representative 'to secure three "companhos menestriers" in Paris to come to serve the city council'.[50] The three minstrels were to be compensated for their expenses and interest in coming to speak with the city council of Toulouse. Unfortunately, as this document is only a list of expenses accrued on the trip, no information is provided as to why they were brought to Toulouse or what occurred during their meeting with the city council. Based on the accounts of the city, the ensemble from Paris did not replace the current personnel of the civic wind band, who were all from a single family.

Not surprisingly, however, the city in south-central France that appears to have had the largest number of foreign minstrels was the extremely cosmopolitan Avignon. Over 25 per cent of the minstrels identified in Avignon have been documented as foreigners, particularly from Italy, but also Germany and northern France. In 1378, when Pope Gregory XI ordered the 'Liber Divisionis' to determine the legal status of inhabitants of Avignon, three of the five minstrels on this list identified themselves as courtiers, rather than as citizens, meaning that they immigrated to Avignon specifically on account of the papal court.[51] Italian and German minstrels have been identified among the members of the confraternity of Notre-Dame de la Major, including a Guiqardo Franco di Parenca, a Guillo de Rens (Reims), and an Angelin de Francfort. Other foreign musicians in Avignon in the second half of the fourteenth and early fifteenth century records include the Brocardus

[49] AMMo, BB 36, fol. 7.

[50] AMT, CC 2333, No. 7, 'sercar tres companhos menestriers a parrias per venir servir mes d senhos de capitol'.

[51] Vatican Archives, Registra Avenionensia 204, fols. 428–507, 'Liber Divisionis Cortesianorum et Civium Romane curie et civitatis Avinionis', 1378.

de Campanino de Pavia 'tactor instrumentorum musicorum' from northern Italy mentioned earlier, a Johannes de Bray from northern France, a Siuerino de Alamania from Germany and a Mosse de Lisbonne from Portugal. Contributing to an international instrumental scene in late medieval Avignon were the frequent visits of nobility with minstrels in their entourage, some of whom were the most sought after instrumentalists in Europe and came from German lands. Papal accounts from the fourteenth century include payments to the minstrels of the dukes of Normandy, Bourbon, Burgundy, Brunswick and Anjou, as well as those of Prince of Achaia, the Duke of Brunswick and the Count of Geneva, among others. Other examples include a Pontius de Francafort de Alamania who accompanied the Viscount of Turenne to Avignon in 1371 and three German 'ioculatores' who received a special gift from Clement VII in 1383.[52]

From this international musical setting, skilled instrumentalists emerged who found employment in courts throughout Europe. At the court of Aragon in the early 1390s, among the numerous minstrels from northern Europe was a 'Johanni dAvinyo'.[53] In the early fifteenth century, another minstrel from Avignon was highly sought after and appears to have worked in a number of the major European courts. A 'Jean d'Avignon' appears among the royal French minstrels in 1416, a 'Johannes de Avignione' is paid by the Duke of Savoy in June of 1424, and in July of that year a 'Giovanni d'Avignon', identified as a 'piffaro', appears at the court of Ferrara.[54] When Giovanni was brought to Ferrara, in addition to his salary he was offered a house and court stable privileges and 'word was passed that he was to be well treated because he had been sought in France for two years'.[55] In 1437, a 'Giovanni d'Avignon piffaro' again appears in the records of Ferrara, though his activity for the thirteen intervening years is unknown, if indeed it is the same man.

[52] Tomasello, *Music and Ritual*, pp. 24 and 166.

[53] H. Anglès, 'Cantors und Ministrers in den Diensten der Könige von Katalonien-Aragonien im 14. Jahrhundert', in *Bericht über den Musikwissenschaftlichen Kongress in Basel* (Leipzig, 1925), pp. 56–66, at p. 64.

[54] C. Wright, *Music at the Court of Burgundy, 1364–1419: A Documentary History* (Henryville, Pa., 1979), p. 49. R. Bradley, 'Musical Life and Culture at Savoy, 1420–1450' (Ph.D. diss., City University of New York, 1992), p. 356.

[55] L. Lockwood, *Music in Renaissance Ferrara, 1400–1505* (Cambridge, Mass., 1984), p. 17.

More evidence for Avignon's vital instrumental culture has been cited by Frank D'Accone in his book on music in Siena. In June of 1446 a 'maestro Garino of Avignon' received an invitation from the city of Siena which read, 'Having learned of your talents and of your mastery of wind instruments, and desirous of having you in our service, we have, together with our colleagues, nominated you and two other pifferi and a trombone, whom you will choose, for a lifetime [appointment in our Palace]. . .'.[56] Garino accepted the invitation and brought with him to Siena two pifferi, Germano and Ferrino de Francia, and a trombonist, Giovanni de Alamannia. Less than a year later, only two of the four musicians remained in Siena: Garino and Germano had overstayed a two-month leave to go to France and were fired. While the other three have not been identified in the city records of Avignon, it is possible that the leader of the wind band, 'Garino', was a 'Garinus Bornheti' who appears in city records of Avignon from 1449 through 1458. Perhaps after a brief stay in Siena, Garinus returned to Avignon where he and 'his associates' were frequently hired by the city for local celebrations, attesting to the high quality of instrumental music in this city.[57]

PROFESSIONAL RELATIONSHIPS

In at least the two principal cities of late medieval southern France, Montpellier and Toulouse, a professional guild of minstrels existed. By at least 1353, the minstrels of Montpellier had formed a professional guild, only three decades after that in Paris. Registers from the second half of the fourteenth and the fifteenth centuries record the officers of the different professional guilds, who were identified as 'consuls des métiers'. For each year from 1353 to 1393, again from 1412 to 1422, and then sporadically throughout the fifteenth century, the officers of the minstrel's

[56] F. A. D'Accone, *The Civic Muse: Music and Musicians in Siena during the Middle Ages and the Renaissance* (Chicago, 1997), p. 522.

[57] For example, for the procession of Rogations in 1449, payment was made to 'Petro Peyroni et Garino Borheti mimis tam pro se et pro sociis suis . . . in associando processione generali Rogationum . . . cum suis chalamelis sive instrumentis festivando et fistulando': AMA, CC 363, Mandat 192. In 1467 the city of Siena again hired a minstrel, trombonist Petro Tristano de Valenza, from a southern French city, Valence. D'Accone, *The Civic Muse*, p. 792.

guild are recorded.[58] For the first three years, 1353–5, not only the name of the minstrels is identified, but the instrument he played as well. For each of these years, there was a combination of trumpeters, 'cornamuse' players and percussionists ('nacharayre' and 'taboroyayre'), suggesting a concern for diverse instrumental representation. In the fifteenth century, officers represented different categories of musicians. For most of this century, until 1472, one officer was selected to represent the 'menestriers' and one for the 'trompayres'; an additional officer appears during the last decades of the century to represent the 'taborins'. The only reference to soft instrumentalists among these officers is to a lute player in 1477 and a rebec player in 1490, raising the question whether they had lower status within the guild, or even whether they were not a common element of the guild. Throughout this 150-year period, officers were not limited to city-employed musicians, as many of these officers never appear on the city's payroll. The members of the civic wind band, however, do appear to have served more frequently. For example, in the second half of the fourteenth century, civic musicians served as an officer every three to five years.

Further evidence of the profession's organisation and prominence in Montpellier is the participation of musicians throughout the fifteenth century in the annual custom on Ascension Day of the distribution of bread contributed by the city council and the different professions to those in need. The amount of bread donated by a profession was related to its size and social prominence. In 1416 when the musicians, identified as 'menestriers' and 'les trompayres', contributed seventy-one loaves, the city council donated 1,000 loaves, the notaries donated 200, the tailors donated 100, the dyers donated eighty, and the hat makers and the crossbowmen each donated twenty.[59] (See Table 3 for the number of loaves donated by musicians throughout the fifteenth century, as well as the manner in which the musicians were identified.)

Without a set of statutes, it is impossible to determine the nature of the guild in Montpellier, whether it was concerned with professional issues or whether it primarily addressed the social

[58] AMMo, Inv. 6, 'Regestre des senhors consoulz et curials de la villa de Montpelier'; GG 1–16, 'Livres des consuls des métiers'.

[59] AMMo, GG 1–16, 'Livres des consuls des métiers', 1416–96.

Table 3 *Number of loaves of bread donated to charity by musicians in Montpellier*

Date	*Categories of musicians*	*Number of loaves*
1416	Menestriers	40
	Les Trompayres	31
1444	Menestriers and Trompayres	40
1460	Lo haultz menestriers	16
	Trompayres	20
1472	Menestriers et trompetas	20
1477	Los autz menestriers	12
	Trompetas et taborins	20
1479	Los menestriers	32
1481	Menestriers	32
1482	Menestriers	34
1484	Menestriers	25
1485	Menestriers	25
1486	Menestriers del consolat	12
	Los autres menestriers qui sont trompetes et taborins	24
1489	Menestriers del consolat	12
	Les autres menestriers qui sont trompetes et taborins	25
1490	Menestriers del consolat	12
	Los autres menestriers qui sont trompetes et taborins	20
1491	Menestriers del consolat	12
	Les autres menestriers qui sont trompetes et taborins	25
1495	Menestriers et trompetes	25
	Aultz menestriers	12
1496	Los trompetas	20
	Los aux menestries	12
	Los taborins	24

welfare of its members. Other sources from Montpellier do reveal a concern among minstrels for the well-being of their colleagues. In the wills of minstrels and their relatives in Montpellier, which frequently include bequests of money and clothing to colleagues or their families, a sense of responsibility for the welfare of their colleagues is evident.[60] A wife of a civic minstrel of Montpellier specified that she was to be buried at another minstrel's grave site and appointed him as the executor of her will, a function given

[60] ADH, II E 95/436, fol. 36^{r-v}, 1411; II E 95/414, fols. 63^{v}–65, 1420.

only to a person in whom the testator had full confidence.[61] Describing the relationship between executor and testator, Louis de Charrin, in his study on the wills in Montpellier during the Middle Ages, writes: 'In general the testator chose two or three friends in whom he had full confidence, very often people of the same craft or of the same profession . . .'.[62] In addition, a notarial contract from 1421 documents the donation of a vineyard by one of the wealthier civic minstrels of Montpellier to one of his poorer colleagues.[63] Further legal interactions between minstrels, involving selling property to one another and serving as witnesses for each other's various legal contracts, suggest a close minstrel community.

For Toulouse, a set of statutes for a minstrel's guild exists from 1492.[64] As is customary in professional guilds at this time, the minstrels of Toulouse identify their patron saint, in this case the Virgin Mary, and establish an annual celebration in her honour at the church in the Convent of the Carmelites. Many of the statutes reflect the important confraternal function of caring for fellow colleagues, including helping in the burial and celebration of mass on the occasion of a minstrel's death, and special considerations for minstrels who fall ill or become destitute. Another important concern is to ensure honesty within the profession, insisting that minstrels faithfully fulfil all obligations and never treat their partners dishonestly. To control competition, an entry fee is placed upon all foreign minstrels arriving in town and requires them to present themselves to the officers of the guild before performing for money. Unlike the statutes from Paris dating from 1407, no stipulations are made as to the conditions of admittance into the guild, including requirements of serving as an apprentice.

Even in the much smaller town of Marseilles, at least some cus-

61 ADH, II E 95/414, fols. 56v–57v, 1420.

62 'En général le testateur choissisait deux ou trois amis en qui il avait pleine confiance, très souvent des gens du même métier ou de la même profession . . .'; L. de Charrin, *Les Testatments de la région de Montpellier au moyen âge* (Ambilly, 1961), p. 125.

63 ADH, II E 95/415, fol. 94.

64 AMT, HH 66, fols. 433–438v and ADH, E 1318. For a detailed discussion of this set of statutes, see Charles-Dominique, *Les Ménétriers français*. For a discussion on the formation of minstrel guilds, particularly in Paris, see K. B. Slocum, 'Confrérie, Bruderschaft and Guild: The Formation of Musicians' Fraternal Organisations in Thirteenth- and Fourteenth-Century Europe', *Early Music History*, 14 (1995), pp. 257–74.

toms of a professional guild were in place. For example, the common custom and obligation of attending and assisting in funerals of colleagues seems to be reflected in the will of Petrus Alaman alias Tamborin, a public crier in Marseilles from at least 1378 to 1395.[65] In his will, Petrus' gratitude to his colleagues who would come to the funeral is evident through his provision of a meal of bread, mutton, and wine for all of the 'minstrels of Marseilles' and allocation of 1 gr. to each minstrel who helped bury him.[66]

In addition to rules and customs controlling the behaviour and activities of the minstrel profession as a whole, individuals entered into legally recognised and complex relationships with their fellow musicians. Private notarial contracts have proven to be the richest and most illuminating source of information concerning these professional agreements between minstrels.[67] For example, in a master–journeyman relationship in Aix-en-Provence in 1450, a trumpeter leased his services to a well-established civic trumpeter for one year for a stipend, clothing and housing.[68] Another option was the master–apprenticeship relationship, as in the above-mentioned example from Aix-en-Provence. In this arrangement, a young man promised to serve a well-established trumpeter for a period of five years in exchange for being taught the 'arte tromparie sive de la trompeta'.[69] A partnership in Marseilles in 1432 involving two minstrels of equal status was identified as a 'societas'. In this arrangement, a local minstrel from Marseilles and a minstrel from the northern Italian town of Chieri promised to perform exclusively with each other at festivities for one year and to share profits.[70] While actual contracts documenting partnerships between musicians are rare in the fourteenth and fifteenth centuries, the frequent references in account books of cities and confraternities from this period to a particular minstrel and his 'socius' raise the possibility that this type of professional rela-

[65] According to Steven Epstein, 'the death of a member brought forth one of the most pervasive guild customs – the obligation to attend the funeral'. *Wage Labor and Guilds in Medieval Europe* (Chapel Hill, N.C., 1991), p. 165.

[66] ADB, 351 E/86, fols. 41^{r}–42^{r}.

[67] For further discussion of the following notarial contracts see Peters, 'Urban Musical Culture'.

[68] ADB, Dépôt annexe d'Aix-en-Provence, 306 E 277, unfoliated.

[69] See above, n. 38.

[70] ADB, 351 E/194, fol. 109^{r-v}.

tionship, with varying conditions and degrees of commitment, was not uncommon.

A professional arrangement among 'two to six or more' minstrels is identified as a 'couble' in the statutes for the minstrels' guild in Toulouse. Honesty among partners in a 'couble' was a central concern in the statutes. It is stated that if a member of the 'couble' received money for an engagement, he must immediately inform his partners of all the money received.[71] Implicit in the use of the term 'couble' in these statutes was the ability of the minstrels to play instruments with different functions and ranges. The statutes read that

> any foreign minstrel who comes to Toulouse to play instruments and to make money in Toulouse, trained and expert in entertaining *(jogar)* and playing 'en Couble', as 'tenor, dessus, contra et sobradessus', is held to pay for his new entry 10 s., one-half to the confraternity and the other half to the reparations of the city of Toulouse. All other foreign minstrels, as it is said, not expert nor trained to make 'couble', 1 s. only to the confraternity.[72]

It appears that in Toulouse in the late fifteenth century, as elsewhere in Europe at this time, instrumental ensembles that could perform counterpoint were in demand.[73]

In conclusion, the rich archives of south-central France allow us to recover a rather detailed image of a vital urban musical culture during the late Middle Ages. While it was customary for minstrels to receive employment from cities throughout this region, freelance activities were essential to their livelihood. These freelance opportunities ranged from representing confraternities in processions in which they served a ceremonial function much like that

[71] ADH, E 1318: 'quant alcun del couble logat en alcuna festa levaria largent del couble et sos companhons, Que incontinent tal companhon que ainsi auria levat largent per tout lo couble sia tengut de rendre bon et loyal compte aldit son couble de tout so que aura levat et so sus pena de una liura . . .'.

[72] AMT, HH 66, fol. 435^{r-v}: 'Item staturen et ordeneren, Que tout menestrier estrangier qui vendra en tholosa per sonar de instrument et gasanhar argent en tholosa, excercitat et expert a jogar et sonar en couble com es, tenor, dessus, contra et sobradessus, sia tengat de pagar per sa novuela intrada, detz soulz de tournes applicadors per la mytat aladita confreyria, et lutra mytat alas reparacions de ladita villa de tholosa, Et tout autre menestrier estrangier ainsi com dit es non expert ny excercitat per far couble, ung solz de tournes, aladita confreyria tant solament.'

[73] K. Polk, *German Instrumental Music of the Late Middle Ages: Players, Patrons and Performance Practice* (Cambridge, 1992), p. 165.

of civic wind bands, to playing on the streets and in bathhouses. Through these diverse means of support, minstrels were able to provide a comfortable lifestyle for their families and were a stable element of the community. At least in Montpellier and Toulouse, the two principal cities in the region, the minstrels formed professional guilds, entered into complex professional relationships, served civic obligations and contributed to the welfare of fellow citizens and musicians. By the mid-fourteenth century and throughout the fifteenth century, minstrels were a highly visible and respectable element of medieval urban society in southern France, presenting a striking contrast to the popular image of the itinerant minstrel who was forced to live on the outskirts of society.

University of Wisconsin at Eau Claire

APPENDIX

Lists of Minstrels in Major Cities, 1300–1500

Name	*Dates*	*Identification*[1]
Minstrels in Montpellier		
Pierre Marti	1301	trompayre
Guilhem Ayle (father)	1322	trompator
Guilhem Ayle (son)	1322	trompator
Sanchonus de Fanassio	1327	
Jean Arnaud	1342	trompette
Bartolmieu Pezo	1353	trompayre
Michelet de la Sala	1353	cornamuzayre
Jon Mota alias Pancamicha	1353–82	cornamuzayre
Pos Canayre	1353	
Perrot Floret	1354–82	nacharayre
P. Martin	1354–76	trompayre
Robert de Paris	1354–83	cornamusayre
Peire Bonet	1354–86	trompaire
G. Boyssier	1355–64	trompayre
Jon Cordier	1355	trompayre
Jonet Aymes	1355	cornamuzayre
Michelet Cani	1355	taboroyayre
Raymondus Salamon	1356–98	trompaire
P. Arnaut	1356	
Andrieu Joza alias Sanca Boyssos	1356–60	
B. Bonet	1357	
Michelot	1357	
Martinet	1357–83	
Raymondus Frayssenet	1358–83	
Johan Ayle	1358–92	
Durant Angelier	1360–82	trompette
Raymon Folquier	1362–69	
B. Dieu	1364	
Poy Rostanh	1366	
Jacme Dieu	1369–84	
Johan Remieu	1370–1	trompeta
Petrus de Murato (Ayle)	1370–1404	tubicinator
Astorc	1371–84	lo trompil
Johannis Martin alias Blandin	1371–89	

[1] Only identifications other than 'menestrier' or 'mimus' are provided.

Name	*Dates*	*Identification*
Jacme Duran	1374–87	
Bn Garnier	1378–89	
Johannes Carpini	1379–1420	
Ascort Besso	1380	
Tibaut	1382	
Posset	1382	cornamusayre
Miqualet	1382	
Colin	1383	
Nicholaus la Charrua	1384–1426	
G. Tarrabust	1384–92	trompaire
Colin Dreus lo fes	1387–91	
Johan Paret	1388	
Huliqui	1390	
Artaut Masuyer	1390	
Henricus le Champenois	1393–1410	
Marinus Parpetuis	1398	tubicinator
Johan Guart	1392–1403	trompeta
Guilhmus Alberqui	1403–13	
Petrus de Medie Camporum	1403–12	
Simonet Riqueri	1403–46	trompeta
Martinet	1404–17	
Johannes Lamen	1406	
Jacobus de Mereleto	1406	
Petrequin de Stamps	1412	
Johannes Roch	1412–17	tubissinator
Johannes Boeri	1412–21	tubissinator
Arnaudus Assaut	1415	trompeta
Johan Araguo	1415	trompayre
Roget	1416	trompayre
Bengimer Andrieu	1416	trompayre
Guilhem Sabbatier alias Carmez	1416–20	trompayre
Johannes Capelani alias Piseti	1415–18	
Jacquet Bobin	1416–19	
Johannet Lanandrer	1417–21	trompayre
Jonhan Canayre	1417	trompayre
Raymon Duranton	1418–20	trompayre
Peyre Vyan	1419	trompayre
Berthomei Flanant	1419	trompayre
Jacominus Mutonis	1419–51	
Peyre de Mala	1419–50	

Name	*Dates*	*Identification*
Johanis Bonet	1420	tubicinator
Durandus de la Vinha	1420–48	
Jacobus Campanhac	1425–49	trompeta
Jaufredus Julian alias Verdellet	1432–55	
Cleofas Bosqui	1428–40	trompeta
Johan Mahut	1431–4	trompeta
P. Manti	1432	trompeta
Raymundus de Bussargues	1434–43	trompeta
Johannes Sarralhon	1435–80	trompeta
Peyre Genssa	1435	trompayre
Johan Fongi	1435	
Petrus de Fonte	1441–7	tubicinator
Johannes Montels	1441–9	tubicinator
Domergues Daremes	1444	trompayre
Peyre Nicholau	1446	trompeta
Antonius Rochier	1449	trompeta
Hugoninus Mellery	1449–94	ault menestrier
Peyre Amelier	1449–55	
Joseptus Peseloux	1450	
Jaquetus Jordan	1451–5	
Johan Verdelet	1455–60	
Michael Michael	1460–91	trompayre
Guillo Mayete	1467–70	
Marsal Fabre	1469–98	menistryer tornyer
Loys de Senarsi	1469–82	trompeta
Guille Palhassi	1472–80	trompayre
Johan Pigetier	1472–89	
Jehan Hueri	1477	sonador de laut
Coston Fabre	1477–88	trompeta
Jaumet Labejac	1477–96	trompeta
Jehan Arnaud	1479	taborin
Bernat Salles	1479–90	trompeta
Dionisis Martin	1479–85	trompeta
Bernard Dolcet	1480–97	trompeta
Johannon Pouton	1481	trompeta
Frances de las Lanas	1481–9	taborin
Raymonet Cabrie	1482–97	ault menestrier
Guille Baillc Proulle	1484	taborin
Gonin Agulhatier	1484	hault menestrier
Peyrot Cabrier	1485	

Name	*Dates*	*Identification*
Glaude Dedet	1485–99	taborin
Anthony Cassan	1486	trompeta
Anthony Messonin	1486	taborin
Estene Doulcet	1487–94	trompeta
Jehan Gely	1489	trompeta
Odinet	1490–6	rebec
Anthony Quisac	1493–9	haut menestrier
Thanet lo Fromagier	1495	
Ghuiraut Roziero	1495	
Custol Costans	1495	
Glaude Cayratar	1496–9	
Johan Mellery	1496	
Bernard Fabry	1498	haut menestrier
Minstrels in Toulouse		
Guilhem Johan	1330–42	cornayre
Raymon dAuriac	1342	trompaire
Pons de Sanctas	1342	trompaire
Johan dAlbas	1383–4	trompayre
Johan Andrieu	1383–1407	trompayre
Raymon Arguier	1383–1406	
Bernat de Cazamaior (vielh)	1384–1420	
Raymon del Falgar	1384	cornayre
Bernat Gasc	1384	gayca
Johan Capel	1391–1407	trompayre
Arnaut Marti	1397–98	cornamuzayre
Mathieu	1397–98	la trompeta
Bernat de Casamaior (jone)	1405–20	
Guilhem Robert	1416	trompayre
Loys de Bosi	1416–59	trompayre
Raymon del Portal	1417–55	trompayre
Peyre Gautier	1432–65	
Johan Guayfius	1420	trompayre
Johan de la Haya	1432	
Andrieu Priand	1434	
Johan del Portal	1443–60	trompayre
Nicolau Semaliera	1443	charaminayre
Peyre Semaliera	1443	charaminayre
Laurens Arnaud	1445	
Guillem Prisvesia	1450–61	cornaire

Name	*Dates*	*Identification*
Guilhem Gautier	1444–55	
Johan Gautier	1455–9	charmayre
Nicholau de Sivelhie	1456	joueur de pipeau
Johan Vens	1459	charmayre
Laurens Arnaut	1459	charmayre
Marsel Arnaut	1459	charmayre
Panisi Portal	1459	trompayre
Johan de Toyn	1460	trompeta
Peyre Baudi	1460	guaya
Sansat de Casanova	1460–88	cornayre
Nicholas Chamelera	1461	
Peyre Espinart	1464	
Peyre Audran	1485–1504	
Bertolomeo Serda	1485	
Anthoni	1485	trompeta
Guilhem de Tanis	1487–98	
Peyre de Ressies	1488–1504	trompeta
Peyrot	1489	lo tanboret
Jacob Desi	1488–94	trompeta
Petro Menadier	1492	
Guillermo Baleret	1492	
Johanne Briconnet	1492	
Gaultier du Chans	1492	
Michaele Visiani	1492	
Gaspar Fabri	1492	
Guillermo de Marcaus	1492	
Johana de Sant Laurens	1492	
Josse Betinc	1492	
Andrea Chastanhier	1492	
Glaude de Rezies	1494–5	trompeta
Minstrels in Avignon		
Brocardus de Campanino de Pavia	1366–7	tactor instrumentorum musicorum
Guiqardus Franco di Parenca	1369–91	
Cornerius	1370–8	
Ghilion de San Michel	1370–90	
Albertinus Raynaudi	1372–90	trompeta
Giccardo de Mora	1373	
S. Giahnetto	1377	

Name	*Dates*	*Identification*
Guicciardus Franasti	1378	
Raynaudus Gauballie	1378	
Ottuvius	1378	
Jacomin Pancheti	1378	
Jan Chassrte	1380	
Bertrandus Bernard	1389–91	
Johannes de Carpentorate	1390	
Pier Rogeti	1391	
Guille de Rens	1393	
Angelin de Francfort	1407–20	
Tortoyin	1410–28	trompeta
Johannes Boruete	1410	trompeta
Monetus de Puteo	1411	trompeta
Guillius	1413–16	
Poncius Blaconi	1415–46	
Nesle	1419–28	
Johan Aucher	1423–63	cornemuse
Symonetus Menerbe	1427–51	trompeta
Jacobus Bobenti	1429	trompeta
Remonet Martin	1439–44	trompeta
Johannes de Bray	1447–62	
Johanin Galey	1449–50	
Lazarus de Pugeto	1449–51	trompeta
Mahuetus Michaelis	1449–51	trompeta
Petrus Peyroni	1449–51	
Garinus Bornheti	1449–58	
Johanne Menerba	1449–75	trompeta
Mosse de Lisbonne	1449–83	
Antoine Girard	1449	
Jacques Boysseau	1473	
Stephan Molheti	1474–81	taborin
Micheleto Vileti	1474–5	taborin
Petrus de Nabes	1475–7	trompeta
Anthonius Menerbe	1475–81	trompeta
Johan Menerbe	1478	trompeta
Minstrels in Marseilles		
Antonius Daranha	1349–53	trombador
Tibaut de Castillon	1350–3	cornamusayre
G. Rostanis	1351	tronbador

Name	*Dates*	*Identification*
Possilon	1351	cornamuza
Estevem Songefesta	1351	cornamuza
P. Pelos	1351–3	naquarar/cornamuza
G. Almaric	1353	cornamuza
Roman Faranc	1353	cornamuza
G. Dalbans	1353	trombador
Petrus Alaman alias Tamborin	1366–95	
Guillmus Roscagni	1373–80	trombator
Julian Galli	1375–81	
Johannes Johanin	1375–86	cornamusayre
Petrus Cassanus	1376–1402	trombator
Pones Jordan	1376	tubicinator
Andree Maurelli	1376–93	tubicinator
Guilles	1378	
Guilles Cayssard	1380–96	
Monuetus Farnosii	1382	tubicinator
Ludovicus Gosini	1382–6	
Antonius Henrici	1383	trompeta
Buguete Stosene	1384	tanborinus
Peyrinus de Savoya	1387	
Antonius Grutonis	1393	tamborinus
Monuetus Bathalheri	1398	trompator
Guillem	1398	cornamusayre
Cola Danta Richa	1420	trompeta
Louis Scorte	1424–6	trompette
Trophimus Gimundus	1427–35	
Stephanus Laurenci	1428–30	trompeta
Martinus Andree	1429–39	corneiator
Johannes Dayguina	1432	
Johannetus Johannis	1434	fistula/flahutayre
Petrus Gay	1434	tubicinator
Monet Johan	1452–7	
Jeaner Johan	1457	
Peyre Bonifay	1457	
Lontron Blanc	1458	
Guilhem Porquier	1458	
Tonon Guauthier	1458	
Antonin Arnaut	1487	taborin

Early Music History (2000) Volume 19. © Cambridge University Press
Printed in the United Kingdom

MAGNUS WILLIAMSON

ROYAL IMAGE-MAKING AND TEXTUAL INTERPLAY IN GILBERT BANASTER'S *O MARIA ET ELIZABETH**

This essay stems from the recent discovery of the cantus firmus of the motet *O Maria et Elizabeth* by Gilbert Banaster (d. 1487).[1] The chant, which will be discussed in detail, is the respond *Regnum mundi*. Banaster's motet is known to the scholarly community on account of its unusual text, which concludes with a prayer for an unspecified king. It will be argued that Banaster chose *Regnum mundi* as his cantus firmus on account of its thematic relevance to

* I should like to record my thanks to Dr Margaret Bent, Dr Ian Biddle and Professor Andrew Wathey for reading earlier drafts of this essay, and for their helpful suggestions.

1 This discovery was made independently by the author and by Dr Catherine Hocking (see C. Hocking, 'Cantus Firmus Procedures in the Eton Choirbook' (Ph.D. thesis, Cambridge University, 1995), pp. 78–86). Several other cantus firmi deployed in repertory of the Eton choirbook (Eton College Library MS 178 [= MS 178]) have recently been identified. Dr Hocking has suggested cantus firmi for the following motets: Robert Wylkynson, *O virgo prudentissima* (MS 178, openings e1–e3, now incomplete), whose cantus firmus is *Angelus autem Domini* (psalm antiphon at Lauds, Easter Sunday: see *Antiphonale Sarisburiense*, ed. W. H. Frere (Plainsong and Mediæval Music Society; London, 1901–24; repr. Farnborough, 1966) [= *AS*], pl. 237); Richard Davy, *O Domine celi terreque creator* (MS 178, openings k4–k6) = *Simon, dormis* (antiphon to Benedictus at Lauds, Thursday in Holy Week: *AS*, pl. 214); and John Browne, *O Maria salvatoris mater* (MS 178, openings a2–a4), whose cantus firmus appears to be based rather loosely on *Venit dilectus meus* (psalm antiphon, Matins, on the feast of the Assumption: *AS*, pl. 495); see Hocking, 'Cantus Firmus Procedures', pp. 64–73, 133–5 and 135–7. I have also been able to identify cantus firmi for the following compositions: John Hampton, *Salve regina* (MS 178, openings k2–k3) = *Gaudeamus omnes* (Mass introit on numerous feasts: see *Graduale Sarisburiense*, ed. W. H. Frere (Plainsong and Mediæval Music Society; London, 1894; repr. Farnborough, 1966), plates 142, s, 181, 191, 196, 199); and Richard Davy, *Gaude flore virginali* (MS 178, openings b6–b8, now incomplete) = *O lux beata Trinitas* (hymn, Vespers, Sundays from Corpus Christi until Advent) and *Virgo flagellatur* (respond at Matins, feast of St Catherine); see M. Williamson, 'The Eton Choirbook: Its Institutional and Historical Background' (D.Phil. thesis, Oxford University, 1997), pp. 322–4; H. Benham, *Latin Church Music in England c.1460–1575* (London, 1977), p. 92.

the motet text, and that in so doing he collaborated in the appropriation of devotional means to serve dynastic ends.

When Henry VI founded Eton College in 1440, his primary intention was to endow a 'powerhouse of prayer' which would not only expedite his passage through purgatory, but would also advertise the pious credentials of his dynasty.[2] To this end he codified within his statutes an elaborate cycle of intercessions which were to be recited by the members of his college in chapel, at work, at mealtimes, and at the bedside.[3] No day passed without some form of intercession on behalf of the king and his family, and one of the most significant rituals in which these prayers were said was the memorial to the Virgin Mary which was recited every evening. As part of this memorial, polyphonic motets (or votive antiphons) were sung by the clerks and choristers of the chapel; in the early 1500s, long after the founder's death, the choir's repertory of votive antiphons, accumulated during the previous thirty years, was copied into the codex now known as the Eton choirbook.

Among these antiphons is Gilbert Banaster's *O Maria et Elizabeth*.[4] This is one of the oldest antiphons in the Eton choirbook, representing later fifteenth-century English polyphony at a stage of transition. It was almost certainly composed for performance within the royal household chapel, and it contains textual references to the biblical story of the Visitation, whose liturgical feast was a new feature in the English Kalendar in the 1480s.[5] But its most conspicuous feature is the inclusion within its text of a prayer for the reigning king. The community for which the Eton choirbook was copied was acutely aware of its royal pedigree, sporting the title 'collegium regale' in its official documents, and the royal arms appear within one of the choirbook's illuminated initials.[6] The singing of Banaster's motet, and its inclusion in the

[2] See K. E. Selway, 'The Place of Eton College and King's College, Cambridge, in the Polity of the Lancastrian Monarchy' (D.Phil. thesis, Oxford University, 1993), pp. 6, 22–3, 27 and 207–19.

[3] See Williamson, 'The Eton Choirbook', pp. 81–138.

[4] See *The Eton Choirbook*, ed. F. Ll. Harrison, ii (Musica Britannica, 11; London, 1958), pp. 117–27 for an edition of this piece.

[5] On the feast of the Visitation and its belated incorporation into English liturgical kalendars, see R. W. Pfaff, *New Liturgical Feasts in Later Medieval England* (Oxford, 1970), pp. 40–51.

[6] In opening k4L, stave 1 (the *Triplex* part of Richard Davy's *O Domine celi terreque creator*).

choirbook, was therefore a suitable expression of the college's royal pedigree as well as a fulfilment of its intercessory obligations.

Banaster's antiphon probably did not originate at Eton College, however, and its existence reveals as much about his situation as a beneficiary of royal patronage, his methods as a composer, and his manipulation of devotional rhetoric, as it does about the ritual patterns of Eton College. Although it is arguably less technically accomplished than many of the later motets in the Eton choirbook, *O Maria et Elizabeth* is a complex devotional artifice constructed out of the interwoven and interdependent elements of text, music and cantus firmus. It was most probably written as an occasional piece, located within a specific (though now unspecifiable) historical context. The wider context, a period of political instability and dynastic uncertainty, is central to our understanding of the motet.

COMPOSER AND CONTEXT

Gilbert Banaster is well known to the scholarly community as a gentleman of the royal household chapel during the 1470s and 1480s, until his death in 1487. Several elements within his biography need clarification, however, particularly his birthdate, his early career, and the year in which he entered royal service. His father was possibly Henry Banaster, a yeoman of the royal household until his death in 1456; if this was so, Gilbert may also have begun his musical training as a boy chorister in the royal household chapel, as John Caldwell suggests.[7] His birthdate is not known, and has been estimated as either 1420–5 or *c.* 1445.[8] An

7 J. Caldwell, 'Banaster, Gilbert', *The New Grove Dictionary of Music and Musicians*, ed. S. Sadie (London, 1980), ii, p. 104. There is no record of Gilbert Banaster's boyhood membership of the royal household chapel, neither is there any contemporary documentation which unequivocally associates Gilbert with Henry Banaster. Henry Banaster was probably from Lancashire: on 20 December 1445 William Akenshawe, citizen and barber of London, gave all his goods to Robert Broune, saddler and citizen of London, Henry Banastre, 'one of the yeomen of the crown' and Thurstan Banastre of Lancashire, 'gentilman' (*Calendar of the Close Rolls, Henry VI*, iv: *A.D. 1441–1447* (London, 1937), p. 294). Although it is not stated explicitly, it would seem that Henry and Thurstan were related.

8 Caldwell, 'Banaster', p. 104; *Early English Versions of the Tales of Guiscardo and Ghismonda and Titus and Gisippus from the Decameron*, ed. H. Wright (Early English Text Society [EETS], O.S. 205; London, 1937), p. xxiii. In 1424 a Gilbert Banastre was indentured to serve John, Duke of Bedford, as a soldier in France (PRO E 101/71/2/820). This is unlikely to have been the composer, whose mother was still alive when he made his will in 1487.

earlier birthdate is predicated upon the attribution to Banaster of a rhymed English translation of a tale from Giovanni Boccaccio's *Decameron*.[9] This is present in two mid-fifteenth-century manuscript sources: Oxford, Bodleian Library, MS Rawlinson C. 86 (fols. 143v–155), and London, British Library Add. MS 12524 (fols. 17v–28v), which includes Banaster's name in the concluding two-stanza Envoy.[10] This attribution would seem to indicate a birthdate no later than 1425. Although none of his three daughters had yet come of age when he made his will in 1487, it is less likely that Banaster died young than that he married late.[11] He joined the Fraternity of St Nicholas, the London guild of parish clerks, in 1456, at which time he is unlikely to have been younger than twenty or thereabouts;[12] he would certainly not have been as young as eleven, which rules out 1445 as a birthdate. It therefore seems likely that he was born in the 1420s.[13]

Very little is known of Banaster's early career. His life almost certainly began and ended in London; in his will he described himself as 'of Est Grenewich in the Counte of kent gentilman'.[14] He was most probably resident in London when he joined the Fraternity of St Nicholas.[15] By 1469 (not 1471 or 1475, as is suggested elsewhere), he had entered royal service as a clerk in the royal household chapel;[16] on 25 February of that year he was granted a corrody in Daventry Priory by Edward IV, as 'one the

[9] See *Early English Versions*, ed. Wright: 'The Tale of Guiscardo and Ghismonda', pp. 2–37.

[10] In *Catalogue of Additions to the Manuscripts in the British Museum in the Years MDCCCXLI–MDCCCXLV* (Trustees of the British Museum, 1850), Add. MS 12524 is dated to the end of the fourteenth century. But the style of the scribal hand suggests a later dating.

[11] In his will (PRO, PROB 11/8, sig. 11, fol. 94), he left 'to Alice my doughter my Wedding gowne that I was last weddid in', suggesting that he had been married previously.

[12] See below, n. 15.

[13] *Calendar of Patent Rolls, Henry VI*, ii: *A.D. 1429–1436* (London, 1907), p. 183: pardon to 'Henry Banastre of Suthwerk, co. Surrey, gentilman', 28 November 1431. Banaster's withdrawal from active duty in the royal household chapel in 1486 also suggests an earlier rather than a later birthdate (see below, n. 22).

[14] PRO, PROB 11/8, sig. 11, fol. 93V.

[15] H. Baillie, 'A London Gild of Musicians 1460–1530', *Proceedings of the Royal Musical Association*, 83 (1956–7), pp. 15–28, at p. 20.

[16] See Caldwell, 'Banaster', p. 104; S. R. Charles, 'The Provenance and Date of the Pepys MS 1236', *Musica disciplina*, 16 (1962), pp. 57–71, at p. 63. See also A. Wathey, 'Musicology, Archives and Historiography', in B. Haggh, F. Daelemans and A. Vaurie (eds), *Musicology and Archival Research* (Archives et Bibliothèques de Belgique, 46; Brussels, 1994), pp. 3–26, at pp. 13–14, n. 15.

clerks of our chapell'.[17] It is possible that Banaster had already been appointed to the royal household chapel some time before 1469; it is equally possible that he found work outside London between 1456 and 1469, in or near Canterbury. This is suggested by the inclusion of two of Banaster's compositions in Pepys 1236, a miscellany of polyphonic compositions, musical treatises, astronomical tables, calendars, poems and charters which was compiled in the mid to late 1460s; this manuscript appears to have originated in the Almonry Chapel at Christ Church Cathedral Priory, Canterbury, and contains pieces by composers with proven Kentish connections.[18] Further evidence – albeit circumstantial – that Banaster either worked at Canterbury or had close associations with the cathedral is the inclusion of his poem, *Miraculum sancti Thome martyris*, within the chronicle of John Stone, monk of Canterbury, in 1467.[19]

Banaster's career spanned a momentous period in both political and musical terms. His lifetime was almost exactly coterminous with the dynastic upheavals of the Wars of the Roses; these events need to be rehearsed in detail, as they are inextricably linked with Banaster's most ambitious musical composition. Banaster was born during the minority of Henry VI, who had succeeded his father, Henry V, as a baby in 1422. During his youth, the political structures which had held together during the king's long minority disintegrated with the loss of territories in France and the erosion of political and social stability in England. Henry VI was deposed in 1461 by Edward, Earl of March, who took the throne as Edward IV.

It was under Edward that Banaster was appointed to the royal household chapel. A year after Banaster's appointment Edward

17 PRO C 81/824/2748; I should like to thank Mr Jonathan Hall and Dr Andrew Wathey for this and other references to Banaster's royal grants.

18 R. Bowers, 'Magdalene College, Pepys Library, MS 1236', in *Cambridge Music Manuscripts 900–1700*, ed. I. Fenlon (Cambridge, 1982), pp. 111–14. The contents of Pepys 1236 are published in *The Music of The Pepys MS 1236*, ed. S. R. Charles (Corpus mensurabilis musicae, 40; American Institute of Musicology, 1967); this includes Banaster's three-voice *alternatim* setting of the hymn *Exultet celum* (pp. 18–19) and two-voice *Alleluia: laudate pueri* (pp. 146–7).

19 Christ Church Cathedral MS 417 (see *Early English Versions*, ed. Wright, pp. xviii–xx, and below, Appendix 1, for a transcription). The name 'Gylbartus Banystre' was added to Stone's manuscript in a different hand, which caused Wright to question Banaster's authorship (*ibid.*, p. xx). There seems, however, no reason to doubt this attribution (perhaps based on a now-lost concordance) unless a more convincing attribution is posited.

fled to the Netherlands during the brief Readeption of Henry VI (October 1470 to May 1471). Soon after Edward regained the throne, Banaster was granted corrodies in the abbeys of Abingdon, Berkshire (now Oxfordshire), and Crowland, Lincolnshire.[20] He continued to receive royal grants until Edward's death in 1483. All his corrodies were received from Edward: he is not known to have received royal grants during the Readeption of Henry VI, or during the brief reign of Richard III or from Henry VII.[21] By the time Edward died in 1483, Banaster had been appointed master of the children (in 1478); working at court, and living in Greenwich, he would almost certainly have witnessed the events of early summer in 1483, when Edward IV's brother, Richard, Duke of Gloucester, deposed his thirteen-year-old son, who subsequently disappeared. The two-year reign of Richard III was overshadowed by the rebellion of the Duke of Buckingham, one of Richard's key supporters, in 1483, and the threat posed by Henry Tudor, an exile in Brittany. Henry, having eluded Richard's attempts to have him extradited, assembled an invasion army, landed at Milford Haven, marched into the Midlands, and defeated Richard, who was killed at the Battle of Bosworth in 1485. After his coronation, Henry VII married Elizabeth of York, Edward IV's eldest daughter (in January 1486), thus symbolically uniting the rival houses of Lancaster and York; Banaster was almost certainly present on both occasions. The Wars of the Roses finally came to an end on 16 June 1487, at the battle of Stoke; later that summer, Banaster died, having relinquished his duties as master of the children the previous year.[22]

[20] See below, Appendix 2.

[21] This is excepting the allocation of £26 13*s*. 4*d*. which was made to Banaster 'for the exhibicion of the childryne of the chapelle' and recorded in Edward V's book of household expenses compiled in May–June 1483 (R. Horrox (ed.), 'Financial Memoranda of the Reign of Edward V: Longleat Miscellaneous Manuscript Book II', *Camden Miscellany*, 39 (Camden Society, 4th ser. 34; London, 1987), pp. 197–272, at p. 241). This was not a grant as such, but an element in the audit of the royal household undertaken after the unexpected death of Edward IV; the financial allocation was, moreover, intended for the boys' upkeep and not as a personal reward to Banaster himself.

[22] A. Ashbee, *Records of English Court Music*, vii (1485–1558) (Aldershot, 1993), p. 3: grant of 40*s*. annuity to Lawrence Squier as master of the children of the royal household chapel, dated 8 November 1486. *Materials for a History of the Reign of Henry VII*, ed. W. Campbell, i (Rolls Series; London, 1873), p. 547: grant of corrodies in St Benet Hulme and Bardney Abbeys to Robert Colet on surrender by Gilbert Banaster, dated 22 August 1486. These surrenders suggest that Banaster relinquished his duties, probably on account of old age.

He made his will on 18 August 1487; he was dead by the end of that month, and his corrodies were distributed to other members of the royal household between 1 and 10 September.[23] Like later members of the royal household chapel, Banaster had used his position to accrue property; he owned tenements and land (over twenty acres) in Greenwich, including a riverside house with its own wharf, and had amassed a quantity of silver gilt by the time of his death.[24]

THE TEXT: CONTEXT, CONSTRUCTION AND MEANINGS

As a gentleman of the Yorkist and early Tudor royal household chapel and as a resident of the environs of London, Banaster would have been familiar with the themes of dynastic image-building which had been employed since the usurpation of Henry IV in 1399:[25] these themes were shaped within the orbit of the royal household and played out most publicly in the capital. Perhaps the most pressing dynastic issue of the fifteenth century was the question of legitimacy. The occupation of French territories, and the dual monarchy uneasily embodied in Henry VI, reopened the vexed question of dynastic legitimacy which had been raised in 1399.[26] The young English king's allegedly superior claim to the French throne was advertised in churches both in France and at home in England in the 1420s, with pictorial and poetical genealogies.[27] The French poem, by Jean Calot, was translated into English by John Lydgate, the dominant poet at Henry VI's court, who

23 Prerogative Court of Canterbury Wills, Milles 11. See J. C. C. Smith, *Index of Wills proved in the Prerogative Court of Canterbury 1383–1558* (London, 1893). Probate was granted on 31 January 1488. This will is kalendared in A. Ashbee and D. Lasocki (eds), *A Biographical Dictionary of English Court Musicians 1485–1714*, i (Aldershot, 1998), p. 62.

24 PRO, PROB 11/8, sig. 11, fols. 93v–94v. On property-holding among members of the royal household chapel, see F. Kisby, 'Courtiers in the Community: The Musicians of the Royal Household Chapel in Early Tudor Westminster', in *The Reign of Henry VII: Proceedings of the 1993 Harlaxton Symposium*, ed. B. Thompson (Harlaxton Medieval Studies, 5; Stamford, 1995), pp. 229–60.

25 For a comprehensive critique of Lancastrian political literature, see P. Strohm, *England's Empty Throne: Usurpation and the Language of Legitimation, 1399–1422* (New Haven and London, 1998).

26 See J. W. McKenna, 'Henry VI of England and the Dual Monarchy: Aspects of Royal Political Propaganda, 1422–1432', *Journal of the Warburg and Courtauld Institutes*, 28 (1965), pp. 145–62.

27 *Ibid.*, pp. 151–4.

repeated the same themes of royal legitimacy in numerous texts. Although the currency of these texts was circumscribed by the loss of the French territories in the 1440s, they nevertheless established a pattern of literary validation which was followed by Edward IV and Henry VII in their own attempts to justify their usurpation of the English throne.[28] Given his literary interests and his likely knowledge of Lydgate's work, Banaster would have been familiar with the legitimising discourse which responded to successive kings' propagandising impulses. The text of *O Maria et Elizabeth*, outwardly an antiphon in honour of the Virgin Mary, is in fact a piece of carefully wrought propaganda, whose themes stemmed from an established tradition of dynastic image-making.

Banaster set the following text:[29]

O Maria et Elizabeth; O fecunde cognate, omnium matres matrum felices ex quibus deus novum commercium prolis educandi natura mirante specialiter operatus est. Tu Maria velut rubus moysi igne haud concupiscencie conbusta eundem filium et non alium quem pater ab eterno genuit ihesum ex tempore mater et virgo peperisti. Et tu Elizabeth ut arida virga aaron miro ordine florida cunctis sanctiorem prophetis procreasti sterilis Johannem.

Sic ambarum ubera de celo plena sed Maria superplena de cuius plenitudine demones conculcantur homines salvantur angeli reintegrantur et quicquid partus Elizabeth boni habet ex donis gracie filii Marie est. O viscera celi rore onusta[30] quarum obsequiis devote salutando humilitatis invicem prestitis; Eve peccamina veteris abolita preconia Trinitatis audita et nostre redempcionis primordia declarantur.

Ac obtrusis ventre creatorem servus regem salvatorem cognovit et more tripudii mutuo filii congaudebant. Matres quidem[31] gratam societatem floridum aspectum ac colloquia celica cum dulcibus ad invicem osculis ad libitum habuerunt.

Suscipe igitur piissima mater has preces nostras et ad solium defer filii tui ubi iuxta se te ipsam posuit, nam nephas est alibi te esse quam ubi est id quod a te genitum est. Protege quesumus tibi devotum athletam regem nostrum .N. graciam dans huberem qua clemens cum iustitia diu regnet. Da virtutem illi in armis triumphantem hostesque rabidos iugo premat iusto et prosperitatem nobis confirmet. Et post felices grandevi patris annos succedant liberi regno in paterno et avito virtute antiquos exsuperantes celebratos. Ac ecclesiam et regnum et fidem et pacem habeat populus, amore timeat deum regem et legem, et nobis peccatoribus det veniam et graciam immortalis deus tuus gloriosus filius. Amen.

[28] McKenna, 'Henry VI of England', p. 162.

[29] It is with gratitude that I acknowledge the generous help of Professor Jonathan Powell of the Classics Department of Newcastle University and Leofranc Holford-Strevens in unravelling the complexities of this text.

[30] MS 178 has 'omista'.

[31] MS 178 has 'quidam'.

O Mary and Elizabeth, O fruitful kindred, blessed mothers of all mothers, through whom God especially wrought the new work of bringing forth offspring, to the wonder of nature. You, Mary, gave birth to the same Son, and none other, that the Father begat from eternal into worldly time; just as the bush of Moses was unconsumed by the fire, you – a mother and a virgin – were in no way consumed with lust. And you, Elizabeth, although sterile, bore John, holier than all the prophets, like the barren rod of Aaron flowering by a miraculous order.

Thus these women's wombs were filled, Mary's indeed to overflowing, from heaven above: by whose fullness the demons are crushed, people saved, and angels restored; and whatever was good in Elizabeth's childbearing is given by grace of Mary's Son. O wombs, laden with the dew of heaven, by whose reverences in devout salutation the sins of the former Eve have been abolished, the announcement of the Trinity has been heard and the beginnings of our redemption are declared.

And, after the wombs were filled, the servant recognised the saviour-king, and the sons rejoiced together in a mutual dance; the mothers at their pleasure enjoyed a pleasant companionship indeed, a blooming countenance, and a heavenly discourse with sweet kisses in turn.

Therefore receive these our prayers, most gentle Mother, and convey them to the throne of your Son, where he placed you by his side: for it is contrary to divine order that you should be anywhere but next to the one to whom you gave birth. Protect, we beseech you, the devout champion, our king, .N., giving copious grace whereby he might reign for a long time with clemency and justice. Give him triumphant valour in arms; may he subdue his raging enemies under a just yoke, and may he also increase our prosperity. And after the long-lived father's happy years, may his lineage succeed in their father's and ancestors' realm, surpassing in virtue their famous forebears. And, as for the king's subjects, let the church, the faith, the kingdom and peace be their inheritance, and may they lovingly fear God, the King and the Law. And may your glorious Son, O Immortal God, give to us sinners grace and forgiveness. Amen.

Banaster's text simultaneously invites and eludes historical contextualisation. In broad terms it follows the binary format of many fifteenth-century votive antiphon texts, in which the first half is addressed to a saint (usually the Virgin Mary), establishing her biblical pedigree or praising her miraculous powers; the second half is usually an exhortation to her to intercede on behalf of the sinner's soul in its passage through purgatory. Although the overall structure of *O Maria et Elizabeth* adheres to this pattern, its rhetoric differs in some important respects. First, and most conspicuously, it opens with an exhortation to two saints, Mary and Elizabeth, meditating at length on the theme of the Visitation, which had only recently become established as a liturgical feast at the time the piece was written.[32] Secondly, it concludes not just

[32] Pfaff, *New Liturgical Feasts*, p. 47.

with a prayer for the intercession of the Virgin Mary, but with a prayer for the king and his heirs, the Church, the realm and its people. This is unusual, not only because of the intrusion of dynastic and political concerns into what was customarily a devotional form, but also because this intrusion effects a shift of emphasis from the realm of Christian redemption to the political health of the worldly kingdom. Only at the last moment, in the concluding clause of the text, does the issue of redemption reassert itself.[33]

The worldly concerns of the second half of the text, moreover, influence the way in which the first half is interpreted. What might otherwise be read purely as a biblical narrative is retrospectively invested with political and dynastic significance: in the binary structure of the votive antiphon text, the second half is the necessary corollary to the first half. The Visitation story concerns the pregnancies of the Virgin Mary and her cousin, Elizabeth.[34] Both pregnancies were miraculous: Mary, though a virgin, was made pregnant through the agency of the Holy Spirit; Elizabeth conceived John the Baptist after years of infertility, a mark of God's favour and a release from the stigma of barrenness. Read in conjunction with the prayer for the king which follows it, the Visitation narrative as recounted in *O Maria et Elizabeth* implicitly alludes to a royal pregnancy, either as the celebration of a *fait accompli* or as the statement of a desired objective.

The second half of the text yields further important clues as to its intended audience. It is hoped that the king might reign for a long time with clemency and justice: clearly he had not yet reigned for long, and was therefore implicitly not an old man at the time the text was written. Looking into the distant future, the author prays that the king's successors may come to the throne after he has reigned for many happy years, entering into the kingdom of their father ('paterno') and ancestors ('avito'). The theme of parenthood, raised in the first half of the text, is also alluded to earlier in the second half, when Mary is depicted in her rightful place next to the throne of her Son, conveying to him the petitions of those who pray to her. But the royal succession evoked here

[33] See below, n. 36, regarding the recitation of prayers *ab inimicis* within the royal household.

[34] The story of the Visitation is taken from Luke 1:39–56.

extends beyond the immediate, nuclear, family of the king and his children. The king's 'liberi' included not only his children, but all of his descendants; similarly, the 'regno . . . paterno et avito' is the realm not only of the children's father and grandfather, but of their ancestors as a whole. The king and his prospective children are thereby located within their royal line, past, present and future.

Considered in the light of later fifteenth-century English politics this is significant. Except for Edward V, king for just six weeks (April–May 1483), none of the English kings between 1461 and 1509 was himself the son of an anointed monarch. The kings for whom *O Maria et Elizabeth* was most likely to have been written, Edward IV and Henry VII, came to the throne, not through peaceful accession, but through military enforcement of their claims, which rested on their descent from Edward III (d. 1377). Both kings were disposed towards the kind of dynastic image-making which is implicit within the text. In usurping the throne, both Edward and Henry had violently interrupted the normal modes of dynastic succession, but sought to justify their usurpation by virtue of their royal lineage which could be traced back to the fourteenth century. The issue of the royal succession raised in *O Maria et Elizabeth* is therefore politically coloured: the reality of the king's usurpation is veiled in the rhetoric of dynastic continuity and legitimacy. This factor is an important clue to the dating of the motet and its text.[35]

Fifteenth-century dynastic upheaval, and the political violence ensuing from it, underlies the stated hope that the king might triumph on the battlefield, subduing his enemies under a just yoke. This rhetorical emphasis suggests that these enemies were a threatening reality rather than a literary abstract.[36] Who were

[35] See below, 'Date of Composition'.

[36] A less emphatic echo of this form can be found in the standard prayer for the king, *Quesumus omnipotens Deus*: 'viciorum voraginem devitare et hostes superare' ('[may the king] destroy the pit of vices, overcome his enemies', etc.) (J. Wickham Legg, *The Sarum Missal* (Oxford, 1916), p. 397). But in this context the nature of the enemies is less overtly military. A more analogous instance of a context-specific reference to the king's enemies in a polyphonic motet is Cooke's *Alma proles regia/Christi miles inclite/Ab inimicis*, which was apparently written during Henry V's wars in France (F. Ll. Harrison, *Music in Medieval Britain* (London, 1958), p. 246). The tenor, *Ab inimicis defende nos, Christi* ('Defend us from our enemies, O Christ'), was taken from the litany for Rogation Days in time of war (*ibid.*, p. 246 and M. Bukofzer, *Studies in Medieval and Renaissance Music*

they? An allusion to domestic enemies was problematic, implying a negative critique of the king's governance (why should an effective king have domestic enemies?).[37] This problem is carefully diffused: the king's enemies are mad ('rabidos') and their hostility stems from their madness. Textual analysis therefore suggests that the text was written during a royal pregnancy when there was simultaneously a perceived threat to the security of the king and his polity. The various themes raised within the text, and their implication with regard to the date of composition, will be considered in due course.

THE CANTUS FIRMUS: INTERTEXTUAL RELATIONSHIPS

Banaster's use of cantus firmus is unusual. He wrote his Tenor part in short note values, freely subtracting from and adding to the chant model, transposing some passages, omitting others, using quotation and paraphrase extensively, and introducing apparently extraneous material.[38] Frank Harrison concluded, perhaps not surprisingly, that the cantus firmus was invented by Banaster.[39] Hugh Benham found apparent quotations from the psalm antiphon *Benedicam te, Domine* which, by coincidence, would have been sung at Lauds the Sunday before the wedding of Henry VII and Elizabeth of York in January 1486.[40] But a closer match with Banaster's Tenor part can be found in the Matins respond *Regnum mundi*.[41]

This respond, whose incipit matches that of *Benedicam te*, was from the Common of Virgins; it was also sung in procession when one of these feasts fell on a Sunday;[42] it was also used at the

(London, 1951), p. 68). *Ab inimicis* was also sung during the processional litany in the royal household chapel, at which the king was sometimes present and from which the queen was seldom absent (*Liber Regie Capelle: A Manuscript in the Biblioteca Publica, Evora*, ed. W. Ullmann (Henry Bradshaw Society, 92; London, 1961), pp. 17, 59–60).

37 Strohm (in *England's Empty Throne*, pp. 173–95: 'Advising the Lancastrian Prince') draws attention to the avoidance of direct criticism of the king in earlier fifteenth-century literature, even in ostensibly admonitory texts.

38 Banaster's treatment of the cantus firmus is considered below. This piece and its cantus firmus are also discussed briefly in Hocking, 'Cantus Firmus Procedures', pp. 78–87.

39 Harrison, *Music in Medieval Britain*, p. 307.

40 Benham, *Latin Church Music*, p. 76 (where Benham posits the marriage as a likely date of composition, largely on the strength of this coincidence).

41 *Antiphonale Sarisburiense*, ed. Frere, plates 666–7.

42 *Processionale ad Usum Sarum* (William Pynson, 1502), fols. 161v–162.

Consecration of Virgins, in which it was sung during the concluding procession out of church after the veiling of nuns.[43] Banaster chose this chant with care, more for its textual correspondence with the themes of *O Maria et Elizabeth* than because it happened to be liturgically appropriate on the day for which (or on which) Banaster wrote the motet. Like Banaster's text, the words of *Regnum mundi* comprise two elements: the respond refrain, which contains a distillation of New Testament (mainly Pauline) theology, denying the pleasures of the world,[44] and the verse, which is taken from Ps. 45 (Vulgate 44) (see Example 1):

> I have counted as nothing the kingdom of the world and all transient things, on account of the love of my Lord Jesus Christ; whom I have seen, whom I have loved, in whom I have believed and in whom I have delighted.
>
> My heart overflows with a goodly theme: I address my verses to the King.
> Glory be to the Father (etc.)

There can be little doubt that Banaster used *Regnum mundi* deliberately to create a multitextual synthesis of words, music and cantus firmus.[45] The primary relevance of *Regnum mundi* as cantus firmus derives from the subject matter of its psalm verse. Nevertheless, the refrain is interesting in itself. The theme of the refrain, a denial of the worldly kingdom and its trappings, seems discordant with Banaster's own text, which is a supplication on behalf of an earthly king. This may account for one of Banaster's musical evasions: the chant to which the words of worldly denial ('seculi contempsi propter amorem Domini mei Ihesu Christi') would have been sung in the respond is never quoted literally.[46] But he would have been familiar with contemporary theological interpretations of the Visitation story, such as contained in the homiliary *Speculum Sacerdotale*, which suggested a way of reconciling the apparently conflicting themes of his text and his chosen cantus firmus. Here, at the end of the sermon on the Nativity of

[43] A. B. Yardley, 'The Marriage of Heaven and Earth: A Late Medieval Source of the *Consecratio virginum*', *Current Musicology*, 45–7 (1990), pp. 305–24, at pp. 311, 324. The melody was also used as a *Benedicamus* verse (Harrison, *Music in Medieval Britain*, p. 75 and pl. VII).

[44] Rom. 8; Phil. 3:8; 1 John 2:15–16; see also 1 John 1:1, 1 Pet. 1:8 and Rev. 11:15.

[45] See M. Long, 'Symbol and Ritual in Josquin's *Missa Di Dadi*', *Journal of the American Musicological Society*, 42 (1989), pp. 1–22 for an analogous musical–textual–conceptual synthesis by Josquin.

[46] See below, 'Articulating the Text'.

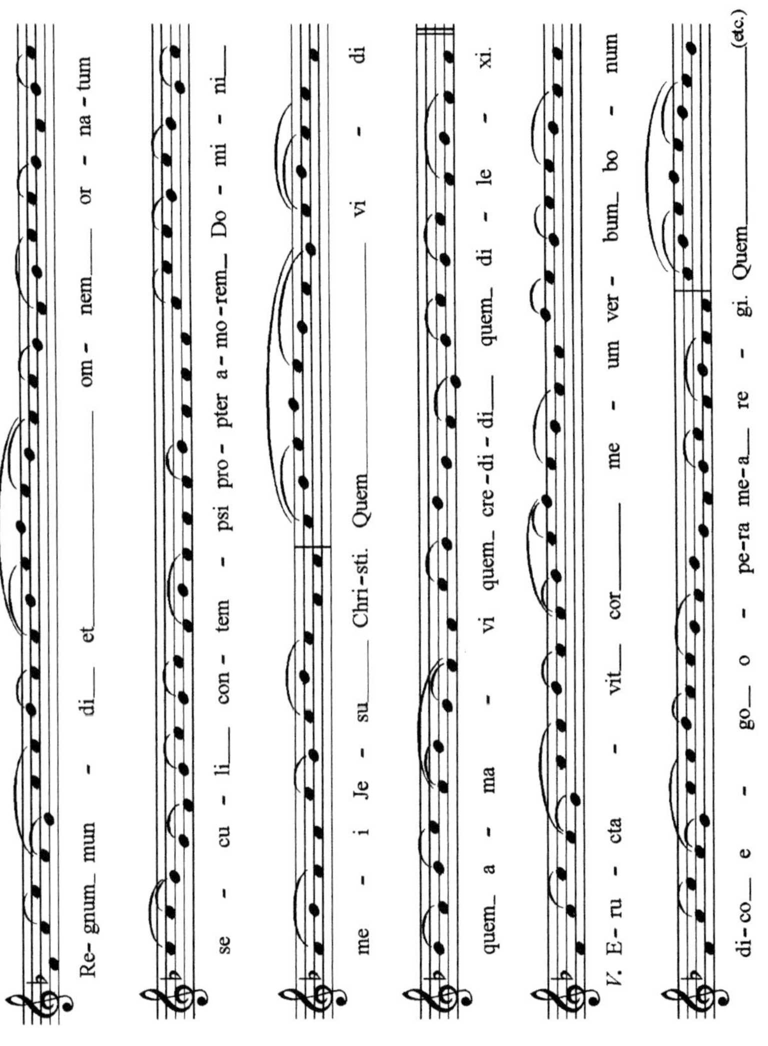

Example 1 Respond: Regnum mundi

John the Baptist, in which the Visitation narrative is rehearsed, the preacher reminds his listeners of the central themes of John the Baptist's ministry – preparation and penance:

Bretheren, we knowe wele that mynde of man is deuyct and ouercommen with dyuersitees of lustis and likynges of the world, for he loueth noght laboure but luste, ese, and ydelnes, and unnethe he is brought to entent for to leve siche unlawefull lyf. But yf he begynne for to thynke of the nede of his laste day and of the burthyn of the dome that is to come and thynketh hertely of the peyne and sorowe that may falle that day and of the mede and joye that is in that to be grauntyd eke, then he wold here make batel bitwene his body and passiones and do penaunce and leve his olde foule desires.[47]

Whatever the suitability of the respond refrain, its respond verse, *Eructavit cor meum*, displays an almost perfect thematic alignment with Banaster's text. It is the first verse of a frequently sung and well-known psalm (Ps. 45) which, in both secular and monastic uses, was sung as a proper psalm at Matins on feasts of virgins (including feasts of the Virgin Mary), and on feriae at Matins (Monday in monastic use, Tuesday in secular).[48] *Eructavit cor meum* was also the psalm verse for the mass introits *Gaudeamus* and *Dilexisti* on the feast days of numerous female saints.[49] The text of Ps. 45 is an epithalamium encompassing a number of potent themes: regal dignity, victory over the king's enemies, a royal wedding (with kings' daughters in attendance), the prospect of sons, and the promise of future glory:[50]

[47] *Speculum Sacerdotale edited from British Museum MS. Additional 36791*, ed. E. H. Weatherly (EETS, O.S. 200; London, 1936), p. 168 (sermon on the Nativity of St John the Baptist).

[48] J. Harper, *The Forms and Orders of Western Liturgy from the Tenth to the Eighteenth Century: A Historical Introduction and Guide for Students and Musicians* (Oxford, 1991), pp. 244–5, 256–7. Psalm 45 (44) was the first psalm at second nocturns on the feasts of St Agnes (21 January), the Purification (2 February), the Annunciation (25 March), the Visitation (2 July), St Mary Magdalene (22 July), St Anne (26 July), St Catherine (25 November), and the Conception of the BVM (8 December); *Breviarium ad Usum Insignis Ecclesiae Sarum*, ed. F. Procter and C. Wordsworth, iii (Cambridge, 1886), cols. 45, 89, 136, 237, 399, 518, 546, 1108).

[49] *Missale ad Usum Insignis et Praeclarae Ecclesiae Sarum*, ed. F. H. Dickinson (Burntisland, 1861–83), cols. 668, 707, 793, 817, 825, 865, 895, 917 (as verse to *Gaudeamus* on feasts of the Conception, Visitation, Assumption, Presentation and Nativity of the BVM, Mary Magdalen, St Agatha and Anne, mother of Mary); cols. 710 and 890 (as verse to *Dilexisti* on feasts of St Scholastica and St Cuthberga). Various verses of Ps. 45 (44) were used in the Common of Virgins and other female saints (*Missale*, ed. Dickinson, cols. 718*–734*).

[50] A commentary on Ps. 45 can be found in D. Kidner, *Psalms 1–72: An Introduction and Commentary on Books I and II of the Psalms* (Tyndale Old Testament Commentaries; Leicester and Downers Grove, Ill., 1973), pp. 170–4.

1. My heart overflows with a goodly theme; I address my works to the king; my tongue is like the pen of a ready scribe.
2. You are the most handsome of men; grace is poured upon your lips; therefore God has blessed you forever.
3. Gird your sword on your thigh, O mighty one, in your glory and majesty.
4. In your majesty ride on victoriously for the cause of truth and to defend the right; let your right hand teach you dread deeds.
5. Your arrows are sharp in the heart of the king's enemies; the peoples fall under you.
6. Your throne, O God, endures forever and ever. Your royal sceptre is a sceptre of equity;
7. you love righteousness and hate wickedness. Therefore God, your God, has anointed you with the oil of gladness beyond your companions;
8. your robes are all fragrant with myrrh and aloes and cassia. From ivory palaces stringed instruments make you glad;
9. daughters of kings are among your ladies of honour; at your right hand stands the queen in gold of Ophir.
10. Hear, O daughter, consider and incline your ear; forget your people and your father's house,
11. and the king will desire your beauty. Since he is your lord, bow to him;
12. the people of Tyre will seek your favour with gifts, the richest of the people
13. with all kinds of wealth. The princess is decked in her chamber with gold-woven robes;
14. in many-coloured robes she is led to the king; behind her the virgins, her companions, follow.
15. With joy and gladness they are led along as they enter the palace of the king.
16. In the place of ancestors you, O king, shall have sons; you will make them princes in all the earth.
17. I will cause your name to be celebrated in all generations; therefore the peoples will praise you for ever and ever.[51]

Banaster would have been aware of the thematic content of this psalm, and his use of *Regnum mundi* as a cantus firmus may be regarded as a careful ploy: the cantus firmus recalls the text of the respond which, in turn, evokes the themes of the psalm. When recited on feasts of female saints (especially virgins), the psalm clearly alluded to the virgin saint as *sponsa Christi*, a bride of Christ or the Church; but, in the context of *O Maria et Elizabeth*, the marriage evoked so vividly in the psalm becomes a biblical allusion to a contemporary event. The psalm therefore serves to unify the two constituent parts of Banaster's text: biblical pregnancy and contemporary kingship. Taken together, the motet text and the

[51] *The Holy Bible containing the Old and New Testaments: New Revised Standard Version* (New York and Oxford, 1989), pp. 570–1.

respond text simultaneously look backwards to the royal wedding, and forwards to the imminent birth of heirs, aligning the legitimacy of the ruling dynasty with the bestowal of divine favour ('whatever good is in Elizabeth's childbearing is given by grace of Mary's Son') and the prospect of a flourishing dynastic line ('I will cause your name to be celebrated in all generations; therefore the peoples will praise you for ever and ever').

The ephemeral topicality of the motet text raises the question of its authorship: was Banaster the author? The composer's position within the royal household would have brought him into contact with distinguished authors and poets, both native and European.[52] To John Skelton, for instance, are ascribed the surviving unrhymed Latin inscriptions on Henry VII's tomb in Westminster Abbey (as well as the versified elegies on vellum, which are said to have hung on the grille surrounding the tomb).[53] Not long after his accession, Henry VII granted corrodies to the blind French Franciscan poet Bernard André.[54] André, the king's poet laureate and an early architect of the Tudor version of contemporary English history, was the author of *Vita Henrici Septimi*, which covered the first twelve years of the reign (1485–97).[55] As court panegyrists either Skelton or André would have been authors of first choice, especially if *O Maria et Elizabeth* was commissioned by the king himself or by another member of his immediate family.

Militating against Banaster's authorship of the text is the preference of most fifteenth-century composers for pre-existing texts, such as *Salve regina*, *Gaude flore virginali* or *Gaude virgo mater Cristi*, which might easily be found in books of hours. Quite possibly the text was contained in Banaster's own book of hours.[56] It is also possible that the text had been in circulation prior to Banaster's

[52] The following discussion of authorship is largely predicated upon the dating of the motet to 1486: see below, 'Date of Composition'.

[53] H. J. Dow, *The Sculptural Decoration of The Henry VII Chapel, Westminster Abbey* (Durham, 1992), pp. 42–4; the funerary inscription has been dated 1512 (*ibid.*, p. 43). Skelton also wrote verses on the death of Edward IV in 1483.

[54] *Materials*, ed. Campbell, i, p. 203: grant to 'Bernard Andrewe' of a corrody in Crowland Abbey, Lincolnshire (8 December 1485).

[55] *Ibid.*, ii (1877), p. 62: grant of ten marks *per annum* to 'Bernard Andrew . . . poet-laureate' (24 November 1486); *Historia Regis Henrici Septimi a Bernardo Andrea Tholosate conscripta*, ed. J. Gairdner (Rolls Series; London, 1858), pp. 3–75.

[56] PRO, PROB 11/8, sig. 11, fol. 94^{v}: 'Item I bequethe to Johan Combe my prymer now of late bownden'.

composition of *O Maria et Elizabeth* and may even have been written under a previous monarch, although the lack of concordances suggests otherwise: Banaster's motet is the only extant source for the text.

Banaster's long-standing track record as an author, however, suggests that he himself might have written the text. Moreover his position as master of the children at the royal household chapel entailed literary and dramatic activity under the Tudors.[57] The degree of thematic control and schematic planning evinced by the text and its treatment suggests either that Banaster was the author of both text and music, or that he worked in close collaboration with a text-writer, or even that he (or his putative collaborator) wrote the motet text *after* the cantus firmus had already been chosen. This, combined with the implicitly occasional, context-specific, nature of the text suggests that it was purpose-written by (or for) Banaster, as has been suggested elsewhere with regard to other textual *unica* in the Eton choirbook, such as Browne's *O Maria salvatoris mater*.[58]

The final quotation of the cantus firmus (bars 255–74) appears at first sight to constitute a declaration of authorship on Banaster's part: here the Tenor quotes the respond verse, 'My heart overflows with a goodly theme: I address my works [or 'verses'] to the king.'[59] The cantus firmus is concealed elsewhere in the motet;[60] in these bars, however, it is easily recognisable. Banaster's unequivocal quotation of his chant source at the very end of the

[57] F. Kisby, 'A Courtier in the Community: New Light on the Biography of William Cornysh, Master of the Choristers in the English Chapel Royal 1509–1523', *Bulletin of the Society for Renaissance Studies*, 16 (1999), pp. 8–18; see also W. R. Streitberger, 'William Cornish and the Players of the Chapel', *Medieval English Theatre*, 7 (1985), pp. 83–100.

[58] N. Sandon, 'The Manuscript London, British Library Harley 1709', in S. Rankin and D. Hiley (eds), *Music in the Medieval English Liturgy: Plainsong and Mediæval Music Society Centennial Essays* (Oxford, 1993), pp. 355–80, at p. 366.

[59] A contemporary translation with which Banaster would almost certainly have been familiar, from the Brigittine *Myroure of oure Ladye*, brings an even clearer authorial voice into the psalm verse: 'Myne harte hathe shewed a good word. I telle my workes to the kynge' (*The Myroure of oure Ladye*, ed. J. H. Blunt (EETS, extra series 19; London, 1873), p. 298). Hocking ('Cantus Firmus Procedures', p. 83) suggests that bars 255–71 quote material from the respond itself ('Regnum mundi et' and 'amorem Domini'). But the melodic allusion to the respond verse is clear, and makes more sense than the dislocated quotations which Dr Hocking posits: Banaster's reference, not only to the respond refrain, but also to the psalm from which the respond verse is taken, is central to our understanding of this piece's intertextuality.

[60] See below, 'Articulating the Text'.

motet corresponds with the psalmist's declaration of authorship, suggesting an analogous authorial signature on the composer's part. In the Envoy to his *Decameron* translation, Banaster had declared his authorship unambiguously:

Go forth, lytill tayle, full bare off eloquense,
With humble sprete make thi supplicacioune;
Prey all tho, theras thou comyst in audiens,
To have piete on thy symple translacione,
Oute off prose by myne unkonnyng directioune
Made in balade; wherfor myne innocence
Submytting lowly unto coreccioune
And supportacion of youre benevolence,

Besekyng all the maisters of this science
Me holde excused, for goode ys myne entencion,
Thogh I florysh nat with metyr and cadence,
Off rethoryk and poetry makyng mencioune;
Such clerkly werkys passith my discrecion;
Natwithstonding, if here be fawte or offens,
Speke to Gilbert banester, which at the mocioune
Off Iohn Raynere this made aftir the sentence.[61]

But Banaster's quotation of the respond verse in bars 255–71, while unmistakable, is nevertheless incomplete, if not evasive. The final phrase of the respond verse (sung in *Regnum mundi* to the words 'dico ego opera mea regi') is marked by the omission of 'ego' (completely) and 'mea' (partially), thus implying a dissociation between the composer and the act of versifying.[62] Unless the resulting aporia was incidental, rather than intentional, the final cantus-firmus quotation may not only be disregarded as a declaration of authorship, but may even be interpreted as a deliberate disclaimer. Taken as a whole, therefore, the available evidence is circumstantial and inconclusive: despite his earlier work as a poet and translator, authorship of the motet text cannot confidently be attributed to Banaster.

[61] *Early English Versions*, ed. Wright, p. 36.
[62] See below, Example 5.

MUSICAL LANGUAGE: STRUCTURE, TEXTURE AND SONORITY

In comparison with the audaciously conceived, subtle interplay between the motet text and the cantus-firmus text, Banaster's polyphony is imperfectly realised. The piece is long, occupying three openings in Eton MS 178, as opposed to the normal two, and Banaster seems to have struggled unsuccessfully to reconcile the length of his text with the need for structural coherence. This gave rise to a number of consequences: the texture is unusually syllabic, with as much text crammed into as short a space as possible; this in turn restricted opportunities for melismatic elaboration, hence the unusually frequent incidence of near-homophonic part-writing (bars 50–60, 96–7, 242–6).[63] The text – prose instead of verse – becomes a liability, as the composer is unable to overcome the shapelessness of his textual phrase structures. His structural planning is undercut by his over-reliance on a limited repertory of stock compositional stratagems: small-scale cellular imitation and syncopation (bars 13–14, 29–30, 185, 218–20, 230–2), uncontrolled scalic writing (bars 181–4), and overused and sometimes mishandled cadential forms.[64] Banaster also appears to have been unable to meet the competing requirements of linear vitality and harmonic coherence (Medius, bars 50–60), a symptom of a successive, rather than simultaneous, polyphonic realisation of his carefully planned programme.[65]

These apparent shortcomings suggest that Banaster's motet – his only surviving five-part piece – was only a partially successful essay in extended five-part writing. *O Maria et Elizabeth* is among

[63] Frequent use of homophony is also a characteristic of other early repertory in MS 178, for instance William Horwood's *Gaude flore virginali* (openings m6–m7). Horwood died in 1484, shortly before Banaster.

[64] The penultimate structural cadence at bar 255 is particularly incongruous, exacerbated by a seemingly mistaken added accidental in the Contratenor.

[65] For an extended discussion of successiveness and simultaneity in fifteenth-century polyphony, see B. J. Blackburn, 'On Compositional Process in the Fifteenth Century', *Journal of the American Musicological Society*, 40 (1987), pp. 210–84. See also M. Bent, 'The Transmission of English Music 1300–1500: Some Aspects of Repertory and Presentation', in H. H. Eggebrecht and M. Lütolf (eds), *Studien zur Tradition in der Musik: Kurt von Fischer zum 60. Geburtstag* (Munich, 1973), pp. 65–83, at p. 68, for a consideration of a different (though analogous) form of textual interpenetration in a fourteenth-century motet to St Thomas of Canterbury (d. 1170) and St Thomas of Dover (d. 1295), in which the texts are 'as much simultaneously (rather than successively) conceived as the musical lines to which they are attached'.

the earliest surviving pieces in the Eton choirbook (a lost five-voice setting of *Gaude flore virginali* was attributed to John Dunstaple (d. 1453) in both of the choirbook's indexes).[66] It bears the hallmarks of an early example of a form which was perfected only by the next generation of composers, an impression which is confirmed when *O Maria et Elizabeth* is compared with Banaster's less ambitious vernacular song, *My feerfull dreme*.[67] In this three-part meditation on the Passion, the same devices used in *O Maria et Elizabeth* – cellular imitation, syncopation, occasional homophonic writing – are employed more purposefully, regulated by the structural clarity of the vernacular text. A clumsy (or, perhaps less likely, archaic) compositional technique is also indicated by the prevalence of direct or scarcely avoided consecutive fifths and octaves in *O Maria et Elizabeth*.[68] These 'solecisms' do not occur in *My feerfull dreme*, and by the end of the fifteenth century were largely absent from other English composers' work. In *O Maria et Elizabeth* they are mostly confined to full sections written for all five voices singing together, and involve the Triplex, the uppermost voice-part, in most instances. Was the Triplex an added part, clumsily overlaid onto a piece which had originally been written for four voices? This is unlikely: Banaster used boys' voices to exemplify the theme of childhood, so that the Triplex part was, *ab initio*, figuratively essential to the design of the motet.[69] But his indifferent handling of the Triplex part suggests that composing in five parts for a chorus

[66] This setting was copied into openings o8 and p1; gatherings n, o and p are now missing. Like Banaster's motet, Dunstaple's *Gaude flore* had an overall compass of twenty-one notes. Concerning the attribution of this lost setting to Dunstaple, see I. Bent and M. Bent, 'Dufay, Dunstable, Plummer: A New Source', *Journal of the American Musicological Society*, 22 (1969), pp. 394–424.

[67] British Library Add. MS 5465, fols. 77^{v}–82; published in *Early Tudor Songs and Carols*, ed. John Stevens (Musica Britannica, 36; London, 1975), pp. 110–13.

[68] These occur in bars 47 (Triplex/Tenor), 49 (Triplex/Medius), 54 (Triplex/Tenor), 58 (Triplex/Contratenor), 62 (Triplex/Medius), 63 (Tenor/Bassus), 73 (Triplex/ Medius at unison; Medius/Contratenor simultaneously at fifth); 102 (Triplex/Medius); 149 (Medius/Tenor), 160–1 (Triplex/Tenor), 240 (Triplex/Tenor), 244 (Medius/ Contratenor), 254 (Medius/Contratenor), 261 (Triplex/Medius), 266 (Triplex/ Contratenor), 273 (Triplex/Contratenor). Banaster's awareness of this problem is suggested by his awkward avoidance of consecutive intervals between Contratenor and Bass in bar 241 and Contratenor and Tenor in bar 246.

[69] See below. Christopher Page (in 'Marian Texts and Themes in an English Manuscript: A Miscellany in Two Parts', *Plainsong and Medieval Music*, 5 (1996), pp. 23–44, at pp. 41–3) has drawn attention to the 'affective appeal' of the boy's voice, and the notions of 'prepubescence and innocence' which were configured around the unbroken voice.

of men and boys was – for him at least – a new and unmastered technical challenge. This might be considered in any assessment of the motet's date of composition.[70]

Occasional instances of word-painting provide further clues to the date of composition. The textual image of the king as a young man is represented in Banaster's polyphony with a Tenor–Contratenor duet (bars 164–87); the aspiration that he might reign for a long time ('diu regnet') is mirrored by an extended melisma, whose florid vocalisations represent the king's hoped-for longevity and also his present vitality (bars 181–7). The parts of the king's children ('liberi'), implicitly not envisaged as mature heirs in the text, are played in the polyphony by Triplex in *gimell* (bars 207–21), crossing over each other, swapping motifs in playful melodic cartwheels (bars 215–21); the image of the grandparent (bars 221–34) is configured around a Bass–Triplex duet, the Bass part clearly mimetic of age and maturity. Similar instances of melismatic word-painting can be found at 'florida' (bars 38–40) and 'congaudebant' (bars 99–103), where cadential melismata appear to have been used consciously to highlight particular textual images ('flourishing', 'rejoicing'). Like the text, the polyphony appears to portray a vigorous king in his prime without an adult heir, but with the birth of heirs in prospect.[71]

ARTICULATING THE TEXT: CANTUS-FIRMUS USAGE

Banaster's use of his chosen cantus firmus, the respond *Regnum mundi*, exemplifies the problems he encountered in realising his conceptual design. Perhaps because of the respond's asymmetry, the cantus prius factus is never stated in its entirety, despite the

[70] On the development of the English choral ensemble in the fifteenth century see R. Bowers, 'To Chorus from Quartet: The Performing Resource for English Church Polyphony, c.1390–1559', in J. Morehen (ed.), *English Choral Practice 1400–1600* (Cambridge, 1995), pp. 1–47; *idem*, 'Choral Institutions within the English Church: Their Constitution and Development, 1340–1500' (Ph.D. diss., University of East Anglia, 1975), pp. 6026–90.

[71] A further case of word-painting, but one which does not impinge on the dating of the motet, occurs in bars 239–47, when the chorus temporarily intrudes into an extended soloistic section of the motet (164–255). The chorus here represents the collective people ('et pacem habeat populus, amore timeat Deum'). This prefigures John Browne's use of the chorus as *turba* in his six-part *Stabat mater* (see Benham, *Latin Church Music*, p. 86).

unusual length of the motet. The second half of the refrain and the whole psalm verse are quoted almost note for note during the last thirty-four bars, but the first half of the refrain, either through accident or – perhaps more likely – through design, is heavily disguised. Banaster's deviation from his chant model is especially evident during the first 163 bars, in which extended, literal quotation is avoided in favour of paraphrase, motivic regeneration, and the interpolation of extraneous material.

Regnum mundi is a comparatively long respond, with a two-section refrain, the second half of which (from 'Quem vidi') is repeated after the psalm verse and after the doxology. It is in the fifth mode, and shares the characteristic fifth-mode psalm incipit with the antiphon *Benedicam te*. This is elaborated in both the respond and the antiphon, incorporating the fifth-mode mediation to give the following motif, which appears four times in *Regnum mundi*:

Banaster quotes this incipit, motif 1, either as part of an extended plainsong quotation, or – more usually – as an isolated motif in bars 45–50 (Tenor), 104 (Triplex, elaborated), 207 (Triplex Primus, elaborated), and 255 (Tenor).[72] But these exact quotations are outnumbered by his use of a subsidiary, simplified, motif (motif 1a: F–A–C–D–C) which occurs at bars 67–8 (Tenor), 94–5 (Tenor and, possibly, Triplex), and 109–10 (Triplex). This five-note motif recalls the fifth psalm-tone from which both the respond and the antiphon are derived.

Similarities between the respond *Regnum mundi* and the antiphon *Benedicam te* cease after the eighth note, and it becomes clear at this point that *Regnum mundi* is the primary source for Banaster's

[72] Hocking ('Cantus Firmus Procedures', pp. 83 and 86) suggests that both literal and paraphrased quotations of motif 1 were used by Banaster to elide the unheard respond text, 'Regnum mundi', with royal references in the motet text, e.g. 'tibi devotum athletam regem nostrum .N.' (bars 169–75), 'et post felices grandevi patris' (bars 207–9) and 'liberi regno in paterno' (bars 214–19). This is a convincing hypothesis, especially with regard to the latter two quotations.

cantus firmus. Following the incipit, the melody of *Regnum mundi* continues with two circular motifs, one of four notes (motif 2) and one of three (motif 3, which is sung twice):

Banaster makes extensive use of these. Motif 2 appears in bars 35–7 (Triplex and Medius in imitation), 59–61 (Medius), 69–70 (Medius, in migration from the Tenor), 211–13 (Triplex Secundus, ornamented as answering phrase to Triplex Primus), 234–9 (Medius, migrating in bar 239 back to the Tenor).

Unlike motif 2, motif 3 is seldom quoted unless as part of an extended statement of the chant; an exception can be found in bars 212–13 (Triplex), where it is used in conjunction with motif 2, and another, less plausibly, in bars 70–1 (Tenor), used as a cadential figure, which might be coincidental. But both motif 2 and motif 3 are deployed strategically elsewhere, motif 2 extrapolated from one statement of the cantus firmus and relocated elsewhere and motif 3 similarly reworked and repeated. Tracing Banaster's use of these motifs throughout the motet as a whole reveals three phases of activity in his Tenor part: bars 45–103, dominated by motif 3; bars 144–63, whose hallmark is the repetition of motif 2; and bars 239–end, in which the chant is finally quoted literally.

The entry of the Tenor part at bar 45, beginning with motif 1 in long notes, initially appears to herald the expected first statement of the cantus firmus, but this does not materialise: the next twenty-five bars consist of repetitions of motif 3 (motif 2 is omitted altogether), and a passing quotation of motif 1a, concluding at bar 78 with a cadential figure derived from the chant.[73] The next entry of the Tenor cantus firmus, at bar 89, continues this process of selective quotation and free interpolation. Its melodic material bears a scant resemblance to the remainder of the first

[73] There are several instances of this figure in *Regnum mundi* (at 'contempsi', 'dilexi', 'mea regi' and at the end of the doxology: see above, Example 1).

half of the respond refrain ('propter amorem Domini mei Ihesu Christi'), except for some extraneous material in bars 89–92, which echoes the opening phrase of the Contratenor part (bars 1–4); both phrases share a kinship with motif 2, but can only tentatively be said to be derived from it (see Example 2). Taken as a whole, therefore, these two sections (bars 45–103) constitute a free paraphrase of the first half of the respond refrain, in which the Tenor is defined as much by its deviation from the chant model as by its adherence to it.

Example 2 Tenor paraphase, bars 89–103

The next phase of Tenor cantus firmus (bars 144–63) takes place after the change of mensuration to *tempus imperfectum* (bar 104). This largely freely written material includes motifs 1a–3 inverted, transposed and alternated (see Example 3). Taking advantage of the inherent symmetry of motifs 1–2, Banaster creates in the middle of this passage an implied retrograde statement of motifs 1–3 combined (see Example 3). The dominance of motif 2 within this section, and its absence earlier on, imply that it had been deliberately extracted for use at a later stage in the motet. Indeed, Banaster's premeditated use of motif 2 is manifested in a musical pun (bars 144–7). Here an inversion of motif 2 is sung to the text 'nam nephas alibi' ('for it is contrary to divine order [that you should be elsewhere]'): the inversion of divine order is matched by the inversion of one of the principal motivic elements.

If Banaster's apparent fixation with motif 2 after bar 144 stemmed from his earlier omission of the same theme earlier, this omission had arisen from a practical problem. Either through choice, or because of the tessitura of his singers, the compass of his Tenor (*c–d′*) lies lower than the range of *Regnum mundi* (*e–f′*): motif 2, therefore, exceeded the upper end of his Tenor register. His solution was simple, but ruled out a literal quotation of the entire cantus firmus. Rather than using 'high' clefs, which would indicate 'transposition' in performance, Banaster merely transposed the offending passage down an octave where possible (at bars 144–7, 150–2, 259–67 and, possibly, 89–92).[74] This is a procrustean solution to a problem which he could have resolved more elegantly: his contemporary, William Horwood, used 'high' clefs in his *Salve regina*, whose twenty-one-note compass was the same as that of *O Maria et Elizabeth*.[75] Banaster clearly saw the limitations of his own solution: at bar 51, he excised motif 2 from the Tenor part, so avoiding the ungainly transposition which his own compositional stratagem would otherwise have necessitated (see Example 4).[76] Once removed from its melodic context, motif 2 assumed an independent life of its own, appearing at bars 35–7 and 59–61, 144–7, 150–2, 211–13 and 265–7 as an interpolated or paraphrased motif.

[74] By using the term 'high', I refer to written pitch, rather than any implied performing pitch.

[75] In Eton College, MS 178, openings g2–g3: Horwood used C4 clef in his Bass part, rather than F4.

[76] Hocking ('Cantus Firmus Procedures', p. 83) suggests that motif 1 migrates to the Medius part in bar 51 ('superplena': C–D–E–F). This apparent (and very partial) quotation, however, bears less resemblance to motif 2 than a more literal quotation which appears in the same voice-part in bars 59–61 ('reintegrantur, et quicquid').

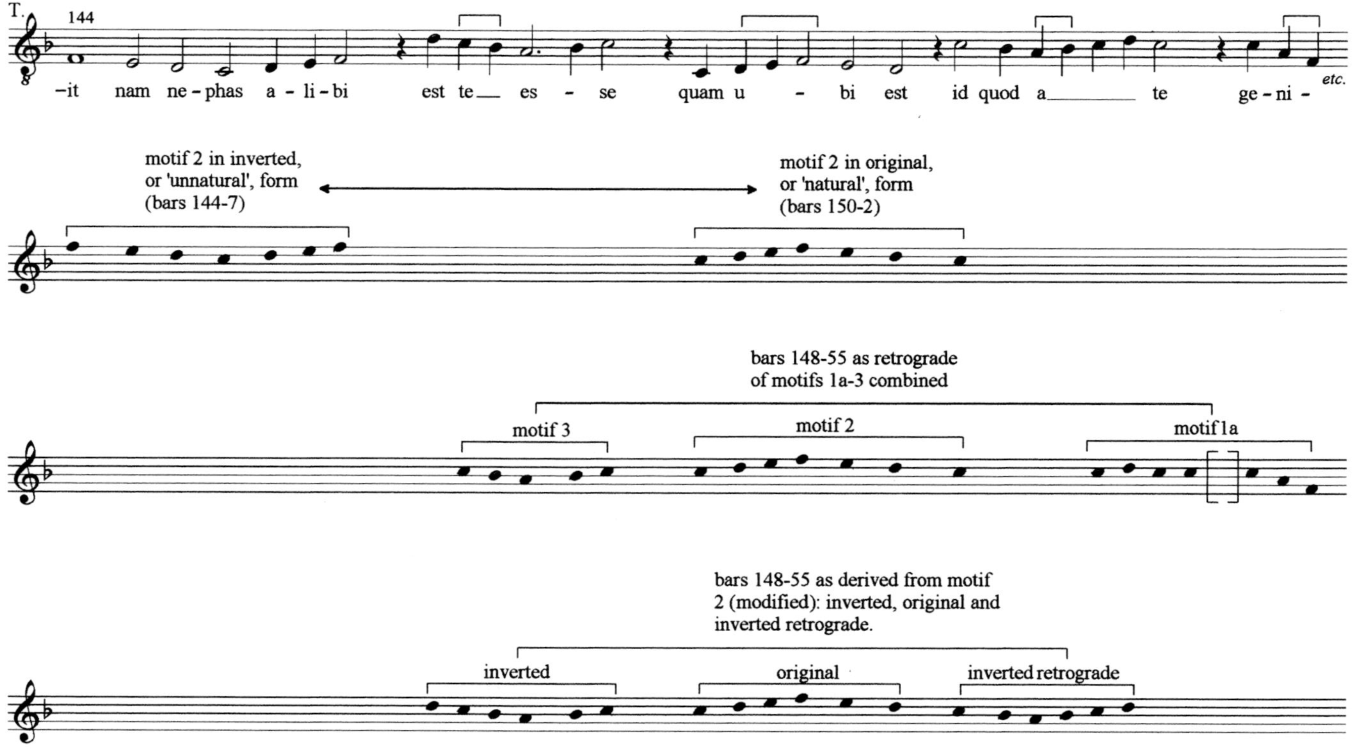

Example 3 Motivic inversion and retrograde, bars 144–63

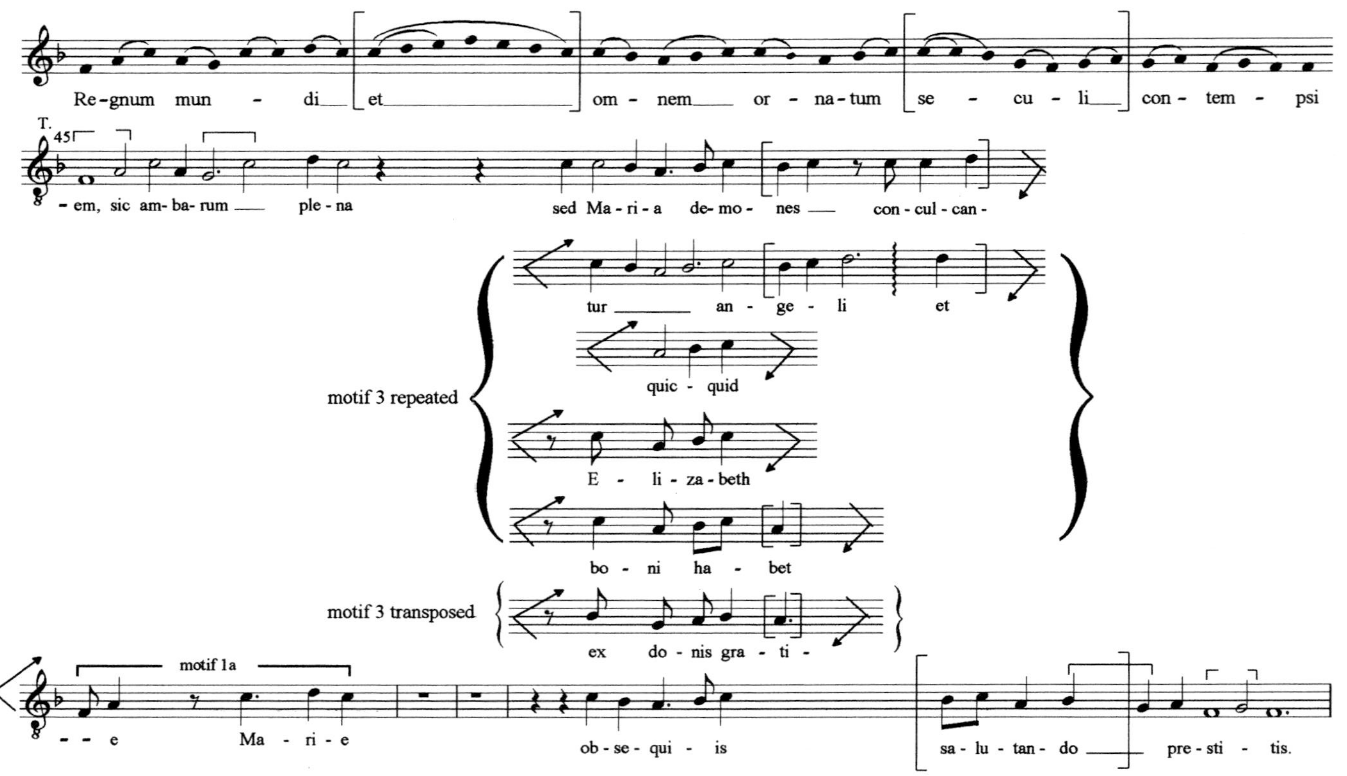

Example 4 Selective quotation and motivic repetition, bars 45–78

The cantus firmus is at last quoted literally during the final thirty bars, although the quotation begins in the Medius, migrating to the Tenor in bar 239 (see Example 5). This 'false' statement in the Medius is, in fact, real: for the first time, motif 2 is heard at its original pitch, thus 'correcting' the pitch change which Banaster had made earlier. In contrast to his earlier periphrasis, an extended, almost literal, quotation of the cantus firmus is made within this last statement (from 'Quem dilexi' to 'opera mea regi'); indeed, more of the original chant is used in the last thirty bars than in the preceding 244. Banaster's explicit reference to his chant model is significant at this point: the climax of the motet text, when attention is finally drawn from the worldly to the heavenly kingdom (and hence towards the hope of salvation), is marked by the first overt reference to the respond, which stresses devotion to Jesus above love of worldly trappings, and its psalm-verse, which draws together the corresponding themes of the motet text.[77]

DATE OF COMPOSITION: THE FEAST OF THE VISITATION AND THE ESTABLISHMENT OF THE TUDOR DYNASTY

The composition of *O Maria et Elizabeth* has been associated with Henry VII, either at the time of his marriage to Elizabeth of York, or following her conception of Prince Arthur, in 1486.[78] Although 1486 is the likeliest date, it cannot be proven: the absence of the king's name from the text in Eton 178 (where it is rendered as '.N.') is not made good in the only surviving concordance, which is fragmentary.[79] Any dating of the motet depends upon the coincidence of a number of factors: a royal pregnancy; dynastic or polit-

[77] There is also, as Catherine Hocking has astutely observed, an elision of themes between the motet text in bars 234–42 ('ac ecclesiam et regnum et fidem et pacem habeat populus amore timeat Deum') and the respond text at this point ('quem vidi, quem amavi, quem credidisti, quem dilexi') (Hocking, 'Cantus Firmus Procedures', p. 84).

[78] W. H. Grattan Flood, *Early Tudor Composers* (London, 1925), p. 15, and Benham, *Latin Church Music*, p. 76 (both suggest the marriage of Henry and Elizabeth of York); Harrison (in *Music in Medieval Britain*, p. 309) suggests that the motet was written during Elizabeth's pregnancy.

[79] Eton College Library, MS 178, openings m3–m5; Chester, Town Archive, MS CX/1, fol. 17^{v} (see G. Curtis and A. Wathey, 'Fifteenth-Century English Liturgical Music: A List of the Surviving Repertory', *Royal Musical Association Research Chronicle*, 27 (1994), pp. 1–69, at p. 23).

Example 5 Literal quotation in Medius and Tenor, bars 234–74

ical insecurity; a young king; a queen (probably) called Elizabeth; the possible occurrence of the feast of the Visitation (2 July) during the pregnancy. Several royal pregnancies in the 1470s and 1480s fulfilled some of these criteria: in 1470, for instance, Edward IV's queen, Elizabeth Woodville, was pregnant at a time of unprecedented political instability which culminated in her husband's (temporary) deposition. But the 1486 pregnancy is the only one to fulfil all the criteria.

Prior to his invasion of England in August 1485, Henry Tudor had contracted to marry Elizabeth of York, the oldest surviving child of Edward IV and Elizabeth Woodville.[80] The marriage was a key component in the establishment of the Tudor dynasty. Henry's claim was validated first in his victory in battle at Bosworth on 22 August; he was then anointed at Westminster Abbey on 30 October; a month later he received parliamentary recognition.[81] On 18 January 1486, having established his own claim to the throne, Henry married Elizabeth, thus uniting the rival houses of York and Lancaster (Elizabeth had to wait until November 1487 for her own coronation). With the birth of their first child in the autumn of 1486, the establishment of the dynasty was complete.

Prince Arthur was born thirty-five weeks after the king's marriage, on 20 September 1486, and must therefore have been conceived soon after the wedding. Henry had good reason to give thanks for an early pregnancy: the legitimacy and security of his dynasty were predicated upon the birth of a male heir who would continue the Tudor line and embody the union of the rival dynasties. Early in Queen Elizabeth's pregnancy, during April 1486, the new regime encountered its first armed challenge, the rebellion of Viscount Lovell and the brothers Humphrey and Thomas Stafford.[82] Although this rebellion flopped, it was a precursor to the much more threatening uprising in 1487, centred on the Yorkist imposter Lambert Simnel, and gave substance to the new

[80] The ceremony of betrothal took place at Rennes Cathedral (Brittany) on Christmas Day 1483.

[81] See S. Anglo, 'The Foundation of the Tudor Dynasty: The Coronation and Marriage of Henry VII', *Guildhall Miscellany*, 2/i (1960), pp. 3–11.

[82] See S. B. Chrimes, *Henry VII* (London, 1972), pp. 68–94.

king's insecurity.[83] The threat of rebellion, invasion or treason dominated Henry Tudor's first decade as king, and the manifestation of this threat so soon in the queen's pregnancy was sobering.

The feast of the Visitation (on 2 July 1486) coincided with the mid-term of the queen's pregnancy. Following his royal progress in the spring of 1486, Henry had returned to the capital in June and would have celebrated the feast at Westminster.[84] The Visitation was a new feast. It had originally been promulgated by Pope Boniface IX in 1389, with the stated aim of healing the papal schism, but its adoption in England had been slow.[85] Only after Pope Sixtus IV renewed the feast's institution in 1475 did the Visitation make inroads into the English kalendars; in 1480 the Convocation of Canterbury petitioned the Archbishop, Thomas Bourchier, to order the feast's adoption as a major double.[86] In the same year Caxton printed the mass and office of the Visitation; subsequent prints in 1493 and 1495 indicate that the feast had at last achieved widespread acceptance. Although there were localised devotions to the feast earlier in the fifteenth century, its late dissemination in England militates against *O Maria et Elizabeth*, a motet specifically directed towards the Visitation, having been written before 1480.[87] The feast's adoption by the Yorkist court in the early 1480s is indicated by Queen Elizabeth Woodville's letter to Pope Sixtus IV inquiring how the octave of the feast should be celebrated concurrently with other feasts in 1481;[88] the pope's

[83] This rebellion came to a head in June 1487, shortly before Banaster's death, at the battle of Stoke. This was the last pitched battle of the Wars of the Roses.

[84] *Calendar of Patent Rolls, Henry VII,* i: *A.D. 1485–1494* (London, 1914), pp. 106 ff.: among the places visited by Henry VII were Cambridge, Ely, Lincoln, Nottingham, York, Worcester and Bristol. The king returned to Westminster in June and was there for the feast of the Visitation, which would have been celebrated on 3 July (2 July fell on a Sunday in 1486).

[85] Pfaff, *New Liturgical Feasts*, pp. 40–3.

[86] *Ibid.*, pp. 45–7, 59; in his statutes of 1480 for Magdalen College, Oxford, William Waynflete described the feast of the Visitation as 'de novo solennizatur'; *Statutes of the Colleges of Oxford with Royal Patents of Foundation, Injunctions of Visitors, and Catalogues of Documents Relating to the University, Preserved in the Public Record Office*, ed. E. A. Bond, ii (London, 1853), p. 67).

[87] Pfaff (in *New Liturgical Feasts*, pp. 45 and 57) cites Syon Abbey (in 1419) and St Albans Abbey (in 1430).

[88] *Ibid.*, pp. 47–8; the octave coincided with the Translation of St Martin (4 July), the octave of Sts Peter and Paul (6 July) and the Translation of Thomas Becket (7 July).

response, which also granted indulgences for those reciting the Rosary, drew attention to the queen's 'singular devotion' to the feast.[89]

But it was Henry VII's mother, Lady Margaret Beaufort, who was the most zealous royal sponsor of new liturgical feasts, particularly the Transfiguration and the Name of Jesus.[90] Henry Hornby, Margaret's chancellor, devised for her the office of the Name of Jesus approved by the Canterbury Convocation in 1488; he also had the rhymed office of the Visitation, 'Aeterni Patris Filius', copied into her service books.[91] At the time of her son's accession in 1485, the Visitation feast was well established in England, having spread rapidly in the early 1480s.[92] In her veneration of new feasts, Margaret demonstrated the devotional dynamism of the new regime; because of the feast's origins during the papal schism, moreover, a political message could be attached to the Visitation: liturgical rhetoric against religious divisions could also be understood as an appeal against political divisions.[93] In *O Maria et Elizabeth* we can see the same appeal for spiritual and social concord within the common weal ('Ac ecclesiam et regnum et fidem et pacem habeat populus'). The motet text, which so vividly rehearses the theme of Mary's visit to Elizabeth, suggests that *O Maria et Elizabeth* was written for performance on or around that feast day. Given the multiplicity of themes inherent in the texts of the motet and its cantus firmus – a royal wedding, the birth of heirs, the perpetuation of a dynasty,

[89] *Calendar of Entries in the Papal Registers Relating to Great Britain and Ireland*, xiii/1: *Papal Letters 1471–1484*, ed. J. A. Twelmlow (London, 1955), pp. 90–1.

[90] Pfaff, *New Liturgical Feasts*, p. 48; M. G. Underwood, 'Politics and Piety in the Household of Lady Margaret Beaufort', *Journal of Ecclesiastical History*, 38 (1987), pp. 39–52, at pp. 47–8; F. Kisby, 'A Mirror of Monarchy: Music and Musicians in the Household of the Lady Margaret Beaufort, Mother of Henry VII', *Early Music History*, 16 (1997), pp. 203–34, at pp. 220–1: among the liturgical items listed in Margaret Beaufort's *post mortem* inventory were '.v. quaires of the Feest of the visitacon of our lady' (Kisby, 'A Mirror', p. 220).

[91] Underwood, 'Politics and Piety', p. 47; Pfaff, *New Liturgical Feasts*, p. 48. This office, which includes the psalm *Eructavit* in second nocturns, can be found in *Breviarium ad usum Sarum*, cols. 391–408 (see also above, n. 87). Partly because of the delay in the feast's adoption in England, variant forms of the same office achieved circulation: a radically different rhyming office, 'Accedunt laudes virginis', was adopted in Hereford Use (*The Hereford Breviary*, ed. W. H. Frere and L. E. G. Brown, ii (Henry Bradshaw Society, 40; London, 1911), pp. 223–31), although this too included the psalm *Eructavit* in second nocturns (p. 226).

[92] Pfaff, *New Liturgical Feasts*, p. 59.

[93] *Ibid.*, p. 55; *Missale Sarum*, col. 796 (secret and postcommunion at high mass).

and the well-being of the church, the king and his realm – *O Maria et Elizabeth* would have been politically apposite in the summer of 1486. The feast of the Visitation, which celebrated two miraculous biblical pregnancies, marked the mid-point of the queen's pregnancy. In prospect was the birth of an heir: a propitious token of God's favour for the new dynasty, an opportunity for public rejoicing (for which preparations were probably already under way), and a promise of security for a regime still struggling to assert its authority and legitimacy.[94]

The probability that *O Maria et Elizabeth* was written with Elizabeth of York's pregnancy in mind is further increased by Elizabeth's commissioning of a similar piece later in her husband's reign, which suggests she shared her mother's (and her mother-in-law's) devotion to the Visitation. At St Albans on 28 March 1502, Elizabeth paid 20*s*. to Robert Fayrfax 'for setting an Anthem of oure Lady and Saint Elizabeth';[95] this coincided with a visit to Eton by William Barton, Elizabeth's chaplain, during which he made an offering of 20*d*. to 'oure lady of Eton' on the queen's behalf, and these two events may be related.[96] The piece which Fayrfax wrote for the queen is probably *Eterne laudis lilium*, whose text, outlining the genealogy of the Virgin Mary (and thereby alluding to the queen's own ancestry), comprises the acrostic 'Elisabeth Regina Anglie'.[97] Thematic correspondences between the texts of *Eterne laudis lilium* and *O Maria et Elizabeth* are numerous: genealogy (and hence dynastic legitimacy), pregnancy, motherhood and, of course, redemption. (Fayrfax's later antiphon, *Lauda vivi alpha et O*, which concludes with a prayer for Henry VIII, provides another parallel to Banaster's motet.)[98] It is therefore possible that Elizabeth, or her mother-in-law Margaret Beaufort, or even her own mother

94 See K. Staniland, 'Royal Entry into the World', *England in the Fifteenth Century: Proceedings of the 1986 Harlaxton Symposium* (Woodbridge, 1987), pp. 297–314. Henry and Elizabeth were related in the fourth and fifth degrees of consanguinity, requiring papal dispensation for their marriage (and hence their offspring) to be legitimised; the dispensation granted by Innocent VIII (2 March 1486) was subsequently printed and distributed (Chrimes, *Henry VII*, pp. 330–1).

95 *Privy Purse Expenses of Elizabeth of York: Wardrobe Accounts of Edward the Fourth with a Memoire of Elizabeth of York*, ed. N. H. Nicolas (London, 1830), p. 2.

96 *Ibid*., p. 3.

97 An analysis of this text by Andrew Carwood can be found in the notes to the third instalment of The Cardinall's Musicke, *The Works of Robert Fayrfax* (CD GAU 160).

98 Harrison, *Music in Medieval Britain*, pp. 329–30, n. 3.

Elizabeth Woodville, had commissioned Banaster to write *O Maria et Elizabeth* during the 1486 pregnancy, following her wedding to Henry.[99]

Further corroboration of 1486 as a date of composition is provided by the correlation between the state of the Tudor family in 1486 and the young family depicted in Banaster's motet. Textual references to Elizabeth, mother of John the Baptist, could be addressed also to a Queen Elizabeth (either Elizabeth Woodville, wife of Edward IV, or her daughter, Elizabeth of York, wife of Henry VII). But the presence of royal grandparents within the text ('avito') makes Elizabeth of York the likeliest dedicatee. Unlike her parents, Edward IV and Elizabeth Woodville, Elizabeth of York was the daughter of a reigning king, and it was through her that Henry VII, a usurper without royal parentage and a weak claim to the throne, consolidated the Tudor dynasty: their children derived legitimacy both from Tudor father and grandmother (Henry VII and Margaret Beaufort) and Plantagenet mother and grandfather (Elizabeth of York and her father, Edward IV). The allusion within the motet to grandparent(s), whose gender is delicately unspecified, could apply either to Henry's mother, Margaret Beaufort (a powerful patroness and the most prominent figure at the early Tudor court save her son, the king himself) or to his queen's deceased father, Edward.[100] If, as therefore seems likely, *O Maria et Elizabeth* was composed in the summer of 1486, it was one of the first cultural products of Henry VII's quest for legitimacy.

THE ETON CHOIRBOOK: TRANSMISSION AND REDACTION

Banaster's motet was performed at Eton College and copied into the Eton choirbook (despite the likelihood that his musical lan-

[99] The singing of *Regnum mundi* at the veiling of nuns (see above, p. 249) would have lent the respond significance to Margaret Beaufort, who took a vow of chastity in 1499, which she renewed in 1504 (M. K. Jones and M. G. Underwood, *The King's Mother: Lady Margaret Beaufort, Countess of Richmond and Derby* (Cambridge, 1992), pp. 187–8). Elizabeth Woodville retired from court in July 1486, withdrawing first to Westminster Abbey, and then to Bermondsey Abbey in 1487.

[100] Having received numerous royal grants from Edward IV, Banaster (if he was the author of the motet text) had good reason to perpetuate Edward's memory (see below, Appendix 2).

guage was becoming outmoded by the time the choirbook was copied in the 1500s) for a number of reasons. Eton College, although a royal (Lancastrian) foundation, ceased to attract significant royal patronage after 1461. Nevertheless the community continued to configure its identity around its royal name and pedigree. This was facilitated by its geographical proximity to Windsor and by informal, personal contacts within the royal court.[101] The daily recitation of prayers for the king, an obligation which lay at the heart of the college's statutes, served further to entrench the community's perception of itself both as a chantry for the person of Henry VI and as a 'powerhouse of prayer' for its founder's royal successors. This self-perception manifested itself in a variety of ways. In 1473/4, for instance, a picture of Edward IV's infant son, Richard, was bought for the college chapel:[102] a seemingly trivial (and certainly cheap) purchase, but one which neatly illustrates not only the continuing preoccupation of the community with its royal status, but also the permeation of dynastic images into devotional space.[103] This pictorial analogy to Banaster's text predated the well-known use of Tudor heraldic devices at King's College, Cambridge, and in Henry VII's Lady Chapel in Westminster Abbey.[104]

The abiding perception by members of Eton College of their corporate royal privilege relates to one of the more anomalous aspects of Banaster's text as transmitted in the Eton choirbook: the use of '.N.' as substitute for the proper name of the king. This marks a decisive shift in the nature of the text from occasional, written with the specific circumstances of one king in mind, to generic, analogous to standard liturgical forms such as the collects

[101] H. C. Maxwell Lyte, *A History of Eton College* (4th edn, London, 1911), pp. 81–3, 92.

[102] Eton College Library, MS 231 (bursars' draft book, 1473/4), fol. 5^{v} (under *Custus necessariorum pro ecclesia*); an artisan of Windsor was paid 8*d*. for an 'ymago domini Ricardi principis filii Regis Edwardi iiij^{ti}'. This picture may have been made in commemoration of Prince Richard's creation as Duke of York on 28 May 1474.

[103] For a comprehensive survey on this subject, see Andrew Martindale, 'Patrons and Minders: The Intrusion of the Secular into Sacred Spaces in the Late Middle Ages', in D. Wood (ed.), *The Church and the Arts* (Studies in Church History, 28; Oxford, 1992), pp. 143–78.

[104] See H. M. Colvin, D. R. Ransome and J. Summerson (eds), *The History of the King's Works*, iii: *1485–1660 (Part I)* (*HKW*) (London, 1975), pp. 192–3 and 213. In Henry VII's Chapel, the display of John Skelton's eulogy on the bronze enclosure to Henry VII's chantry in 1512 recalls the earlier exhibition of Jean Calot's/John Lydate's dynastic panegyric to the Dual Monarchy (*HKW*, 213); see above, pp. 243–4 and 253.

in the mass *pro rege*.[105] Although the dearth of concordances precludes a definitive answer to this, the explanation probably lies in the date at which the Eton choirbook was copied: between 1500 and 1504.[106] By the early 1500s, fifteen years after Banaster's death, the political circumstances which had given topicality to *O Maria et Elizabeth* had passed: the king was no longer young and the Tudor dynasty appeared to be securely established on the throne. The king's heir, Arthur Prince of Wales, was in his mid teens, betrothed (and then married) to Catherine of Aragon, and in all appearances a credible successor to his father. The scribe of the Eton choirbook, aware of the possibility that 'Henricus' might in the near future be succeeded by 'Arthurus', wrote '.N.' instead, so as to circumvent the need for emendation at a later stage: although it was becoming stylistically outmoded, *O Maria et Elizabeth* was an established part of the college choir's repertory, and its inclusion in the lavish new choirbook suggests that it was expected to remain current for some years more. In the event, Henry VII reigned until 1509, to be succeeded by another Henry: Prince Arthur died prematurely on 2 April 1502.[107]

CONCLUSIONS

Despite its technical shortcomings, *O Maria et Elizabeth* reveals more about the role of polyphony within the late medieval English devotional mindset than many of the more polished essays in this form contained within the Eton choirbook. It exemplifies the interdependence of religious practice and dynastic priorities in the later Middle Ages; the coalescence of these concerns earlier in the fifteenth century had been manifested in the foundation of institutions such as Eton College.[108] Banaster's elision of biblical and royal themes in his text, and the context in which the piece was

[105] See *Missale Sarum*, cols. 784*–786*.[106] On the copying of the choirbook, see Williamson, 'The Eton Choirbook', pp. 183–338.

[107] According to this hypothesis, *O Maria et Elizabeth* was copied into MS 178 before April 1502. This accords with the *terminus ante quem* I have suggested elsewhere (See Williamson, 'The Eton Choirbook', pp. 287–99) of *c.* 1504: the scribe of MS 178 had assembled approximately a third of the manuscript by the time he came to copy Banaster's antiphon.

[108] See P. McNiven, *Heresy and Politics in the Reign of Henry IV: The Burning of John Badby* (Woodbridge, 1987), and W. N. M. Beckett, 'Sheen Charterhouse from its Foundation to its Dissolution' (D. Phil. thesis, Oxford University, 1992), p. 10.

sung, at one of the focal points in the liturgical day, underline the extent to which the rhetoric of Marian devotion could be (and had been) appropriated to serve wider purposes. These purposes included royal image-making as well as pious intercession: the text of Banaster's motet paints the portrait of a young, dynamic exemplar of virtue, a dynast on whom the health, wealth and happiness of the wider community depended.

Although Banaster's formula is unique in the Eton choirbook, the survival of settings of 'royal' texts by Robert Fayrfax suggests that *O Maria et Elizabeth* was not an isolated instance of dynastic image-making. The explicit rehearsal of biblical pedigree in Fayrfax's text and, most especially, the fact that he was given a generous commission to write his 'Anthem of oure Lady and Saint Elizabeth' open up wider questions of patronage and listenership. Although doubt has been cast elsewhere on the question of patronage in pre-Reformation English church music,[109] the composition of a small quantity of pre-Reformation polyphony can be linked to a client–patron transaction (rather than being the incidental by-product of an employer–employee relationship). The commissioning of occasional polyphony, often with context-specific texts such as *Eterne laudis lilium* or *O Maria et Elizabeth*, suggests that these pieces had an intended audience. Like the other antiphons in the Eton choirbook, Banaster's *O Maria et Elizabeth* was sung in the nave of the chapel, in the public space, not the private collegiate space which lay beyond the choir screen; while the laity may not have understood the Latin text, they would certainly have comprehended its devotional significance. Similarly, the explicit rehearsal of dynastic pedigrees and imagery in motets such as *O Maria et Elizabeth* speaks against the suggestion made elsewhere that sacred polyphony was regarded with indifference or hostility in ecclesiastical and courtly communities.[110] *O Maria et Elizabeth* stems from a culture in which private piety was given public expression.

The degree of artifice evident within *O Maria et Elizabeth*, how-

[109] R. Bowers, 'Obligation, Agency and *Laissez-faire*: The Promotion of Polyphonic Composition for the Church in Fifteenth-Century England', in I. Fenlon (ed.), *Music in Medieval and Early Modern Europe: Patronage, Sources and Texts* (Cambridge, 1981), pp. 1–19.

[110] J. Dean, 'Listening to Sacred Polyphony *c*.1500', *Early Music*, 25 (1997), pp. 611–38, at pp. 611–12.

ever imperfectly it was executed, contradicts the suggestion that fifteenth-century English composers paid little heed to their texts, or that polyphony – either sacred or secular – was conceived entirely independently of the text in which it was embedded and which it was intended to convey.[111] As has been argued, Banaster's *O Maria et Elizabeth* was conceived as a polytextual unity, drawn together in a web of thematic signifiers by a composer with a track record as an author and translator. Partly because he was not using a well-established text, like *Salve regina* or *Stabat mater*, with a ready fund of musical exemplars, Banaster was obliged to find novel solutions to the issues raised by the text; in his cantus firmus he found a means of drawing text and polyphony into a closer union. This unified artefact had a specific function: to commemorate a royal pregnancy and to celebrate the continuation of the ruling dynasty which this pregnancy brought into prospect; to give royal sanction to a newly established liturgical feast; and to advertise royal legitimacy, through the elision of biblical and dynastic themes and the appropriation of devotional language for the purposes of late medieval statecraft.

University of Newcastle

[111] See, for instance, John Stevens, *Music and Poetry in the Early Tudor Court* (Cambridge, 1979), pp. 325–6 ('None of these [composers, including Banaster specifically] were learned men in any sense of the word'); see also R. Bowers, 'Early Tudor Courtly Song: An Evaluation of the Fayrfax Book (BL, Additional MS 5465)', in *The Reign of Henry VII*, pp. 188–212, at pp. 205–6 ('. . . music and text were independent . . . When a poem was set to music at this period the role of the composer was to supply an artefact parallel to and simultaneous with the poetic text, but not especially integrated with it.'). In 'Cantus Firmus Procedures', pp. 21–87, Catherine Hocking discusses intertextuality (between motet texts and cantus firmi) in the works of John Browne. See also Noël Bisson, 'English Polyphony for the Virgin Mary: The Votive Antiphon, 1430–1500' (Ph.D. diss., Harvard University, 1998), pp. 35–115, for a detailed consideration of votive antiphon texts, their sources, imagery and ritual significance.

APPENDIX 1

Gilbert Banaster, *Miraculum sancti Thome martyris*[1]

Not longe ago [bifell] a meruelys thyng,
Which was don the vijth day of July.
Pylgrymys with grete deuocyon comyng
To Seynt Thomas of Canterbury,
The wyckyd fende therof he had grete envy,
Yet seynt Thomas conseruyd them, I wys:
Nouis fulget Thomas miraculis.[2]

Vppon the see suche tempest ther felle,
Ther with Sathan apperyd in figur
As a dragon with fyry flamys of helle,
On the watyr brennyng a long leysur
The shippys to wracke, vnnethe myght endur.
Withoutyn fayle, trew it was and is:
Nouis fulget Thomas miraculis.

Also ther was an horryble ayer,
No wyght almost myght the savour abyde.
The peple were almost at the poynt of dysspayr,
With dredefull noyse on Seynt Thomas thei cride,
Which that was seyne be the shippis syde
As a bisshop and dede all hem blys:
Nouis fulget Thomas miraculis.

Whan this swete syght thus dyde apper,
Sathan he fled with all his myght,
The firmament began for to clere.
Vppon the see there they restyd all nyght
And thankyd god with hertys lyght
And Seynt Thomas that dyd here paynys lysse:
Nouis fulget Thomas miraculis.

Off all the flok nat oon was lost,
The Shepperde kepte hem all so surely
And put to flyght Sathan with all his ooste.
So forthe they came vnto Cauntirbury,
Vnto which place who gothe devoutly,
Off his request ne shall he fayle nor mys:
Nouis fulget Thomas miraculis.

[1] Originally published in *Early English Versions*, ed. Wright, p. xx.

[2] *Novis fulget Thomas miraculus* was the eighth respond at nocturns on the feast of St Thomas (*Breviarium ad Usum Insignis Ecclesiae Sarum*, ed. F. Procter and C. Wordsworth, i (Cambridge, 1882), col. cclvii).

APPENDIX 2
Corrodies Granted by the Crown to Banaster

Daventry Priory	granted 25 February 1469 (PRO C 81/824/2748)
Forde Abbey	granted 18 January 1470 (PRO C 81/829/2985)
Abingdon Abbey	petition 20 July 1471; granted 20 July 1471 (and 10 April 1477); surrendered 23 April 1480 (PRO C 81/1502/47, C 81/871/5095, C 261/5/45, C 261/5/58, C 261/5/59; *Calendar of Close Rolls, Edward IV, A.D. 1468–1476* (London, 1953), p. 199)
Crowland Abbey	granted 28/29 August 1471 (PRO C 81/836/3319; *CCR, 1468–1476*, p. 209)
Cerne Abbey	presented 20 May 1474; surrendered 1 June 1476 (PRO C 81/1507/32, C 81/857/4364, C 261/5/36)
St Benet Hulme Abbey	granted 21 November 1474; surrendered 9 August 1486 (PRO C 1/855/4274, C 82/13/16)
Abbey of St Mary of Graces by the Tower of London	granted 13 August 1479; surrendered 20 October (PRO C 81/869/1986, C 81/870/5015, C 81/869/4980, C 261/5/52)
Athelney Abbey	granted 19 October 1479 (PRO C 81/870/5014)
Muchelney Abbey	granted 25 October 1479; surrendered 23 April 1480 (PRO C 81/870/5018, C 81/871/5096)
Norwich Cathedral Priory	granted 9 January 1482; granted *post mortem* to Edward John, gentleman of the royal household chapel, 1 September 1487 (C 81/878/5447; Ashbee, *Records*, vii, p. 189)

Bardney Abbey	surrendered 9 August 1486; regranted 22 August 1486 (PRO C 82/13/16; *Materials*, i, p. 547)

Early Music History (2000) Volume 19. © Cambridge University Press
Printed in the United Kingdom

REVIEWS

KENNETH LEVY, *Gregorian Chant and the Carolingians*. Princeton, Princeton University Press. 1998. x + 271 pp.

Musicologists and liturgical scholars have together been concerned not only with the existence and maintenance of Roman chant in Rome throughout the early Middle Ages, but also with the development of Frankish and Carolingian chant in Gaul, that is, 'Gregorian' chant. Discussion has focused on the various stages of that process. It is a widely held view that rather than Frankish/Gregorian chant developing independently from a late antique and probably Roman base, the injection of Roman influence into Francia is to be dated to the middle of the eighth century to create the Romano-Frankish hybrid known as 'Gregorian'. In Rome the Roman chant was still fostered, especially in the eleventh century. In the light of the meagreness of the surviving evidence, however, there remains doubt concerning the extent of 'Roman' input in the eighth century and about the documentation of the late antique and early medieval melodies to which Père Jean Claire of Solesmes contributed so influentially with his ideas of *modalité archaïque*. The other major preoccupation of early medieval musicologists is the notion of a progression from memory to written record with respect to musical notation: what was the origin and development of neumes and how do these fit into our understanding of the relationship between orality, memory and literacy?

It is to these fundamental debates about the development of Gregorian chant that Kenneth Levy has made so many seminal contributions. Six of his articles, published between 1982 and 1995, are gathered together in this book, without revision. Indeed, oddly enough they are photographic reprints, preserving all the original typefaces. These are the articles on 'The Gregorian Processional Antiphon', 'Toledo, Rome and the Legacy of Gaul', 'Charlemagne's Archetype of Gregorian Chant', 'On the Origin of Neumes', 'On

Gregorian Orality' and 'Abbot Helisachar's Antiphoner'. Levy has added five new chapters which take up and extend the themes addressed in his earlier work and provide a firm statement of his thinking, notably on the subject of the development of neumes. All the same it is a pity that the opportunity was not taken to update the essays from the 1980s and early 1990s as far as references, editions of Latin texts and correction of detail are concerned. An instance is the preservation in chapter 2 of the erroneous reference to the predominance of Benedictine monasticism in the early Middle Ages and the chronology of its introduction into England, long since revealed to be unfounded in the work of Josef Semmler and others.[1] Further, it would have been more useful had Levy more obviously engaged with the arguments of Arlt, Treitler, Rankin and others on points of detail and taken account of them *in situ* rather than making the reader wait until the last few chapters for the culmination of his arguments.[2]

As a whole, Levy's book witnesses to the consistency and ever further refinement of his views. His expertise and integrity, quite apart from the sheer volume of the extraordinarily interesting musical evidence he presents, inspire both admiration and respect.

[1] The Rule of Benedict was certainly known in England from the seventh century, but Benedictine monasticism was not promoted as the most desirable form of the religious life there until the later tenth century. In Frankish Gaul, despite the promotion of the Rule of Benedict as the desired norm by the Carolingian church in the late eighth and early ninth century, many houses continued to observe different approaches to the monastic life: see J. Semmler, 'Karl der Grosse und das fränkische Mönchtum', in W. Braunfels (ed.), *Karl der Grosse: Lebenswerk und Nachleben*, ii: *Das geistige Leben*, ed. B. Bischoff (Düsseldorf, 1965), pp. 255–89; idem, 'Zur Überlieferung der monastischen Gesetzgebung Ludwigs des Frommen', *Deutsches Archiv für Erforschung des Mittelalters*, 16 (1960), pp. 309–88; *idem*, 'Studien zum Supplex Libellus und zur anianischen Reform in Fulda', *Zeitschrift für Kirchengeschichte*, 69 (1958), pp. 268–98; *idem*, 'Corvey und Herford in der benediktinischen Reformbewegung des 9. Jhts', *Frühmittelalterliche Studien*, 4 (1970), pp. 289–319. On the unlikelihood of Augustine of Canterbury having brought Benedictine monasticism to England see C. Holdsworth, 'Saint Boniface the Monk', in T. Reuter (ed.), *The Greatest Englishman: Essays on St Boniface and the Church at Crediton* (Exeter, 1980), pp. 47–68. On Gregory the Great's praise of Benedict (as distinct from his Rule) in his *Dialogues* see R. Markus, *Gregory the Great and his World* (Cambridge, 1997), pp. 68–72. For a brief general account see R. McKitterick, *The Frankish Kingdoms under the Carolingians, 751–987* (London, 1983), pp. 109–24 and 279–86 and for an up-to-date discussion: M. de Jong, 'Carolingian Monasticism: The Power of Prayer', in R. McKitterick (ed.), *The New Cambridge Medieval History*, ii: *c. 700–c. 900* (Cambridge, 1995), pp. 622–53.

[2] For excellent discussion and useful bibliography see Susan Rankin, 'Carolingian Music', in R. McKitterick (ed.), *Carolingian Culture: Emulation and Innovation* (Cambridge, 1994), pp. 274–316.

He raises issues of crucial importance to anyone, not just medieval musicologists, wishing to understand the cultural and intellectual history of the period from the eighth to the tenth centuries in western Europe. In what follows, therefore, I offer a Carolingian historian's perspective on the problems discussed by Levy in both his earlier work and the new chapters, and air some questions that still seem to me to remain unresolved in all discussions of the early medieval chant repertory, the Carolingian context, the supposed contribution of Rome, and notation.

Levy's new introduction provides, first of all, a clear survey of the state of play in discussions of the development of 'Gregorian' chant. In his own words and with his distinctive emphases:

> Between the sixth and tenth centuries, European plainchant went through three more or less simultaneous processes of change. In one of these the local chant repertories, with their distinctive musical dialects, were suppressed, and the single authoritative Gregorian melodic repertory was substituted. In another the melos went from something that might vary between one delivery and the next to one that was fixed and should, in principle, always sound the same. In a third change there was a turn from solely aural transmission to one where verbatim memory had the support of memory-aid neumes. These three changes affected one another. They came about largely before neumes were introduced, or before there is record of their use. The changes were essentially complete by the time of the first extant Gregorian neumings, ca. 900.[3]

Levy is convinced, furthermore, that 'by 800 an authoritative Carolingian–Gregorian repertory had supplanted the local chant dialects in most Carolingian domains'. He concedes that as no neumes survive from before the second quarter of the ninth century[4] little is known of earlier dialects. There is no documentation of Roman music at Rome before the eleventh century, for example, and none for Milan before the twelfth. Of other regional repertories there is evidence but, as I understand it, not only does secure documentation of these also post-date the Carolingian period but the differences in both style and detail between the various repertories have proved very difficult to account for. Here, for Levy as for other musicologists, is where there is scope for creative and necessarily speculative interpretation. The reconstruction of ear-

[3] Levy, *Gregorian Chant*, p. 6.

[4] *Ibid.*, p. 7.

lier music repertories has had to be done by ingenious and very learned back-projection from, and interpretation of the possible routes travelled to, the structures of particular melodies as we have them in an extant notated form. It seems somewhat analogous to the discussion of historical linguists in suggesting hypothetical vocabularies and words as a consequence of vocalic sound changes. Levy is particularly good at such reconstruction, as is most evident in his article 'Rome, Toledo and the Legacy of Gaul'. Yet, as he himself acknowledges, such reconstructions can only be hypotheses.

Much of this interpretation on the part of early medieval musicologists is weakened by insufficient attention to the non-musical historical background. Further, it is influenced, implicitly or explicitly, by unfounded assumptions about other aspects of the wider cultural context. Let me focus first of all on the idea of the move from the variable to fixed repertory, dated *c.* 800 and associated with notions of the 'suppression' of local chants and variety.

The apparent consistency in the repertory, established from a small number of manuscripts, is by all accounts only discernible in the evidence from the late ninth or early tenth century onwards. What has influenced Levy's choice of *c.* 800, a century earlier, for the fixing of the repertory, is the undoubted insistence in Carolingian royal capitularies and ecclesiastical legislation on the need for correct Christian texts to be used by everyone within the Carolingian empire.[5] Efforts were indeed made to promote uniformity in religious observance and practice.[6] In this context it may be helpful to compare the success of the simultaneous promotion of such texts as the Bible, the Homiliary (sermons for use throughout the liturgical year), the liturgy of the Mass, canon law and the Rule of Benedict. In each case the emphasis of the Carolingian ruler and his advisers was undoubtedly on the production and empire-wide dissemination of *correct* texts as distinct from insistence that everyone use the same text.

5 The prime example is the *Admonitio Generalis* of 789 (see also below, p. 284) and the *De litteris colendis* of *c.* 800, in *Monumenta Germaniae historica, capitularia regum francorum*, ed. A. Boretius, i (Hannover, 1883), nos. 22 and 29, pp. 53–62 and 79–80. See G. Brown, 'The Carolingian Renaissance', in R. McKitterick (ed.), *Carolingian Culture: Emulation and Innovation* (Cambridge, 1995), pp. 1–51.

5 To save space here I refer readers to my book, *The Frankish Church and the Carolingian Reforms, 789–895* (Royal Historical Society Studies in History, 2; London, 1977).

Although the corrected version of the Bible produced at Tours and associated with Alcuin has achieved modern fame, Bonifatius Fischer's work established that Tours was by no means the only centre producing a corrected text of the Vulgate or various combinations of *Vetus Latina* and Vulgate versions of the Old and New Testament books in the ninth century.[7] Paul the Deacon's Homiliary, produced at Charlemagne's request, undoubtedly achieved wide dissemination, but older Homiliaries remained in use throughout the Carolingian realm and in Italy, and others were compiled.[8] The receiving of the *Hadrianum* Sacramentary or Mass book from Pope Hadrian between 784 and 791 precipitated a flurry of liturgical production, most notably in association with Benedict of Aniane, Hildoard, bishop of Cambrai, and the Saint-Amand scriptorium.[9] The subsequent liturgical history of Mass books in the Frankish realm indicates that the older Mass books (the 'Gelasian', the 'Gregorian', the 'Eighth-century Gelasian', and local adaptations of all of these) continued to be produced and used in different centres.[10] The late ninth-century Sacramentary of Echternach, for example, adhered to older liturgical traditions and incorporated elements of the so-called Gelasian, eighth-century Gelasian and a supplemented *Hadrianum* of the Saint-Amand type.[11]

Although Charlemagne and his advisers recommended the adoption of the canon-law collection known as the Dionysio-Hadriana, it is clear again that older collections remained in circulation and more local collections were compiled by individuals

[7] B. Fischer, 'Bibeltext und Bibelreform unter Karl dem Großen', in: Braunfels (ed.), *Karl der Grosse*, ii: *Das geistige Leben*, ed. Bischoff, pp. 156–216, and *idem*, *Lateinische Bibelhandschriften im frühen Mittelalter* (Freiburg, 1985); R. McKitterick, 'Carolingian Bible Production: The Tours Anomaly', in R. Gameson (ed.), *The Early Medieval Bible: Its Production, Decoration and Use* (Cambridge Studies in Palaeography and Codicology; Cambridge, 1994), pp. 63–77.

[8] R. Grégoire, *Homéliaires liturgiques médiévaux: analyse des manuscrits* (Bibloteca di Studi Medievali; Spoleto, 1980).

[9] J. Deshusses, *Le Sacramentaire grégorien* (Spicilegium Friburgense, 16; Fribourg en Suisse, 1971) and *idem*, 'Chronologie des grands sacramentaires de Saint-Amand', *Revue bénédictine*, 87 (1977), pp. 230–7 and 'Encore les sacramentaires de Saint-Amand', *Revue bénédictine*, 89 (1979), pp. 310–12.

[10] C. Vogel, *Medieval Liturgy: An Introduction to the Sources*, trans. and rev. W. G. Storey and N. K. Rasmussen from the French edition of 1981 (Washington, D.C., 1986), pp. 61–104.

[11] *The Echternach Sacramentary*, ed. Y. Hen (Henry Bradshaw Society; Woodbridge, 1997).

in particular dioceses.[12] Despite the sterling efforts, especially under Louis the Pious in his Aachen decrees of 816 and 817, to promote the Rule of Benedict, many religious houses retained or adopted alternative guides to the religious life, including the rules for canons.[13] The extant evidence witnesses, in other words, to continuing diversity rather than uniformity throughout the ninth century. Harmony and diversity, as well as unity, indeed, have been constant themes in many recent assessments of Carolingian political and cultural life.[14]

In such a context, therefore, although a remarkable degree of consistency in the repertory may well have been achieved by the tenth century, parallel liturgical and textual evidence would suggest that harmony rather than uniformity prevailed in the Carolingian kingdoms before that. Indeed, the degree of consistency in the repertory is in any case less thorough than is implied by modern scholars. It is simply not possible to be certain that the promotion of what is claimed as Roman chant as part of the political programme of Pippin III and his son Charlemagne, and the recognised value of liturgical singing as a symbol of social unity, entailed the instant 'suppression' of local musical dialects. Instead, both enriched existing chant practice. Surely one of the points of Notker Balbulus of St Gall's famous story, written *c.* 880 about Charlemagne's reactions to hearing different chants in the churches he visited, is that it reflects the diverse musical traditions of the Frankish empire and how well entrenched they were and continued to be.[15] It is unlikely that music could have achieved

[12] H. Mordek, *Kirchenrecht und Reform im Frankenreich* (Berlin, 1975) and R. Kottje, 'Einheit und Vielfalt des kirchlichen Lebens in der Karolingerzeit', *Zeitschrift für Kirchengeschichte*, 76 (1965), pp. 323–42 and the references in R. McKitterick, 'Knowledge of Canon Law in the Frankish Kingdoms before 789: The Manuscript Evidence', *Journal of Theological Studies*, n.s. 36/1 (1985), pp. 97–117, repr. in R. McKitterick, *Books, Scribes and Learning in the Frankish Kingdoms, 6th–9th Centuries* (Variorum Collected Studies; Aldershot, 1994), chapter II.

[13] See above, n. 1.

[14] See K. Morrison, '"Know thyself": Music in the Carolingian Renaissance', in *Committenti e produzione artistico-letteraria nell'alto medioevo occidentale* (Settimane di studio del Centro italiano di studi sull'alto medioevo, 39; Spoleto, 1992), pp. 369–479 and R. McKitterick, 'Unity and Diversity in the Carolingian Church', in R. Swanson (ed.), *Unity and Diversity in the Church* (Studies in Church History, 32; Oxford, 1996), pp. 59–82.

[15] Notker Balbulus, *Gesta Karoli*, I, c. 10, ed. R. Rau, *Quellen zur karolingischen Reichsgeschichte*, i (Darmstadt, 1974), p. 336. I have discussed this in 'Royal Patronage of Culture in the Frankish Kingdoms under the Carolingians: Motives and Consequences', in *Committenti*

a uniformity which cannot be observed in any other category of cultural or intellectual endeavour in the Carolingian realms. I concede willingly, however, that the small number of extant manuscripts do witness to the remarkable consistency of the melodic repertory in the tenth century. Thus, one does need to posit some period before that of such consistency in process of fulfilment. But to my mind, a period of a whole century beforehand, and the apparently arbitrary choice of the year 800 for the fixing of the musical repertory, conflict with the evidence from every other sphere and especially that most closely related, namely, the liturgical texts. Concentration on similarities may be in danger of obscuring the differences and investigation of their implications.

Carolingian texts of the later eighth and early ninth century undoubtedly insist that Roman chant was to be sung, and refer to Pippin's abolition of Gallican chant for the sake of unanimity.[16] So far all of us have accepted this as a statement of fact as if it makes sense, but all the same it is awkward to prove in the absence of either musical or textual material of any kind before the eighth century. As mentioned earlier, the Roman music that can be documented from the eleventh century is often very different from the Carolingian-Gregorian repertory. Further, the earliest Mass texts surviving in the Sacramentaries are all from eighth-century Francia apart from the so-called Leonine Sacramentary (in fact a private collection of liturgical prayers) of the late sixth or early seventh century, possibly from Verona.[17] The *Hadrianum* sent from Rome in the late eighth century was inadequate, for it contained only the prayers the pope used at the stational churches of Rome.[18] It had therefore to be extensively augmented for Frankish use. In other words, the repeated claims that Roman use was introduced by Pippin may have as much to do with ideological positioning as

(Spoleto, 1992) (as in n. 14), pp. 93–129, reprinted in R. McKitterick, *The Frankish Kings and Culture in the Middle Ages* (Variorum Collected Studies; Aldershot, 1995), chapter VII.

16 *Admonitio generalis* 789, c. 80, in *Monumenta Germaniae historica, capitularia regum francorum*, ed. Boretius, i, no. 22, p. 61.

17 Verona, Biblioteca Capitolare, Cod. LXXXV (80). See E. A. Lowe, *Codices Latini antiquiores*, iv (Oxford, 1947), no. 514 and D. M. Hope, *The Leonine Sacramentary: A Reassessment of its Nature and Purpose* (Oxford, 1971).

18 The earliest extant copy, made for Bishop Hildoard of Cambrai, is Cambrai, Médiathèque Municipale 164, dated 811–12. Two others from the first half of the ninth century are both from Verona.

with statements of fact. We should be careful not to assume that we are really presented with survivals of Roman, as distinct from Frankish, use and creativity.[19] The Franks acknowledged the authority of Rome in ecclesiastical matters to an ever increasing extent, but Pippin and Charlemagne also commissioned, as we have seen, corrected texts of many kinds. Claiming that these corrected, authoritative and specially commissioned versions were Roman would clearly have enhanced the status of these texts.

Certainly the musicians and scholars of the Carolingian period were extraordinarily creative, with their shaping of the Gregorian chant repertory, their systematisation of modal behaviour, and their written articulation of the theory of modes. The treatises on music and other discussions of music from the Carolingian period are also of crucial importance for what they may reveal of their authors' assumptions about the means in existence for recording music in writing. Levy's article on Abbot Helisachar's antiphoner suggests that Helisachar is alluding to notation, a suggestion rendered more plausible by the early date now assigned to the earliest extant examples of neumes, namely the neumed *Psalle modulamina* in Munich, Bayerische Staatsbibliothek Clm 9543, of the second quarter of the ninth century. Neumes for the Gregorian repertory are said to be testified in manuscripts no sooner than the later ninth or early tenth century, half a century or so after prosulae, tropes and sequences were being neumed. Only about a dozen Gregorian antiphoners survive from the period between the eighth and the later ninth century and none is neumed.[20] The earliest witness to Gregorian neuming, according to Levy, is Albi, Bibliothèque Municipale 44 from southern Aquitaine, dated to the late ninth century, though since redated by Bernhard Bischoff to the tenth century.[21] Other fragments, however, seem to be push-

[19] Important work is in progress on the history of the Frankish liturgy by Yitzhak Hen in a monograph for the Henry Bradshaw Society and on the *Missale Gothicum* by Els Rose for a Ph.D. at the University of Utrecht.

[20] How many antiphoners have been lost is clear if we remember that at Reichenau alone in 821 ten antiphoners are recorded. A trawl through all extant ninth-century book catalogues and treasure inventories would be worthwhile: see, for example, Bernhard Bischoff (ed.), *Mittelalterliche Schatzverzeichnisse*, i: *Von der Zeit Karls des Großen bis zur Mitte des 13. Jahrhundert* (Veröffentlichungen des Zentralinstituts für Kunstgeschichte in München, 4; Munich, 1967).

[21] Though one wonders if Bischoff was influenced in this by assumptions about the dates of neumes: *Katalog der festländischen Handschriften des neunten Jahrhunderts*, i: *Aachen–Lambach* (Stuttgart, 1998), p. 11.

ing Gregorian neuming back into the last few decades of the ninth century.[22] It is clear, therefore, that work remains to be done and that some of the manuscripts may have been dated too late.

Levy positions himself clearly in relation to the debate about the forms taken by neumes, arguing for a directional or gestural rationale as the generating principle for notation. There is no reason why principles of punctuation could not also have been drawn on by those attempting to record musical sound with written signs. Whoever first adapted the concept of sign for sound was bound to draw on conceptualisations already in existence. Equally, alternative solutions may have been tried. The foundation of Levy's exposition of neumes, however, is the idea that authoritative neumation was promulgated simultaneously with authoritative melodic formulations. As I have indicated above, there is evidence of attempts to promote authoritative texts, so the idea of the same for melodies and for neumes is not inherently implausible. Yet for melodies and texts, anything introduced had to compete, largely unsuccessfully, with existing practice. Was this also the case for neumes? The obvious comparisons would be with the insistence on correct Latin orthography and grammar and the development of Caroline minuscule, its rapid spread throughout the Carolingian realm, and introduction into Italy, Spain and England.

Carolingian Latin undoubtedly moved closer to its classical ancestor. This development appears to have been a consequence of deliberate policy, combined with the fact that east of the Rhine at least it was introduced to so many peoples incorporated into the Frankish realm as a second language for use in religion, education and government.[23] Caroline minuscule, on the other hand, was not a reformed script. It had evolved slowly from the letter forms of the Roman script system, and especially cursive and half

[22] Laon, Bibliothèque Municipale 266 (flyleaf). See Peter Jeffery, 'An Early Cantatorium Fragment Related to Laon 239', *Scriptorium*, 36 (1982), pp. 245–52 and plate 29. This fragment, dated to the last quarter of the ninth century, indicates development between it and Laon, Bibliothèque Municipale 239, and also represents a slightly divergent musical tradition from that in the Laon cantatorium.

[23] See R. Wright, *Late Latin and Early Romance in Spain and Carolingian France* (Liverpool, 1982); R. Wright (ed.), *Latin and the Romance Languages in the Early Middle Ages* (London 1991, repr. Philadelphia, 1996); and Michel Banniard, 'Language and Communication in Carolingian Europe', in *The New Cambridge Medieval History*, ed. R. McKitterick, ii: *c.700–c.900* (Cambridge, 1995), pp. 695–708.

uncial. It reached its distinctive form in the 780s in a number of different regions of the Carolingian empire, with many regional variants sustained thereafter.[24] We have no undisputed examples of scribes learning to write, only the polished products in books prepared for libraries and liturgical use.

So for neumes a sudden invention is unlikely, as distinct from the emergence of a similar idea in a number of different places which, because of the vibrant network of communications fostered by the intellectual activities of the Carolingian period, gradually influenced one another. The sophistication of the developed forms of neumes to be observed in manuscripts such as Laon, Bibliothèque Municipale 239 and Sankt Gallen, Stiftsbibliothek 359 does suggest a period of experimentation beforehand. Levy's notion of a simple, 'nuance poor' system gradually developing into a complex, 'nuance rich' one as its potential was realised is probably right. It is not impossible that the court may have given impetus to such developments.

The problems remain of how long a period of development one should allow for and how much of a role the court played. In the absence of firm evidence, no answer is possible. If there were a court archetype with a system of neumes invented for the purpose of promoting a fixed repertory of Gregorian melodies, one ought to be able to identify its descendants. One might wish to focus on developments in Lotharingia and Metz as Levy argues in chapter 10, though one should be very wary of following nineteenth-century nationalistic justifications in proposing clear cultural divisions to accompany the political partitions of the middle of the ninth century and thereafter.[25] But the distribution of the neumed books and the rich variety of notation does pull in a different direction, suggesting that if the royal court did play a role it was a supporting one in a cast with no main protagonists.

[24] Bernhard Bischoff, *Latin Palaeography and the Middle Ages*, trans. D. Ó Cróinín and D. Ganz (Cambridge, 1990, from the 1986 German edition), pp. 112–18.

[25] Levy, *Gregorian Chant*, p. 243. The two works he cites in support of his 'basic cultural division' do not mention this but are accounts of the political divisions in 843; secondly, the Strasbourg oaths, as I have tried to make clear elsewhere, are not to be taken as a literal account of what happened (Introduction to *The New Cambridge Medieval History*, ii: *c.700–c.900*, pp. 11–12). The chronological leap Levy makes back from the tenth and eleventh centuries to 843 is putting too much on a political event, especially when one of the most lasting divisions created in 843 was not so much east and west but the creation of the Middle kingdom, namely, Lotharingia.

What is the function of neumes in relation to the development of chant? How pervasive were neumes and did they exist for a long time alongside alternative means of remembering melodies? How was Gregorian melody remembered before the advent of neumes? On all these Levy has much of great interest to offer. In Chapter 9, therefore, on 'Plainchant before neumes', he distinguishes four classes of Gregorian chant: remembered melodies; accommodated melodies; psalmic matrices; centonate formulaic compounds. This chapter needs to be read against the background of his insistence elsewhere that memory without the support of neumes falls short of verbatim recall. Neumes make possible the precise memory control that is the essence of the transmission. Pitch descriptions are only approximate but exact enough about rhythmic and other nuances of melodic contour to support memory. It is perhaps significant that neumes first appear in relation to new compositions of tropes and sequences before they are applied to the Gregorian melody as well. Presumably in the case of the latter a stronger remembered tradition could be relied upon. Surely trained cantors were the last people who would have needed memory aids for Gregorian melodies. Yet somehow the new melodies needed to be communicated and it is conceivable that notational means were devised to augment the aural. Nevertheless, ninth-century accounts of chant refer to singing masters and teachers. Would they not also have referred to the wonderful new writing system if it were being used to the extent that Levy suggests?

Levy is insistent that 'conjectures about ninth-century melodic states and notational usage come down in the end to matters of memory'.[26] But they come down to more than that. Ultimately, whether one follows Levy in his insistence on the necessity for neumes depends, firstly, on one's understanding of what was possible in terms of human memory. Secondly, however, it has to do with attitudes towards, and uses of, literacy in the early Middle Ages.

With respect to the former, all commentators have been able to do is point to what is expected of memory in the Middle Ages and instances of prodigious feats of memory. It would be possible to regard the maintenance of a chant tradition without neumes as

[26] *Gregorian Chant*, p. 192.

just such a feat. Yet the various functions neumes acquired as a 'silhouette of melodic substance', an aid to memorisation and a means for the stabilisation of the repertory, so meticulously and convincingly documented by Levy, may need to be distinguished from the original and continuing intention of them. Musical notation is to be understood not so much in relation to any assessment of the capacity for memorisation as in the context of Carolingian attitudes to the written word and to texts.

Neumes record melodic gestures linked to units of text with details of inflection, expression and rhythmic nuance. These neumes, varying from place to place but representing similar musical detail, are a documentation of performance practice of extraordinary subtlety. They articulate a reading of texts with dimensions of colour and rhythm which enhance the impact of the text itself to far greater an extent than if it were merely spoken.[27] What the scholars in the Carolingian period were most concerned with was texts. It was in this period that many dramatic developments were made in the representation and expression of, as well as arguments advanced about the relationship between, text and image.[28] In the abundant biblical and theological exegesis of the time, different layers of understanding (figurative, literal, allegorical) of the text are unpeeled.[29] Music, too, was a form of understanding and of interpreting texts. Neumes do not just represent sound. They are indeed a form of writing of meaning, expressing more than the words or adding extra meaning to the words to enrich a part of human sensibility and understanding beyond speech. Neumes are thus an indication of how to interpret the text in a musical language.

[27] I here follow Susan Rankin, 'Carolingian Music', pp. 292–300.

[28] See the magnificent new edition of Theodulf of Orleans's *Libri Carolini*, ed. A. Freeman (Monumenta Germaniae historica, Concilia II, *Suppl.* I: *Opus Caroli regis contra synodum*; Hannover, 1998); the essays gathered together in *Testo e immagine nell'alto medioevo* (Settimane di studio del Centro italiano di studi sull'alto medioevo, 41; Spoleto, 1994), especially H. Kessler, '"Facies bibliothecae revelata": Carolingian Art as Spiritual Seeing', and B. Brenk, 'Schriftlichkeit und Bildlichkeit in der Hofschule Karls d. Gr.', pp. 532–84 and 631–82; and C. M. Chazelle (ed.), *Literacy, Politics and Artistic Innovation in the Early Medieval West* (Lanham, Md. and London, 1992).

[29] J. Contreni, 'The Carolingian Renaissance: Education and Literary Culture', and D. Ganz, 'Theology and the Organisation of Thought', both in *The New Cambridge Medieval History*, ed. McKitterick, ii: *c.700–c.900*, pp. 709–85, and the articles collected together in 'The Power of the Word: The Influence of the Bible on Early Medieval Politics', ed. M. de Jong, *Early Medieval Europe*, 7 (1998), pp. 261–358.

Literacy is not just about how many lay people could read or write.[30] This is to miss the point. It is the understanding of writing and its meaning, the attitudes towards the written word and the qualitative use of it that are crucial.[31] Thus musical notation in the ninth and tenth centuries is an extraordinarily rich and nuanced manifestation of a literate mentality. It is as much crucial evidence for the development of music as it is of the interpretation of written texts in the early Middle Ages. Those preoccupied with the books incorporating music from this period must necessarily engage, therefore, with Carolingian and Ottonian culture as a whole.

Rosamond McKitterick
Faculty of History, University of Cambridge

CLAUDIA BURATELLI, *Spettacoli di corte a Mantova tra Cinque e Seicento*. Storia dello spettacolo: saggi, 3. Florence, Casa Editrice Le Lettere. 1999. vii + 278 pp.

Musicologists are now used to lying abed with historians of the other arts – even with (political, social, economic...) historians *tout court* – and some may claim that we are all in the same boat, although it is usually easier to mix a metaphor than the disciplines, whatever the current academic fashion for so-called interdisciplinarity. We have also sought to occupy the cultural–historical high ground, in part as a reaction against the lowly place normally accorded music in most broader 'history of...' compendia, and also because we have evolved away from the text- (or image-)based studies that some would say still dominate histories of art or literature. Indeed, we now turn to curious advantage the dubious status of the musical 'text' – which reaches fruition in sound only by way of evanescent performance – and also the well-known prob-

[30] *Pace* both D. Bullough, 'The Carolingian Liturgical Experience', in R. N. Swanson (ed.), *Continuity and Change in Christian Worship* (Studies in Church History, 35; Woodbridge, 1999), pp. 29–64, and M. Richter, '*...quisque scit scribere, nullum potat abere laborare*: Zur Laienschriftlichkeit im 8. Jahrhundert', in J. Jarnut, U. Nonn and M. Richter (eds), *Karl Martell in seiner Zeit* (Beihefte der Francia, 37; Sigmaringen, 1994), pp. 393–404.

[31] R. McKitterick, *The Carolingians and the Written Word* (Cambridge, 1989) and McKitterick (ed.), *The Uses of Literacy in Early Mediaeval Europe* (Cambridge, 1990).

lems of musical semiosis: music that means nothing starts to mean everything, nurturing a wealth of readings that offer unique (we claim) insights into given times and places.

Our specific alliances forged to bolster the perceived relevance of music to broader cultural understanding have variously tended to move in the directions of political and social history (broadly defined), art history and literary theory. It is strange that we have often tended not to look at the performing art perhaps closest to our own, that of the theatre. This statement may reflect a national bias: 'historical' theatre studies, as distinct from the literary–historical study of theatrical works, would seem to have a less strong tradition in the UK (and perhaps the USA) than in, say, Italy, where 'Storia dello spettacolo' is more firmly grounded as a university discipline. Also, opera studies must be a special case, if not always, it seems, a theatrical one. And we can all bring to mind Renaissance musicologists who have engaged fluently with music on the stage. But even the finest examples are emblematic of the problems: for example, Nino Pirrotta's magnificent *Li due Orfei* of 1969,[1] which includes an extended essay by the distinguished theatre historian Elena Povoledo, falls into two unequal parts that do not sit quite happily together.

Perhaps that is because theatre studies would seem to force a focus on text as performance with which many musicologists feel uncomfortable outside the narrow confines of historical performance practice. The primary sources do not help: archival or similar material usually reveals more about the fact than about the act of performance, and accordingly we are accustomed to construing more the cultural, social, political and other meanings of performance than its precise nature. We can tell what was done, and where and even why, but much less often how. In part that is because of the requirements and interests of those compiling the documents that end up in official archives; in part, it is also because the 'how' of performance is usually a matter of professional competence the elements of which were of limited concern outside a small circle, and indeed were often kept secret for fear of competition and loss of status. Even seemingly comprehensive 'how to...'

[1] N. Pirrotta, *Li due Orfei* (Turin, 1969, 2nd edn 1975); *Music and Theatre from Poliziano to Monteverdi*, trans. K. Eales (Cambridge, 1982).

treatises – and there are plenty of sixteenth-century examples in both music and theatre – tend to obscure as much as they clarify, telling us only something, but never everything, of what we need or want to know. Both the theatre historian and the musicologist are thus left with ever-problematic texts whose realisation through performance is essential to their understanding – and for that matter, to our love of the art – and yet whose performance is in several senses unrealisable.

In her study of court entertainments in Mantua in the late sixteenth and early seventeenth centuries, the theatre historian Claudia Buratelli adopts a solution similar to that of many older-fashioned musicologists in dealing with this thorny issue, which is in effect to ignore almost entirely both text and performance. Thus she focuses largely on context on the one hand, and biography on the other. For historians of music in late Renaissance and early Baroque Italy, her subject might seem well known, and also well documented, thanks to the remarkable work of late nineteenth- and early twentieth-century antiquarians such as Alessandro Adimari, Antonino Bertolotti and Angelo Solerti,[2] and also recent scholars such as Iain Fenlon, Susan Parisi and Don Harrán.[3] Her period stretches from the accession of Duke Vincenzo I Gonzaga (1587) to the death of Vincenzo II (1627), which provoked a disastrous dispute over the Gonzaga succession leading to the horrific sack of the city by Imperial troops in July 1630. Many would call this a golden age of Mantuan culture – in particular the reign of Vincenzo I (1587–1612) – with the city playing host to the likes of poets such as Battista Guarini, musicians such as Claudio Monteverdi, and artists such as Peter Paul Rubens.

The story goes back further. Duke Guglielmo Gonzaga – not quite the ascetic Counter-Reformation zealot that some believe – made considerable headway in establishing a permanent theatre, and permanent players, in Mantua, thanks not least to the activ-

[2] A. Adimari, *La bell'Adriana ed altre virtuose del suo tempo alla corte di Mantova* (Città di Castello, 1888); A. Bertolotti, *Musici alla corte dei Gonzaga in Mantova dal secolo XV al XVIII: notizie e documenti raccolti negli archivi mantovani* (Milan, 1890; repr. Bologna, 1969); A. Solerti, *Gli albori del melodramma* (Milan, 1904; repr. Bologna, 1976).

[3] I. Fenlon, *Music and Patronage in Sixteenth-Century Mantua* (Cambridge, 1980, 1982); S. H. Parisi, 'Ducal Patronage of Music in Mantua, 1587–1627: An Archival Study' (Ph.D. diss., University of Illinois at Urbana-Champaign, 1989); D. Harrán, *Salamone Rossi: Jewish Musician in Late Renaissance Mantua* (Oxford, 1999).

ities of Leone de' Sommi as playwright and *corago* ('director' comes closest in English, but the term embraces the creative management of all aspects of a production). To emphasise the place of the theatre in Mantuan life, Buratelli quotes (p. 181) Luigi Rogna's letter to Pietro Martire Cornacchia of 6 July 1567:

> The crowd of people of all kinds gained every day by one and the other of these two troupes of comedians is unbelievable. Consider, Your Lordship, that the artisans [*artisti*] and the Jews leave their work aside to go and hear them, nor does one pay less than half a *reale* per person. The gentlemen stand there the whole day, and some of the lord officials, such as the Lord Steward [*il signor massaro*] and some of the Lord Masters of the Receipts [*signori maestri dell'entrate*] also go there. I leave aside speaking of the gentlewomen, for whom are reserved the windows and certain other places.[4]

The letter merits close reading. Rogna refers to the presence of two commedia dell'arte troupes, to the wide range of social and other classes permitted attendance at theatrical entertainments (but to the restrictions placed on women), and to seemingly mixed modes of production and finance combining courtly patronage (however defined) with a paying audience. For the most part, these remain characteristic during Buratelli's period, with the added twist of Duke Vincenzo I's own special, personal interest in the stage. The theatrical result depended upon a tautly constructed infrastructure of artists and artisans carefully managed by a court establishment to serve Vincenzo I's apparent love of spectacle and, in broader terms, the so-called politics of prestige. The whole came together in remarkable ways in the splendid performances of Guarini's *Il pastor fido* in 1598 that served to put Mantua on the theatrical map (surprisingly, Buratelli says very little about them) and culminated in the magnificent festivities for the wedding of Prince Francesco Gonzaga and Margherita of Savoy in May–June 1608 (the subject of chapter 2), which outshone contemporary festivities in Florence and Savoy and indeed set a new standard for theatrical splendour and artistic achievement. It is not surprising – and typical of the literature – that Vincenzo's successors, Francesco II, Ferdinando I and the sickly Vincenzo II, appear in a much less favourable light.

4 Mantua, Archivio di Stato, Archivio Gonzaga, *busta* 2577, fol. 23^{r}.

The 'heroes' of Buratelli's account are not so much the actors, musicians, dancers and stagehands – or even the poets and composers – who worked so hard to bring these entertainments to life; rather, they are the 'ideologi e tecnici della spettacolarità mantovana' (the title of chapter 3). These 'ideologues and technicians' are individuals for whom no straightforward functional title exists but who played a major role (among other duties) as masters of ceremony and directors of entertainments: the court functionary Federico Follino, the architects and stage-designers Antonio Maria Vaini and Gabriele Bertazzolo, and the ducal secretaries and sometime librettists Alessandro Striggio and Ercole Marliani (or Marigliani). The latter two are well known to musicologists for their collaborations and correspondence with Monteverdi. Vaini was prefect of the ducal buildings from 1595, and thus responsible for, among other things, the on-going construction of the duke's palaces and villas; Bertazzolo was a remarkable jack-of-all-trades, able to turn his hand as much to digging canals as to organising firework displays. Follino emerges far more strongly than just as the author (perhaps better, collator) of the description of the 1608 festivities: he was closely involved in court celebration and ceremonial from the late 1580s until at least 1613 – by all account he staged good funerals as well – and he was also a playwright, with a list of works including the 'favola boschereccia' *L'amor reale* (Carnival 1590), the pastoral play *La Modesta* (Carnival 1602), and the comedy *Le quattro età del mondo* (Carnival 1611) as well as texts for *intermedi*, tournaments and the like.

Buratelli then turns to the two main groups of performers involved in these dramatic endeavours. Chapter 4 deals with the all-male Jewish companies which regularly provided a comedy at least for carnival, although not usually for other, grander court festivities, where, I assume, the social rules were different and carnivalesque or other licence did not apply. Chapter 5 focuses on the commedia dell'arte troupes employed on a more or less permanent basis by the duke and which could be 'lent' to other courts in Italy and abroad (Paris, Vienna) if the time and price were right (often they were not) or if there was diplomatic advantage to be gained. The Jewish community was in effect held to ransom by Duke Vincenzo and his heirs to provide financial and other support for entertainments in return for more liberal conditions in the ghetto; in this context, the supposedly enlightened treatment of the Jews in Mantua takes on a more sinister air. In broader terms, Buratelli also offers a timely reminder that the growth of Mantuan theatrical activity from the late 1560s coincided with the darkening clouds of Inquisitorial persecution and ducal oppression – from which the theatre was a deliberate distraction to placate the populace – while the later Gonzagas' support for competing groups of comedians was often not so much enlightened patronage or a strategic use of resource as an attempt to maintain loyalty by a process of divide and rule. For all the celebratory images, Mantua was not the happiest of places in this period.

The stars of the commedia players in Mantua included the famous Tristano Martinelli (Arlecchino) – he whose portrait has often been confused for Monteverdi's – and Pier Maria Cecchini (Fritellino), plus Giovan Battista Andreini (Lelio) and his wife Virginia (Florinda). They did not always reap significant rewards from Mantua and regularly attempted to engineer periods of service elsewhere. Buratelli is surprised that they and their comedian colleagues were never placed on the court salary rolls, unlike the musicians. This raises the question of what in fact a court 'salary' means in this period. It also makes sense in the context of 'mixed' modes of production (the comedians gained receipts from a paying audience and from other privileges), while one-off donations or payments in kind such as clothing (costumes?) and jewellery – shades of the 'necklace' given to Monteverdi for the dedication to the Duchess of Mantua of his Seventh Book of madrigals – tend to disappear from the archival record. According to Buratelli, only Martinelli made himself rich by way of the theatre, in part by cannily depositing his earnings in investment funds outside Mantua; Cecchino lost money in the silk trade and property speculation, and Andreini ended his life in poverty.[5] Yet Duke Vincenzo and his successors became adept at wielding carrot and stick to maintain the comedians in service, offering privileges, exemptions, property rights and citizenship while at the same time having scant regard for security of tenure: it was not just the musicians who suffered from the reforms of the court establishment in 1611–12.

[5] But for a rounder view, see P. Besutti, 'Da *L'Arianna* a *La Ferinda*: Giovan Battista Andreini e la "comedia musicale all'improviso"', *Musica disciplina*, 49 (1995), pp. 227–76.

All this places Monteverdi's bitter feelings about Mantua, and about his treatment by the Gonzagas, in a much clearer light.

On the whole, Buratelli pays scant attention to Mantuan music and musicians save where occupations and responsibilities overlapped as matter of record (practice is, of course, a different matter); it is unclear whether her omission reflects issues of court organisation – i.e., systemic divisions of labour as yet not fully understood – or of archival serendipity. Or perhaps she should just have read the work of Susan Parisi. She does discuss the singer, lutenist and dancer Isacco Massarani ('Isacchino hebreo'), and the singer Filippo Angeloni, the latter for a time superintendent of the comedians. Massarani was involved in devising the staging of the problematic *Giuoco della cieca* in Guarini's *Il pastor fido*, and he deserves significant recognition for his role in establishing particular patterns for sung and danced entertainments in Mantua that were to reach fruition in the 1608 festivities with the Rinuccini–Monteverdi *Ballo delle ingrate* and the Striggio–da Gagliano *Il sacrificio d'Ifigenia*.[6] Clearly he was an outstanding professional – if probably not a father as Buratelli suggests (p. 158; he was a castrato) – and he cannot have needed the fussy advice of the playwright Muzio Manfredi, who wrote to him on 19 November 1591 concerning the potential staging at court of his 'favola boschereccia' *Semiramis* (p. 159):

> In the [*favola*] *boschereccia* that have I sent to your Lord Duke, the four canzonettas of the chorus are certainly sung, but they are also danced. And since it will be your job to create the dances, I tell you that the first should have little movement and no gesture; the second, little movement as well, but some small gesture of desire; the third has to be like the second, but varied in terms of its sections [*purché variato di partite*]; the fourth should have somewhat greater movement than the others, and gestures of grief and scorn. At the end there is a fairly lively *moresca*, done with spears and darts; and I say 'fairly lively', and not too much so, given the concern one should have for the nymphs. The final dance of Hymen is lively in terms of movement and gesture, and not very slow. I know that you are a capable man, and so I will not tell you any more.[7]

[6] See I. Fenlon, 'The Origins of the Seventeenth-Century Staged *Ballo*', in I. Fenlon and T. Carter (eds), *'Con che soavità': Essays in Italian Baroque Opera, Song, and Dance, 1580–1740* (Oxford, 1995), pp. 13–40; T. Carter, 'New Light on Monteverdi's *Ballo delle ingrate* (Mantua, 1608)', *Il saggiatore musicale* (forthcoming).

[7] Archivio Gonzaga, *busta* 2231, unfoliated.

Nor, I imagine, did Giaches de Wert need a similar letter sent the next day (p. 176, n. 84):

> Just as I write to Messer Leone [de' Sommi] and Messer Isacchino, giving the one some instruction concerning the costumes and the other concerning the dances, thus I beg Your Lordship that the songs [*canti*] of the four canzonettas of the chorus should follow their affects, and should be so free of fugal artifice [*e siano tanto sinceri d'artificio fugato*] that the words should not be lost in terms of their understanding, noting that all the chorus should sing, now together, now in two groups, correspondingly in the stanzas and in the refrains, and always dancing and with several instruments. As for the dance of Hymen, even though it should have a great noise of voices and instruments, I would be grateful if even its words could be understood, and likewise understood those of the madrigal in praise of the goddess, even if, given that this is to be done without any instrument, it might have some brief little imitation [*alcuna brieve fughetta*] because of its joyfulness.[8]

Presumably these letters are so detailed because they are by an outsider. On the whole, however, Buratelli's documentary pickings are relatively thin (and as she notes, even these two letters are known to scholars),[9] assiduous though she has been in following up and checking the archival sources. Perhaps one should not blame her for the nature of her materials, and she does offer a few important corrections of dates and other readings of well-known documents. But there are certain notable absences from the book, some of which are surprising for a theatre historian while others may just reflect unreasonable expectations from a musicological reviewer. One is any extended discussion of the location, layout and resources of the theatrical spaces used by the Gonzagas (so there is nothing added to the problematic issue of the location of the première of Monteverdi's *Orfeo*). Another is the role of women performers in a court that seems to have been more enlightened than most on the matter, albeit within certain constraints: only (and predictably) Virginia Ramponi-Andreini receives coverage for her performances as an actress–singer, not least in Monteverdi's *Arianna* (1608) and, if I interpret a contemporary hint correctly, in the role of Dafne in his lost 'eclogue',

[8] *Ibid.*

[9] They were included in A. d'Ancona, *Origini del teatro italiano* (2nd edn, Turin, 1891), ii, pp. 424–5. D'Ancona presents many of the documents discussed by Buratelli.

Apollo (Carnival 1620).[10] The book also cries out for a chronological listing, however preliminary, of theatrical works performed in Mantua: search though I might, I was unable to find details of the comedy that was performed in Carnival 1607 two evenings before *Orfeo*, which could have suggested how much music was involved and therefore how it might have conflicted with rehearsal schedules for Monteverdi's opera.

As for those Mantuan gentlewomen who reportedly, and famously, wept at the fates of Monteverdi's Arianna and of most of the other maltreated heroines variously represented in speech, song and dance in the entertainments for the 1608 wedding,[11] one assumes that they were offered more comfortable seats than the window ledges 'and certain other places' to which Luigi Rogna relegated them in 1567. But exploring the implications of that requires a very different book from the one written by Buratelli, for all that any subsequent work in this field will have to take hers into account.

Tim Carter
Royal Holloway, University of London

[10] For Andreini's impact on *Arianna*, see T. Carter, 'Lamenting Ariadne?', *Early Music*, 27 (1999), pp. 395–405. The preparations for the 'egloga' (elsewhere called a 'ballo') *Apollo* (to a text by Alessandro Striggio) are discussed in P. Fabbri, *Monteverdi*, trans. T. Carter (Cambridge, 1994), pp. 171–4; it seems to have received two performances in Mantua, one in late February or early March 1620 and the other the following summer; parts of it were also heard in Venice. Buratelli (p. 230, n. 1) cites a letter from Virginia Andreini of 22 April 1623, perhaps to Alessandro Striggio (Archivio Gonzaga, *busta* 2761, no. 216), in which Andreini refers to 'that feeble service which I then did for you who deigned to have me do [the role of] Dafne in your most gracious *balletto*'. We know from Monteverdi's letters that *Apollo* included the characters Apollo (who had a lament), Amor and Peneius (Daphne's father; sung by a bass singing *alla bastarda*), and Daphne is, of course, central to the Apollo myth.

[11] See S. Cusick, '"There was not one lady who failed to shed a tear": Arianna's Lament and the Construction of Modern Womanhood', *Early Music*, 22 (1994), pp. 21–41; A. MacNeil, 'Weeping at the Water's Edge', *Early Music*, 27 (1999), pp. 406–17.

Early Music History (2000) Volume 19.
Printed in the United Kingdom

INSTRUCTIONS FOR CONTRIBUTORS

EDITORIAL POLICY

Early Music History is devoted to the study of music from the early Middle Ages to the end of the seventeenth century. The journal demands the highest standards of scholarship from its contributors, all of whom are leading academics in their fields. *Early Music History* gives preference to studies pursuing interdisciplinary approaches and to those developing new methodological ideas. The scope is exceptionally broad and includes manuscript studies, textual criticism, iconography, studies of the relationship between words and music, and the relationship between music and society.

1. SUBMISSIONS

All contributions and editorial correspondence should be sent to: The Editor, Dr Iain Fenlon, *Early Music History*, King's College, Cambridge CB2 1ST, UK. The Editor can also be contacted via email at iaf1000@cus.cam.ac.uk.

Submission of an article is taken to imply that it has not previously been published, and has not been submitted for publication elsewhere. Upon acceptance of a paper, the author will be asked to assign copyright (on certain conditions) to Cambridge University Press.

Contributors are responsible for obtaining permission to reproduce any material in which they do not own copyright, to be used in both print and electronic media, and for ensuring that the appropriate acknowledgements are included in their manuscript.

2. MANUSCRIPT PREPARATION

All contributions should be in English and must be double spaced throughout, including footnotes, bibliographies, annotated lists of manuscripts, appendixes, tables and displayed quotations. In the event of the manuscript being accepted for publication the author will be asked to submit the text on computer disk (Apple Macintosh or IBM compatible PC) as well as in hard copy, giving details of the wordprocessing software used (Microsoft Word or WordPerfect). However, the publisher reserves the right to typeset material by conventional means if an author's disk proves unsatisfactory.

Typescripts submitted for consideration will not normally be returned unless specifically requested.

Artwork for graphs, diagrams and music examples should be, wherever possible, submitted in a form suitable for direct reproduction, bearing in mind the maximum dimensions of the printed version: 17.5 × 11 cm (7″ × 4.5″). Photographs should be in the form of glossy black and white prints, measuring about 20.3 × 15.2 cm (8″ × 6″).

All illustrations should be on separate sheets from the text of the article and should be clearly identified with the contributor's name and the figure/example number. Their approximate position in the text should be indicated by a marginal note in the typescript. Captions should be separately typed, double spaced.

Tables should also be supplied in separate sheets, with the title typed above the body of the table.

3. TEXT CONVENTIONS

Spelling

English spelling, idiom and terminology should be used, e.g. bar (not measure), note (not tone), quaver (not eighth note). Where there is an option, '-ise' endings should be preferred to '-ize'.

Punctuation

English punctuation practice should be followed: (1) single quotation marks, except for 'a "quote" within a quote'; (2) punctuation outside quotation marks, unless a complete sentence is quoted; (3) no comma before 'and' in a series; (4) footnote indicators follow punctuation; (5) square brackets [ ] only for interpolation in quoted matter; (6) no stop after contractions that include the last letter of a word, e.g. Dr, St, edn (but vol. and vols.).

Bibliographical references

Authors' and editors' forenames should not be given, only initials: where possible, editors should be given for Festschriften, conference proceedings, symposia, etc. In titles, all important words in English should be capitalised; all other languages should follow prose-style capitalisation, except for journal and series titles which should follow English capitalisation. Titles of series should be included, in roman, where relevant. Journal and series volume numbers should be given in arabic, volumes of a set in roman ('vol.' will not be used). Places and dates of publication should be included. Dissertation titles should be given in roman and enclosed in quotation marks. Page numbers should be preceded by 'p.' or 'pp.' in all contexts. The first citation of bibliographical reference should include all details; subsequent citations may use the author's surname, short title and relevant page numbers only. *Ibid.* may be used, but not *op. cit.* or *loc. cit.*

Abbreviations

Abbreviations for manuscript citations, libraries, periodicals, series, etc. should not be used without explanation; after the first full citation an abbreviation may be used throughout text and notes. Standard abbreviations may be used without explanation. In the text, 'Example', 'Figure' and 'bars' should be used (not 'Ex.', 'Fig.', 'bb.'). In references to manuscripts, 'fols.' should be used (not 'ff.') and 'v' (verso) and 'r' (recto) should be typed superscript. The word for 'saint' should be spelled out or abbreviated according to language, e.g. San Andrea, S. Maria, SS. Pietro e Paolo, St Paul, St Agnes, St Denis, Ste Clothilde.

Note names

Flats, sharps and naturals should be indicated by the conventional signs, not words. Note names should be roman and capitalised where general, e.g. C major, but should be italic and follow the Helmholtz code where specific (*C,, C, C c c′ c″c‴; c′* = middle C). A simpler system may be used in discussions of repertories (e.g. chant) where different conventions are followed.

Quotations

A quotation of no more than 60 words of prose or one line of verse should be continuous within the text and enclosed in single quotation marks. Longer quotations should be displayed and quotation marks should not be used. For quotations from foreign languages, an English translation must be given in addition to the foreign-language original.

Numbers

Numbers below 100 should be spelled out, except page, bar, folio numbers etc., sums of money and specific quantities, e.g. 20 ducats, 45 mm. Pairs of numbers should be elided as follows: 190–1, 198–9, 198–201, 212–13. Dates should be given in the following forms: 10 January 1983, the 1980s, sixteenth century (16th century in tables and lists), sixteenth-century polyphony.

Capitalisation

Incipits in all languages (motets, songs, etc.), and titles except in English, should be capitalised as in running prose; titles in English should have all important words capitalised, e.g. *The Pavin of Delight*. Most offices should have a lower-case initial except in official titles, e.g. 'the Lord Chancellor entered the cathedral', 'the Bishop of Salford entered the cathedral' (but 'the bishop entered the cathedral'). Names of institutions should have full (not prose-style) capitalisation, e.g. Liceo Musicale.

Italics

Titles and incipits of musical works in italic, but not genre titles or sections of the Mass/English Service, e.g. Kyrie, Magnificat. Italics for foreign words should be kept to a minimum; in general they should be used only for unusual words or if a word might be mistaken for English if not italicised. Titles of manuscripts should be roman in quotes, e.g. 'Rules How to Compose'. Names of institutions should be roman.

4. PROOFS

Typographical or factual errors only may be changed at proof stage. The publisher reserves the right to charge authors for correction of non-typographical errors.

5. OFFPRINTS

Contributors of articles and review essays receive 25 free offprints and one copy of the volume. Extra copies may be purchased from the publisher if ordered at proof stage.